HONUS WAGNER

HONUS WAGNER

A BIOGRAPHY

DENNIS DeVALERIA AND

JEANNE BURKE DeVALERIA

UNIVERSITY OF
PITTSBURGH PRESS

Published 1998 by the University of Pittsburgh Press, Pittsburgh, Pa. 15261
Originally published by Henry Holt and Company, Inc.

Library of Congress Cataloging-in-Publication Data
DeValeria, Dennis.
Honus Wagner : a biography / Dennis DeValeria and Jeanne Burke DeValeria.
p.   cm.
Originally published: New York : H. Holt, 1996. With new front matter.
Includes bibliographic references (p.   ) and index.
ISBN 0-8229-5665-9 (pbk. : alk. paper)
1. Wagner, Honus, 1874–1955.   2. Baseball players—United States—Biography. 3.
Pittsburgh Pirates (Baseball team) I. DeValeria, Jeanne Burke. II. Title.
GV865.W33D38   1998
796.357'092—dc21
[B]   97-45771

FOR OUR PARENTS

Bob and Gert DeValeria,
Jack and Dee Burke

CONTENTS

ACKNOWLEDGMENTS

To our friends whose love, talent, and expertise show within these pages, we offer a very special salute. Thanks to: Paul Adomites, our confidant over the last three years, whose effort and wisdom were essential; Jack Carlson, longtime fan and historian of the Pittsburgh Pirates, who pored over our work, picking it apart for the better; Joe Santry, a most underappreciated baseball history superstar, who reviewed our text for accuracy and readability; Sally O'Leary, a perennial all-star who, in our minds, is second only to Wagner in her value to the Pirates; Mark Alvarez, the Society for American Baseball Research's talented publications director, for reviewing our early draft and providing much needed direction and advice; Bob Bailey, whose deep knowledge of both nineteenth-century and Louisville baseball was a perfect match for our project; Dan Bonk, for frequently lending his considerable ballpark expertise; Marilyn Holt and the staff of the Pennsylvania Room of the Carnegie Library of Pittsburgh, for patiently answering a steady stream of questions; Jack Kavanagh, who shared research and encouragement over the last few years; Marcella and Dan McGrogan, who keep the spirit of Carnegie alive at the Historical Society of Carnegie, Pennsylvania; and the entire membership of the Society for American Baseball Research, for so willingly contributing a wealth of information.

We want to thank the following people and organizations whose professional assistance guided our research: Bill Guilfoile, Peter Clark, Pat Kelly, Ginny Reinholdt, and Bill Burdick at the National Baseball Library in Cooperstown, New York; Linda Brown and the Paterson Public Library; Bill Williams and Rex Bradley of Hillerich & Bradsby in Louisville; Margaret Merrick at the University of Louisville Record Archives; Derek McKown of the Warren County (Pennsylvania) Historical Society; Frank Zabrosky and John Thompson of the University of Pittsburgh Archives; Don and Sharon Oberriter and the staff of the Cooperstown Bat Company; Katy Feeney of the National League offices in New York City; and Tim Rozgonyi at *The Pittsburgh Post-Gazette*.

We are grateful to all of our friends who opened their hearts, minds, libraries, and homes to us over the last few years—Dave Arrigo, Will Baker, Mike Blake, Frank Boslett, Rick Bradley, Betty and Jim Brown, John Burk, John Butch, Bill Carle, Gene Carney, Richard J. Cerrone, Pat Collins, Frank Cunliffe, Bill Deane, Dutch Doyle, Morris Eckhouse, Howard Elson, Chris Erskine, Leigh Fightmaster, Jim Freeman, Bill French, Larry Gerlach, Michael Gershman, Barbara Gregorich, Bill Gustafson, Bill Haber, Morley Harris, Tom Hetrick, Bob Hoie, Bill Humber, Bill Jakub, Dave Kelly, Geoff LaCasse, Len Levin, Ed Luteran, Norman Macht, Jerry Malloy, Bob McConnell, Margaret McCrum, Dan Miller, Mike Monschein, Neil Munro, Scott Neill, Ray Nemec, Eric Nicholson, Pete Palmer, John Pardon, Denise Petro, Bill Phelps, Christy Pretzinger, Fred Ralston, Denis Repp, Rob Ruck, Cindy and Tom Sanderson, Fred Schuld, Norm Schumm, Corey Seeman, Tim Shepherd, Tom Slater, Darlene and Greg Smith, Bob Smizik, Mike Sparrow, Ron and Sue Stacy, Alan Steinberg, A. D. Suehsdorf, Brad Sullivan, Lou Swartz, David Vincent, Phil Von Borries, John Winston, Marty Wolfson, and John Zajc.

Invaluable personal memories and reminiscences were graciously shared with us by Wagner's friends, acquaintances, townspeople, former ballplayers and Pirates personnel. Thanks to Violet Ahlquist, Milton Aranson, Mabel Aston Thornhill, Jim Barr, Leslie Blair, Joe L. Brown, Mace Brown, Jim Cancilla, Chuck Cavanaugh, Greg Chaberski, John Ciptak, Dr. Klaus Conermann, Myron Cope, Al Cusick, Frank Damiani, Clyde Davis, Carol Dlugos, Vincent Dlugos, George Duda, Jiggs Eckels, Charles Eisenhuth, Richard Esch, Joe Finegold, Elbie Fletcher, Mary Flory, Jim France, Jim Freeman, Al Gionfriddo, Joe Goodworth, Joe

Gooter, Bob Gustine, Bob Heinrich, Julia Hendzel, Sam Jarkesy, Myron Jewell, Tom Johnson, Bill Kehoe, Lefty Kendall, Ralph Kiner, Jim Knepper, Jane Davis Kolts, Jim Kriek, Judy Kueshner, Jeff Lewellyn, Pat Livingston, Vic Lombardi, Al Lopez, Ed Lysakowski, Bob Massick, Louis May Jr., Socko McCarey, Bill McCue, Jim McCully, Roy McHugh, Art McKennan, Sally Motto, Joe O'Toole, Tom O'Toole, Dick Phillips, Tot Pressnell, Pee Wee Reese, Frank Sgro, Murray Shapiro, Fred Smith, Jim Smith, Delores Stevens, George Strickland, Gus Suhr, Frank Thomas, Lou Vitale, Herman Welsh, John Welsh Jr., and John Wishart.

We also tip our caps to the staffs of the Hillman Library at the University of Pittsburgh; The Filson Club of Louisville; and the public libraries in Steubenville, Akron, Mansfield, Columbus, and Cleveland, Ohio; Adrian, Michigan; Carnegie, Warren, New Castle, and Franklin, Pennsylvania; Wheeling, West Virginia; Wilmington, Delaware; Hartford, Connecticut; New York, New York; and Louisville, Kentucky.

A final note of appreciation to our editor, Ben Ratliff, for having an open mind to our project and for helping us improve it.

HONUS WAGNER

PRELUDE:
A DAY IN COOPERSTOWN

A group of boys dressed in knickers was playing ball in an open field. The young runner was breaking for second as his teammate cocked his bat, awaiting the delivery from the pitcher in full windup. In the distance, in the boys' deep center field, an American flag was waving in front of a schoolhouse, symbolically flanked by a cottage, a barn, and a steepled church. It was a celebration of baseball and America, played out on a three-cent postage stamp.

The stamp was the United States government's contribution to the commemoration of the one-hundredth anniversary of the birth of baseball, placed by folklore in 1839 at Cooperstown, New York. Of the total production of sixty-five million special stamps, one million were allotted to the little Cooperstown Post Office, and as it opened its doors on June 12, 1939, the first man in line quietly approached the window. Handsomely attired in a crisp summer suit with a snug-fitting, red-white-and-blue baseball cap, he carefully and ceremoniously placed three pennies on the metal counter and was presented with a single stamp. As if it were a most critical business deal, the two parties posed for several minutes while cameras snapped.

The dapper customer was Kenesaw Mountain Landis, commissioner of baseball, and the clerk fulfilling the transaction was James A.

Farley, postmaster general of the United States. It was the first official act in a day of ceremonies and activities that highlighted an entire summer's worth of events across the nation for the game's centennial.

Outside the post office, Main Street swelled with fifteen thousand people, five times the town's normal population, as anticipation grew for the formal opening and dedication of the National Baseball Hall of Fame and Museum. Visitors arrived from around the country. Radio broadcasters and newsreel cameras were on hand to report the experience to the rest of the nation. After years of fund-raising, planning, and effort on the part of many, all of America could now enjoy baseball's shrine.

Three years earlier, in January 1936, the idea of a National Baseball Museum was still in its infancy when the first-ever Hall of Fame poll was conducted. Two hundred twenty-six members of the Baseball Writers' Association of America voted for the ten players since 1900 who were most deserving of Hall of Fame immortality. In order for a player to earn induction, he would have to be named on 75 percent of the ballots. The votes were tallied, and five men would receive baseball's ultimate honor in the inaugural year.

The names roll from the tongue, as recognizable today as they were during their heyday—Ty Cobb, "The Georgia Peach"; Babe Ruth, "The Bambino"; Christy Mathewson, "Big Six"; Walter Johnson, "The Big Train"; and Honus Wagner, "The Flying Dutchman." They were grand masters whose contributions to baseball far surpassed their own remarkable statistical achievements. These men transcended baseball, molded it in their own unique images, and forever changed the public's perception of the game.

Ty Cobb was relentless. Daring his opponents to stop him and forcing mistakes with apparent recklessness, Cobb was always pushing, pushing for more: Get on base at all costs, take an extra base no matter who stood in the way. The bag, the plate, the baseline were his and his alone. He was the American League's first homegrown star.

Babe Ruth and his home run feats were larger than life and were a vital component of the Roaring Twenties. His style of baseball represented a new version: A single base or a single run became less significant when runs could be made in bunches with one swing. Ruth's outlook—if one is good, two are better, and if two are good, ten are better yet—applied unequivocally to everything he pursued.

Christy Mathewson, a devout young man with a college background, seemed out of place in the unruly world of early-twentieth-century baseball. He not only survived but was ultimately worshiped by fans and teammates. His cunning matched his talent, and both were astounding. He was calm and calculating, pacing himself through games and studying batters to find their weaknesses. With a wholesome image, magnetic looks, and acute intelligence, he was a role model for the youth of the country and contributed to an increased respectability for baseball.

With an effortless, whiplike motion that unleashed blazing fastballs, Walter Johnson racked up incredible shutout and strikeout totals. His long arms had batters claiming they could almost hit Johnson's fingers with their bats on his follow-through. He was a self-effacing, compassionate man and was actually fearful of hurting someone with a pitch. For twenty-one years Johnson graced the team of the nation's capital and the game of baseball.

Honus Wagner was a man who could win with his glove, his arm, his bat, or his head. He set new benchmarks for hitting, baserunning, and fielding. As a major leaguer, he played every position except catcher, and many who watched him said he would have been a Hall of Famer at any of them. Still regarded as the greatest shortstop in baseball history, Wagner earned tremendous recognition. But he was a humble, simple man who shied away from glorification.

Between the first voting and the opening of the Hall, seven more outstanding players joined the elite class. Nap Lajoie, Tris Speaker, and Cy Young were elected in 1937, Grover Cleveland Alexander in 1938, and George Sisler, Willie Keeler, and Eddie Collins in 1939. In addition, a Centennial Committee selected the most deserving "Builders of Baseball" and pre-twentieth-century greats for enshrinement. June 12, 1939, was the day they were saluted for their accomplishments.

◆ ◆ ◆

Having completed his stamp-buying errand, Commissioner Landis joined other dignitaries on a platform in front of the museum door, while the Hall of Famers remained inside the building. At noon, a brass band played the national anthem, and Charles J. "Chilly" Doyle—Wagner's friend, a Pittsburgh newspaperman, and president of the Baseball Writers' Association of America—opened the festivities with a brief speech. Cooperstown Mayor Rowan D. Spraker followed Doyle to the podium for a few words, and then Landis stepped up and dedicated the "shrine of sportsmanship" to the entire nation. "Take Me Out to the Ball Game" played as the red-white-and-blue ribbons that stretched across the doorway were cut and the door was unlocked and opened.

A drum roll accompanied the reading of a list of the thirteen "Builders of Baseball" and nineteenth-century players honored within. As the final name from this list was recited, the only surviving "pioneer" emerged from the doorway and approached the microphone. Seventy-six-year-old Connie Mack, "The Tall Tactician," was no stranger to awards or public speaking. But he was visibly struck with emotion as he uttered, "This is one of the most memorable days in the history of my days in baseball."

The exclusive list of the twelve players to be enshrined was presented next, and "Hans Wagner" was the first name announced. Now sixty-five years old with thinning white hair, Wagner carried a barrel chest, bursting through a suit that could not have fit him for at least a decade. His gnarled fingers were obviously not up to the task of knotting his tie. It had been said that his legs were so bowed he "couldn't catch a pig in an alley," and even his baggy trousers could not disguise that fact as he ambled through the doorway onto the platform.

In the folksy, casual manner that always connected him to ordinary fans, he told the crowd, "When I was just a kid, I said, 'I hope someday I'll be up there playin' in this league.' And by chance I did. . . . I remember walkin' fourteen miles just to see [Connie Mack] play ball for Pittsburgh. But it was worth it." Pausing momentarily to gaze at the surroundings, he added with total seriousness, "A nice, quiet town you have here. Reminds me of Sleepy Hollow." The audience chuckled. Writer Ken Smith, in attendance that day, recalled, "Instantly the lid was off the formal proceedings. The celebration was back in its homespun ice-cream-and-cake-picnic atmosphere." It was vintage Honus Wagner.

Each of the others took a turn expressing his pleasure and appreciation for the tribute. Commissioner Landis wrapped up the ceremony by proclaiming, "I now declare the National Baseball Museum and the Baseball Hall of Fame in Cooperstown, New York—home of baseball—open!"

◆ ◆ ◆

The entire group assembled that afternoon at an overflowing Doubleday Field, Cooperstown's little ballpark, for the day's primary event, the Cavalcade of Baseball. Re-creations of mid-1800s style ball were performed in full regalia, and then it was time for the major leaguers. The National and American Leagues had rearranged their schedules, clearing two days to shine the sporting spotlight on the tiny New York village. In addition, each of the sixteen major league teams sent two active players to the occasion as ambassadors, as well as to play a few exhibition innings. Some were stars, others were not. They were there to pay respect to baseball's past.

The eleven living members of the new Hall of Fame were still center stage for the Cavalcade. Of the eleven immortals, as they would be called, nine served on an esteemed "board of strategy," while Honus Wagner and the great second baseman Eddie Collins discarded their suits to don uniforms and manage the two squads. Like schoolchildren, the two retired ballplayers gripped a bat, alternating hand-over-hand to see who would have first selection for the choose-up game. Wagner's huge paw ended up on top, and he immediately headed for home plate with bat in hand. Challenging former moundsman Alexander to throw him a curve, Wagner called out to the crowd, "Every time you get one of those things in your hand, you think you can hit." Alexander declined, responding, "And every time I saw you with one, I thought you could hit, too."

Asked about the pace he expected from his men in the exhibition, manager Wagner replied, "I don't know about the other fellows, but I'm playing for keeps, to win. I'm not playing for marbles." It was the only way he knew to play, and it turned out to be the only way for the others as well. What began with hitters swinging at the first pitch, seemingly in a hurry to finish the scheduled three innings, turned into seven innings and an hour and forty minutes of major league baseball. Though no one placed much importance on the outcome, Wagner did get his victory. Ironically, it was a Pittsburgh Pirate shortstop of a later generation who was one of the game's heroes: Arky Vaughan, a Wagner favorite and future Hall of Famer (class of 1985), doubled and scored the tie-breaking run as the "Wagners" rallied for two runs in the sixth to beat the "Collinses," 4–2.

◆ ◆ ◆

Wagner was in his glory all day long, expounding his same time-honored tales to anyone within earshot. There was the one about the time he hit a home run into the smokestack of a locomotive, only to have the ball blown back in a cloud of black smoke and caught for an out. He also told of the time a fielder snagged his belt on a nail protruding from the outfield fence and dangled helplessly as Wagner circled the bases for an inside-the-park home run. Every story ended with Wagner's trademark: "How about *that?*" Perhaps no one enjoyed the day more than he did—

talking baseball, swapping memories and lies with his old friends, and even getting onto a ball field for a few hours.

By that summer of 1939, Wagner was a balding, beer-drinking story-teller whose awkward frame struggled to carry his own weight. However, during his prime, he had epitomized the American hero—successful, steadfast, hardworking, and unpresumptuous. In Wagner's playing era, America was thinking on a grand scale. It was a country with a short history and a vast expanse. Powerful giants such as Andrew Carnegie, John D. Rockefeller, and Henry Ford walked the land, amassing immense fortunes as the country settled into its role as the world's industrial leader. The nation's game was baseball. It was played by children in countless country fields and on the ever-increasing number of city streets. Long before other sports would gain a foothold, men played baseball while representing their companies or communities. Semiprofessional and professional leagues were abundant, and fans coast to coast followed the major leagues through the newspapers. It was in this setting that Honus Wagner became a baseball giant.

Wagner was always a private person, causing much speculation about what he was like. Even later in his life, when he actively participated in the banquet circuit, he maintained a personal distance from the public. Rather than talk candidly about himself, he fueled already formed misconceptions with more exaggerations. And decades after his death, his celebrated 1909 baseball card continues to spawn new myths.

In our research of Wagner's life in and out of baseball, we discovered that the truth was every bit as absorbing and entertaining as the many fabrications previously told. But as lore is very much a part of what Wagner was and has become in the minds of people today, it cannot be left out of his story. Our goal is to provide an accurate understanding of the facts and share the circumstances that became foundations for the legends. Wagner's talents afforded him the opportunity to meet, associate with, and even become one of the great figures during America's maturation. We have striven not only to chronicle his life but also to offer the flavor of his times.

Wagner participated in and helped shape baseball's evolution for more than half a century. His accomplishments remain conspicuous, and he will continue to be a standard for comparison in the future. In a recap of the 1939 formalities in Cooperstown, respected sportswriter Fred Lieb wrote, ". . . if [Wagner] lives until baseball's next centennial in 2039, he still will be a baseball man."

O N E

FROM COAL FIELDS
TO BALL FIELDS

Upon the 1866 arrival in America of Peter and Katheryn Wagner, it was not surprising that they were quickly stirred into the melting pot that was western Pennsylvania. As industrial trade rapidly expanded during the 1800s, the country became increasingly dependent upon the resources of the region, including quality natural gas, oil, and coal. Aided in its growth by a network of rivers and railroads, Pittsburgh became the nation's leader in iron production, earning the title "The Forge of the Universe." Because a tremendous amount of manpower was required, disembarking immigrants were commonly recruited off the docks at Baltimore, Philadelphia, and New York to come inland for work at the mines, mills, and manufacturing plants.

The Wagners, married two years and each twenty-eight years old, had left the oppressive military nation of Prussia, where property was owned by the small ruling class, industrial growth was slow, and work was scarce. Like millions of others over the decades, the Wagners sailed to America in search of better economic opportunities. Only the Irish outnumbered the Germans as waves of European immigrants, most unskilled, flooded into the Pittsburgh area throughout the late nineteenth and early twentieth centuries. Between 1860 and 1880, the population of

Allegheny County, Pennsylvania, doubled, and the number of residents in the city of Pittsburgh more than tripled—from roughly 50,000 to more than 156,000.

Peter Wagner found work in the coal mines, and he and his wife set up housekeeping in Chartiers, Pennsylvania. Though only four miles apart as the crow flies, Chartiers and Pittsburgh were separated by mountains and the Monongahela River. The Wagners, as well as their neighbors, had little reason to travel into Pittsburgh; they walked to their jobs, and everything they needed was available in Chartiers or its sister community of Mansfield, just across tiny Chartiers Creek.

Katheryn Wagner gave birth to nine children, but only six survived infancy, five sons and one daughter. The children were christened with German names but would be known by the English equivalents. Johannes (John) Peter, born on February 24, 1874, was the fourth surviving son. He was preceded by Charles (Charley) in 1869, Albert (Al) in 1871 (a date misidentified in many baseball publications), and Ludwig (Louis or Luke) in 1873. The Wagner's only daughter, Caroline (Carrie), was born in 1877, and Wilhelm (William or Bill) rounded out the family in 1880.

Born with bowed legs and always big for his age, Johannes was never described as graceful. His family called him by the shortened "Hans" or "Honus" (pronounced HAH-nus) which, ironically, was often a term of endearment for big, awkward kids. This moniker fit the fourth Wagner son perfectly, and it stuck with him throughout his eighty-one years. But he was just as frequently referred to as Hans, and as an adult, he usually signed his name J. Hans Wagner or John H. Wagner. Only later in his life did he use the name Honus in a signature.

The Wagners resided in a poor, working-class section of town. Their house, later addressed as 119 Railroad Avenue, was situated along a dirt road, only a stone's throw from a railroad yard and the fourteen sets of tracks that ran along Chartiers Creek. Though modest, the home must have been comfortable enough, for they lived there long after members of the household could afford another; in fact, both Peter and Katheryn would die there. The elder Wagners' indifference to ostentatious living was a character trait they passed on to their children.

The parents preferred to speak German at home, and their English carried a thick accent. The children, however, became bilingual, learning at an early age to read and write in English. Some have believed that Honus had a German accent, but he did not—like each of his siblings, he spoke in the dialect of the Pittsburgh area and considered himself an American, often correcting any misconception.

The Wagners were Lutherans and quite religious. In 1882, the first German Lutheran church came into existence in the Chartiers-Mansfield area. Peter Wagner was among a group of men who recruited a minister, E. F. A. Dittmer, from Missouri to preside over the new St. Johannis Evangelisch Lutherische Kirche (renamed in 1925 as The First Evangelical Lutheran St. John's Church), where services were held in German until the 1920s. The younger Wagner children attended the parochial school attached to the chapel, and Honus received the latter part of his six-year education there. It was not until 1895 that secondary education became available to the children of the area with the opening of the first local high school, so in 1886, like many twelve-year-old boys of western Pennsylvania, Honus went to work.

The older Wagner sons—Charley, Al, and Luke—had all followed their father into the coal fields, and now Honus joined them. Though there were laws regulating child labor, they specified an age limit of thirteen for working in factories and twelve for boys in the coal mines. Each morning, the Wagners walked to the site near their home where, as in much of the region, they mined coal by digging it out of a hillside rather than by sinking a shaft into the ground. At the time, mining was done primarily by adults using pick axes; children often functioned as "breaker boys," separating the coal from the mined rock. But Honus remembered operating a ventilation unit as a "trap-door boy" and doing "general work . . . for pay," adding, "It was hard work, but good exercise."

Less than a year later, he was legally old enough to work in a steel mill and he sometimes did. Mining and mill jobs were irregular, especially for youngsters, and when the oldest brother, Charley, made the family proud by becoming a barber, yet another opportunity opened up for Honus. He frequently helped out in Charley's shop, doing chores, running errands, or shaving a drifter—when there wasn't a ballgame.

◆ ◆ ◆

Although they often spent their daylight hours working, the energetic Wagner boys still managed to have time for fun. Racing up and down their street, Honus showed some of his natural talent at an early age and surprised his brothers with the good speed that always belied his bandy legs. Baseball was a crucial part of the boys' childhood. They played catch at lunchtime or under the gas street lamps in the evening and took advantage of the extra summer daylight hours to play ball. On Sundays, they rounded up others in the neighborhood for pickup games on an empty lot on Main Street in Mansfield, and Honus often pitched. He later liked to brag about the Wagner family team, but with an age spread of eleven years between Charley and Bill, it hardly could have struck fear in the hearts of opponents.

Baseball was thought by much of society to be rough and its players uncivilized, but it seems as though Mr. and Mrs. Wagner had no objections to their sons playing ball. However, the sport did cause a few family problems. Sometimes when Honus was assisting in his brother's barber shop, he would sneak out to get in on a game, leaving a frustrated Charley in the lurch.

While in their teens, Al, Luke, and Honus began competing regularly on local squads. Al, a tall and stocky young man, was developing into one of the best players in the community. Although two and a half years younger than Al, Honus was even taller and heavier. He showed signs of becoming a strong right-handed pitcher, a potent right-handed batter, and a fast baserunner. He had an advocate in Al, who often persuaded his teammates to let his brother fill in when they needed someone.

Perhaps even more important, Al, a versatile fielder and right-handed thrower and hitter himself, encouraged Honus to learn every position so that he could always find a spot on a team. It was advice that Honus took to heart, and incredibly, he was thirty-four years old before he played one position for an entire season.

Representing several loosely structured community- as well as church- and company-sponsored teams during a single summer, the Wagners occasionally had to disguise their true identities. Honus usually played under the name of John, but if a schedule conflict caused Al or Honus to miss a game, one brother would assume the other's name and take his place, or simply play as William. Honus later admitted that he could make up to five dollars per week for a pair of games, and with wagers sometimes made between the clubs, he and his brother did not want to bypass any contests.

In 1893, Honus and Al became more visible when they joined the Mansfield Indians in the four-team Allegheny County League. With a single league game each Saturday, the club supplemented its schedule with exhibitions (though in April, a contest against the National League Pittsburgh Pirates was rained out). The Wagner brothers played sporadically and at a variety of positions for the last-place Indians but faced much better competition, including some of the best amateur talent in the area and players from Western University of Pennsylvania (now the University of Pittsburgh).

The Indians were under the management of thirty-year-old ironworker Shadrach "Shad" Gwilliam, a remarkably solemn man who was also an up-and-comer in sports circles, although his reputation would come in the realm of gambling. Following the season's closing contest, Gwilliam challenged first-place Tarentum to a game for a whopping one hundred dollar purse—copped by his Indians with a convincing 10–3 victory.

◆ ◆ ◆

Things were looking up for the Wagners as 1894 began. Railroad Avenue had been paved and sewers installed. In February, Peter Wagner was one of an overwhelming majority of citizens who voted in favor of consolidating the two small boroughs of Chartiers and Mansfield. The new municipality was named Carnegie in honor of western Pennsylvania's foremost citizen, Andrew Carnegie. A Scottish immigrant of humble beginnings, Carnegie started working at age thirteen as a bobbin boy in a Pittsburgh-area cotton mill. Through diligence and shrewdness, he amassed a fortune by age twenty-four and eventually became a multimillionaire in steel manufacturing and other industries. He came to share much of his wealth, donating millions of dollars to support education, free public libraries, and the world peace movement. (Mr. Carnegie was so pleased by the residents' gesture that in 1901, he endowed the town with a library.)

In the spring of 1894, Charley's business was expanding, allowing him to make a few improvements to his shop, while Al, Luke, and twenty-year-old Honus prepared for another active baseball summer. One of the teams they played for was the newly formed Carnegie Athletic Club, managed by Shad Gwilliam, in the Allegheny County League. With the Wagners and their friends James "Toots" Barrett and Patrick "Patsy" Flaherty showing promise, the *Carnegie Union* took notice that the town "has some splendid amateur baseball players." The weekly paper used the term "amateur" loosely. Teams commonly bet one another and small payments were made to some individuals, but since league rules disallowed contracts, the players were not considered professionals.

In perhaps their last appearance as a brother act, the three were in the same lineup for the second game of a July 4 doubleheader. Al was at second base for both games, while Honus moved from shortstop in game one to the mound in game two. Luke played in just the one game, going hitless and making an error in left field.

Earlier in 1894, Al had tried his hand at pro ball in Frankfort, Kentucky, but returned in May, saying that he did not care for that part of the country. Apparently more to his liking was eastern Ohio where, after the Allegheny County League folded in July, he hooked up as a paid member of the Twin Cities club representing the villages of Dennison and Uhrichsville.

The Twin Cities team was one of the best semipro outfits in Ohio, playing a number of exhibition games against National League clubs, including an 11–10 win over Connie Mack's Pittsburgh Pirates. On at least one occasion, Honus joined his brother in Dennison. On July 29, Honus played right field and had two hits from the eighth spot in the order. Al, primarily an infielder, hit .410 and scored fifty-three runs over thirty-seven games for the Twin Cities Real Estates in 1894. He was also paving the way for his brother to get a crack at a professional contract.

◆ ◆ ◆

Over the decades, Honus Wagner treated many to some of his best tales when asked to reflect on his first stint in professional baseball. Typical Wagner yarns were lightly sprinkled with facts and liberally laced with embellishment. This one usually began with what he claimed was his first and last attempt to get more money for playing ball. His friends thought he had hit the big time when he received a telegram from a minor league team offering thirty-five dollars per month. But when they found out Al was getting sixty dollars, they convinced Honus to ask for an additional five spot. He boldly acted on their advice but received the reply, "If you can't accept thirty-five, you had better stay home."

What happened next could—depending on the receptivity of his audience or the creativity of his interviewer—take on epic proportions in later years. In one popular version, Honus feared he had blown his only chance when his request was denied, and in desperation, he hopped a coal train to meet his new team just as the season was about to get under way. Wearing his uniform under his clothes and carrying no luggage, he was hustled from the depot to the field. No baseball shoes could be found that fit him, so he was forced to play barefoot until a suitable pair of spikes were located the following day.

Other subplots included brother Al having to show him the correct way to put on a uniform, and Honus walking a dozen men and hitting seven more with pitches before the visiting team insisted he be removed from the mound. In yet another variation, Al had to retrieve Honus from home when he quit after his first game.

The events which led to Wagner's entry into professional ball actually began in the fall of 1894. A few Pittsburgh men joined a group of Ohioans in an effort to form a new minor league for 1895. George L. Moreland, a Pittsburgh sportswriter and the secretary of the now-defunct Allegheny County League, was itching to get into baseball in an official capacity. He began to beat the drum for the formation of a league and agreed to own, operate, and manage a club in Steubenville, Ohio. The Inter-State League would comprise clubs from seven Ohio towns as well as Wheeling, West Virginia.

One of the first players Moreland pursued and secured was Al Wagner. By February 2, 1895, Moreland reported that he had signed all of his players. The roster he submitted to the league president did not include any other Wagners, but over the next few days, Moreland was convinced by Al that Honus would be an asset as a pitcher and utility man.

Moreland had been impressed with Honus when he saw him play the previous summer and made out a contract with the name of William Wagner—the name Honus had played under. Honus was not about to let a minor technicality like the wrong name stand in his way. The two copies of the agreement were made out with William's name, and that is how Honus signed them in the presence of his eighteen-year-old friend Patsy Flaherty.

Honus was now a professional ballplayer. The document stipulated that his thirty-five-dollar monthly salary was "payable on the first and fifteenth of each month or as soon as possible" and that he was responsible for paying for his own uniform and shoes out of his first earnings. One Wagner memory was that after the expense was deducted, he netted three dollars; at other times, he would recount that payday "never did become possible."

Moreland received Honus's signed contract on February 10. The Wagners and their hometown friend Toots Barrett, who had agreed to pitch for Moreland, arrived together uneventfully in Steubenville on April 10, 1895, the day all players were to report. Throughout his life, Honus would be considered a homebody, but his first extended venture away from home was made easier by the fact that the Ohio River town of Steubenville was just an hour or so from Carnegie, and he made the trip with his brother and friend.

Now twenty-one years old, Honus was off to a late start compared with many other budding professionals. Though not handsome, he had a pleasantly rugged face with a somewhat oversized nose, high cheekbones, a strong jaw, and sleepy brown eyes. At five feet eleven inches tall and weighing about 185 pounds, he was a large man for his time, though he was not quite fully grown. But the physical characteristics that would become his trademarks were already evident—broad shoulders, long arms, huge hands, and those soon-to-be-famous bowed legs.

T W O

ANYWHERE AND
EVERYWHERE

During the 1890s, many minor leagues lacked organization and finances, making them extremely volatile. Leagues came and went, often lasting less than a season before folding. And even if a league survived, sometimes individual clubs would not, causing the circuit to limp along with less than a full contingent. Frequently, the result was confusion over player contracts, scheduling problems, and controversy about records or standings. Storm clouds were gathering over the Inter-State League as early as February 1895, and *Sporting Life,* a leading sports magazine of the era, called the league "a sickly babe from the start." As the season drew near, optimism grew somewhat after a 112-game schedule had been finalized, but the cities that were to be represented were in doubt until a few days before games were to begin. Finally, it was decided that the eight teams would be Steubenville, the Twin Cities team of Dennison and Uhrichsville, Findlay, Columbus, Kenton, Canton, and Mansfield in Ohio, and Wheeling, West Virginia.

Moreland encouraged his Pittsburgh friends, Al C. Buckenberger and Edward G. Barrow, to buy into the Wheeling franchise. The Pittsburgh Pirates' indecisive ownership had bounced Buckenberger from acting president to team manager during the previous three years. After

piloting the Pirates to a surprise second-place finish in 1893, Buckenberger was displaced for good in late 1894 by catcher and rookie
manager Connie Mack. Barrow had been a mainstay of the Pittsburgh
sports scene and managed the scorecard concession at Exposition Park
for scorecard magnate Harry M. Stevens. Buckenberger and Barrow
jumped at the chance to get the Wheeling club.

Buckenberger soon accepted a National League managerial position
with St. Louis (a tour of duty that would last only fifty games into the
season) and turned over responsibility of the Wheeling club to Barrow.
Barrow, a big, good-natured fellow and a hustler, would handle the business affairs and player contracts of the Wheeling Mountaineers, sometimes called the Stogies. It was Barrow's first official role in professional
baseball and began an executive career in the game that spanned more
than fifty years, culminating in his induction into baseball's Hall of
Fame. His path would cross Honus Wagner's several times over the
years, always under favorable circumstances.

Moreland had grave reservations about Steubenville's ability to support his club, not to mention the lack of adequate grounds. Huntsman
Park did have its problems: The outfield was short and uneven, with the
left field fence only 290 feet away. The right field fence was even closer
at a mere 210 feet, necessitating a ground rule stating that a ball hit over
it would be just a double. Compared with the outfield, the infield was
considered good, even if it did slope from first to third. In addition, a hill
just beyond the short outfield fence allowed freeloaders to see games
without paying.

Expressing confidence that he had assembled a good team, Moreland expected third baseman Al Wagner to shoulder much of the load,
saying, "[He] is one of the coming ballplayers of the country. . . . His
great hold is baserunning and batting; in the latter he is considered by
many an equal of many a player in the [National] League. Last season,
while the Pittsburgh team was playing the Twin Cities, manager [Con-
nie] Mack made the remark that [Al] Wagner would be found in the big
league inside of two years. . . ." Unclear about the name of his new
pitcher but enthusiastic about his prospects, Moreland said, "William
Wagner . . . is a young blood with an arm on him like one of Rusie's
and speed as great." It was quite a compliment, since celebrated fireball-
er Amos Rusie "the Hoosier Thunderbolt," had won thirty or more
games in the National League four years running and had led the league
in strikeouts four of the previous five years.

By mid-April, the team's new gray uniforms were on hand. The jerseys featured a traditional collar and a blue "S" on a breast pocket. (Of course, there was no number or name, since those would be adopted by the sport much later.) The outfit was completed with a blue cap and stockings. Two dozen "Kentucky Sluggers" were delivered, and Moreland's squad was ready. The first exhibition game, on April 19, was a 19–6 blowout over a local nine. Al Wagner provided the heroics—four doubles and a single in six trips to the plate. Honus was only a spectator. In this he was not alone, as there were an estimated one thousand people at the grounds but only three hundred in Huntsman Park. The rest were scattered on the hillside and in nearby trees, avoiding the twenty-five-cent admission charge.

Honus, or "Will," as he was being referred to now, got his first game action as a true professional the following day as the right fielder in a victory over Holy Ghost College of Pittsburgh (renamed Duquesne University in 1911). Batting seventh, he collected a single and a double in his five at bats. He stole a base and immediately drew acclaim for his play in the outfield. *The Steubenville Star* stated that a fly to Will was "like knocking a ball in a well . . . as he is sure death to any fly that goes into his territory."

Al continued to pound the ball through the final three exhibitions as Moreland's men won all five of their tune-up games against weak competition. Honus alternated between left field and the mound. In one four-inning pitching stint, he struck out eight batters and lost a ninth to a dropped third strike.

Honus was in left field and batting seventh for the Inter-State season opener at Steubenville on May 2. The home team jumped on Canton pitching for six runs in the first and four in the second, but Honus struck out in each inning. In the third, Canton rallied for five runs to make it a 10–7 game, but Honus ended the inning when he gunned out at the plate a runner who tried to score from second on a single. Steubenville added five more runs in the fourth, with Honus's three-run homer capping the inning. The home team cruised to a 29–11 win in a game that featured ten home runs, many of which would have been outs "if that peskey [*sic*] fence had been back a few yards," *The Steubenville Star* noted. While the pitching was shaky, the offense amassed twenty-four hits, five by Al. The defense turned four double plays and, even more impressively, did not commit a single error. Honus failed to get a ball out of the infield in his final three at bats and ended his professional debut 1 for 6 with the three-run home run.

Steubenville scored forty-five runs in winning two of their next three games in front of dwindling attendance. On May 7, Honus went 3 for 5 with a triple and made his first official pitching appearance with two innings of relief that included four strikeouts and a walk in a 7–6 loss to Kenton. He was on the mound the next day, and after an hour-and-fifteen-minute rain delay, Steubenville scored nine runs in the first inning, sixteen in the second, and then hurried to squeeze in the required five innings while Kenton purposely tried to stall in hopes of a called game. Honus rapped two doubles and pitched a five-inning complete game, surrendering three walks and seven hits, including three home runs, before Kenton (aptly nicknamed the Babes) quit after five. The turnout at the shortened affair was estimated at twenty-five, and Moreland, having already received league approval to move the team to a more suitable location, was off to Akron, Ohio, to meet with interested parties there.

Money men in Steubenville made last-ditch efforts and promises, but Akron's backers agreed to give Moreland five hundred dollars cash, purchase fifty season tickets, and allow him to use the Buchtel College grounds, which could be reached by three different sets of street railways. These inducements, coupled with the fact that Akron's population of roughly forty thousand was three times larger than Steubenville's, made it easy for Moreland to agree to the move.

A final three-game series was to be played against the Mansfield Kids before the team left Steubenville; Honus sat out the first one but took the mound to mop up the last few innings of the second game, allowing one run in a 10–5 loss. The final contest was rained out, with Steubenville holding a 4–0 lead in the third, and on Monday, May 13, the club—holding a record of 5–3—played its first game representing Akron. "Will" was off to a solid start, batting 11 for 30 with a homer, a triple, three doubles, and three stolen bases in his seven games for Steubenville.

◆ ◆ ◆

Akron newspapers began calling the team the Akrons well in advance of its arrival, and the squad was treated to a welcoming parade. The *Akron Beacon Journal and Republican* assured the locals that the members of the team were "gentlemanly players and not rowdies," but the turnout for Akron's Inter-State opener was a disappointment. The team did endear itself to the few who were present with a 21–5 massacre of Findlay. Left fielder Honus, batting sixth, had two doubles and a home run, and Al had two homers.

The Wagner brothers were clouting more than their fair share of home runs in the first few weeks of the 1895 season. The rubber-center baseballs of the era did not carry well and were allowed to remain in play until they were gray and misshapen. As a result, the home run was not as common as it would be a few decades later or is today. (During the 1890s, major league home run leaders most often finished with season totals in the teens.) Honus was already demonstrating the unique combination of power and speed for which he would become well known. He had both the strength to punch the "dead" ball through the infield, into a gap, or even over a wall, and the swiftness to turn singles into doubles and drives between outfielders into inside-the-park home runs.

After Akron split the next two games, Honus pitched on May 17, allowing seven hits and four walks. He hit two batters and threw a wild pitch but muddled through a complete game as his team took advantage of nine Canton errors for a 14–7 win.

A few members of the Inter-State League were on shaky financial ground, and Moreland's situation was the most critical. Attendance was so dismal for the four games in Akron that the gate receipts for the best day were only forty-seven dollars, and he was unable to pay the visiting club's guarantee. Hoping for better support, Moreland rescheduled the May 18 contest as a road game at Canton. But after forfeiting that game because one of his players refused to leave the field after being ejected, Moreland disbanded his club, and the league admitted a team from Lima, Ohio.

George Moreland's turbulent minor league experience was over for the year, and he returned to *The Pittsburgh Press* as a sportswriter. He was destined to become one of baseball's foremost statisticians and a strong supporter of major league baseball.

The *Ohio State Journal* reported, "A lively scramble is expected to take place over Akron's players," and the paper encouraged the local Columbus team management to get involved. Al Wagner and Toots Barrett signed with Canton. Shortstop Claude Ritchey and a few of the others moved on to Warren, Pennsylvania, of the Iron & Oil League, which had been rumored to be tampering with some of the Inter-State League players for the last few weeks.

Honus, staying in the fragile Inter-State League, signed with the Mansfield Kids, winners in just two of their first fourteen games. The *Mansfield Daily Shield*, a chronic complainer, or "kicker," about league affairs, relished making fun of the league and its leadership. It referred to league president Howard Zigler as "Fathead Ziegler [*sic*]," conveying that he "seems to know as much about managing a base ball league as a hog does about algebra," but explained, "His ignorance is pardonable because it is laughable." Its comments on the league itself were just as positive, referring to it as "a big farce" and the "interchangeable league." Not to be outdone, the *Uhrichsville Chronicle* proved it could do a little kicking of its own when it described nearby Mansfield as "the deadest of dead towns, strewed with stinking corpses, where never a breath of fresh air stirs, and the green scum of creation is inches deep around the roots of the moss that grows on the backs of the inhabitants." Amid this spirited feeling of cooperation and sportsmanship, the Inter-State League and Wagner made yet another start.

Frank O'Brien, manager of the Mansfield team and another Pittsburgh-area man, gave Wagner his first professional try at shortstop when the young player arrived on May 20. John, as he was now being called, made three errors in his first game—not good, but certainly common in a time of poor playing surfaces and tiny gloves only slightly larger than a player's hand. Despite his three errors, he remained at shortstop, and the Kids won three straight.

On May 23, he had a rocky relief outing as brother Al's Canton club knocked off Mansfield, 14–10. But Honus hit two home runs, and the *Mansfield Daily Shield* admitted, "J. Wagner is a good all-around player," and wished, "Oh, for nine men like Wagner." The first professional head-to-head matchup between the two brothers became another Wagner tall tale. According to Honus, his Mansfield team thought he was Al because his brother had signed two contracts when the Akron team dissolved, one with Canton and one with Mansfield. In securing two positions Al was looking out for his younger brother—and turned the Mansfield job over to Honus. Mansfield only caught on to the scheme when Canton came to town with the real Al. All was forgiven after Honus socked those two home runs that day.

The Kids avenged their loss to Canton by winning the next two, and Honus went 5 for 9 with a triple and home run over the two games. He was not, however, receiving much praise for his fielding. He had two more three-error games and was chastised by his own teammate for his over-aggressiveness at shortstop after he collided with the left fielder on a pop fly. Moved off the shortstop position, he logged playing time in center field, at second base, and at third base the rest of the way with Mansfield.

On June 2, Kenton and Al's Canton team tried to play a game on a

Sunday, an immoral act for much of the nation, which still adhered to a strong puritan ethic. Local authorities arrested both teams. The Kenton ball club paid the exorbitant sixty-five-dollar fine and moved on, but the amount proved too much for Canton management, and the team disbanded. The *Ohio State Journal* again urged the Columbus manager to secure some of the now available talent from Canton, such as pitcher Toots Barrett, catcher Harry Smith, or "Home-run [Al] Wagner," but all three players joined their friends, who had already signed with the Warren organization.

Mansfield manager O'Brien assured all that his club was in the race to stay, but within a week, he was rescheduling home games to the road in order to secure enough gate receipts to pay off his players and provide each of them with a train ticket. After the team's brief resurgence when Wagner arrived, it lost ten of eleven, its record now standing at a woeful 8–23, solidly in last place. Delightedly announcing the team's demise on June 14, local coverage included a final parting shot with, "[The *Mansfield Daily Shield*] politely bows and says, 'I told you so.'"

Al expressed an interest in having his younger brother join the gang at Warren, but Honus already had another team lined up. Feeling he had nothing to lose, he wired Al on June 15, collect: "Will come for sixty five [dollars per month] send ticket." His terms were way too steep for Warren, so Honus pursued his first opportunity.

◆ ◆ ◆

One of the backers of the now defunct Mansfield club was businessman William H. Taylor. His son, Rolla L. Taylor, was part owner and manager of a club in Adrian, Michigan, of the Michigan State League. Father convinced son that Wagner would prove a good addition, and Rolla signed the younger Wagner to a contract calling for fifty dollars per month.

Along with Adrian, the Michigan State League consisted of teams representing the Michigan communities of Port Huron, Owosso, Kalamazoo, Battle Creek, and Lansing. Adrian, a farming town of about ten thousand people and the county seat of Lenawee County, billed itself as a "beautiful residence city in the center of a rich agricultural district." To Wagner, the flat terrain and rural setting must have seemed very foreign.

With the six-club Michigan State League season only a few weeks old, the Adrian club was in third place when Wagner arrived. But the boys from Adrian could not even claim to be the best team in town, as Adrian was also home to the Page Fence Giants, a successful barnstorming team of black ballplayers. The Giants, sponsored by the Page Woven Wire Fence Company, traveled throughout the Midwest in their own ornamented railway car, which the Adrian *Evening Telegram* referred to as "a veritable palace on wheels." Shortly before Wagner's arrival, Adrian was clobbered 20–10 by the Giants, who sometimes lent players to the Adrian team. In addition, two of Adrian's full-time players were obtained from the Giants, pitcher George Wilson and catcher Vasco Graham. (As was typical of the times, the press referred to the two as "the watermelon battery.") While the unwritten color line in Organized Baseball had not yet solidified into an absolute, blacks and whites playing ball on the same team was still very rare.

The sales pitch given by the elder Taylor on Wagner's behalf must have been a good one because in his first game with Adrian on June 20, Wagner batted fourth. (Not yet labeled "cleanup," the fourth position in the batting order was known as a "post of honor.") Wilson threw a one-hitter and struck out eleven as Adrian beat Owosso. Wagner provided no instant heroics in his newest city as he went 1 for 4 and made an error while playing second base; nonetheless, the *Evening Telegram* wrote, "The local team has been greatly strengthened by the addition. . . ."

Two days later, Wagner had a single, double, and triple in a come-from-behind, ten-inning victory as Adrian completed a three-game sweep. In Adrian's fourth straight win, he tripled home two runs in the first inning. "Wagner's work on second and at the bat was excellent," cited the *Adrian Daily Times*. "Some of the ground stops he made were handsome plays in every respect. He is undoubtedly a strong point on our team." Adrian won its first seven games with Wagner. It lost the next game only when Graham, the black catcher, was grabbed between third and home as he was trying to score the winning run in the ninth inning, hit with a thrown ball, and called out. Wilson was then ejected from the bench for arguing, and Billy Holland, another black player for Adrian that day, refused to continue to pitch. The game was lost in extra innings.

The winning ways continued, and by Independence Day, Adrian was fighting for first place. As the second baseman and nearly .400-hitting cleanup batter, Wagner made a significant contribution to the team's success. But he played his last game with Adrian on July 5 and headed back to Carnegie. His reasons for leaving are not entirely clear. Thirty-five years later, in 1930, just two years before his death, Rolla Taylor recalled that the reason for Wagner's abrupt departure was that he did not like playing with Adrian's black players. Fifty years after the fact, Wagner's explanation for leaving Adrian was simply homesickness. Neither man elaborated.

While not a pioneer in race or ethnic relations, Wagner most likely would have had no unusual difficulty associating with blacks. Carnegie was a diverse community and home to a number of ethnic groups— albeit, like all of America at that time, the black population was disconnected from whites, worshiping, working, and living apart. Wagner's feelings would have echoed the prevailing separatist attitude, but he certainly did not harbor the feelings of racial hatred exhibited by other ballplayers, most notably Cap Anson and Ty Cobb. In fact, there are indications that Wagner was mostly indifferent to race. Throughout his major league career, his teams employed two black trainers, Ed LaForce and George Aston. Not only were Wagner's relations with them cordial, he stood up on their behalf when anyone showed them discourtesy. John Henry "Pop" Lloyd, a tremendous shortstop and one of the greatest black ballplayers of the early twentieth century, was nicknamed "The Black Wagner." When asked his opinion on having a black namesake, Wagner answered, "It's an honor to be compared with him."

Wagner's departure most likely resulted from a number of factors. He suffered a spike wound in his last game with Adrian, and he was concerned for his father, who had sustained a broken arm in a mine accident a few days earlier. In addition, his brother and friends in Warren were about to get a fresh start with the opening of the Iron & Oil League's second half-season. Honus had been promised a roster spot (although at only thirty-five dollars per month), and he was back home by July 9.

◆ ◆ ◆

It was a short stay in Carnegie. Two days later, Wagner made the picturesque five-and-a-half-hour train journey through the mountains of northern Pennsylvania to Warren. It was a trip he would make many times over the years. This section of Pennsylvania would become a favorite hunting ground and retreat for Wagner. He formed lasting ties with Warren and was honored by its citizens in 1938 and again in 1946.

In 1895, the city of Warren was thriving due to its proximity to vast natural resources of petroleum and timber. This Allegheny River community of about seven thousand people was a hotbed of carriage and furniture manufacturers, oil refineries, and iron works. Patrons of Warren's brand-new Recreation Park, built in midseason, had a view of both the scenic Allegheny River and the many oil wells and refineries that pocked the landscape.

In Warren, Honus was reunited with Toots Barrett, Claude Ritchey, brother Al, and a number of other friends and escapees from the Inter-State League. The group that preceded Honus to Warren was receiving quite a bit of recognition. *Sporting Life* reported that the major league Pirates had their eye on Barrett, Ritchey, and Al Wagner. Ritchey was said to be a crowd favorite, and it was noted that when he reached first, he "almost invariably steals second." Locally, Al was considered "a heavy hitter," having recorded several multi-hit games. Barrett's career would end in the minors, but a few of the others who caught on with Warren would eventually get to the majors, including shortstop Ritchey, outfielder Joe Rickert, pitcher Bill Carrick, and catcher Harry Smith, later one of Honus Wagner's closest friends. Despite such noteworthy additions earlier that season, Warren was destined to finish the first half at 20–24, fifth in a six-team race.

Honus, arriving just in time for the July 11 game, played first base and batted fourth. He singled, scored twice, and stole a base, but Al made three of the team's nine errors as Warren lost 14–11. The next day, Honus was in right field and went hitless as the team played its final game of the first half, winning 8–5. A few exhibition wins followed, with Honus playing shortstop and batting second, where he had a four-hit day that included a home run.

The team representing Franklin won the first-half championship from its northwest Pennsylvania competitors of Oil City, Titusville, Sharon, New Castle, and Warren. For the season's second half, the Sharon club was relocated to Celoron, New York, and two clubs of the now defunct Inter-State League—the Twin Cities Twins from Ohio and Ed Barrow's Wheeling Mountaineers—were added to the ranks to make an eight-team, four-state Iron & Oil League.

The second half began on Tuesday, July 16, with Warren bagging a 7–6 victory over Celoron, thanks to Al's tie-breaking triple in the ninth. It earned him a dollar from an admirer and a mention in the *Warren Evening Democrat* that "the prize third baseman . . . [was] a pretty good man to have around in an emergency." Honus started in right field, then moved to left for the bottom of the ninth; batting fourth, he had a single and scored a run.

On Wednesday, Warren played an exhibition against the Pittsburgh Pirates, who were making a midseason run at first place in the National

League. Warren let a 7–4 lead slip away by giving up eight runs in the eighth inning. The Pirates were aided by seven Warren miscues, but Honus, Al, and Toots were each errorless. Barrett, a left-hander, allowed only four hits and no earned runs until the disastrous eighth. Al smacked a homer and dropped down two sacrifice bunts. Honus had a single, and each brother swiped a base off Pirate catcher Connie Mack.

Mack had a reputation in the National League for his incessant talking behind the plate. It was not the vulgarities of many players of the era, just continual banter intended to distract an opposing batter. When Honus took his place in the batter's box for his first at bat, Mack began chatting about the weather and a number of meaningless subjects and happened to mention what pitch would be coming next. Mack continued to tip off pitches to Wagner, but the young hitter was so confused he could barely take advantage of the information, getting just one single on the day. Later in the contest, with the bases full, Wagner approached the plate. Mack shook his head and simply said, "You're on your own this time, kid." To Mack's delight, Wagner made an easy out.

The Wagner boys' versatility was on display in Warren. Honus played a few more games in right field, but when Al moved to second base while nursing a leg injury, Honus took his place at third. The *Warren Evening Democrat* recognized his good work there, pointing out that it "seems to be a regular Wagner base."

Honus's tenure at third lasted just three games. The *Warren Ledger* reported that on July 26, while running to catch a train after a rainout in Titusville, "He fell against a picket fence and received quite a gash under his right arm-pit, which is quite painful but not serious, as none of the muscles were injured." Several stitches were required to mend the wound, and it kept him out of action for three full weeks. While Honus watched and rehabilitated during a long homestand, his teammates put together a twelve-game winning streak and moved comfortably into first place.

In the middle of a road trip, Honus, Al, and a few of their teammates spent an off Sunday at the Wagner home in Carnegie before moving on to the Twin Cities. There, Honus was back in the lineup as Warren won two games, one thanks to a twelve-error performance by the Twins, and the other due to the crowd taking control of the field in the eleventh inning, causing a forfeit. One day later, the moneyless Twin Cities team folded. Within a few days, Oil City and Titusville disbanded for similar reasons, and Franklin was teetering as well.

The Warren club was still on relatively secure financial footing. The

Warren Evening Mirror stated that "salary day in Warren means checks for the players in full . . . [and] there are plenty of people here to give $5, $10 or even $20 or $25 to make good any defficiency [*sic*]." Indeed, local support was adequate, and silver dollars were often the rewards for Warren players who hit home runs at Recreation Park. Wheeling, though, was the most—perhaps the only—profitable team in the league. Barrow and Buckenberger were alleged to have broken even on their investment by the first of July, and home games played on the July 4 holiday and an exhibition game with Brooklyn of the National League netted another one thousand dollars. However, the league situation was dire.

Late in August, sensing the inevitable demise of the circuit, Barrow challenged first-place Warren to play his second-place Wheeling club in a seven-game series. The victor would win the second half-season and earn the right to face Franklin, winner of the first half, for the Iron & Oil League's 1895 championship. To capitalize on attendance at the West Virginia State Fair, all of the Wheeling-Warren games were to be played at Wheeling's Island Park. Gate receipts would be split, with 65 percent going to the winners and 35 percent to the losers. Wheeling had made a late-season charge thanks to recent acquisitions "Pebbly Jack" Glasscock and Harry Staley, both of whom finished their big league careers earlier that year. Barrow coaxed Glasscock, a Wheeling native, out of a brief retirement after his midyear release from Washington's National League club, the end of a seventeen-year big league career as an accomplished shortstop in the bare-hand days and as the 1890 National League batting champ. Staley had pitched eight seasons in the bigs and won 137 games before being released by St. Louis and signing on with Wheeling.

The series opened on Friday, August 30. Honus went 1 for 4 and Al had a double, but Barrett surrendered three runs in the eighth inning to lose 4–3. Warren's only highlight came when catcher Harry Smith, chasing a foul pop, slipped and fell on the wet grass but managed to make the catch with his bare hand while lying on the ground. In front of an estimated Saturday crowd of fifteen hundred, Honus made two errors and went hitless as Warren lost 9–4 to go down two games to none. Even worse for Warren, Smith had a thumbnail torn off in the first inning and was forced to the sidelines for the remainder of the series.

West Virginia's blue law prohibited Sunday baseball, so the series resumed on Monday, September 2. Honus and Al each had two hits, and Warren took advantage of nine Wheeling errors to roll to an easy 11–2 win, despite Al's three errors at second base. Honus committed three errors at third the following day as Warren lost 10–4 to go down three games to one. Warren scored sixteen runs to win the next one, but in game six, Barrett gave up two runs in the ninth and lost 3–2. Wheeling won the series four games to two, but Warren won a meaningless seventh contest, staged to secure a few more dollars from the fairgoers.

The series proved to be a financial windfall, and the management and players of both teams were pleased with the result. In addition, Barrow and Buckenberger were impressed with some of the talent on the Warren squad and approached a few of the boys before they left town. Honus Wagner, 8 for 29 with no extra-base hits and five errors in the series, Al Wagner, 9 for 28 with three doubles and a triple, and Claude Ritchey, 10 for 30 with five doubles, all expressed a willingness to play for Wheeling the following year. With the uncertainty of each franchise and the entire Iron & Oil League, any plans for the future were premature.

Wheeling proclaimed itself league champ when the Franklin team disintegrated before a final series could be played. Despite the outcome of the postseason series, the Warren papers were quick to point out that their hometown team should be considered the league champion because its second-half record was still better than Wheeling's. When Warren dropped two of three games in New Castle following the Wheeling series, the New Castle press curiously asserted that its team should be crowned as champs. After deliberating, the league president declared Wheeling the winner and forwarded a pennant to club management. In later years, Ed Barrow derived great pleasure in stating that his first year in professional baseball resulted in two championships—the Inter-State and Iron & Oil Leagues of 1895.

Warren's season ended after a two-game drubbing of a team of local amateurs. Management tried to keep the team assembled and to schedule a few more exhibitions, but they finally called it quits in mid-September.

It had been an incredibly hectic year for the Wagner family. Peter Wagner suffered a broken arm. Charles lost his barber shop and was forced to ply his tonsorial trade elsewhere when his landlord skipped out with a year's rent. Eighteen-year-old Carrie had become quite a socialite around Carnegie. And Al and Honus spent the summer hopping from one city and team to another, attempting to earn a living playing baseball.

In just over five months, Honus played for five different teams in three states and three leagues. He played eight different positions, all four in the infield, all three in the outfield, and had also pitched. Displaying the talents that would define his career—an ability to play virtually anywhere in the field, a strong and accurate throwing arm, surprising speed on the base paths, and power with the bat—he competed and succeeded at a better quality of play than he had experienced before.

In addition, Wagner later said that the season of 1895 was when he began to study baseball. He strived to refine his skills, eliminate his weaknesses, and emulate the techniques of the players he admired. He also began observing his opponents, especially pitchers, looking for ways to get a better swing at the plate or a better jump on the bases. It was a practice he continued throughout his long career.

Honus and Al arrived home for the winter on Saturday, September 21. Their offseason got off to a rocky start that very evening, as five chickens were stolen from their mother's chicken coop.

◆ ◆ ◆

Ed Barrow is commonly credited with the discovery of Honus Wagner. By the winter prior to the 1896 baseball season, Barrow was quite familiar with the developing, but as yet unrefined, young player. However, it was Barrow's recognition of Wagner's true potential that was significant. Wagner's "discovery" is considered of such importance in Barrow's career that the executive's Hall of Fame plaque in Cooperstown notes it as one of his greatest achievements.

Barrow's own story of the event begins when he was spending some time at a Pittsburgh taproom, Johnny Newell's Cafe, in late February 1896. He mentioned to his friend and local "sport," Shad Gwilliam, that he was looking for baseball talent. Gwilliam knew the Wagner brothers well from when he managed them in their semipro days, and he informed Barrow that Al and Honus were presently unsigned for the coming year. Barrow, who liked what he saw of the Wagners when they faced his Wheeling club, thought Al to be the better ballplayer but regarded him as difficult to manage. Barrow was unsure about the younger Wagner, who had turned twenty-two a few days earlier, thinking he might be too awkward. But remembering the strength and power Honus displayed the previous summer, and valuing his amicable, easygoing nature, Barrow decided to give Honus an offer.

It was a bright but cold winter day, and Barrow headed for a Carnegie pool hall, the Wagner boys' hangout. Finding it nearly deserted, he asked where he could find Honus Wagner and was directed to the railroad yard where some of the boys were having a "throwing match." Honus and his buddies spotted Barrow coming toward them and, taking him for a railroad bull, were ready to run. Barrow immediately recognized Wagner, who was wearing a silly derby hat adorned with a chicken feather in the band, by his bowed legs and long arms.

Getting straight to the point, Barrow asked Wagner if he wanted to play ball that summer. Wagner hesitated, perhaps recalling the chaos of the previous year, and continued to fire rocks and lumps of coal down the railroad tracks. As he saw the distance Wagner's powerful arm hurled the rocks, Barrow became increasingly convinced that he had to have the young man on his ball club. Ignoring a league salary limit of $100 per month, he lured Wagner with the figure of $125. It meant that he would make more that summer than the average 1896 worker would earn for the entire year ($439). The two returned to the pool hall to finalize the arrangement.

◆ ◆ ◆

Earlier in the winter of 1895–1896, the Pittsburgh Pirates had made a play for Wagner. Pirate president William W. Kerr, prodded by George Moreland and Connie Mack, extended an offer of $100 per month, which Wagner later admitted had him "right smartly smoked up." But the contract included the stipulation that he be sent to Kansas City of the Western League to gain experience. (Major league clubs of that era sometimes signed players and sent them to a minor league for seasoning while reserving rights to the player. This practice was often harshly criticized for giving wealthy teams an advantage by allowing them to sign many unused players to contracts. While individual players were "farmed," this process predated the farm system as we know it today, in which entire minor league clubs are tied to a major league team.) Mack and Kerr wanted to add Wagner to their reserve list but agreed he was not quite ready for big league ball.

Wagner was unsure. He asked Kerr where Kansas City was and who played on the team. Despite the opportunity to sign a contract that might lead to playing in nearby Pittsburgh, Wagner declined: He didn't recognize any of the names Kerr told him were on the roster, and Kansas City seemed like a million miles from home.

Ed Barrow's immediate success in Wheeling had convinced him that there were monetary gains to be made in baseball. But the instability of both the Inter-State and Iron & Oil Leagues for 1896 left him looking elsewhere. He and Charles I. McKee, a Pittsburgh cafeteria operator, purchased for eight hundred dollars the Paterson, New Jersey, franchise in the Atlantic Association (soon renamed the Atlantic League), an upstart minor league on the eastern seaboard.

The Atlantic League was recognized from the outset as a strong organization. With clubs in Connecticut, New Jersey, Delaware, and eventually New York and Pennsylvania, it was backed by a few of the most influential businessmen and politicos on the east coast and was dotted with former and future major leaguers. Al Buckenberger, Barrow's former partner in Wheeling, tried to organize a club in Trenton, New Jersey, and signed the Wagner brothers and Toots Barrett to contracts in early January. But a lack of local cooperation led Buckenberger to throw in the towel on Trenton a month later, leaving the three Carnegie boys without jobs. Buckenberger soon agreed to manage Toronto in the Eastern League and within a few weeks signed Barrett and Al Wagner. But by then, Barrow had Honus's signature.

The day after Honus signed his contract with Paterson, Kerr was informed and approached Barrow to ask about Wagner's availability. Barrow, realizing the value of his discovery, refused but promised the Pirate magnate first shot at Wagner should his contract ever be for sale. This commitment, and Wagner's previous contract discussion with Kerr, caused speculation that while Wagner was playing for Paterson, he was "at the end of a string" tied to the Pirates.

◆　◆　◆

Ironically, Honus Wagner's debut for Paterson was in Pittsburgh against Al Buckenberger's Toronto club, with both Al Wagner and Toots Barrett on the roster. Barrow and Buckenberger decided to conduct their teams' spring training together in balmy Pittsburgh, since the two managers and several of their players resided in the area. They planned to wrap up with a week of head-to-head exhibition games at Exposition Park, home of the Pittsburgh Pirates. Rain and snow cut the schedule down to two games, both played in less than ideal conditions. With a total of twenty-five errors committed in the two contests (one by Honus and none by Al), only two of the thirty runs scored were earned in the 9–3 and 10–8 Toronto wins. Honus had a single and double in the first game from the unfamiliar leadoff spot and went hitless in game two. Barrow's team moved on to Paterson.

Founded in 1791 by Alexander Hamilton, Paterson had become an industrial center through its transportation links to New York City. Silk production was introduced into the area in the 1840s and at one time made up 70 percent of the city's commerce. By 1896, the city was known as a world leader in silk dyeing and production, and it had earned the nickname it still holds today—Silk City.

Paterson had its first professional baseball club ever, and W. L. Dill, local correspondent to *Sporting Life*, was promptly convinced that Barrow was the right man to lead the team. Dill immediately pegged Barrow as a "hustler," and went on to state, "What the people of Paterson want is when a stranger comes to the town with the idea of catering for their patronage [that he] mingle with all classes, and this is the kind of man Barrows [*sic*] appears to be." Unlike the previous year in Wheeling, Barrow would handle field manager duties of the Paterson team and make most of the off-field decisions.

In years past, Paterson had successfully supported semipro ball, but it was only played on Sundays (permissible in New Jersey), the day the local mills were closed. Barrow felt a better, more accessible facility was needed for professional ball to flourish, and he succeeded in finding a backer for the project in Garret A. Hobart. Hobart, a New Jersey politician and a prominent Paterson citizen, was also president of a local streetcar line. With an eye on increasing ridership, Hobart agreed to spend four thousand dollars to construct a 1,500-seat grandstand featuring "opera chairs" rather than the standard bench seats.

When Olympic Park, situated between Passaic and Paterson, was completed in mid-April, it was surpassed as the class of the East Coast only by the Polo Grounds, home to the National League's New York Giants as well as an Atlantic League club. Andrew Freedman, majority owner of the Giants, had purchased the Jersey City franchise in the Atlantic League. Finding no suitable ballpark in that city, Freedman decided to rename his new team the New York Metropolitans and play home games at the Polo Grounds when his Giants were on the road.

(One year later, Garret Hobart was elected vice president of the United States under President William McKinley. Referred to as "the assistant president," Hobart died in office in 1899. His replacement on the winning Republican ticket for 1900 was Theodore Roosevelt, who would become president upon McKinley's 1901 assassination.)

In one year, Barrow and Wagner had come a long way. By the spring of 1896, Barrow was rubbing shoulders with prominent and powerful people. The Atlantic League's level of play and high visibility proved valuable to many players in establishing their baseball credentials, and Wagner would take advantage of his opportunities.

◆ ◆ ◆

A festive atmosphere surrounded the season opener at Olympic Park on Thursday, April 23. A band welcomed the more than two thousand people who filled the new grandstand and surrounding area. The mayor extended a greeting to the crowd, wished the team success, and threw out the first pitch, yelling, "Play ball!" Wagner batted fifth and played first base. He drew a walk in one of his first three trips to the plate, but Paterson could not catch up to the Wilmington, Delaware, Peaches's twenty-year-old left-hander, Jerry Nops. Wagner's ninth-inning, bases-loaded double broke up a four-hit shutout, but Nops prevailed 7–2.

The next day, Paterson banged out twenty hits, five by Wagner including a double and a triple. The team lost four of its first six, all against Wilmington. Three of the four losses were to the young hurler Nops, although Wagner wasn't intimidated, twice slapping two hits in a game with a double, triple, and homer from the cleanup spot against the pitcher. (Nops went on to make his major league debut later that same year and put together a 20–6 season for the Baltimore Orioles in 1897.)

Wagner was hot. After only eight games, he had seventeen hits, had scored eleven times, and was gaining attention for his fine work at first base. The *Paterson Daily Guardian* declared, "Many a throw that would be an error with an ordinary first baseman is raked in by Hannes with consummate ease."

He was now known to the baseball world simply as Honus. The print media re-created his name phonetically as "Hannis," "Hones," "Hannes," and various other ways, but there were no more references to "J.," "John," or for that matter, "Will." Although only twenty-two years old, his obliging temperament had him affectionately referred to in local accounts as "Old Hannis," "Old Reliable," "Big Hannis," and "the German Warhorse," and the attention paid by the local press was considerable. Even his bats were of interest—at the time, he was swinging a bat with a unique reddish-brown tint. His legs brought comparison with the most notable bowlegged big league player of the day, Philadelphia Phillie Lafayette "Lave" Cross. In a brief player profile, the *Paterson Daily Press* insightfully pointed out that Honus "plays the game because he likes it."

◆ ◆ ◆

The Paterson club's first trip to Newark, New Jersey, started on a bad note when Wagner and pitcher Sam McMackin complained to their teammates that Scheutzen Park in Newark wasn't big enough for shooting marbles—not to mention the notable drawback of the big tree growing in left field. A running feud soon developed between the two teams. In the first game of the series, Paterson came back from a 5–0 first-inning deficit to win 10–6, but the visitors were forced to dodge rocks thrown at them by some of the rowdies in the stands. In game two, it was baseballs the Paterson players were dodging. At this, they were unsuccessful, as seven of them were hit by pitches, Wagner once, while they rolled to a 28–10 win.

The Newark team, referred to in Paterson as "The Robbers," was continually accused of inflating its record by adding exhibition wins to its victory totals. Terse words flew between the two rivals each time they played. In one late-season visit to Newark, Barrow was stopped at the gate and refused admission. Barrow, who loved boxing almost as much as baseball and had successfully promoted several professional matches, took offense. The incident did not end until he was fined for popping a security man in the nose. Bad blood between the two teams lasted the remainder of the season.

In mid-May, Paterson took over first place, and by the second week of June, its record stood at a league-best 30–15. The club was getting tremendous support at Olympic Park, often by crowds of more than three thousand, and Barrow was said to be making a "barrel of money." He quashed open gambling in the stands, but on two different occasions he had to fine and suspend pitchers for taking the mound while drunk. In another episode, former big league pitcher Lee Viau arrived at the park in an altered state. Several players were upset with him for sampling the spirits when they needed him to pitch, and Wagner expressed their displeasure. Viau, only five feet four inches tall but a stocky power pitcher, grabbed a water bucket and emptied it over Wagner's head. An unamused Wagner wrapped his large hands around the pitcher's throat, lifting him off the floor. After a few seconds, Wagner regained his composure and dropped the shaken man. It was a seldom-seen side of the mild-mannered Wagner.

Honus was moved around in the batting order, continuing his prolific hitting from the fourth to sixth spots, and there was talk of moving the team's "star first baseman" to second base. But on June 11 against arch rival Newark, Wagner badly injured his kneecap when he violently collided with catcher Bert Elton while chasing a foul pop. Over the next few days, Wagner's condition worsened, and when the team played at the Polo Grounds, Barrow took him to a New York City hospital to have the knee drained. He missed three weeks with the injury, during which time Paterson went 11–12 but kept its grip on first place.

◆ ◆ ◆

Barrow took his team to Wilmington for what would prove to be a very special Fourth of July celebration. The day gave birth to a baseball legend that both he and Honus Wagner recounted again and again. A common event was the morning-afternoon doubleheader, two games with a time interval in between so that the stands could be cleared and a second admission charged. Wagner was still out of the lineup as Paterson dropped both games of the holiday twin bill. A total attendance of 4,300 helped make the day a financial success, but that was not enough for the tireless promoter Ed Barrow.

He and his opposite number with Wilmington had a scheme to cash in on yet another gate charge. Advertised well in advance was a third game that Independence Day. This one was an exhibition to start at 8:00 P.M. and continue past dark under temporary electric lights erected specifically for the event at Union Street Grounds. It was a very novel plan, and the two teams had no idea what to expect. (Official league baseball under lights was still many years away, and the major leagues would not commence night baseball until thirty-nine years later, in 1935.)

Only two hundred people paid to see what the Wilmington *Sunday Morning Star* described as "the most unique and comical exhibition of the national sport that has been seen in this city, and although not a glowing success, [it] will long be remembered." A large "indoor" ball, resembling today's softball, was used for better visibility—but once it rose more than forty feet in the air, it disappeared from sight. The *Wilmington Morning News* called the contest "a burlesque on base ball" and explained, "The ball became lost so often and so many runs were made that they were not counted."

Picking up the story as Barrow and Wagner remembered it, the game ended after the Paterson manager set up his star player for a holiday gag. Earlier in the day, Barrow had purchased a round "torpedo" firework. The Wilmington pitcher for the nightcap was Doc Amole, whose flamboyant windup was once likened to the gyrations of an exotic dancer. Barrow convinced Amole to substitute the white torpedo for the ball, and when Honus met the target with a mighty cut, it exploded into the night in a shower of sparks. By now, the fans had seen enough of the farce and, storming the field, chased Wagner out of the park and down the street. Just ahead of him was Amole, and out in front of them both were their teammates. Leading the pack and beating everyone back to the hotel was the Wilmington club secretary, who had the gate receipts safely tucked away in his satchel.

Wagner would never again play in a game under lights, but his memories of that night in Wilmington lasted forever. Over the decades, as Barrow continued to rise through the ranks of the minor and major leagues as a manager, general manager, club owner, and league president, he remained wary of night baseball due to the fiasco of July 4, 1896. In 1935, the Cincinnati Reds introduced baseball under lights to the major leagues, and many clubs followed suit. Four years later, Barrow, now president of the New York Yankees, still referred to night baseball as "a passing attraction," and when he was approached about lights for Yankee Stadium, responded, "As long as I have anything to say about the running of the Yankees, they will not play night ball in the stadium." He was true to his word. The first night game at Yankee Stadium was in 1946, one year after Barrow was replaced in the day-to-day handling of the Yankees.

◆   ◆   ◆

Upon his return to regular game action on July 6, Wagner was again at first base but was placed in the seventh spot in the batting order. Initially unable to regain his stroke, he contributed only five hits as the team dropped five of their next eight. After much discussion, league officials decided not to divide the season into two halves. But in mid-July, New Haven dropped out, and with the officials saying owner Andrew Freedman had been "obnoxious and unfair in his dealings," his Metropolitans were expelled. An abrasive man with significant Tammany Hall connections, Freedman was known throughout baseball and elsewhere as a most unpleasant character. He filed suit to no avail, and teams representing the Pennsylvania cities of Philadelphia and Lancaster were added to the ranks of the Atlantic League.

Attendance at Olympic Park continued to be strong, but the Silk Cities, or Weavers as they were sometimes called, limped along the rest of the season. Though it lost as many as it won, the team remained within sight of first place. Wagner bounced between fourth, sixth, and seventh in the batting order before finally being placed for good in the cleanup spot on July 27.

He made some appearances at second and third, and he even pitched a few innings, mopping up in a loss to hated Newark. But he was used primarily at first base, where one of Wagner's stock anecdotes came to pass: He had reached into his back pocket for a fresh supply of "scrap" (loose chewing tobacco) when his hand became entangled in the fabric. He frantically signalled to his pitcher not to deliver, but it was too late, and the batter slapped the first pitch in the infield. The shortstop made the play and fired the ball to Wagner, who made the catch literally with one hand behind his back. While receiving a razzing from his teammates, he sheepishly retreated to the bench, explaining his predicament to his manager. The bench jockeys howled as Barrow rescued Wagner by cutting his pocket to free his hand.

While playing first base on August 15, Honus and catcher Elton let a fly ball drop between them as they cautiously avoided a repeat collision. Two days later, Wagner sustained another injury when he broke a finger on his glove hand. As a result, he spent the next week shuttling between right and left fields before being moved to third base on August 23, when he was about to go on a sizzling hitting streak.

Starting August 25, Paterson won eight of its next twelve, and during the stretch, Wagner scored thirteen runs and had twenty-six hits, including four doubles, three triples, and three home runs. One performance was a 5 for 5 day against pitcher Cornelius "Con" Lucid, who had just been released by a National League club. Another was a two-homer day that included a grand slam. Wagner was in full gait as the season wound down.

Going into the final week, it was a three-way fight among Paterson, Newark, and the Hartford, Connecticut, team, led by longtime major league manager Billy Barnie. Accusations of cheating and unfair umpiring flew among the three teams, and each claimed it owned the league's best record. As Paterson and Hartford met head-to-head for their last five games, they held differing opinions on which team was in the lead. When Hartford swept the first three games, Paterson players wailed about the umpiring. In the third inning of the third game, Wagner disputed a call and was ejected. In the eighth, George Smith, Paterson's ace pitcher, second baseman, and team captain, refused to leave the field after being tossed and had to be removed from the premises by a police officer. Having seen enough, a disgusted Barrow pulled his men from the field, forfeiting the game.

On Saturday, September 12, Paterson came back to pound Hartford 10–2 and on Sunday, more than four thousand people filled Olympic Park to see Paterson cruise to a 10–4 win and, in their opinion, to a first-place lead by half a game; Hartford disagreed, saying it had won the pennant by taking three of the five against Paterson. Meanwhile, Newark proudly declared itself the victor. Special celebrations were held in all three cities, with each proclaiming to be Atlantic League champion. For the Paterson team, a local clothing firm awarded each player a new suit of clothes, and a banquet was held at the Clifton Hotel, where the players were congratulated and presented with watch charms. The occasion was Wagner's first formal affair, and fortunately for him, the players were not expected to speak—Barrow was more than willing to talk on the team's behalf. (Wagner eventually would become very familiar with events like this but would never feel completely comfortable.)

◆ ◆ ◆

Barrow and Barnie saw eye to eye long enough to cry foul against Newark. The two protested that, during the season, Newark management refused to allow league umpires into its park, preferring to use its own players as umps, and that the team had padded its record by including as many as eight exhibition victories in its win total. Barrow and Barnie, acting on their own, decided the pennant should fly over either Hartford or Paterson and agreed to play a best-of-seven postseason series. The winning club would receive 60 percent of the gate receipts and a silver cup donated by Charles Soby, a wealthy cigar manufacturer in Hartford. The Soby Cup, a beautiful three-foot-high trophy valued at eight hundred dollars, would not become a team's property unless it could be won three consecutive years.

Prior to the Soby Cup Series—and amid rumors that Newark was seeking an injunction to prevent it—Paterson played a tune-up game against the National League Boston club. In a tight pitcher's duel, Wagner had one of only two hits Paterson could muster off Fred Klobedanz, who would become a twenty-six-game winner for Boston's pennant-winner the following year. Paterson's George Smith allowed only five hits and walked no one but lost 2–0.

Perhaps Barrow should have saved Smith for the Soby Cup opener on September 24: Sam McMackin was rocked for fifteen hits in a 13–3 loss at Hartford. The next day, in front of two thousand Hartford spectators, the teams played eleven innings before the game was called due to darkness, with the score 1–1. On Saturday, September 26, fifteen hundred people paid the twenty-five-cent admission and saw the two teams split a doubleheader. Smith pitched Paterson to a 6–2 win in the first game, but his teammates dropped the second 10–4, giving Hartford a two-games-to-one lead in the series. Wagner went hitless and committed an error in each of the first three contests (including the tie game), but he finally broke through with a double in the second game of the doubleheader.

During a three-day layoff in the series, Barrow scheduled another National League opponent. A Sunday crowd in Paterson of more than three thousand watched the home team thump Brooklyn's Bill Kennedy for fifteen hits and fifteen runs, only to lose 18–15. Wagner stole a base and scored three runs but was erratic afield; the *Paterson Evening News* noted that he "made some remarkable stops and also made some glaring errors." Just as he had been against Boston a few days earlier, Smith was the star of the game versus Brooklyn. Only a .256 hitter for the year, Smith clobbered two grand slams and two triples off Kennedy.

The Soby Cup Series resumed in Paterson on Wednesday, September 30. Wagner led the charge with four hits, including a double and two triples, as Paterson won 8–7, evening the series at two games apiece. Wagner had two singles the next day as Paterson won 17–4 in front of only four hundred midweek fans. And Smith wrapped up the Soby Cup for Paterson, four games to two, with a 4–3 triumph on Saturday, October 3. Attendance was disappointing for the last few games, but it was a profitable series for Barrow and his players nonetheless.

Ignoring the agreement between its two rivals, Newark claimed it was the Atlantic League champion. In recapping the 1896 season, *Spalding's Official Base Ball Guide* included Newark's exhibition wins in its totals, listed Newark at the top of the league standings, and made no mention of the Soby Cup. But Barrow felt he had won another league title and hurriedly gathered the team for a photograph with the Soby Cup before the players dispersed. His reputation as a shrewd baseball man was growing, and in the offseason he was offered the presidency of the Atlantic League for 1897. He eagerly accepted.

Wagner's career was starting to blossom. He finished the year with a .348 batting average, best on his team and fifth highest in the league for players appearing in more than fifty games. He stole bases and hit for power. By his own admission, he "would play anywhere anybody suggested," but his defense was still suspect. He held his own at first base with a .968 fielding average, adequate for the era, but his mark at third base was a dreadful .866.

Wagner was beginning to think there was quite a future in playing ball. To be sure, it was strenuous. He played in more than one hundred games in 1896 and suffered continuous injuries. But it was fun, and it beat the rigor and danger of coal mining and the boredom of the barber shop. He was earning more money than he had thought possible, and unlike the previous year, the pay was right on time. He even had a girlfriend, Miss Millie Guptill of Brooklyn, whom he called on and escorted to a few vaudeville shows. And he looked forward to another summer in Paterson—Barrow had reserved him for 1897.

◆ ◆ ◆

Barrow now had the responsibility for coordinating all league affairs, in addition to handling Paterson personnel decisions. It forced him to turn over the managerial duties of the team to his partner, Charles McKee, but Barrow was never far from the scene. The typical comings and goings of minor league franchises preceded the Atlantic League's second season. For 1897, its makeup included the three contenders for the previous year's honors, Paterson, Hartford, and Newark; holdovers Lancaster and Philadelphia, Pennsylvania; and newcomers Richmond and Norfolk, Virginia, and Reading, Pennsylvania. The league's territory and reputation were spreading.

Despite a rudimentary education, Wagner was capable of clearly expressing his thoughts on paper. In the custom of the period, he wrote an offseason letter to Paterson explaining that he was maintaining good condition and looking forward to giving his maximum effort for the club in the coming year. Another Carnegie boy who was ready for professional ball was the Wagners' friend, Patsy Flaherty. Paterson signed the left-handed pitcher, now twenty years old, and he and Wagner arrived together on April Fool's Day. Within a few days, they were preparing for baseball.

Barrow splurged on new uniforms for 1897. The traditional quilted knickers were back from the previous year, but Barrow now clad his team in collarless jerseys, rare for the time. Thin black pinstripes ran vertically down these "modern" jerseys, and dark red piping circled the neckline and sleeve openings; PATERSON was emblazoned in red block letters across the chest. Modeling their new uniforms, Paterson split two games with Toronto as the Wagner brothers opposed each other as third basemen for their respective teams.

The year was not even under way when Paterson and Newark began bickering as six exhibition games had been foolishly scheduled between the two enemies. Amid all the bad feelings, Wagner picked up where he left off the previous year. In the first matchup, he clouted a three-run homer that cleared a house beyond the left field wall and walked around the bases. He totaled four home runs in the first four games against Newark. By the fifth head-to-head contest, nerves were frayed. The Paterson players walked off the field in the fourth inning when they felt they had been mistreated by the umpire, who also happened to be a Newark player. The next day, Newark refused to travel to Paterson for a scheduled game, and the feud was on again.

Though still in the preseason, Wagner was already receiving accolades. *Sporting Life* referred to him as a "jewel" and (preferring the synonymous term *crank* instead of fan) remarked, "Wagner is the idol of the cranks and is growing in favor daily." In a season-opening victory before two thousand people in Hartford, he socked two doubles from the cleanup spot. A disheartening home opener loss followed as Ned Garvin, on his way to a big league career, threw a one-hitter against Paterson.

Soon afterward, Wagner's hits were coming in bunches. In Paterson's first nineteen contests, he had twelve multi-hit games. By May 20, the team was in first place at 13–6, Wagner was hitting .425, and Flaherty's early season mark stood at 3–1. After a poor start at third base, Wagner put together twelve consecutive errorless games. But it was his stick work that had the *Paterson Evening News* proclaiming HAIL HERO "HANNES" after a two-triple performance. The hits were constant, but so were the injuries. He retired from one game when he took a pitch in the stomach, and when he was struck in the hand by a line drive two days later, he was forced to play first base and the outfield for the next two weeks.

Word of Wagner's performance spread quickly, but with only twelve major league teams and shorter player rosters than today's, opportunities were limited. Nevertheless, the wheels determining his future were in motion. National League representatives surveyed the Atlantic League continuously, and in May and June a parade of managers and magnates came specifically to observe Wagner. Many of these scouting trips were for Sunday games, which fortunately for Wagner were permissible in Paterson. (The club was rumored to be skirting the issue by providing the ballpark's neighbors with free Sunday admission.)

Seeing Wagner in a single game, sometimes two, most baseball men were put off by his physical appearance, assuming him to be clumsy. Frank Selee, Boston's manager, said he would not pay a dime for Wagner, and Brooklyn president Charles Byrne and manager "Scrappy Bill" Joyce of New York were equally unimpressed. And Philadelphia manager George Stallings asserted he wouldn't even pay Wagner's train fare to the City of Brotherly Love.

◆ ◆ ◆

One of the teams Wagner was assaulting in the spring of 1897 was Norfolk. In the first month of the season, Wagner was 8 for 21 with two home runs and two triples against the league's new entry. Norfolk outfielder Claude MacFarlan took notice. MacFarlan, a Louisville native with evidently a great deal of hometown pride, wrote a letter extolling Wagner's achievements to Harry C. Pulliam, president of the Louisville Colonels National League club. The letter was ignored. Pulliam had seen Wagner play a few games and thought him too bowlegged to be a success in the "fast company" of the National League. MacFarlan persisted, firing off telegrams to Pulliam expressing the urgency of signing Wagner before another big league outfit grabbed him. Receiving no response to his wires, MacFarlan took the short trip from Newark, where his Norfolk team was playing, to New York, where Louisville was in the middle of an eastern road trip. At the Sturtevant Hotel, where the Colonels were staying, MacFarlan expounded the quality of both Wagner's skills and disposition to Louisville management.

On June 6, Louisville had an off Sunday in the middle of a series with Brooklyn, and Pulliam decided to spend it in Paterson. Accompanied by his star outfielder, Fred Clarke, Pulliam took another look at Wagner. Playing left field, Honus had two singles in four at bats and stole a base in a rather uneventful 3–2 win over Hartford. With Pulliam and Clarke commenting that Wagner was not "so warm," and Barrow and McKee stating they had no intention of selling their best drawing card at any price, the posturing began.

Meanwhile, there were other visitors to the Silk City. Phil Auten, number-two man of the Pittsburgh Pirates, and his team's manager, Patsy Donovan, who had taken over for the deposed Connie Mack, journeyed to Paterson on Sunday, June 13. With their team riding an eight-game losing streak, Auten and Donovan took advantage of an off day to see Wagner, then the Atlantic League's leading hitter. Notwithstanding a 1 for 5 performance, Auten offered Paterson management fifteen hundred dollars for Wagner's contract—and was immediately rebuffed.

Negotiations continued, with each of the three sides (Louisville, Pittsburgh, and Paterson) feigning disinterest. But rumors were flying. The Pittsburgh and Louisville clubs were known to be actively looking for players. In mid-June, with Louisville in the midst of a typically dismal year, the team's manager was fired, and the reins were turned over to twenty-four-year-old Clarke, who had made a rapid rise to prominence in the National League. More gossip followed that other changes were imminent, and Pulliam wired to Louisville for another uniform, giving no word of who was to fill it.

Almost as if staged, Sunday, June 20 was designated Wagner Day at Olympic Park. A group of rooters, sensing Wagner was only days away from being sold to the highest bidder, presented him with a gold watch when he approached the plate in the first inning. It was the first time Wagner had been honored in this way, and he struggled for a response, causing the *Paterson Evening News* to state, ". . . if brevity is the soul of wit, his reply was extremely witty." The watch would be a cherished memento for the remainder of his life.

Realizing he was being shopped, Wagner felt both excited and apprehensive about the prospect of playing in the National League. Big league ball was certainly alluring, but he had achieved a level of success and popularity in Paterson that would be tough to match. Paterson provided Wagner with some of his fondest baseball memories. Reminiscing about his time there, he would say, "I never had so much fun in my life. . . . To me it seemed like a vacation. When I went south training in my later years, it always made me think of Paterson. We had fun and excitement all the time."

As Wagner was being showcased, he began another hitting tear. On July 1, he smacked two homers and stole two bases. July 3 saw another homer, and on July 5, he went 3 for 4 with a double. Upon reflection, Wagner felt that there were two games in the middle of this torrid stretch that were the most dazzling to the big shots who were watching—July 6, when he hit for the cycle, going 4 for 4, and July 11, when he was 4 for 5 with two doubles and two triples. The streak helped him land the Atlantic League batting title with a mark of .379. At third base, his fielding average had improved to .898, third best in the league—completing nine of ten chances flawlessly was roughly the norm for a third baseman. But his team was slumping, and Wagner was still accused by the *Paterson Evening News* of "playing for his release," not giving his all.

Pulliam stepped up his efforts to obtain Wagner, offering Barrow $2,000 for the third baseman. It was a tremendous figure at the time, an amount thought to be excessive by some Atlantic League people, and one that Pulliam was unsure the club treasury could cover. Barrow, satisfied with the price but recalling his verbal commitment to President Kerr of Pittsburgh a year and a half earlier, wired Kerr to see if he would match the offer. Kerr answered affirmatively, but Pulliam immediately upped his bid to $2,100. A second telegram from Barrow to Kerr went unanswered, and after a few days, Barrow and Pulliam closed the deal. On July 17, it was announced that Wagner was a Colonel, and that evening, he was accompanied by Pulliam on a train bound for Louisville, Kentucky.

Honus Wagner was actually Ed Barrow's second discovery to reach the major leagues. As a young man in Des Moines, Iowa, Barrow had worked for a local newspaper, supervising a number of young news carriers. With the intention of creating camaraderie among the boys, Barrow also managed a baseball team for the group. One of his carriers and the star of his youth team was Fred Clifford Clarke. By July 1897, Clarke was a superb big league outfielder and the manager of the Louisville Colonels—the man Wagner was to report to upon his arrival.

THREE

THE COLONEL AND THE CAPTAIN

A poor team to begin with, and one riddled with injuries, the Louisville Colonels' performance so far in 1897 was inept. In mid-July when Wagner came on board, Louisville was wallowing near the bottom of the standings and recently had been slaughtered 36–7 by Cap Anson's Chicago Colts. Calling the Colonels' offense "the laughingstock of the league," *Sporting Life* reported, "The team seems to be in the slough of despondency, and the boys seem to . . . lack nerve and spirit . . . 'they are very much Louisville,' and the future . . . does not appear to be particularly encouraging." Certainly, the publication did not consider the purchase of Wagner as the solution to the club's struggles, commenting, "It is to be hoped that Louisville didn't throw away very much money on the Wagner deal. . . ."

But Fred Clarke viewed the acquisition in a much different light:

> We think we have made a deal which will materially help us out.
> After negotiating for some days we have succeeded in securing
> Hans Wagner, the famous hard-hitting first baseman. . . . Bat-
> ting is his long suit. . . . He will make a most serviceable utility
> man for us. Several of the National League teams have been
> after him, but we succeeded in landing him, because we bid the

highest price, which was a pretty stiff one, too. . . . Everybody in the East, who knows anything about the baseball of the Atlantic League, is stuck on old Hans, as they call him. . . . Wagner will come in very handy lots of places. . . . He is a big, heavy German, with very large hands, and is powerful as a bull. He kills the ball . . .

Five years earlier, Clarke had placed a small advertisement in *The Sporting News* offering his services as a ballplayer, and the Hastings, Nebraska, club had given him a contract. After spending parts of three seasons in the minors, including stops in St. Joseph, Missouri, Montgomery, Alabama, and Savannah, Georgia, Clarke burst into the National League on June 30, 1894, going 5 for 5 with a double in his Louisville debut. Appointed manager in mid-1897, he became the Colonels' seventh skipper in the last five and a half years. Referred to as the "Boy Manager," his behavior and appearance—including a rapidly receding hairline that led to complete baldness within a few years—contradicted the term. The left-hand batting and right-hand throwing Clarke was regarded as a solid hitter as well as a fleet-footed outfielder and baserunner.

Clarke was an intense, driven, fiery man. Two-fisted and vocal on the diamond, he occasionally would run from the outfield to the mound to chastise his own pitcher. He enjoyed his image as a scrapper and played it up by gnawing on a toothpick during games. In contrast, his new player Wagner was easygoing and unassuming. Though their personalities could not have been more different, the two men rapidly developed a mutual admiration for each other and became close friends. From their earliest days together in Louisville, Clarke called Wagner by his recently acquired nickname "Dutch" that, along with "Dutchman," would stick with him throughout his life. (These terms were applied to people of German descent as far back as the 1600s, a result of the similarity to the German word *Deutsch*.) Wagner always referred to Clarke simply as Cap, short for Captain. In July 1897, the two men began a long trek together that would eventually lead them both to the Hall of Fame.

◆ ◆ ◆

Hall of Famer Cap Anson's hits total varies widely by source. While some maintain that he never amassed three thousand hits at all, others credit him with achieving this milestone on July 18, 1897. One day later, July 19, Wagner—who would become the first or second batter (depending on which source is believed) to reach the three-thousand-hit mark—made his National League debut, as a center fielder for the Colonels. In the bottom of the first, both Clarke and Colonel right fielder Tom McCreery singled. Batting third against Washington's James "Doc" McJames, the league's strikeout leader that year, Wagner placed a bunt to the first base side of the mound and came close to beating it out. The successful sacrifice moved two runners into scoring position as part of a four-run first inning. Honus walked and struck out in his next two trips to the plate and, in the seventh inning, lined a single to right, driving in a run. On the day, he went 1 for 2 in the Colonels' 6–2 win, collecting several big league firsts: single, run driven in, base on balls, sacrifice bunt, strikeout, stolen base, and outfield assist.

Only six hundred paying customers witnessed Wagner's big league debut, but *The Louisville Commercial* called him "the main feature of the game" and referred to him as "Count Hans Von Wagner." The paper noted that he "is a splendidly built man, cut on a generous pattern," elaborating, "In fact his whole build is very much after the order of a one-story brick house." Favorably impressed, the paper also maintained, "He throws like a shot . . . and is remarkably fast." His baserunning aggressiveness also nearly cost the team a rally. With Clarke at third and Wagner at first, Wagner stole second, rounded the bag, and headed for third when the throw skipped a few feet away. Clarke, who was anchored to third, reacted to Wagner barreling toward him by setting out for home, where he narrowly avoided a tag at the plate.

The following day, Wagner made a sensational catch in center field and over the next few games secured many of his other career firsts. On July 21, in game one of a doubleheader, he scored his first run and hit his first double off Washington's Lester German. German, coincidentally, had surrendered Napoleon "Larry" Lajoie's first double less than a year earlier. In the second game of the doubleheader, Wagner had his first two-hit game and first triple, also off McJames (though he tried to stretch the triple into a home run and was thrown out at the plate). His first big league homer would come five weeks later, on August 27, when he drove a Jack Dunn pitch over the left field fence at Brooklyn's Eastern Park. (Dunn is best remembered for being the minor league magnate-manager who, years later, would sign Babe Ruth, a young recruit out of the St. Mary's Industrial School for Boys, to his first professional contract.)

Wagner was off to a flying start. He had at least one hit in each of his first nine games, totaling fourteen hits and giving him a .424 batting average. Within three weeks of his debut, *The Sporting News* touted his hitting prowess as well as the strength and accuracy of his throwing arm, calling him "a glittering success" and the "bright particular star of the Colonels just now." The St. Louis–based sports weekly continued with, "Every day he gets cheers and verbal and typographical bouquets and his place in the affections of the rooters is disputed only by Fred Clarke."

Within a month of his first game with Louisville, Wagner was already making himself the butt of a joke in describing his introduction to Cincinnati Reds' center fielder William "Dummy" Hoy. Changing sides between innings, the two crossed paths but Hoy gave no response to Wagner's repeated requests for a chew. Honus confided to teammate Perry Werden that Hoy must be "the worst stuck-up guy I've ever seen." In admitting his gaffe to others with the story, Wagner quoted Werden's reply, "Why, you slob, he's deaf and dumb." It was obvious that Wagner was already comfortable with his new surroundings, but then again, he never felt above telling one on himself.

Wagner's agreeable combination of cheerful good nature and superior baseball ability helped pave the way to his acceptance and eventual popularity at the major league level. He confessed, "I was a green, awkward kid, unused to big league ways. . . . I kept my mouth shut, though, and went right along about my business. The one thing that saved me from a lot of extra joshing, I suppose, was [that] I could always slam the ball."

◆ ◆ ◆

Though Wagner was used most often in the third spot of the order, he also batted cleanup a few times. He played primarily center field and filled in at second base, making his first infield appearance on August 25. The Colonels' middle infield was a sore spot throughout the season. Joe Dolan hurt his arm and was limited to thirty-six games, batting an anemic .211. Albert Johnson hit .242 over forty-eight games. Jimmy Rogers, who managed and played second base before being dumped, hit just .147 in forty-one games. Other shortstops and second basemen came and went. In a few exhibitions, Clarke himself played shortstop, thinking he might be the answer. There was even talk of trying Wagner at short, a move not recommended by many and rejected by Clarke.

Then again, problems were nothing new to Louisville baseball. In 1876, the city fielded its first National League team, but it was dropped after a scandal in its second year, when four of the team's players were found to have thrown the 1877 pennant. Louisville was a charter member in the American Association in its first season as a major league in 1882. In 1885, the team name was changed from the Eclipse (after the famous British racehorse that was an ancestor to many modern thoroughbreds) to the Colonels, and despite talent such as Pete Browning, Guy Hecker, and Chicken Wolf, Louisville teams were mostly mediocre. The Colonels did capture the 1890 Association title—due in part to talent being stretched over three major leagues, including the Players' League, which lasted just one season. But two years later, when the club re-entered the National League, few of the players from the championship team remained.

In 1892, the Association shut down, and Louisville, Baltimore, Washington, and St. Louis joined the eight National League teams of Boston, Brooklyn, New York, Cincinnati, Pittsburgh, Cleveland, Philadelphia, and Chicago to create a single major league, a cumbersome twelve-team "big league." (Though this term was not new, it was now catching on as a synonym for major league.) Louisville had been pitiful since joining the National League, and after an eleventh-place effort in 1893, finished last from 1894 through 1896, more than fifty games out of first place each year.

Wagner was just happy to be in the National League. Years later, when he was asked about his purchase by Louisville in mid-1897, he responded, "Personally, I didn't care where I went. All I wanted was to play baseball, the bigger the league, the better." An increase in salary to $250 per month was the reward for his promotion—he would earn more in two summer months than the average American did in a year.

However, there was a price to pay. Minor league ball was rough, but play in the National League was downright hostile. The 1890s saw a marked increase in both on-field violence and the players' (and at times, fans') abuse and even brutalization of umpires. The players' antics often cast them as undesirables and rogues. There were calls to crack down on "rowdiness" and "kicking." *Sporting Life* cautioned, "Magnates, beware! There are other sports in the world besides base ball. And the best and most permanent patrons of base ball do not attend ball games for the purpose of witnessing prize fights or heavy slum language."

The Colonels felt right at home with this style of ball, however, and Wagner's indoctrination was immediate. A few days after Wagner's arrival, Louisville pitcher Bert Cunningham allowed the only run of a 1–0 affair to score from third while conducting a heated argument with the umpire. Within a week, Cunningham had lost another game for the club by provoking an umpire until the official declared a forfeit. Three days later, in the first game of an August 4 doubleheader in Louisville, the Colonels were the beneficiary of a forfeit: Cleveland great Jesse Burkett, a man so cantankerous he was called "the Crab," approached the plate and cursed the umpire, resulting in ejection. After Cleveland player-manager Patsy Tebeau refused to name a hitter to take Burkett's place, the game was awarded to Louisville. In game two of the doubleheader, Burkett again lit into the umpire and had to be removed from the grounds by two policemen.

The events at Louisville, though, were mild in comparison with what transpired in Cincinnati that same day. After umpire Tim Hurst made an unfavorable call against the home club, a Reds fan launched a beer glass in the umpire's direction. Hurst picked up the glass and threw it back into the stands, where it struck an innocent spectator in the head. A mob descended on Hurst. Police moved in, barely averting a riot, and arrested the umpire for assault.

At the forefront of "rowdy ball" were the Baltimore Orioles. Led by manager Ned Hanlon and a talented, aggressive cast of characters that included shortstop Hughie Jennings and hot-tempered third baseman John McGraw, the Orioles had won the National League championship in each of the last three years. Hanlon's Orioles refined the "inside game" of baseball through the polished, strategic use of such plays as the sacrifice bunt and the hit and run. The goading of umpires and opponents, and unscrupulous acts on the base paths, were also part of the Oriole attack.

The volatile and controversial McGraw saw this style of play as not only within the bounds of the rules but out-and-out necessary, saying that he knew "several men who influence probably fifty runs in the course of a season by calling the umpire's attention to a point at the critical moment when a decision is just about to be made." He contended, "The idea that every protest must end in an assault and battery affair is all dead wrong. The only kind of kicking is judicious kicking, and that calls to mind the fact that kickers are born, not made."

An upcoming monthlong road trip would take the Colonels through all six eastern cities, including Baltimore.

◆ ◆ ◆

A Sunday game on August 29 provided Wagner with a brief reunion at Paterson as the Colonels played an exhibition against his former team-mates—a game that may well have been arranged as part of Wagner's sale price. The largest crowd that had ever seen a game in Olympic Park turned out, and estimates of the total ranged from five to six thousand. The hundreds of people who poured over the outfield wall made an exact count impossible.

The game was a bust, and few of those in attendance stayed for the entire contest. Clarke chose not to play, and the Colonels were said to look lazy as they collected only six hits off Lee Viau in a rather embarrassing 4–1 loss. But Wagner was on center stage. Pregame practice was disrupted by a flock of hero-worshiping boys who trailed Wagner all over the grounds. During the game, the boys sat in left field, where Wagner was playing, and cheered his every action. He singled in three trips to the plate and did his best to ignore the attention and the razzing from his teammates. He could not wait for the day to end.

◆ ◆ ◆

With the Colonels playing miserably on a long road trip, allowing three teams to pass them in the standings, Clarke made a few changes. On September 8, a new second baseman, catcher, and southpaw pitcher all made big league debuts in the first of a three-game series with the first-place Orioles. At second base was Wagner's Paterson teammate George Smith, who as it turned out was not the solution to the Colonels' infield problem. The new battery was not a huge success either. Catcher Ossee Schreckengost went 0 for 3 and had a passed ball in his only Colonels appearance, although he would resurface the following year with Cleveland. The twenty-year-old pitcher proved he wasn't ready for the big league quite yet, giving up eleven hits and four walks while striking out only two in a 5–1 loss. But George Edward "Rube" Waddell would make his mark eventually.

Louisville lost again the next day as both teams moaned about every call the umpire made. In the third game of the series, the Colonels faced Wagner's torpedo-throwing Atlantic League rival Doc Amole, and this time there were also fireworks. A Louisville player was ejected in the second inning after arguing over balls and strikes, and one Oriole and two Colonels were fined twenty-five dollars apiece for kicking. In the seventh inning, after an umpire's decision against Louisville, Clarke refused to let his team continue playing, and the game was forfeited.

Wagner went 5 for 12 in the series with a triple and, of course, emerged with a vivid memory of his first encounter with the rough-and-tumble Orioles:

They used to call them the rowdy Orioles, and they weren't fooling. I hit a long ball deep into the outfield and should have made an easy home run out of it, but when I got to first base, Jack Doyle gave me the hip and Heinie Reitz almost killed me when I rounded second. Hughie Jennings tripped me at short, and when I got to third, John McGraw was waiting for me with a shotgun. I did well to get a triple out of it. After the game, Fred Clarke, our manager, said to me: "What the hell kind of a way is that to play baseball? Letting everybody kick you around! If you can't do any better than that, you won't be with us when we leave Baltimore. . . ." So the next day, I hit a ball down to McGraw, and it was a close play at first. But if Doyle had any idea of giving me the works again, I beat him to it. I banged into him with my shoulder and knocked him into right field. McGraw's throw sailed into the outfield and finally bounded into a stand, and it worked the same as a home run. After I scored and returned to the bench, Fred Clarke smiled his approval. "That's the way to play the game, Dutch," he said. "Make 'em respect you."

The last stop of the trip was a two-game set in Pittsburgh. Wagner's first opportunity to play in front of his friends a few weeks earlier had ended in a humbling 0 for 7. But in his next trip back home as a big leaguer, he had three hits, including a pair of doubles. The Colonels even managed to win one when four Pirates were ejected for unseemly behavior, one for throwing a ball at the umpire's head.

The team dropped eight of its last nine and finished 52–78, ahead of only an awful St. Louis team at 29–102. Another dismal year for Louisville produced few bright spots: Clarke was commended for his outfield work and for providing a good example to his men. As the team's leadoff hitter, he batted .406, second only to "Wee Willie" Keeler's .432. At the season finale, and in anticipation of better times ahead, Clarke was presented with a diamond ring from admiring fans. (Though Keeler's batting average would later be adjusted to .424 and Clarke's to .390, due to additional information being uncovered, they were still one-two in the league for 1897.)*

Wagner played in sixty-one games—fifty-two in the outfield and nine

* *The Baseball Encyclopedia,* Ninth Edition, Macmillan Publishing Company, 1993, serves as the primary source for the player statistics herein.

at second base. He showed promise but did not vault to stardom in his first few months in the National League. His batting average, announced at the time as .344 and since adjusted to .338, ranked eighteenth in the league in a year when the entire circuit averaged a lofty .292 and the Orioles as a team batted .325. Wagner was still an unknown quantity, and Clarke had trouble judging his capabilities. While impressed with the newcomer's speed and power, Clarke discounted some of Wagner's early success as pure luck because he seemed so awkward, and he later said, "[Wagner] was a three-ringed circus to watch." Pittsburgh Pirate president William Kerr did not lament a missed opportunity in not acquiring Wagner and only commented on how few young players of any caliber were coming into the league.

◆ ◆ ◆

Disputes surrounded many of the 1897 postseason cup series. Since 1894, the first- and second-place finishers in the National League had met in a series for a loving cup donated by William C. Temple, owner of the Pittsburgh Pirates early in the 1890s. In 1897, second-place Baltimore knocked off first-place Boston for its second straight Temple Cup victory. But the teams spent the off days of the series playing exhibitions against each other to collect more money, and rumors swirled that the combatants had agreed to split the Temple Cup receipts evenly, regardless of the outcome. During the offseason, the series was abolished, and the cup was returned to Mr. Temple.

In New Jersey, Barrow and McKee sold the Paterson team late in the season to a local group, and Wagner's former teammates finished sixth in the eight-team league at 68–79. Second-place Newark refused to play for the Soby Cup, and first-place Lancaster was strong-armed into playing a one-game showdown for the cup against the previous year's winner, Paterson, who won the game and killed the credibility of the Soby Cup.

The Eastern League's Steinert Cup was just as controversial. Al Wagner's Toronto club held a three-to-two lead in games over Syracuse, but the two teams could not agree on where the next game would be held, and the series ended incomplete, although the cup was later forwarded to Toronto.

Al, who had split his 1896 season between Wheeling and Toronto, hit .325 and scored 77 runs in 101 games as Toronto's shortstop in 1897. Added to the Washington Senators' reserve list for the coming year, Al was to get his chance in the big league very soon. John Heydler, a Washington writer and a future National League president, said of Al, "if he is as good as his brother, he will do." The two brothers had clearly traded places: Al would live the remainder of his days known best as Honus's older brother.

Honus and Al returned home to Carnegie from different directions in mid-October. They made their first investment with baseball earnings, opening a poolroom in Pittsburgh's West End. Requiring little capital or expertise, billiard rooms were common ventures for ballplayers. The Wagner brothers' pool hall was a place where a fellow could get a sandwich and soft drink—perhaps something a trifle stronger—or just come in out of the cold to talk baseball with the proprietors. During the offseason, when Honus wasn't out hunting small game, he could be found in his establishment. The novelty wore off quickly, however, and profits were not substantial. Within eighteen months, the brothers shut it down.

There was another new business in the family. Charley was back in the barbering trade, opening a new shop in Carnegie in November. It quite possibly could have been Honus's money that staked Charley to the new parlor, for at the opening, a photo of Honus and the Louisville Colonels was mounted in the front window.

◆ ◆ ◆

On February 15, 1898, the battleship USS *Maine* exploded and sank in the Havana, Cuba, harbor, killing more than 250 crew members. Two factions—rebels demanding independence from Spain's rule, and pro-Spanish groups—had been clashing in Havana, and President McKinley sent the *Maine* to Cuba to protect Americans from the rioting mobs. The American public immediately blamed Spain for the tragedy, although the true cause of the explosion was never known. The two countries were approaching war in the spring of 1898.

As the baseball season drew near, Wagner prepared to sign a contract calling for a $1,650 salary. Though a wonderful sum, it was deservedly less than the league maximum of $2,400. Clarke was the only Colonel to earn that amount, and he received an additional $500 for managing. Wagner established a pattern early in his big league career of not signing and returning his contract during the winter, as was the norm. He preferred to wait until he reported to the team before making the agreement official.

Some teams traveled south for spring practice, but the Colonels, representing the southernmost of the National League cities, did not.

With the club's history of faring poorly at the gate, and fearing that attendance would be negatively affected by the coming of war, Colonels management was cost-conscious. An additional expense for 1898 was the assignment of a second umpire for each game in hopes of curbing on-field incidents, even though the league would go back and forth for years between a single- and double-umpire system. In order to recoup some of this expense, and because no Temple Cup games were to be played at the season's end, the schedule was expanded from 132 to 154 games.

Initial preseasons for Wagner were not glamorous. His two springs while playing for Paterson were spent in Pittsburgh and Paterson, and he liked to say that for his first big league spring training, the team actually headed north! When Wagner told this story, it often resulted in the same rolling eyes of disbelief as did most of his white lies, but this one was true. Leaving the Bluegrass State for a week, the club journeyed fifty miles northwest to West Baden Springs, a popular resort community in southern Indiana. Manager Clarke prescribed massive doses of the "medicinal" waters from the local springs. Clarke regarded the water as a "strong stomach strengthener," and Wagner claimed it "put pepper into our blood." Every few hours, whether practicing, running, or simply relaxing in the hotel, each player was to gulp down as much of the liquid as his belly could hold. But Clarke's primary interest was to increase a player's leg strength and wind capacity with a regimen of running, running, and more running. Unlike today's spring trainings, which focus on skills development for players who often maintain a year-round conditioning program, preseason workouts of previous eras centered around "getting your legs back" and sweating off extra winter pounds.

Wagner was no exception. The Wagner brothers and Patsy Flaherty began exercising at the Carnegie Athletic Club hall in early February 1898, running, playing handball, and slugging a punching bag. But when Honus arrived at West Baden, it was obvious that he had filled out his frame, and he was described as "larger than ever." Even at the age of twenty-four, he put on weight in the offseason, expecting to work it off in the spring. By the season opener he would be down to his prime years' playing weight of 190 to 200 pounds.

◆ ◆ ◆

In his first half-season in the National League, Wagner played just twenty-five games at the home grounds, but in 1898, he would have ample opportunity to get to know the city. Louisville grew up at a point where the Ohio River was impassable due to a gradual twenty-six-foot drop through a series of rapids, resulting in the nickname Falls City. It became a stopping point for ships, as their cargo had to be unloaded and carted overland through neighboring Portland (later annexed by Louisville) to waiting ships at the other end of the falls. A canal was completed in 1830, enabling ships to bypass the rapids and leading to even greater river traffic. During the Civil War, Kentucky remained a Union state, and afterward Louisville prospered as its businesses capitalized on relationships fostered in the North. They soon regained their Southern markets as well, adding to the boom economy. By the "gay nineties," Louisville was a thriving city of tobacco processors, paint and chemical plants, and distilleries by the dozens. However, with a population of roughly two hundred thousand, it was the smallest National League city. The area was a center for thoroughbred racing, and both home and visiting players frequented the several tracks, including Churchill Downs.

Ballplayers were also known to visit John "Bud" Hillerich, whose father owned and operated a woodworking shop that manufactured bedposts, porch columns, and butter churns. As a young man, Bud had taken an interest in baseball and, much to his father's chagrin, began turning bats for local players. In 1897, at the age of thirty-one, Bud became a full-fledged partner with his father and took charge of the flourishing bat production. Wagner came to know Bud well in his many calls to the J. F. Hillerich & Son factory, and their friendly business relationship continued for years.

◆ ◆ ◆

The Colonels had long been successful at signing young talent but often had to unload quality players for cash. Other clubs, knowing the Colonels' financial situation was grim, made inquiries about purchasing Clarke prior to the 1898 season. As some suggested, nobody seemed to want anyone else. But he was the one man that Louisville management felt was indispensable. In their only significant deal, the Colonels sent pitcher Bill Hill, 16–45 over the past two years, to Cincinnati for three players. It was a homecoming for Philip "Red" Ehret, a Louisville native who had won twenty-five games for the 1890 champion Colonels but who would win only three games in 1898. More importantly, the trade included fine outfielder Dummy Hoy and infielder Claude Ritchey, Wagner's teammate in both Steubenville and Warren. Wagner and Ritchey continued their development together and remained friends throughout their careers, often sharing a room on the road, but were opposites in most everything. (Despite being slight of build, Ritchey experimented with a vegetarian diet; perhaps a difficulty in locating a good salad in a world of steak eaters aggravated his already surly and unsociable disposition.)

The Louisville City Council declared a half-day holiday for the season opener on Friday, April 15, and an estimated ten thousand fans came out to the ballpark. Loosely labeled League Park because it was home to the city's National League team, it was located in the working-class community of Portland, a lengthy thirty-minute trolley ride from downtown Louisville. Built in 1893 as a successor to Eclipse Park, League Park's most curious feature was that the batter faced due south.

Clarke batted third and had three singles. Wagner played second base and batted fourth, collecting two singles as the Colonels won their first game, 10–3, over Pittsburgh. The team also unveiled new white uniforms, which Clarke referred to as "the neatest in the league." A Gothic L adorned the right breast of the collared shirts, and a somewhat loose-fitting white cap reminded the patrons of a baker's hat and had the bleacher crowd calling the home team the Bakers.

On April 25 against Cleveland, the two teams began jawing at each other, and by the third inning, tempers were hot. In the bottom of the inning, Wagner slid hard into third baseman Rhoderick "Bobby" Wallace, snatched the ball away, threw it into left field, and scored as the ball rolled away. The two umpires discussed the play for a full fifteen minutes and changed their call three times before finally ruling Wagner out for interference. Wagner's answer when asked about the incident was that he believed "in fighting the devil with fire." It was the theme for the day on a much grander scale, as the United States formally declared that a state of war now existed with Spain.

Public concern turned to the battle. While the conflict in Cuba was relatively brief, lasting through mid-July, it spread into other Spanish holdings and was not ultimately resolved until the Treaty of Paris was signed on December 10. The controversial agreement, ratified by the Senate by a single vote on February 6, 1899, called for Spain to grant Cuba its freedom and for the United States to assume control of Guam, Puerto Rico, and the Philippines.

With the commencement of war in the spring of 1898, baseball attendance that had been only discouraging early in the season became horrendous. Compounding the situation for Louisville was the fact that the team quickly sank in the standings. After winning the opener, the team dropped eight of its next nine, and as the *Kentucky Irish American* put it, fans were "getting tired of going down to the park year after year to watch a tail-end club get everlastingly lambasted by one of the other eleven clubs."

Following one particularly dreadful road trip, the team's train was met by a small gathering of loyal but disgusted rooters who brought along a horse-drawn hearse. A few of the players failed to see any humor in the display, but Clarke encouraged them to play along. The Colonels threw their bats into the coach and formed a procession leaving the station.

◆ ◆ ◆

Only six weeks into the 1898 season, Wagner was ailing. A very sore finger was making it difficult to grip the bat, but he had something to look forward to on the team's first eastern swing. Colonel management had made an unsuccessful attempt to secure Al Wagner in the offseason, and he was now a Washington Senator. On June 2, the two brothers faced each other as big leaguers for the first time. As the two teams split four games, Honus went 4 for 16 and Al, 4 for 18. In May, third baseman Al was said to look promising, but by August, Washington magnate Earl Wagner admitted Al "proved an utter and complete failure . . . who would not today bring one dollar on a minor league market." He was benched with an average of only .224 after sixty-three games, but Washington managed to sell him to the Brooklyn franchise. Citing lack of condition, he was slow to report to his new club, and when he did, he hit just .237 over eleven games. During the year, in typical Wagner family style, Al played fifty games at third base, ten in the outfield, eight at shortstop, and five at second base. But even his versatility would not help him at this level. It was his first and last year in the big leagues.

Another brother story taking shape involved Fred Clarke's nineteen-year-old brother, Josh. After practicing with the Louisville club every day in the first few months, Josh finally made his debut on June 15, going 0 for 1 as a pinch hitter. He went on to play in five more games for the Colonels in 1898 but managed only three hits in eighteen at bats. Unlike Al Wagner, Josh would have other chances, although his next big league appearance would not be for seven years.

◆ ◆ ◆

By mid-June, Louisville was in last place, and attendance was awful. The club was losing staggering amounts of money and found itself in deplorable financial condition. Amid rumors that the franchise might need to be bolstered by some of the other league magnates, Barney Dreyfuss, club secretary and the majority stockholder, continued to keep the Colonels afloat by outlaying cash for previously unissued shares of club stock. Players were being released to reduce expenses; one of the casualties was George Smith. Management was also calling for a return of the cost-saving single-umpire system and a roster limit of fourteen so that Louisville would not be at a disadvantage to the big-city clubs, who were putting several unused players under contract.

The press took potshots at the team for its poor performance, and with a batting average hovering near the .250 mark, Wagner was an easy target. *Sporting Life* attested, "The Dutchman is a big favorite, and everybody hopes his slump won't last much longer. . . ." but pointed out, "The greatest disappointment of the team is the complete fall-down of Hans Wagner, who has done absolutely nothing that was expected of him. . . . Some people are mean enough to say Hans is an exploded phenom."

Manager Clarke's midterm evaluation was much the same. He was criticized for castigating his players on the field and swearing too loudly, and *Sporting Life* flatly stated, "Clarke has not done what was expected of him, and you can't find one man in a hundred who believes that he has any ability as a manager, and to make matters worse, his playing is affected by his being manager. . . ." But Clarke was not shaken, and after a July 4 doubleheader, he took advantage of back-to-back off days to head home to Chicago and marry Annette Gray, a sister of the woman who married Louisville pitcher Charles "Chick" Fraser a year earlier. (The Colonel players chipped in for a silver ice cream service, one which no doubt got a great deal of use in a marriage that lasted until Clarke's death in 1960.)

It seemed that the franchise had hit rock bottom on July 19, when after losing twelve of fourteen, the Colonels dropped to thirty-one games under .500, at 24–55. Pitcher Bill Magee helped stop the slide the next day by tossing a one-hitter for the Colonels; Wagner had three hits, including a double. A doubleheader sweep of Brooklyn followed, highlighted by Wagner's game-winning three-run homer in the second game. And on July 28, he helped wrap up the team's eighth consecutive win by driving in five runs, four on his first career grand slam, off the New York Giants' Amos Rusie.

The team pulled itself out of the cellar. And despite a few setbacks like a 24–4 thrashing at the hands of the 1898 champion Boston club, the remainder of the season was marked by progress, including winning streaks of five, six, and seven games. Including Magee's one-hitter on July 20, the squad was a miraculous 46–26 the rest of the way. Its ninth-place finish at 70–81 was Louisville's best showing since joining the National League in 1892.

Wagner remained hot through most of the second half and rebounded to a respectable average of .305 (adjusted in later years to .299) compared to a league average of .271 but just three points higher than the Orioles hit as a team. More notable was the fact that he finished tied for second in the league with ten home runs and was among the leaders in total bases. Splitting his time almost equally between the corners, he fielded his position well at third and adequately at first.

The only fault many could find with Wagner over the last few months of the season was that his uniform was filthy, stained with a mixture of mud, blood, and tobacco juice. Calling his appearance a disgrace, some fans griped that Wagner's white home jersey must not have seen a laundry the entire summer; he was never one who placed a great deal of importance on vanity, particularly on the ball field. In his eyes, the only letdown in late 1898 was a spike wound that kept him out of one game and limited him to pinch hitting in another. But he held up well in his most demanding baseball summer so far, performing in all but two of his team's games.

◆ ◆ ◆

As ball clubs sometimes did, the Colonels gathered for a field events day before going their separate ways for the winter. On October 16, a large crowd of more than four thousand people saw the exhibition at League Park. In the day's running events, Clarke, who became the favorite when Wagner's leg injury prevented him from participating, circled the bases in a time of 14.5 seconds to win the first contest. But in the hundred-yard dash, he was upset by Tommy Leach: The newcomer, who played in just three games for the Colonels late in the season, covered the distance on sod in just over ten seconds.

The highlight of the day was the long-distance throwing competition. Twenty-six years earlier, in 1872, John Hatfield set a record when he threw a baseball a distance of four hundred feet and seven and a half inches at Union Grounds in Brooklyn. For the Louisville affair, a starting position was set up in the right field corner, near the fence. The players were to throw the ball toward a line four hundred feet away that was past home plate, just in front of the grandstand. Clarke and a few others wound up and threw but were well short of the mark on several tries. Wagner's first attempt practically hit the line and had the crowd poised to witness a record-breaking feat. A second throw was lacking, but a third throw, a high, arcing rainbow, sent the congregation at the line scattering as the ball landed four feet past the target. The fans erupted as the players jogged in from the outfield to see the official measurement. An announcement was made that the throw had sailed 403 feet, eight inches, a new record, and Wagner's teammates almost tore his arm off with congratulatory handshakes. The record would stand for ten years, until Larry LeJeune would surpass it in a field events day in 1908.

The players donned costumes and split into two groups, Wagner's Comedians and Clarke's Tragedians. Clarke's men won the game, but according to *The Courier-Journal*, "Wagner was easily the star as far as really humorous work was concerned, and last night the whole town was talking about him. He smoked a huge cigar, played ball with a glass of beer in his hand most of the time and performed a thousand other antics . . . which kept the crowd roaring from beginning to end."

Just as he had in Paterson, Wagner quickly evolved into a fan idol in Louisville. His likable and playful personality, as well as his on-field exploits, were winning him admirers. Cigar manufacturer Henry Reccius, older brother of two former major league ballplayers and member of an influential local family that ran everything from a sporting goods store to a doll hospital, attempted to capitalize on Wagner's appeal. Shown wearing his "baker's" hat and a necktie, Wagner's likeness was used in ads that billed the "Hans Wagner" brand ten-cent cigar as the "Farmers' and Gardeners' Favorite."

◆ ◆ ◆

Despite more games in 1898, league attendance fell to its lowest total in five years. And with less turnout in all but two of the twelve cities, only three franchises showed a profit. It was a miserable year for the Louisville ownership, and estimates of the losses ranged as high as thirteen thousand dollars. Secretary Barney Dreyfuss once again proved to be the Colonels' savior. Over the years, Dreyfuss had become the money, brains, and influence of the club but until now had preferred to stay behind the scenes.

Born Bernhard Dreyfuss on February 23, 1865 (nine years and one day before Wagner), in Freiburg, Germany, he later changed his given name to Barney. Two of his first cousins had emigrated to America,

starting and nurturing a successful distillery and wholesale liquor business in Paducah, Kentucky. The Bernheim Brothers' Distillery was thriving, and the brothers, both in their thirties, were looking for other
family members to join them. At the urging of his cousin Isaac Wolfe
Bernheim, Dreyfuss abandoned his banking apprenticeship in Germany
and set out for the new country while still in his teens.

He liked to claim that his first assignment was scrubbing whiskey
barrels, but he entered the family business as assistant bookkeeper,
where Isaac Bernheim described Dreyfuss as "exceedingly apt, though at
times a somewhat careless young fellow." When the company picked up
and moved the entire operation to Louisville in 1888, Dreyfuss became
what his cousin called a "valuable and trustworthy man." He soon
worked his way to head bookkeeper and eventually credit manager, and
was also granted an interest in the company in 1890 that would prove
very lucrative.

Shortly after arriving in America, Dreyfuss developed an appreciation for the national game. He even formed and played on his own ball
club in Paducah in 1885, a team that lasted two years. Two of the members, playing under the assumed names of Dayton and Colby, were
brothers John and George Dovey, who would later own the Boston National League club. Upon moving to Louisville, Dreyfuss earned a reputation as an avid fan and served a year as president of the City Base Ball
League, a circuit of industrial teams including one fielded by the
Bernheim firm. He also purchased some stock in the American Association Colonels, who were owned by a number of local distillery and brewery men.

In the latter half of the 1890s, Dreyfuss began to increase his holdings and served on the Colonels' board of directors. In spite of being
married and having two young children to support, Dreyfuss was not
shy about taking risks. He was active both in the stock market and at the
racetrack. In 1899, his physician advised him to find an occupation less
confining and one that offered more fresh air than the liquor distillery.
So he resigned his position, disposed of his interest in the Bernheim
firm, and used the proceeds to secure additional control of the Louisville
ball club. In February, he agreed to serve as president, swapping titles
with Harry Pulliam. Dreyfuss was ready to devote himself completely to
baseball and the Colonels.

In addition to being a principal with the Louisville Colonels,
Dreyfuss liked to claim that a governor once appointed him a Kentucky
Colonel—an "honor" bestowed on a significant portion of the state's

male population. He spoke with a pronounced German accent, and with a weight estimated at between 97 and 125 pounds, he was often dubbed the Little Colonel or Colonel Barney. Stubborn, outspoken, and at times extremely critical, he demanded—and rewarded—loyalty from those in his employ. But in the spring of 1899, at the age of thirty-four, he was just beginning his long, exciting, and challenging tenure as a baseball club president.

◆ ◆ ◆

A single person maintaining holdings in more than one National League franchise was nothing new, but the evils of "syndicate ownership" were coming to light. In February, Baltimore owner Harry Von der Horst and owner-manager Ned Hanlon struck a deal with Brooklyn owners Charles Ebbets and Frederick Abell that merged the two ownership groups. With the clubs under joint control, several players were transferred from Baltimore's roster to Brooklyn's. Manager Hanlon moved on to Brooklyn and took with him two twenty-game winners, Doc McJames and Jim Hughes, as well as talented players Dan McGann, Hughie Jennings, Joe Kelley, and defending two-time batting champ Willie Keeler. It transformed the Brooklyn Bridegrooms, a team that was 54–91 in 1898, into the class of the league. Renicknamed the Superbas for 1899, Brooklyn would win 101 games and easily outdistance the field.

Cleveland owners Frank and Stanley Robison gained control of the St. Louis franchise and sent a number of players westward, including player-manager Patsy Tebeau and future Hall of Famers Denton True "Cy" Young, Jess Burkett, and Bobby Wallace. The move turned last-place St. Louis from a 111-game loser in 1898 into a first-division team. The switch devastated the Cleveland team, turning a respectable fifth-place finisher into easily the worst club in the circuit and one of the most farcical teams in history. The Cleveland Spiders of 1899, often referred to as the Misfits, would go on to a 20–134 record, an unbelievable eighty-four games out of first place and thirty-five games behind the eleventh-place finisher.

It had become obvious that the twelve-team league was unmanageable, and there was serious discussion among the magnates about a reduction to eight franchises. With syndicates now controlling the clubs in Cleveland and Baltimore, many owners felt the two could be dropped at the proper time with little repercussion. But two others would still need to be bought out—unless they could be snuffed out first. The powerful owners devised a plan: As the season approached, the original adopted schedule was scrapped, and a new one was quickly drawn up and approved without notifying Dreyfuss or Pulliam. The covert action was targeted at weakening the Louisville club by deleting eleven of its Sunday games. The loss of so many profitable dates could have cost the Colonels up to twenty thousand dollars in revenue.

Dreyfuss raised the roof in protest. Pledging that Louisville was in the race to stay and would not be "frozen out," he threatened legal action and demanded that a vote be taken to reject the new schedule. John T. Brush of the Cincinnati Reds, one of the owners behind the anti-Louisville sentiment, flaunted his coalition's success by smugly responding, "The shock upon my delicate and sensitive nature is so great that I may not recover in time to vote for any change in the schedule until it is too late."

In the end, Dreyfuss was pacified by the restoration of eight Sunday games, including a few that were part of unusual three-team double-headers. But as *The Milwaukee Sentinel* noted, "The row between the National League magnates has done more harm to base ball than all the rowdyism charged against the players during the past six years." The squabble prompted Dummy Hoy, in his spring training correspondence to *The Louisville Times*, to ask why there weren't "anti-rowdy laws for moguls."

Wagner almost missed his first true southern spring practice at Thomasville, Georgia, because of a scrape with death in late February. He was on a hunting jaunt with some friends when the group's buggy and team of horses tumbled down an embankment, spilling the entire party into an icy river. The horses were lost, but none of the hunters perished, despite a long, frigid walk back to safety.

Upon his arrival at Thomasville, Wagner lived up to his growing regard with an outstanding performance during the team's tune-up, becoming an even bigger celebrity than President William McKinley, a recent visitor. Hoy wrote, ". . . since his arrival Hans has monopolized more attention than the President did a few days ago." By 1899, Wagner's adjustment to big league ball was complete. It was to be his coming-out year, in which he would surpass Clarke as the team's biggest star and attraction.

◆ ◆ ◆

More than nine thousand people, including Louisville mayor Charles Weaver and all of the city officials, witnessed an opening day massacre on Friday, April 14, as the Colonels lost 15–1. Chicago scored in eight of nine innings, and Clark Griffith held the Colonels to eight hits and collected a single and triple himself. The only batter he had trouble with all day was Wagner. Now entrenched as the team's cleanup hitter, Wagner went 4 for 4 with a double. He had a second 4 for 4 day on April 25 against the Pirates, a game that he would always recall fondly: He was being taunted by the home crowd, and the fans facetiously—and prophetically—asked the visitors to take Wagner back to Pittsburgh when they left town. By the time he stepped to the plate in the ninth inning of a 1–1 tie, Wagner had already quieted the fans with two singles and a long home run over the left field fence. Facing pitcher Jesse Tannehill, Wagner gave Louisville an abrupt 2–1 win and delighted the local faithful by clouting his second fence-clearing homer.

A third 4 for 4 performance in less than three weeks followed on May 3, when he singled twice and doubled twice at Pittsburgh. Louisville games at Exposition Park were always met with a crowd of well-wishers for Wagner. And no trip to Pittsburgh was complete for him without a sojourn to Carnegie, where two local boys' teams, the "Honus Wagners" and the "Al Wagners," anticipated his visit. The kids knew that a few big league baseballs were sure to find their way into the team's equipment bag.

Cleveland scheduled a doubleheader for its home debut, but it was not a roaring success. Only about five hundred people were on hand to see the Spiders and Colonels split. In the first game, Cleveland first baseman Tommy Tucker attempted to push Wagner off the bag. Wagner shoved him back, and only the umpire's intervention kept the two players from coming to blows. Louisville was having trouble with a very bad Cleveland club, losing four of its first nine contests versus the Spiders. On May 21 against Cleveland, Wagner went 3 for 5 with a home run. But in the ninth inning, he forgot how many outs there were and got doubled off second base to end the game.

Louisville was off to another horrible start and between May 18 and June 16 went 4–20. The team did discover yet another prospect in new pitching acquisition Charles Phillippe (pronounced PHIL-a-pee). Described as having sterling integrity as well as being so unflappable that he did not even complain about his teammates' errors, he earned the nickname Deacon. On May 25, the Colonels had only four hits off the New York Giants' Ed Doheny, but Phillippe, in just his seventh big league game, tossed a no-hitter and walked one in winning 7–0. The tall right-hander would prove a valuable long-term addition to the team, using his above-average fastball and curveball to become the best control pitcher in baseball history—walking just 1.25 batters per nine innings over his entire thirteen-year career.

Stumbling in a six-game losing skid, the Colonels were paced to victory on June 16 by Wagner's first major league five-hit game. In the tenth inning, after his fifth single, he stole second and then scored the winning run a few moments later. The 5 for 6 day ended a personal 11 for 16 stretch that included two doubles and a home run. Wagner stroked a game-winning twelfth-inning single three days later and enjoyed his fourth 4 for 4 game of the season on June 30.

In mid-June, Louisville was in eleventh place and said to be suffering from internal dissension. There were rumblings of a mutiny against manager Clarke, and players were also complaining that Dreyfuss was too critical in his comments. The addition of college man Dave Wills fueled the ill feelings. Players with an academic background were rare, and those who did make it to the big league ranks found it rough going; Wagner recalled that "it was years before the college men were treated as anything but freaks." Third baseman Wagner admitted no guilt but remembered that some of the Colonel infielders would charge a ground ball to within a few feet of first baseman Wills and fire the ball at him, berating him if he failed to make the catch. Wills' major league career consisted of just twenty-four games in 1899.

Over the next few weeks, several roster moves were made to rid the club of the "disorganizers." Some teams thought any and all Colonels were available and made inquiries about Wagner. The most serious overture came from Brooklyn when Hughie Jennings was offered in exchange. Jennings had spent his first major league season in Louisville in 1891 and then jumped to New York of the National League prior to 1892. But later in that offseason, when the American Association folded and four of its teams joined the National League, Jennings was required to return to Louisville. He remained there for the next year and a half before being dealt to the Orioles. In 1899, Jennings did not relish another stint with Louisville. When he received news of a potential deal, he fired off a telegram telling the Colonels that any trade for him would be foolish because his arm was not sound. In fact, earlier that year, he had been shifted from shortstop to first base due to the trouble.

Dreyfuss denied any consideration of trading or selling Wagner and accused Brooklyn of simply seeking headlines. Local fans were used to seeing players dealt, but *The Sporting News* warned that "should

Dreyfuss part with [the Colonels'] slugging wonder there will be the biggest kick ever raised in Louisville over the disposal of a player. Wagner is without a doubt the most popular member of the Louisville club. He is mayor of the bleachers and the idol of rooter's row. . . ."

Dreyfuss was again interested in signing Al Wagner, but negotiations with Toronto broke down when Al was again reported to be out of condition. And although the elder Wagner went to Louisville for a tryout after the Eastern League season ended in September, he ruined any chance at a contract with an unreasonable salary request. After refusing a tryout offer from Boston, he returned home for the winter.

◆　◆　◆

Toward the end of July in Philadelphia, Honus Wagner injured a knee. He missed one game and was moved from third base, his primary position in the first half of 1899, to right field. The bad knee seemed completely healed only a few days afterward when he hit two inside-the-park home runs on July 30. (It was the second time that Wagner had two homers in a game, accounting for more than half his season's total of seven.) On August 13, while in the middle of a road trip the team received word that the wooden grandstand at League Park had burned to the ground in an electrical storm. Team owners, uncertain about their next move, finally approved a hastily constructed temporary bleacher.

Upon the team's return on August 22, the bottom of the first inning was interrupted twice—once as Colonel fans presented Clarke with a baby carriage in anticipation of a new arrival, and a second time as Wagner slid into third and tore a large hole in his pants. Billy Clingman, the Colonel shortstop, hustled a raincoat onto the field for Wagner to wear, and Honus carefully ducked into the clubhouse to swap trousers with one of the other players. Wagner blasted five doubles in the first two games back in Louisville, and the Colonels thrashed the Spiders 15–6 and 13–3. The Spiders were now homeless: Turnouts in Cleveland were averaging fewer than two hundred, so to try to make ends meet, the team took to the road in the first week of July, playing only seven games at home over the last three and a half months.

The Colonels would soon experience this vagabond feeling themselves. Attendance in Louisville was never very good, but now it suffered even further due to the unsatisfactory accommodations of the tiny, uncovered, makeshift bleachers. Although the local citizenry petitioned against the action, Dreyfuss would take the team on the road for the last six weeks of the season. On Saturday, September 2, the Colonels pounded out six home runs and twenty-two hits, beating Washington 25–4 in the last major league game ever played in the Falls City.

A few days into the season-ending, six-week road trip, Wagner bruised a wrist and missed eight games. From the bench, he witnessed a few interesting events. On September 8, Wagner's old pal Patsy Flaherty was introduced to the big leagues as a Colonel. Despite being signed as a pitcher, the good hitting Flaherty ceremoniously took Wagner's place in right field and in the fourth spot of the batting order. A day later, Flaherty made his first major league pitching appearance. Although Wagner did not realize it at the time, he saw one of the greats of the game debut on September 10, in Cincinnati. On his first day as a Red (and hitting his first triple) was future Hall of Famer Sam Crawford, the man who would hit more big league triples than any other player before or since.

September 12, 1899, marked Eddie Waddell's return to the Colonels. After a brief trial in 1897, he had chances to make the Louisville club the previous two springs but was farmed out each time. Waddell's demotion in the spring of 1899 had him vowing to return, and after an overwhelming performance in the Western League, the two hundred-pound left-hander was re-obtained by the Colonels. His unpredictable, bizarre behavior was often likened to a child's and earned him the nickname Rube, a name given to players thought to be hayseeds or country bumpkins. He immediately lived up to his reputation, both as a pitcher and as an eccentric.

In an unusual doubleheader in St. Louis on September 24, the Colonels met the home team in game one and then matched up with the wandering Spiders in a second game. Waddell ran his record to 4–0 in the first game and was so pleased with his showing that he turned a handspring as he left the field.

Wagner contributed three hits, including two triples, as the Colonels beat Chicago on October 3 in what was a landmark day. Thanks to a recent nine-game winning streak, and a very respectable mark since July 1, the team stood dead-even with a record of 72–72. It was the latest in the season a Louisville team had been .500 since joining the National League in 1892. But a losing record was assured ten days later when the Colonels lost a tough game in Pittsburgh. The Colonels scored four runs in the ninth to take a 6–5 lead, but heavy, black smoke from the industry of Pittsburgh enveloped the field. Even though the sun was shining, the umpire was compelled to call the game when he could not see the fielders from home plate through the smog. The score reverted to the end of the eighth, 5–2 Pirates.

The Colonels finished 75–77 and in ninth place but only two-and-a-half games out of seventh. Clarke hit .342, scored one hundred twenty-two runs, and stole forty-nine bases. Ritchey hit over .300 while playing solid defense. And the new additions to the pitching staff, Phillippe at 21–17 and Waddell at 7–2, showed true promise.

Philadelphia great Ed Delahanty dominated the league's offensive statistical categories, but Wagner was among the leaders in batting average at .359 (since adjusted to .336) and second in the league with forty-three doubles. He played third base in seventy-five games, outfield in sixty-one, and also spotted for injured teammates at second and first. Although considered "not an artistic success" at third base, his fielding percentages both at third and in the outfield were acceptable. Wagner's versatility allowed Clarke to use his other players at their best or natural positions. The ability to play anywhere well was admired and valued by his manager, but it may also have hindered Wagner from being recognized as a star. Though he was noted as a budding young hitter, he still was not associated with a single position, making it difficult to compare him with other players.

After the team's fine showing over the last few months, there should have been optimism for the following season, but with the franchise on such obviously shaky ground, many players adopted a wait-and-see attitude.

◆ ◆ ◆

Changes to the structure of Organized Baseball were looming. Most National League owners agreed it was impossible to continue with a twelve-team league and were favoring a cut to eight clubs. Dreyfuss publicly acknowledged that he anticipated the reduction and made it known that he and the other Louisville owners would consider offers by the league or by another club.

Dreyfuss knew Louisville's position was precarious, but he desperately wanted to stay in the baseball business, and he had negotiating leverage due to a number of desirable employees. New York, Chicago, and Cincinnati all made appeals for Colonel players, with much of the interest focused on Clarke and Wagner.

Meanwhile, primary Pittsburgh Pirate stockholders William Kerr and Phil Auten were considering selling their team. After a deal with former manager William Watkins and Cincinnati Reds owner John Brush fell through in late October, Brush met Dreyfuss at West Baden and encouraged him to pursue the Pittsburgh franchise as a way to stay in baseball. Dreyfuss scampered back to Louisville to enlist minority partners. Pittsburgh newspapermen followed the Brush-Kerr negotiations closely and deemed that any sale to an outsider would be a "dire calamity." Kerr was determined to keep further conversations private, and a meeting with Dreyfuss a few days later was hush-hush.

After seeing Kerr on October 30, Dreyfuss stopped in Carnegie to visit Wagner and confided that it looked promising that the executive and his player would represent the Pirates the following year. Wagner passed the good news to a few of his closest friends, and within twenty-four hours, the story was in every Pittsburgh newspaper that Dreyfuss was about to purchase the Pirates. Kerr was immediately plagued with second thoughts and backed out of the arrangement. He acknowledged his desire to bring the best of the Colonels to Pittsburgh in exchange for selling Dreyfuss a share of the Pirates and was even willing to have Dreyfuss appointed club president. But Kerr wanted to keep his hand in the game and refused to turn over controlling interest. The Pittsburgh correspondent to *The Sporting News* praised the popular Kerr for his "honorable record" and wrote, "There is no use trying to conceal the fact that [Pittsburgh] base ball enthusiasts did not take kindly to the prospect of having the local club controlled and operated by foreigners."

Negotiations for Colonel players continued with several teams, but on Friday, December 8, a deal was consummated between Dreyfuss and Kerr. The agreement was actually a series of transactions in which Dreyfuss resigned as president of the Colonels, purchased a 47.3 percent share of Pittsburgh Pirate stock for just under $47,000, and was assured the club presidency. He immediately turned over five seemingly marginal talents—and $25,000—to the Louisville ownership group, now headed by Harry Pulliam. In return, Pittsburgh received the rights to fourteen Louisville players—the pick of the Colonels, featuring Wagner and Clarke, who would soon be named manager.

Dreyfuss was overjoyed. When seen on the streets of Pittsburgh during the offseason, he seemed outwardly pleased, almost gloating. The settlement gave him nearly everything he had hoped for: He remained in baseball, and he had title and status. The only drawback was that he still had to share authority with Kerr and Auten, who together controlled slightly more than 50 percent of the stock.

Honus Wagner and Patsy Flaherty rode a trolley into Pittsburgh on

Saturday, December 9, the same day the new deal was announced. Arriving at the Pirate club office in the Smith Building, the two men expressed their pleasure with the turn of events and wasted no time in signing contracts for the coming season. For Wagner, a raise from $1,950 to $2,100 for 1900 was simply icing on the cake. All he could think of was how he must be the luckiest man alive. He would be able to live at home while playing big league ball.

F O U R

"THIS IS WHERE I BELONG"

The combination of the best of the Pirates and Colonels meant that Clarke had forty men to choose from, and Pittsburgh fans spent their offseason jotting down lineups, envisioning the new team as a contender. No Pirate received as much attention as Wagner. Expectations for him in 1900 were extremely high, and many felt he was on the verge of greatness. Clarke was particularly optimistic about Wagner's future, professing, "I don't think his equal lives today as an all-around ballplayer. . . . Keeler may lead him in batting when the averages are published, but Hans does not bunt them; he hits them out. . . . When his ability to play all the positions on the team is taken into consideration, I say he is the best ballplayer in the business. . . ."

An impressive roster of players accompanied Dreyfuss to Pittsburgh. In addition to Wagner and Clarke, the list included infielders Tommy Leach and Claude Ritchey; pitchers Rube Waddell, Deacon Phillippe, Patsy Flaherty, Bert Cunningham, and Walt Woods; catcher Charles "Chief" Zimmer; and a few lesser talents. In return, Louisville received the rights of five expendable Pirates, the best of them being pitcher Jack Chesbro, who had turned in a meager 6–9 record in 1899.

It was not until March 1900 that the inevitable cut to a league total of eight teams was finalized with a cash settlement to the ownership groups of the four clubs that were axed—Louisville, Cleveland, Baltimore, and Washington. The National League now consisted of New York, Brooklyn, Boston, and Philadelphia in the East, and Pittsburgh, Cincinnati, St. Louis, and Chicago in the West. (The structure of the National League would not be altered again until 1953 when the Boston Braves moved to Milwaukee.) With Louisville eliminated, Harry Pulliam moved to Pittsburgh as club secretary, and the Pirates re-obtained right-hander Chesbro (pronounced cheese-bro), nicknamed "Happy Jack" because of his sunny temperament. None of the four others sent to Louisville before the league reduction would ever play in another big league game.

Among the talented holdovers from the Pirates who would stick with the new team were pitchers Sam Leever, a right-hander, and Jesse Tannehill, a lefty; infielders Jimmy Williams and Fred Ely; catcher Bill "Pop" Schriver; and outfielders Clarence "Ginger" Beaumont and Tom McCreery. Clarke desired a young, hustling, scrappy team and wanted no players "with a past." In trimming down the roster for 1900, he sold ten-year veteran Bert Cunningham to Chicago and unloaded catcher Frank Bowerman, whom Clarke considered too hot-tempered. Perhaps protecting his job and avoiding team cliques, Clarke sold Patsy Donovan, the man whom he had succeeded as manager.

From the time it entered the National League in 1887 until the expansion to the twelve-team format in 1892, Pittsburgh's baseball franchise was in the second division each year. Other than a second-place showing in 1893, it finished no higher than sixth in the twelve-team league and placed seventh in 1899. And turnover had been the rule: Dreyfuss became the seventh club president and Clarke the eleventh manager—fourteenth if you consider that three of his predecessors each had two managerial terms.

The situation was perfect for a rebirth of Pittsburgh baseball. Fans were willing to embrace something new. Friends of William Kerr and Phil Auten were appeased by their continued involvement. Dreyfuss was the resourceful leader the club needed. And the pool of talent provided the nucleus of a powerful team as the franchise was about to begin a prolonged period of success.

◆ ◆ ◆

By the turn of the century, the Pittsburgh region was a leader in the production of steel, iron, glass, and other materials that were keys to progress for the entire nation. These huge firms brought money, jobs, and people to Pittsburgh. But when the factories and mills were active, it was often impossible to see across a downtown street at midday through the black soot puffed out of hundreds of smokestacks. Later in the decade, Professor John R. Commons of the University of Wisconsin would refer to this dichotomy in his comment, "Pittsburgh looms up as the mighty storm mountain of Capital and Labor. Here our modern world achieves its grandest triumph and faces its gravest problem."

The conditions earned Pittsburgh the nicknames of Smoketown and Smoky City—terms in which residents in no way took offense, any more than Boston to "Beantown" or Cincinnati to "Porkopolis." At least the smoke gave the community an identity, something that seemed to be lacking from 1890 to 1911 when the city was alternately spelled Pittsburg and Pittsburgh—a change mandated by the U.S. Board on Geographic Names but never fully accepted by the citizenry and inconsistently adopted by businesses.*

Pittsburgh experienced a phenomenal 33 percent population growth in the decade of the 1890s to more than 321,000, and with at least as many people residing in the immediate suburbs, the region accounted for just under 1 percent of the nation's total population of more than 75 million. Allegheny City, directly across the Allegheny River from Pittsburgh, was populated by 130,000 citizens and served as home to Exposition Park.

With its twin spires of four-sided, pointed roofs visible from downtown Pittsburgh and located just a short walk over a bridge that spanned the river, the ballpark was one of the most accessible in the National League. But separated from the Allegheny River only by the width of a few sets of railroad tracks, the area was highly susceptible to spring flooding, which gave rise to postponements and led to the rotting of the then-traditional wooden grandstand and bleachers. (Exposition Park was situated near the confluence of the Allegheny and Monongahela Rivers, which form the Ohio River, on a site that currently serves as a parking lot for Three Rivers Stadium.)

As spring approached, Dreyfuss had Exposition Park spruced up, and to conform to the recently adopted league standard, a new home plate—at a cost of $7.50—was planted. The traditional twelve-inch square was replaced by the seventeen-inch-wide, five-sided figure we know today. The league felt that there would be fewer arguments over

* For the purposes of this book, the name is written as it appeared in each source.

borderline strikes if there was no longer a corner on the plate, but Pirates pitcher Jesse Tannehill was hardly excited with the change. He pointed out (using terminology that would never quite catch on) that, "We seldom got the corners in the past, and I don't think we will get the flats this year."

◆ ◆ ◆

Plenty of introductions were necessary on the trip south to Thomasville, Georgia. The train was barely out of the Pittsburgh station on March 13 when an excited Wagner broke the ice by challenging his teammates to a sandwich-eating competition. He easily won the contest, and presumably a few dollars, but became so ill that during a scheduled stop in Cincinnati, he considered remaining in town for treatment. He stayed aboard but needed to rest for the first few days of practice and was soon joined on the sick list by Phillippe, who was fighting a losing battle with poison ivy, and Sam Leever, himself nursing a perennially sore arm. The team stayed at a former Baptist church, since renovated as a hotel. Using the four-foot-deep baptismal well as a communal bathing tub, the players quickly became well acquainted.

The itinerary for the trip north included a few days in Louisville, where the team was given a chilly reception. Attendance at the exhibitions was lousy, including a draw of a mere twenty-one fans on a Saturday afternoon that raised all of $5.25 in receipts. Dreyfuss was singled out and chastised for moving the team away. The former Colonels did get to revive some friendships, and the entire squad took a trip to Bud Hillerich's bat factory to pick out their "wagon tongues" for the coming year.

Arriving at the Southern Hotel in St. Louis the day before the season opener on Thursday, April 19, the team found the lobby alive with wagering on the next day's contest. Chief Zimmer and a few others boldly bet some of the local fans that the Pirates would be victorious. Veteran Zimmer should have known better, since his former battery mate with the Cleveland Spiders, the great Cy Young, would be on the hill for the newly named Cardinals. After a delay prior to the game so the new home plate could be dug up and properly inserted, Young shut out the Pirates 3–0. Pittsburgh did not have a hit until Wagner's single in the fifth inning, but he was picked off first base.

Wagner had four singles in helping the Pirates even their record on Saturday. In 1899, the Pirates had refused to play Sunday games. Dreyfuss reversed the policy for 1900 and was immediately rewarded with the largest crowd a Pittsburgh team had ever played to, as more than twenty thousand were on hand in St. Louis. Playing on Sundays generated significantly more revenue, but it meant the team had to make several one-day trips to Chicago, St. Louis, and Cincinnati, the league's western outposts where Sunday ball was permissible. It also required Clarke to tweak his pitching rotation in order to work around Chesbro who, like some others of his time, refused to pitch on the Sabbath.

On Monday, April 23, Wagner began a successful three-game series in Cincinnati by socking two triples in support of a Waddell three-hitter. On Wednesday, Wagner unloaded three doubles, but a furious four-run, ninth-inning Pirate rally was not enough as the Reds won 9–8. The two teams moved on to Pittsburgh for the Pirates' home opener.

A strong Carnegie contingent was part of an enthusiastic overflow crowd of eleven thousand, an Exposition Park record, that came out to welcome the new-look Pirates on April 26. Dreyfuss hired a band to parade down the street to the park, and fans assembled outside the gates two hours before game time. The mood quickly turned sour as Waddell was ineffective, giving up three first-inning runs and a total of eight in five innings. Chesbro gave up four more runs, and the Pirates were down 12–4 after eight. For the second consecutive day, a wild, ninth-inning rally would fall short, as the Pirates scored seven and had the tying run on second before being retired. Pirate pitchers were bombarded throughout the series and into the following week, but Dreyfuss was ecstatic with the early season turnouts as the team's record and Wagner's batting average both fluctuated around .500.

♦ ♦ ♦

Baseball fans, the sporting press, and Pirate opponents were all gaining an appreciation for Wagner's talents as the 1900 season continued. His work in right field was sensational. Fans enjoyed his diving catches and waited with hushed expectation when they knew there would be a Wagner throw to head off a baserunner. After chasing a ball into Exposition Park's right field corner, he made a throw of more than four hundred feet to third base to hold the batter to a double. Another throw to the plate that kept a runner at third had *The Pittsburg Post* describing the crowd's reaction as "an inspiring scene."

Now fully confident in his ability, he was also getting to be a little bit of a showman on the diamond. While at the plate in the tenth inning of a tie game, he grew impatient with pitcher Bill Kennedy's stalling. Wagner stepped from the box and pounded his bat vigorously on the ground, working the crowd into a lather. He promptly hit the next pitch over the center fielder's head for the game winner. Once, as the on-deck hitter, he meandered to the plate during a play and disrupted an incoming throw with his hip while blocking the umpire's view. Another time, after being ejected for arguing, he resumed his position in right field, only to have the umpire point to him and demand that he leave the game. Wagner charged toward the ump, pulled up short, and slapped his glove mockingly against his spikes.

On Sunday, May 6, on the road, Clarke and an old nemesis, Chicago second baseman Clarence "Cupid" Childs, revived a three-year feud. Clarke broke up a pair of double plays by slamming into Childs on the base path, and the second baseman took offense; the two had a brief skirmish before being separated. That evening, the two clubs were scheduled on the same 9:00 P.M. train to Pittsburgh. Awaiting departure at Lake Shore Depot, the short, stocky Childs approached Clarke, cursed at him, and landed the first blow. Clarke returned the punch, and the two combatants clinched and rolled on the platform for several minutes as the players gathered in a ring, shouting encouragement. After a policeman put a stop to the fight, the pair screamed obscenities at each other as they were assisted to the train. The clothes each had been wearing were shredded above the waist, and blood flowed down their faces from cuts.

Eight days later at Exposition Park, Clarke was at it again. He grounded out, but as he crossed the bag, he clipped Boston first baseman Fred Tenney with his spikes. As Clarke ran down the line, Tenney whirled and threw the ball, striking Clarke in the back. The two charged each other and were joined by their teammates before order was restored. Clarke had the final say in this affair when he hit a seventh-inning home run and was pushed off the bench by the other Pirates to doff his cap to the crowd. The Pirate manager was known to target opponents that he felt were due a payback for on-field actions and even rewarded his players with cigars for proper retaliation. He had a reputation for trying to intimidate the opposition by racing around the bases with spikes flashing, but he later confessed that this Tenney confrontation was the only time in his career he deliberately spiked someone.

A few weeks later, against New York's James "Cy" Seymour, the home fans thought Wagner was joining in Clarke's ruffianism. Seymour, a big left-hander with a tremendous fastball but horrendous control, won twenty or more games for the Giants in both 1897 and 1898, but by 1900 his problems in finding the new five-sided home plate seemed insurmountable. On May 26, he walked two of the first three Pirates he faced, and when he plunked Wagner in the back with a fastball, Honus darted toward the mound in a rage. However, he regained his senses after a few steps and upon reaching a shocked Seymour, Wagner slowed, pointed to his own back and asked the pitcher for a rubdown. The fans howled. Before his one inning of work was over, Seymour walked one more batter and hit another.

Two days later, Wagner was nailed again by Seymour, who along with teammate Ed Doheny combined to walk nine and hit four in a 14–0 loss to the Pirates. After an eleven-walk outing in early June, Seymour was sent to the minor leagues to work out his problems. He was a fine hitter and often played the outfield when not on the mound. While he never recovered his pitching prowess, he would return to the majors in 1901 solely as an outfielder and go on to a long, productive career.

◆ ◆ ◆

Led by the thundering bats of Ed Delahanty, Larry Lajoie, and Elmer Flick, Philadelphia was off to a roaring start in 1900, holding first place. The press, reflecting the mood of the times, billed the Phillies' first trip to Pittsburgh as a truly ethnic battle—Delahanty of Irish blood, Lajoie of French, and Wagner of German. Throughout his career, Wagner was a rallying point for many German Americans. To their delight, he won the first round of the matchup in Pittsburgh, banging out seven hits over three games, two of which held Pirate victories. Then on May 31, two days before the Pirates began a series in Philadelphia, Flick and Lajoie sparred in the Phillie clubhouse. Flick was sidelined for two games, but Lajoie had taken the brunt of the abuse, suffering a black eye, several face cuts, and a broken thumb. His injuries put him out of the lineup for more than a month, during which time the Phillies would tread water and relinquish first place to Brooklyn.

In late April, the Pirates acquired veteran first baseman Duff Cooley from the Phillies. Cooley tipped off his new teammates to the Phillie shenanigans that were helping to lead the team to the league's best home record for the season: Morgan Murphy, a little-used catcher, was stationed in the home team's clubhouse beyond the outfield wall at the Baker Bowl. Using a pair of field glasses, he picked up the opposing catcher's sign and relayed the pitch selection to the Phillie third base coach, who in turn passed it to an awaiting batter just as the pitch was about to be delivered. With Leever getting battered in one contest, Clarke complained vehemently to umpire Hank O'Day that the team's signs were being stolen, but the scheme could not be detected and the game continued. What was not clear to umpire O'Day, the Pirates, or even to Cooley, was *how* the signals were being relayed to the third base coach.

Murphy's "signal bureau" would remain a mystery until late in the season, when the Reds visited Philadelphia on September 17. In the practice of the day, Reds shortstop Tommy Corcoran took up the duties as a third base coach. He began scratching the dirt of the coaches' box with his spikes and soon dropped to his knees, clawing the surface with his hands. He emerged with the evidence—an electric buzzer and attached wire, linked underground to the Philadelphia clubhouse, where Murphy crudely telegraphed the pitches to a Phillie coach.

Less than two weeks later, when the Reds were in Pittsburgh on September 29, sleuth Corcoran suspected the Pirates of a similar stunt. In the eighth inning, after holding a conference with the umpire, Corcoran and a few teammates raced to deep center field, climbed the fence, and pulled out a large rod. In recapping the incident a few years later, Alfred Cratty, a colorful correspondent to *Sporting Life*, likened Corcoran's actions to that of "a cocaine fiend running amuck," and the Reds returned to the infield, according to Cratty, "gesticulating like Italian section hands on strike." There they explained the Pirate subterfuge: Zimmer, posted beyond the center field wall, picked up the catcher's signals with binoculars and indicated the upcoming pitch to the batter by positioning the device in a large *O* on an advertising sign posted on the outfield wall. Using the *O* as a dial, the rod would be moved to 12 o'clock, 3 o'clock, or 9 o'clock to indicate fastball, curveball, or changeup.

Although both teams were caught red-handed, in the end no punishment was ever passed down to the Phillies or Pirates. But Dreyfuss was enraged. Fighting was bad enough, but cheating was inexcusable. His belief in winning while maintaining dignity often clashed with Clarke's win-at-all-costs philosophy. Even though the two would disagree on tactics many times over the years, their common goals of winning and money not only helped them work together successfully but also become lifelong friends.

◆ ◆ ◆

Clarke liked what he saw in first baseman Cooley. When the manager left the team in early June due to kidney trouble, he named Cooley to the post of captain and put him in charge of the field decisions. Cooley moved himself into the leadoff spot, where he doubled in six consecutive games, but the Pirates immediately went into a tailspin. After the team dropped seven in a row, Dreyfuss went looking for Cooley, and when he was found at midnight, as Dreyfuss put it, "with two ladies and a batting average of .228," the president was furious. The following day, Fred Ely, a popular veteran who was so skinny he was nicknamed Bones, was appointed the new team captain, and within a few weeks, Tom O'Brien replaced Cooley at first base.

Clarke could not play regularly until June 28, but he was instantly back in form, throwing his cap in protest over being called out at home. At the end of June 1900, the Pirates stood at a mediocre 29–28 and had a team batting average of only .264. Wagner was the only one hitting, although no longer at a .500 clip. After dropping one hundred points from his average in May, he was still fighting for the league lead with the three Phillies—Delahanty, Lajoie, and Flick—who all were around .400.

The Pirate pitching staff that was considered to be a strong point was struggling, and it received another blow when Waddell was suspended indefinitely in early July. As he would be throughout his career, Waddell was often incredible while on the mound and always unpredictable when off it. His nightlife habits and game-day tardiness had the straightforward Clarke boiling. Finally, the manager had had enough, and Waddell was gone.

With a thin staff, outfielder Tom McCreery pitched three innings of mop-up on July 8 in a 17–3 loss to St. Louis. After being shut down without a hit by the Reds' Frank Hahn in Cincinnati on July 12, Philadelphia batters took out their frustration against poor Pirate pitching on Friday, July 13, at Exposition Park. Included in the onslaught were four hits apiece for Lajoie, Flick, and Ed McFarland, and an awesome two-single, three-triple performance by Harry Wolverton. Leever was yanked from the mound after giving up six hits and five runs in the first inning, and Chesbro was clobbered for fifteen hits and fifteen runs over the next four frames.

By the end of five, the Phillies were ahead 20–4, and with the pitching staff depleted, Clarke sent his versatile right fielder to the mound for the sixth. For two innings, Wagner kept the Phillies from scoring. Those who remained in the stands cheered themselves hoarse, and he acknowledged them as he walked from the mound each inning.

When "Big Ed" Delahanty came to the plate in the eighth, Wagner trembled, knocking his knees together in mock fear. The spectators laughed, continuing their merriment as Delahanty popped up harmlessly in the infield. But in the inning, an error, a base on balls, a double, and a triple contributed to three Phillie runs. The game was mercifully halted after eight with the Phillies winning 23–8. In his three-inning big league mound debut, Wagner fanned McFarland for his only strikeout and gave up three unearned runs on three hits and four walks.

After bouncing between second and fourth place throughout July and August, the Pirates began their last long eastern swing on September 3 entrenched in second place, seven games behind Brooklyn. The Pirates began the most successful eastern road trip in their history by sweeping a doubleheader in Boston. Earlier in the season, the Pirates had lost two separate games when Beaneater batters hit home runs at critical times over the shallow left field fence at Boston's South End Grounds. Unlike Exposition Park and many ballparks of the era, which had much deeper fences than do the facilities of today, South End Grounds was pinched between railroad tracks and a city street, making for short foul lines. Wagner avenged the losses by parking a ninth-inning, three-run pop fly over the 250-foot-deep left field fence to give the Pirates an 8–7 win in the first game of the September 3 doubleheader.

Waddell, who had caught on with Connie Mack's minor league club in Milwaukee after his suspension, made his return to the Pirates and in his first appearance fired a four-hitter to complete the sweep. In all, the Pirates won five games in three days from a respectable Boston club. When the Pirates took two of the first three in Brooklyn, the fans back in Pittsburgh were getting wrapped up in a pennant race. A *Carnegie Union* headline proclaimed BASE BALL FEVER RAGING and went on to add that the two questions people in Wagner's hometown were asking each evening were, "How is the score?" and "What did Honus do today?"

◆ ◆ ◆

In 1900, Carnegie was one of Pittsburgh's rapidly growing industrial suburbs, with a population of 7,332. Unfortunately, social conditions were not keeping up with the expanding manufacturing base. Water supplies and sewage treatment often lagged behind a community's growth and periodically resulted in outbreaks of disease. In June, Mrs. Wagner contracted typhoid fever. A housing shortage resulted in the entire close-knit Wagner clan living at the Railroad Avenue home, and it made for a full house. Peter Wagner, who recently found less dangerous employment as a watchman at the First National Bank in Carnegie, was head of the household. All of the grown Wagner children were still single and resided at home—Charley and Bill were both local barbers, Carrie was twenty-three years old and unmarried, Luke was a day laborer, Honus was home year-round when not traveling with the club, and Al spent his offseasons in Carnegie as well. Al was playing in Kansas City in 1900, but when that team sold his contract to Ed Barrow in Toronto, Al refused to report, instead going home to tend to his ailing mother.

In the predawn hours of Monday, September 10, Luke found his sixty-two-year-old mother dead in her bed. Honus hustled home. As the wealthiest member of the family, he purchased a plot of eight grave sites in Chartiers Cemetery the next day. Funeral services were held in the home for the late Mrs. Wagner on Wednesday, September 12. Floral arrangements poured in, including one from the ball club that the *Carnegie Union* called "probably the most magnificent floral emblem ever sent to the town."

Wagner remained at home grieving for four days following the funeral. Then on Sunday, September 16, Bill delivered his older brother to the club in New York and returned home. Wagner missed five games in the week he was gone. Pitcher Tannehill, a good hitter, substituted in right field, and O'Brien took Wagner's cleanup spot in the order. They filled in more than admirably as the team took three of five. The tragic loss of his mother did not interfere with Wagner's play as he went 4 for 5 in his first game back. The Pirates completed a tremendously successful 13–3 road trip by taking the last three games at New York, moving to within three games of first-place Brooklyn.

Back in Pittsburgh, the players were treated to a welcome usually reserved for pennant winners and other conquering heros. An estimated twenty thousand people wearing red badges labeled ROYAL ROOTERS greeted the team at Union Station at 9:00 A.M. on Thursday, September 20, and tens of thousands more paid tribute during a parade through the downtown streets. The festivities continued with a breakfast at Johnny Newell's, the spot of Barrow's "enlightenment" about Honus Wagner in February 1896. Dreyfuss was pressed to explain how the team lost three games in the east. He blamed all three on Wagner being away.

There was more ceremony at the ballpark that afternoon as a midweek crowd of more than six thousand presented Clarke with a seven-foot-high floral horseshoe, and Waddell was given a hat box full of hard-shell crabs. The Pirates also unveiled their new, dark blue stockings with red stripes, which would become their trademark in future years. The stockings added a touch of color to the squad's otherwise nondescript uniforms—plain pants and a simple, buttoned jersey with a left breast pocket and a dull blue collar. With no other identifying features other than a tiny *P* on their caps, the Pirates' striped socks would become symbolic of the powerful early-century Pittsburgh teams.

The team completed the great day for local fandom by jumping out to a first-inning lead and marching to a 10–4 win. Wagner singled three times and drove in three runs, and he delighted the crowd by stealing four bases, including third base twice. It was the first time he stole four bases in one game—a feat he would accomplish five times in his career. He also received a chuckle from the audience when, as the on-deck hitter, he ran to assist Ritchey, who was squirming on the ground after being struck with a pitch. Wagner rubbed his friend's arm and then playfully punted him toward first base.

Wagner provided the spark a few days later as the Pirates pulled to within a game and a half of Brooklyn. Dreyfuss boldly forecasted a pennant and promised each of his players a generous reward if they followed through. This prediction was quite obviously a hoodoo. The team sank six games behind by dropping six of its next seven games, with Wagner contributing only two hits.

Wagner was slumping as the season wound down. The batting title was up for grabs, with Elmer Flick of Philadelphia, Willie Keeler of Brooklyn, and Jesse Burkett of St. Louis all within striking distance of Wagner's league-leading mark. When Wagner chose to sit out the first of five games with St. Louis due to a wrist injury, brackish Cardinal left fielder Burkett accused Wagner of protecting his batting average. Wagner, appearing as a pinch hitter, was livid at the insinuation and was even more disturbed when his tormentor robbed him of a hit by neatly snaring a line drive off the grass in left-center field. Over the next few days, the two men traded hits evenly, each with six over four games. Wagner drew nearer to his first batting crown.

It would be many years before the home run was an everyday occurrence or awards such as the Most Valuable Player and Rookie of the Year would be established. Baseball's most prestigious honor was unquestionably the league batting title. On the final day of the 1900 season, unofficial tallies revealed that Wagner and Flick were still neck and neck for the distinction. The Phillies finished their season at home, as did the Pirates, and when each competitor went 2 for 4, it was thought that Wagner had won by a slim two-point margin, although official figures showed a more sizable spread.

Wagner, the first Pittsburgh National Leaguer to carry the honor since the league's inception in 1876, always considered his first batting crown one of his greatest baseball thrills. One admirer named a bay colt racehorse for him, and Hans Wagner competed over the next two years at Saratoga, Aqueduct, and Coney Island as well as in Memphis, Louisville, and Chicago. The town of Carnegie held a bonfire to mark the occasion, and Al proudly confiscated his brother's bat, mounting it on the wall of the trapshooting gallery they would manage that winter. Years later, a friend recalled the pride that Wagner's father took in the feat. Upon the news of the accomplishment, the elder Wagner primed the neighborhood for a bash by boasting in broken English, "My Honus win the champagne. He bring home the champagne." Honus always discounted the story by saying, "What did those fellows know about champagne? They were all beer drinkers, like me."

◆ ◆ ◆

With a second-place finish virtually assured, the spirits of the Pirates and their fans were soaring. Dreyfuss provided the team complimentary use of Exposition Park and more than four thousand fans showed their growing affections for the team by paying to see the players stage a field events day on October 5. The players wore costumes that made light of their heritage, nickname, religion, or reputation—conduct that would be considered offensive or even intolerable in today's world.

Each player remained in character throughout the day's activities, which were under the strict direction of Chief Zimmer, fully attired in an Indian headdress. Beaumont, whose moniker Ginger came from his tawny hair, was an extremely fast runner, but his appearance and everyday mannerisms, including dragging his bat to the plate, had him pegged as lazy or even slovenly. He played the part for the occasion by lounging in the outfield as a tramp. Sam Leever, nicknamed The Goshen Schoolmaster, had indeed been a teacher in his Ohio hometown and dressed accordingly. Tom O'Brien the policeman, Deacon Phillippe the farmer, wiry Fred Ely the ballet girl, and many others made appearances. Wagner as a plaid-clothes Dutchman with a long-stem pipe and Rube Waddell as a shotgun-toting Uncle Sam received the biggest laughs.

Awards for the traditional sprints and dashes were shared by Beaumont and Leach, while Wagner and Tannehill were the throwing stars. One event consisted of simply sending slow-footed Pop Schriver around the bases and timing him. Schriver's most noteworthy achievement came in 1894, when he became the first player to catch a ball tossed from the top of the Washington Monument. But speed was not his game. In nine of his fourteen big league seasons, he hit a single home run, and after hitting his only one of 1900 he exclaimed, "No more homers for me. They're too hard." On his trip around the diamond, he fell once and was clocked at a not-too-brisk twenty-eight seconds. The fans enjoyed it nonetheless. The greased-pig chase was a debacle. The first animal sustained a broken leg when Uncle Sam flung it onto his shoulder, and as the gang closed in on the replacement hog, it froze and let Wagner grab it.

Cowpuncher Clarke umpired a seven-inning game and at the first sign of a kick pulled his pistol and fired shots into the air. In the fourth inning, Wagner, Waddell, Leever, and Leach sprinted into the outfield. Three of them climbed the fence—Leach's little girl attire not being conducive to the act. Waddell ripped a large, fake clock from the wall and paraded into the infield where it was explained that they had uncovered the opposing team's "signal service." The fans roared.

It was a successful day. The spectators loved it, and the players enjoyed themselves, pocketing more than a hundred dollars apiece, a tremendous sum for their one-day comedy show.

◆　◆　◆

Once it was clearly a two-team race, O. S. Hershman of the *Pittsburgh Chronicle Telegraph* offered a five-hundred-dollar silver cup to the winner of a Brooklyn-Pittsburgh championship series at the season's conclusion. The players were to share all gate receipts from the best-of-five series played at Exposition Park, so Dreyfuss and Brooklyn manager Ned Hanlon, who finished in the top spot for the fifth time in the last seven years, stepped aside to allow Clarke and Brooklyn left fielder Joe Kelley to handle all arrangements. The two agreed that only players under contract as of September 15 would be eligible, that regular-season admission fees would be charged, and that the proceeds would be split fifty-fifty regardless of the outcome.

The Pirates finished only four and a half games off the pace at 79–60. (The league had adopted a shorter schedule in 1900.) But it was not a balanced squad. The team was built solely on Wagner's offense and a fine pitching staff. Wagner was the Pirates' only .300 hitter, leading in most every offensive category. He outhit the league by more than one hundred points and set what would prove to be personal career highs with a .381 batting average, .573 slugging percentage, forty-five doubles, and twenty-two triples—all league highs for 1900.

After a poor start, the pitching staff had been tremendous. Phillippe and Tannehill each won twenty, the second-highest victory total in the league. Leever and Chesbro each went 15–13, and Waddell, despite missing two months of the season, led the league in strikeouts and allowed the fewest earned runs per game at 2.37. (Earned run average, or ERA, was not an official National League statistic until 1912 but is provided herein for comparison purposes.) The staff struck out the most men and walked the fewest, and the team ERA of 3.06 was the lowest in the league by a wide margin.

The Brooklyn team was almost an exact opposite. Its offense was formidable and filled with veterans such as outfielders Joe Kelley, Fielder Jones, and Willie Keeler, who each hit .300. The Superbas scored the most runs, stole the most bases, and hit for the highest average at .293, but their weakness was pitching. Bill Kennedy, a twenty-game winner, was unavailable for the series due to an ailment, and the load fell squarely on the shoulders of Joe McGinnity, the league's best pitcher. McGinnity had reached the National League in 1899 as a twenty-eight-year-old rookie after developing a rising fastball from a devastating underhand delivery. Nicknamed Iron Man (he had once worked in an iron foundry), he lived up to his moniker by leading the league in 1899 with twenty-eight wins and 380 innings. Moving on from Baltimore to Brooklyn in 1900, he again led in both categories, pitching 347 innings and finishing 29–9.

Roughly four thousand fans were on hand for a matchup of Waddell and McGinnity on Monday, October 15. Wet grounds eliminated the running game. In the third inning, Brooklyn struck for three runs on six hits, including three infield bleeders that found the quagmire in front of home plate. It was all the support McGinnity needed, as he surrendered just five singles, walked two, and hit Wagner with a pitch. In the eighth, McGinnity was caught in a rundown, slipped, and crashed his head into Waddell's knee. McGinnity was dazed for several seconds and required assistance to get to the bench, but he remained in the game, closing out a 5–2 Brooklyn win. Wagner was 1 for 3 and scored one of the Pirate runs. But four errors, a pair apiece by first baseman Tom O'Brien and third baseman Jimmy Williams, contributed to three unearned Brooklyn runs.

On Tuesday, Brooklyn fielded flawlessly and Williams made four throwing errors as Leever and the Pirates were defeated 4–2. The Superbas were said to have won a tidy sum betting on themselves in the first two contests. Before the third game, there was some question that the players might allow the Pirates to win a game to prolong the series. Lave Cross, Brooklyn's third baseman, assured the public that the

Superbas were in earnest, saying, "To introduce any crookedness in the series would be to ruin the game, and we cannot afford to do that." The betting was heavy on Brooklyn to win game three. McGinnity warmed up in full view of the stands, but when six-game winner Harry Howell took the mound in the first inning, the "sports" clamored. The Pirates stroked thirteen singles off Howell, three each by Leach and Beaumont and two each by Ritchey and Wagner, as Phillippe whitewashed Brooklyn 10–0.

The Superbas took Thursday's contest, winning the series three games to one. In the second inning, Wagner riled his opponents by fouling off ten balls at the plate in order to make McGinnity throw more pitches. Iron Man was not unnerved. He allowed nine hits, eight of them singles, and bolstered by good defense, he easily wrapped up the cup with a 6–1 win.

Wagner was not enough for the Pirates. In four games, he led all players with a .400 average, going 6 for 15; he stole two bases, drove in three runs, and was errorless in right field. But the team committed fourteen miscues, seven by Williams, and ten of Brooklyn's fifteen runs were unearned. Clarke missed the entire series with a leg injury, and his replacement, Tommy Leach, hit a disappointing .176. McGinnity was awesome, throwing two complete-game wins and not allowing an earned run in eighteen innings. Attendance at game four dropped to 2,335, and with a total turnout of fewer than 11,000 over the four games, the series was not as lucrative as the players had hoped. Still, each received $150 for less than one week's work.

Before departing Pittsburgh, the Brooklyn players voted unanimously to award the beautiful silver cup to McGinnity. The cup competition lasted only one year, and some believed it might be the end of postseason competitions altogether. Dreyfuss stayed completely out of the picture but *The Pittsburg Times* expressed his thoughts, stating that "chances are that it will be the last series of the kind that any Pittsburg Club will ever play, that is so long as the present owners of the club continue in control. . . ."

Dreyfuss and Kerr agreed to kick in a $2,500 pool to be divided among the Pirate players for finishing second. Wagner now felt like he was on Easy Street. He collected an enormous salary for his day and had the added money of the field events day, several midseason exhibitions, the postseason series, and the second-place bonus. With his modest lifestyle and living with his kin at Railroad Avenue, it was an amount that would last for years. His first offseason acquisition was a $400 piano for his younger sister—an uncharacteristically extravagant purchase for Wagner.

◆ ◆ ◆

It was the most profitable year ever for the Pittsburgh franchise, and estimates of the amount ranged as high as an incredible $60,000. Of course, that did not mean the magnates were happy. Soon after the cup games, a squabble began over the position of club secretary. Kerr and Auten wanted to dismiss incumbent Harry Pulliam in favor of Auten's nephew Frank Balliet, who had held the post a few years earlier. Dreyfuss took offense at the action against his comrade and confidant. Over the next few months, a showdown for control of the team was clearly on the horizon. The Pittsburgh newspapers chose sides, and an unofficial count had six preferring the Kerr-Auten interest and only two in favor of Dreyfuss.

At a January stockholders' meeting in New Jersey, the organization's state of incorporation, Dreyfuss, sensing his overthrow by a majority, immediately played his trump card. He cited a technical point that the conference was illegal, in violation of club bylaws because notices had been improperly sent out. As president, he ordered adjournment. *The Pittsburg Post*, obviously not in the Dreyfuss corner, complained, "Dreyfuss and Pulliam ran things to suit themselves, and unfortunately had the New Jersey law on their side. . . ."

Kerr attempted to obtain an injunction, but by mid-February it was clear that he and Auten could not win a legal battle. O. S. Hershman approached Kerr and Auten about the possibility of one of the feuding parties buying out the other, and they agreed to sell. Their 502 shares of stock and a small block of twenty-five shares owned by Wallace J. Tener and his brother John K. Tener, a local banker and former major league player, were purchased for a sum estimated at $66,000. The buying faction was led by Dreyfuss, who enjoyed a prosperous year in 1900 with the ball club as well as with several lucrative investments. Also included were Hershman, who sold his *Pittsburgh Chronicle Telegraph* to acquire a much larger daily, *The Pittsburg Press*, in January; William Kesley Schoepf, executive at the thriving Consolidated Traction Company; and to a much lesser degree, Pulliam.

Dreyfuss, just days before his thirty-sixth birthday, now had a majority of the stock and was in complete control. He proudly announced, "I am a citizen of Pittsburgh and will advance its honors on the ball field as much as in my power." He remained club president until his death in 1932.

Clarke had used his baseball earnings wisely over the last few years and was now considered one of the wealthiest players in baseball. He owned hundreds of acres of land near Winfield, Kansas, and each off-season he returned there to live the ranching life. Coming to Pittsburgh in February, he signed a three-year contract. Now feeling secure in his position with the Pirates, he joined Wagner for a daylong hunting trip—for a Clarke family home.

Wagner's investments were not as far-reaching. In fact, the only notable business in which the twenty-seven-year-old Wagner was involved was chicken farming. Now the proud owner of several coops, he harvested the eggs regularly for sale in Carnegie. In addition to playing poker and pinochle, he also had a new hobby in the growing sport of bowling, claiming it would help him avoid some of the winter flab. Honus, who was becoming quite proficient, led his bowling team to the Carnegie city championship, defeating Al's team and challenging any National Leaguer to a competition.

◆ ◆ ◆

Throughout the last half of the 1890s, Byron Bancroft "Ban" Johnson was president of the Western League. He developed the circuit into perhaps the strongest of the minors and positioned it to become a second major league. Prior to the 1900 season, he renamed the organization the American League and prepared to take advantage of the National's reduction to eight clubs, but his threats of becoming another major league fell through. By early 1901, under the capable leadership of the authoritarian Johnson, and with the deep pockets of energetic Cleveland businessman Charles Somers and a docket of high-powered baseball men turned club operators and managers such as Charles Comiskey, Connie Mack, Clark Griffith, and recent convert John McGraw, it was clear that the rival league was a reality. For the 1901 season, Johnson took Detroit and Milwaukee (the cream of the former Western League), combined them with three of the cities the Nationals had abandoned (Baltimore, Washington, D.C., and Cleveland), and prepared to go toe to toe with existing National League teams in Chicago, Boston, and Philadelphia.

Modest attempts to arrive at a coexistent solution proved fruitless, and the bombastic Johnson boldly proclaimed war. The elder circuit's owners braced for player raids. Johnson and his cohorts agreed to steer clear of any player who was already under contract for the coming season, but players who were simply spoken for under the reserve clause were fair game. (By invoking the reserve clause, a club could bind a player indefinitely even though there was not a contract between the two parties.) The jumping began. Dozens of players, including many stars, hopped the fence for the greener pastures of the American League. Lists of the players defecting were published regularly and contained some of the game's best talent, including Cy Young, Larry Lajoie, Jimmy Collins, Lave Cross, and Joe McGinnity. Of the 185 players Johnson's teams would employ for the 1901 season, 111 were former National Leaguers. The Pirates were relatively unscathed. By season's outset, the only two Pittsburgh players lost to the Americans were Jimmy Williams and Wagner's old Warren buddy Harry Smith, who had yet to play a big league game.

Johnson and company targeted forty-six top National League players. Of course, the Pirate bull's-eye was Wagner. The unavoidable rumors began. In one, Wagner allegedly signed with the Boston Americans. Another had Wagner starring for a Pittsburgh American League team that was to get underway. Wagner would tell a story years later of Clark Griffith, American League emissary and pitcher-manager of the Chicago White Stockings, coming to Carnegie on a snowy night and dangling $20,000 cash in front of Wagner's gleaming eyes. It was "more money than I thought there was in the world," Honus would say. But he rejected the offer.

While the truth was not quite as glamorous as the lore, Wagner had plenty of opportunity to make more money if he jumped. But it was a bad time to be recruiting him. He had just enjoyed his most successful season to date and was happy to be playing for his hometown team. The $2,400 salary limit was ignored by the National League if it meant keeping a player, and Wagner managed an increase to $2,700 for the coming year. Some attributed the loyalty of the Pirate players to Dreyfuss's decency and generosity. Others said that after unsuccessful attempts to lure Wagner, Johnson instituted a hands-off policy for Pittsburgh players, the theory being that if his rivals had a runaway pennant race, public interest would turn to his league.

◆ ◆ ◆

Pittsburgh had reason to anticipate a successful 1901 baseball season. The competition had been weakened by the upstart circuit. The Pirate organization was in Dreyfuss's capable hands. Shrewd field leader Clarke was at the helm. And the fine roster of young and talented players remained intact, including its contented star, Honus Wagner.

While the coming year looked bright for the Pirates, it was a rotten spring for Al. His 1901 destination was in doubt, and just a few days after he signed with Providence, Dreyfuss approached him with an offer to become the Pirates' utility infielder. Al was upset. He had been within a whisker of the majors but made his move too soon. For the second year in a row, Al would return home from his Eastern League assignment prior to season's end.

The family's luck was with Honus. On the return trip from the new spring training site of Hot Springs, Arkansas, the team made a stop in Little Rock, where he won forty-two dollars at the racetrack. (His conservative nature was evident even at the races, as all of his bets were said to be place and show.)

Prior to 1901, foul balls did not count as strikes, with the exception of foul tips. Just like Wagner did during the Chronicle Telegraph games the previous fall, a few batters like Roy Thomas and John McGraw could stand discriminatingly at the plate and foul off innumerable pitches while waiting for a fat one or four balls, whichever came first. A new foul-strike rule, the one we are familiar with today, made all foul balls strikes until two strikes were called on a batter. At the opener in Cincinnati, players immediately began cursing the rule. After fouling one ball off, Wagner fanned and complained to the umpire about the policy. But Clarke, Wagner, and new first baseman William Bransfield all tripled in a four-run sixth inning as the Pirates won 4–2.

First baseman Bransfield, at the age of twenty-three, had played a few games for Boston in 1898. Then in 1900, playing for his hometown of Worcester, Massachusetts, he hit .371 to win the Eastern League batting title by a thirty-four-point margin. Dreyfuss was enthused and bought him in late 1900. Bransfield would spend much of 1901 batting directly behind or ahead of Wagner in the order, as the two men became the team's leading run producers. The two-hundred-pound Bransfield, called Kitty because of his feminine hairstyle, ironically provided competition for Wagner and Waddell as the team's strongest man.

Dreyfuss considered himself a good judge of baseball talent and for years was known to keep a "dope book" of minor league prospects. While many of Dreyfuss's entries became Pirates, it was most often his checkbook rather than his notebook that made the difference in procuring quality players. As *The Pittsburg Dispatch* put it, "He has great faith in the curative powers of gold in baseball. . . ."

Clarke loved to change his batting order, but for much of the season, center fielder Beaumont and left fielder Clarke were the table-setters. The "midgets," Ritchey and Leach, each under five feet seven inches tall, held down second and third but were shuffled around in the order. Ely covered short and batted seventh ahead of the catching pair of Zimmer and Jack O'Connor. The pitching staff that did such a remarkable job in 1900 was intact with one exception.

After two awful performances by Waddell, Clarke finally gave up on the troubled young man and sold him to Chicago in early May. A few days later, as the Pirates began their first four-game sweep at Chicago in club history, Waddell was the losing pitcher. Clarke later took credit for the victory by claiming he distracted Waddell with a promise of giving the big lefty a puppy at the end of the season. Complaining about his teammates' poor support and suffering another suspension later in 1901, Waddell wound up with Connie Mack's American League Philadelphia Athletics the following year. Mack lived with Waddell's peculiar ways as best he could and was able to harness the tremendous talent. Waddell would become one of the best left-handers in baseball history and a Hall of Famer.

♦ ♦ ♦

New York, a last-place finisher the previous year, was a surprise early leader in 1901. Other teams made their run at the top spot, including St. Louis in July, Brooklyn in August, and Philadelphia over the last several weeks of the season, but throughout, Pittsburgh was the club to beat. Although the title would not be secure until the final month, the Pirates were never more than a few games off the pace and took over first place for good on June 15. On June 20, behind a Chesbro three-hitter, Wagner laced two doubles and a single. He stole three bases, including home plate twice—becoming the first player of the twentieth century to steal home two times in a game. "Wagner performed conspicuously," revealed *The Pittsburg Post*. "[He] skipped around the bases with all the abandon of a child playing crack the whip. He was as care free . . . as a bull calf in a ten-acre lot."

A crowd of 12,466 (the largest ever to witness a game in Pittsburgh) turned out for the first game of a July 4 morning-afternoon doubleheader. In addition to the holiday, the attraction was twenty-year-old pitching phenom Christy Mathewson. He was an unimpressive 0–3 in a 1900 trial, and in his first inning of work against the Pirates that year he gave up six hits and six runs, including a three-run homer to Clarke. But in 1901 the former Bucknell College player was taking the baseball world by storm.

The morning game was a twelve-inning thriller. The Pirates had several baserunners but could only manage three runs through nine innings. At one point, with Zimmer at first and Wagner at third, the two tried a double steal. Zimmer broke for second, but Mathewson stretched up, picked off the throw, and fired home to nail Wagner easily at the plate. The Giants scored three times in the twelfth, but the Pirates responded. With two outs, Wagner was at second after driving in a run and Ritchey was perched on first. When Wagner broke for third, the rattled Mathewson committed a balk. With the tying runs in scoring position, Mathewson struck out Ely to end the game and move the Giants back into a first-place tie with Pittsburgh. In the afternoon game, Pittsburgh unloaded fourteen hits and sailed back into first place with a 12–0 victory.

The Pirates won the next two to knock the Giants three games back. New York would hang in the race until mid-July and then drop from sight, finally landing in seventh place, thirty-seven games out. The four games with the Giants drew an unprecedented thirty thousand fans to Exposition Park, one of many franchise records that would fall in the Pirates' first championship season. As the team started to roll, some of the players were getting a little frisky with their success. During one blowout, Zimmer caught an inning without his mask. In another contest, the Pirates scored at least one run in every inning. Leever was coaching first base in the drubbing, and when Tannehill drilled a ball into a gap and began to circle the bases, Leever followed him around the circuit. The two pulled jointly into third with a triple as Leever stomped around, hollering, "Wow! Wow! Wow!" before being ejected.

◆ ◆ ◆

Wagner remained the offensive leader, although the overall team attack was much better in 1901. Clarke and Beaumont were near .300, as were Leach, Bransfield, and Ritchey, all of whom seemed to be blossoming at the same time. The pitching was top-notch, and the team was now in first place to stay. But there were still problems, particularly with umpires and the American League.

The squad continually clashed with arbiters. On June 1, it was Bert

Cunningham, the old Louisville pitcher turned umpire for a brief time in 1901. He was still upset at having been left out in the cold after the Louisville-Pittsburgh deal and warned Tommy Leach that the Pirates would see the worst of a few calls. The players kicked throughout the game, and the fans soon joined the chorus. At the end, it was only through the protection of Wagner and Clarke that Cunningham was allowed to exit the grounds. As it was, he sustained a punch in the neck and soon retired from umpiring altogether.

Later in June, umpire Hank O'Day ejected Wagner for arguing a called strike. Wagner persisted in badgering O'Day from the bench, but once informed that an officer had been summoned to forcibly remove him from the grounds, Wagner clammed up and left the field. In mid-July, he was thrown out again, this time for slamming his glove to the ground in objection to a call. After the game, the crowd surrounded umpire Bob Emslie, but he walked off the field peacefully with two police officers at his side. Less than a week later on July 19, Emslie ruled Clarke out trying to steal second. Clarke blew up at the game-ending call, and the fans again descended on Emslie, making idle threats. In the first few years of the century, it seemed as if the Pirates were bent on replacing the mid-1890s Orioles, both as the might of the league and as grousers.

Ban Johnson's crew was still prowling, and some people believed that they would move a team into Pittsburgh with the financial backing of Kerr and Auten. The Americans were said to have landed a few stars right from under Dreyfuss's nose, such as Wagner, Beaumont, and Tannehill—all reported to have jumped in August. The innuendo proved false, but Dreyfuss was very busy making sure he closed off any potential avenues to his competitors.

He signed a lease to take charge of Recreation Park, predecessor to Exposition Park. He also rented a few large lots, guessing they were potential ballpark sites. And he was trying to exhibit his generosity to the players. He treated the club to a fancy five-dollar hotel in Chicago and sprang for theater tickets when a road game was rained out. He kept injured Leever on the club at full pay and in full view of the others, even though the pitcher's future was in doubt after his arm was badly bruised by a Mathewson pitch. Dreyfuss even sent the team, all expenses paid, to Atlantic City, New Jersey, for some coastal sun during a lull in the schedule. In midseason he began to sign many of his players to contracts for the following year at an increase in salary, and by mid-August, one report had every one of the Pirates already in the fold for 1902. It was a costly maneuver, but Dreyfuss knew he had been lucky in not feeling the worst of the American's assault. He also was raking in the profit generated by his front-running club.

◆ ◆ ◆

Fred Ely was adored by the local fans, but the shortstop's average of .200 and his persistent injury complaints were not endearing him to manager Clarke. A number of solutions were tried in July. Clarke himself played shortstop in one game, abandoning the effort after a three-error performance. Next tried was Lew Carr, a giant by the standard of the day at six feet two inches tall, and the man Wagner called "little boy." The twenty-eight-year-old rookie was found wanting and lasted just nine games. Later in the month, Ely was benched and, within a few days, released unconditionally. Two reasons for the move were made public: The team's acquisition from Brooklyn of outfielder Alfonzo "Lefty" Davis was working out so well that a permanent spot had to be cleared for him; and Tommy Leach was now considered a bona fide big leaguer and had to play every day. The true cause for Ely's release was that he was discovered to be an American League spy and was disseminating its propaganda among the Pirate ranks. Within two weeks he was playing for Connie Mack's Philadelphia Athletics.

On July 23, Clarke announced his intention to play Wagner at shortstop. This news was not welcome, especially not to Wagner. He could finally call right field his own after playing 118 games there in 1900, the most he had ever played at a single position. He was reluctant to move to the unfamiliar spot, so Leach was shifted from third base to shortstop, and Wagner was convinced to come in to play the hot corner temporarily.

Leach recalled in later years that his manager told him to work on Wagner and persuade him that it would be best if he took over at shortstop. The two arguments Leach used were that the big fellow could cover more ground and that since Leach had recently been suffering weakness due to heat stroke, it would make sense for Wagner to play the more strenuous position. After three days of pleading, Wagner agreed to the switch.

He made his first big league appearance at shortstop on Saturday, July 27, 1901, in the second game of an important series in St. Louis. The Cardinals won game one of the series to pull within two games of the first-place Pirates. An enormous crowd of sixteen thousand for the second game was dejected as the Pirates capitalized on eight Cardinal errors to win 7–4. The teams split the next two, including one in front of the largest attendance to date in St. Louis, more than twenty-one thousand, as the Pirates left town with a three-game lead.

Wagner and Leach would swap short and third once more before Wagner settled into the position for the remainder of the year. The responsibility of playing shortstop did not affect his hitting. From July 17 to August 20, Wagner put together a twenty-three game hitting streak, the longest of his career.

There was instant recognition of Wagner's ability at shortstop. After handling ten chances flawlessly in his first contest, *The Pittsburg Dispatch* professed his "game at short was a marvel." Within a few days, *The Pittsburg Post* called his play a "revelation," claiming, "Wagner seems to be at home at short." However, no one appreciated his play at the new position more than his manager, who said, "Wagner is the best shortstop in the country. His record in the scores looks good, but it does not begin to compare with his actual work. . . ." *Sporting Life* reported that Pirate pitchers were no longer moaning over missed double plays: "Wagner is as graceful at short as a steam roller. Yet the clumsy galoot manages to get all over the infield and lays hands on everything that is batted, high or low."

On September 5 in New York, with the bases loaded, Wagner leaped to grab a liner over second base, landed on the bag, and, ignoring an easy chance for a rare unassisted triple play, threw to first base for the final out. It ruined a Giant rally but the New York fans roared, and Wagner acknowledged them by doffing his cap. The following day, the Pirates completed a three-day, six-game sweep of New York. In each of the half-dozen games, the Pirates never tallied less than ten runs and convincingly outscored the Giants in the series 80–23. It finished off the first ten-game winning streak in club annals, with nine of the ten wins coming on the road. During the stretch, Wagner was brilliant in the field and at the bat, going 15 for 27 in the six games versus New York.

Throughout the month of September, Pittsburghers celebrated as the Pirates slowly expanded their lead, and it became apparent that the championship was theirs. At one point, play was halted as Wagner approached the plate so the fans could present him with a huge hollow bat loaded with candy. And when Wagner crushed a grand slam to assure a doubleheader sweep and push the Pirates up by nine and a half games, the fans were so jubilant it was not enough that he simply raise his cap to the crowd. In what was described as the first "encore" ever for a player at Exposition Park, he was compelled to take a bow.

Despite the embarrassment of the day, Wagner was enjoying himself in September. He had a regular girl in Carnegie, though the relationship would prove to be short-lived. He introduced his sister to a couple of his teammates and even a few opponents—Billy Lush and old Warren buddy Joe Rickert, both with Boston. He got Al a position working an Exposition Park turnstile. A satisfied Clarke even rescinded a team rule and allowed the men to play poker on the road.

When Wagner rifled a shot through the pitcher's legs to drive in two runs and then scored on a Bransfield single to cap a three-run, eighth-inning rally on September 27, Pittsburgh clinched its first National League championship. Finishing at 90–49, seven and a half games ahead of Philadelphia, Pittsburgh was the first "western" city to win the National League flag since 1887, and Clarke became the first player-manager to lead a team to the crown since Cap Anson guided his Chicago Colts to the title in 1886.

Dreyfuss hosted a banquet for the squad at the lavish Schenley Hotel and awarded another bonus of $2,000 to be split by the team. Dreyfuss's profit was estimated at $40,000 to $55,000, not to mention the thousands he picked up from side bets with other magnates. He spent some of his take on small, sterling silver pins in the shape of a pennant, which he handed out to his friends. The players received a similar item, although their pins were solid gold.

With the dilution of talent brought on by a second major league, what had been a successful 1900 Pirate squad became a 1901 powerhouse. The effective pitching staff was still intact. Phillippe at 22–12 and Chesbro at 21–10 were the leaders. Tannehill went 18–10, Leever finished 14–5, and midseason acquisition Ed Doheny was 6–2. Wagner was still the hammer in the middle of the order, but the offense was no longer a one-man show. Beaumont (.332), Clarke (.324), Leach (.305), Davis (.313 in 87 games as a Pirate), Ritchey (.296), and Bransfield (.295) all contributed as the Pirates were second only to St. Louis in runs scored.

Wagner had another fine year. For the first time, he played in all of his team's games—a feat he would not accomplish again for another fourteen seasons. He performed sixty-two times at short, fifty-four in the outfield, twenty-four at third base, and once at second base. His fielding percentage in the outfield was among the league leaders. In the infield, while his percentages were not outstanding, he drew acclaim for his range and exciting plays. At the plate, he finished tied for fourth in batting at .353, well behind Jesse Burkett's .382. Wagner was also among the leaders in doubles, slugging, total bases, and hits. He scored one hundred runs for the second straight year and led the league in stolen bases for the first time with forty-nine and in runs driven in with 126 (although like ERA, RBI was not yet an official statistic).

◆ ◆ ◆

At the time, Wagner was frequently heralded as the best ballplayer around, particularly when the discussion focused on overall ability. Most often, he shared the distinction with Larry Lajoie, the American League's prize catch who had led the upstart circuit in most offensive categories. Benefiting by his league's two-year delay in adopting the foul-strike rule, he finished with a batting average of .422. Pitcher Win Mercer and umpire Joe Cantillon, both of the American League, formed a troupe to barnstorm the West in the fall of 1901. Striving for a Wagner-versus-Lajoie headline act, the promoters invited Wagner to come along. For a short while it seemed as if he would accept, but he backed out when the wilds of western Pennsylvania called.

Wagner's hunting exploits were getting more elaborate. He bought the finest dogs, sending many of them by train to his old minor league stomping ground of Warren for professional training by a friend. It was a luxury only the most well-to-do hunters in Pittsburgh enjoyed. The typical Wagner excursion was a few days in the mountains, but some-times a trip would last for a week or more. Many Pirate players, includ-ing Wagner's closest friends on the team, Phillippe and Leever, accompanied him. Usually, he was joined by Al or a few Carnegie pals.

Wagner considered buying a bar in the offseason, but Dreyfuss con-vinced him it would not be a good idea. Phillippe, when asked about the prospect of Wagner's "cafe," commented that the liquor would flow freely if Al was in charge, saying the older brother would "certainly run it to the taste of everyone."

It was no surprise that Wagner would seek his employer's advice before making such a decision. Dreyfuss commonly offered to set up bank accounts for his players, particularly those men with a wife or family. For higher-salaried players, he even volunteered to invest some of their pay with the principle guaranteed. Later in his career, Wagner would often allow his paychecks to accrue. With Dreyfuss using his keen business sense to invest them, Wagner collected a substantially higher sum each fall.

Baseball was America's sports darling, the indisputable national pastime. There were other recreations, but for workplace discussion, dinner-table arguments, and the public's limited entertainment dollar, baseball was king. Football was growing in popularity, but with players wearing little or no padding, deaths were all too common, and most people considered the game extremely violent. Some baseball men were paid to play football in the fall, but the sport never held an allure for Wagner.

Hockey was becoming more prevalent, and Dreyfuss considered organizing a team of Pirate players for some exhibitions. Clarke also liked the sport and a few of the players, particularly Northerners, volunteered. Chesbro, from Massachusetts and no stranger to the game, qualified his interest by saying he wanted no part of it if Wagner was on the ice. Dreyfuss soon dropped the idea.

In early 1902, the ten-year-old game of basketball was booming in Pittsburgh. Teams representing companies, organizations, or entire communities were challenging one another. The somewhat primitive version of the game was generally held in a "cage" of wire or rope netting to protect the spectators and keep the ball in the court. Players shot flat-footed, and the game's laced ball, slightly larger than today's, made for some rather awkward ball handling. On February 4, 1902, Wagner made his basketball debut as a guard for the Carnegie firemen's team, Hose Company No. 3. *The Pittsburg Post* described the 9–5 win over the Pittsburgh suburb of McDonald as "very rough on both sides" and declared, "The feature of the game was a one-handed goal from close to the foul line by Hans Wagner. . . . The roof nearly came down when Hans scored. . . . He looked as proud as if he had cleared the bases with a home run."

Over the next seven weeks, he was in action almost every night for the hose company, the Duquesne Athletic Club, or his own All-Professional squad, which also billed Patsy Flaherty and brother Al. For big games, hundreds of people caught trolleys to follow the locals across town for a contest, and the betting among fans was frenzied. Wagner often led the scoring, but he was also getting banged up. He was not adverse to "dishing it out," but a few opponents preyed on him because of his celebrity. He recalled that fouls were rare and that at times it seemed as if a player had to break through the wire cage before one was called.

At one point, Dreyfuss and Clarke became so concerned about their star that they took in a game in Pittsburgh that matched two of the region's best teams. Wagner, clad in long, baggy shorts similar to the mid-1990s basketball fashion, received a rousing ovation. He was scoreless on two shots before being slammed to the floor on top of his throwing arm. When he had to retire from the game, Clarke and Dreyfuss were beside themselves. The injury did not keep Wagner off the court long, and neither did his two bosses. Clarke convinced Dreyfuss to let Wagner continue—the games meant so much to Honus, and he could maintain better condition than he had in previous winters.

Basketball was an activity Wagner went on to enjoy for the next several years, both as a competitor and referee. He supplemented his summer income by participating in a second sport as the two teams not only split the gate but often made a wager as well. Wagner proved a flashy drawing card, and he often operated his own club. Confessing that organization was never his expertise, he would tell the story of when he scheduled nine games for one week, saying, "There's only one hitch. Seven of them are for Friday."

◆ ◆ ◆

The two baseball leagues were still engaged in full-scale combat. Both of the one-two finishers in the National League batting race, Burkett and Ed Delahanty, jumped soon after the 1901 season. Other stars followed, and by opening day 1902, all but one of the original forty-six on Ban Johnson's hit list were with the American League. Any "steer clear" policy toward Pittsburgh was over, but once again, Dreyfuss was successful at keeping his team together. Esteemed baseball writer and publisher of *Sporting Life* Francis C. Richter, discounting that a hands-off policy ever existed, gave Dreyfuss credit for having the foresight to sign his players to fair and binding contracts well in advance of his counterparts. Whatever the case, Dreyfuss did have some key people who showed uncommon loyalty for the times.

Dreyfuss was always in Clarke's corner. The president provided both support for his manager in tough times on the field and considerable financial rewards. Clarke earned a fine salary and, starting in 1902, received a cut of club profit. The twenty-nine-year-old manager was not about to abandon Dreyfuss for short-term gains, and the American League did not waste much of its breath trying to convince Clarke otherwise.

Throughout the baseball war, Wagner was pursued by the other league, but for him it was not a question of money. He was one of the most recognized men in his field as well as his community and was estimated to be worth a sizable $10,000. He confessed later, "I may have lost a lot of money by it but I feel much happier and satisfied for having stayed in Pittsburgh. . . . I loved my team and associations. They meant much more to me than money." In the end, he signed a one-year contract for 1902 with Dreyfuss for $3,600. Dreyfuss even pulled a coup of his own against the Americans, stealing back Harry Smith from the Athletics and signing shortstop William "Wid" Conroy away from the Milwaukee Brewers—relocated to St. Louis for 1902.

Ban Johnson did not get the runaway race he desired for the National League in 1901, but he surely did in 1902. The full-strength Pirates whipped their depleted opponents throughout the season. Winning its first five and not losing a road game until June 3, Pittsburgh leaped to the front and was out of first place for only a single April day. In 1902, the Pirates never suffered more than two consecutive defeats, clinched the pennant with a month left in the season, set a new big league standard with 103 victories, and finished with a whopping .741 winning percentage. (It was a figure surpassed just once in this century, when the 1906 Chicago Cubs finished at .763.) The Pirates set another mark, this one yet to be broken, when they outdistanced the league's second-best team, Brooklyn, by the incredible margin of twenty-seven and a half games.

Phillippe and Tannehill each won twenty games, and Leever and Doheny won sixteen apiece. The staff threw twenty-one shutouts, struck out the most men, walked the fewest, and threw back-to-back two-hitters and back-to-back three-hitters. But nobody was better than Happy Jack Chesbro, or Algy as his teammates referred to him. He had a twelve-game winning streak, and three shutouts in a row helped him run up a string of forty-one straight scoreless innings. He led the league in wins with twenty-eight and in shutouts with eight.

Top to bottom, the offense was robust, leading the league in almost everything. Clarke hit .321 and scored 104 runs in only 114 games, and two new stars emerged. Little Tommy Leach, referred to as Wee Tommy or Tommy the Wee, had boyish looks that contradicted his shrewdness. He was an accomplished sign-stealer and in 1902 was one of the game's top sluggers. The right-hander drove in eighty-five runs, second in the league, and socked twenty-one doubles and twenty-two triples. In a year in which the entire loop managed just ninety-nine home runs, Leach led with six—a paltry number even for the "dead ball" era, and the lowest league-leading mark since 1878. He hit half his season total in a two-day span, as he squeezed three homers over the short left field wall at Boston's South End Grounds. (Leach is in the unlikely company of power hitters Ralph Kiner and Willie Stargell as one of only three men who have ever won a home-run crown while a member of a Pittsburgh major league club.)

Ginger Beaumont, a right-hand thrower and left-hand batter, was already known as a solid hitter. Despite a chunky five-foot-eight-inch, 190-pound frame, he had exceptional speed that he used to beat out infield hits and bunts. In his first big league season of 1899, Beaumont legged out six infield hits as part of a 6 for 6, six-run game. After having to lose fifteen pounds in the spring of 1902, he went on to lead the league with a .357 batting average and finish among the leaders in runs, total bases, and steals.

Wagner enjoyed big days at the plate throughout the year. He tripled in four consecutive games, won a pair of contests with ninth-inning singles and another with a twelfth-inning home run, and he ended with a .329 average. His baserunning was stunning. He stole home twice during the season, including on August 13, when he stole second, third, and home in the seventh inning of the second game of a doubleheader— the first of three times in his career that he swiped the circuit in one inning. He went on to lead the league in stolen bases for the second straight year. He also led in runs, doubles, slugging percentage, and runs batted in.

Much of his contribution to the 1902 Pirates' success was through his versatility. Despite Wid Conroy's good spring work at shortstop, Wagner began the year at the position, and many felt it was now his permanent home. But when Beaumont went out with a leg injury in early May, newcomer Conroy moved to short and Wagner took over in center field—or, as it was referred to in Pittsburgh for many years, middle field. In his second game in center, Wagner had three assists and snared a looper behind the infield with a headlong catch.

A week later, he was in left field for a few games while Clarke nursed a split finger, and after four more days at short, Wagner moved back to left when Clarke and Fred Tenney were suspended for staging a rematch of their earlier on-field battle. Wagner had not sparkled at shortstop in April, and he wanted to remain in the outfield. There was even talk about him being approached by Johnson's men with a promise that he would be considered only an outfielder if he jumped.

All season, Wagner was called on to fill holes in the unglamorous role as the game's unrivaled utility man—"the best the world has ever produced," in the words of Dreyfuss. Wagner had two extended stints at shortstop, one when Conroy's sub-.200 average frayed Clarke's wits and another when Conroy was suspended for twenty days for a fistfight at second base with Joe Tinker of Chicago. Wagner played right field for a month after Lefty Davis broke an ankle, and he later moved to first base when Bransfield went down with a knee injury. Wagner subbed one game at second base, and on September 5 in Boston, he made his second and final major league pitching appearance.

Harvey Cushman had a few starts down the stretch and in his only big league action compiled an ugly 0–4 record. With Cushman down 10–0 in the second, Clarke brought Wagner into the box. *The Pittsburg Post* reported, "There was a lot of fun for the next five innings, but it was not at the expense of the Dutchman's delivery. . . . He tied himself up in all sorts of knots, threw his legs around and let them come for the plate as best he knew how and it was good at that." In five and a third innings, Wagner allowed two unearned runs on four singles and two walks. He tossed two wild pitches but struck out five, including Fred Tenney, Ed Gremminger, and Herman Long once each, and Gene DeMontreville twice, before the game was called after eight innings in favor of Boston, 12–1.

There were some difficult days for Wagner. Over the years, he was asked several times to name the toughest pitcher he had ever faced. The interviewer most often expected an answer of Mathewson, Brown, Alexander, Young, or one of the other star twirlers of the era. Wagner surprised many with a response of Jack Taylor. And while junk baller Taylor retired in 1907 with a respectable 151–139 record, his was not a name associated with greatness. But in 1902, he threw eight shutouts, tying Chesbro's mark, and had the lowest ERA in baseball, a remarkable 1.33. Taylor was also in the middle of a five-year stretch in which he completed 187 consecutive starts—a string he kept alive by defeating Pittsburgh 3–2 in a nineteen-inning marathon on June 22. They would face each other many times over the years, but in by far Wagner's worst day against Taylor, he went 0 for 8 at the plate in the nineteen-inning affair.

Even though there was no pennant race, the Pirates still did their share of kicking. On July 23, Wagner lifted an eighth-inning foul fly toward the players' bench. St. Louis catcher Jack O'Neill gave chase with his back to the plate, came up with the ball, and Wagner was called out. The Pirates screamed that the ball bounced off the bench before O'Neill corralled it. Wagner stormed around until he was ejected, then maintained the protest from the bench. The umpire ordered Wagner from the grounds, but Honus refused to leave. After a short delay, he retreated to the bleachers and watched the remainder of the game among Cardinal fans. It was the first inning he missed all year. The next day, word came down from the league that he was suspended indefinitely for disobeying the umpire. Wagner spent the next three days in the grandstand, embarrassed about his actions but feeling that he did not deserve the punishment.

◆ ◆ ◆

In mid-June, Wagner's Paterson friend George Smith replaced Horace Fogel as manager of the New York Giants. His managerial position did not last long. It ended in July when the Giant ownership struck the mightiest blow to date against the opposing league by convincing Baltimore's player-manager, John McGraw, and a handful of his best players, including Joe McGinnity, Roger Bresnahan, and Dan McGann, to defect to the Giants in midseason.

The Nationals and Americans continued to spar for players, and most every Pirate (including Wagner and Clarke) was approached at some point. Dreyfuss was even courted about moving his entire franchise to the other league, advances which he flatly but politely refused. For a fleeting moment, it appeared as if the Nationals had a leg up when McGraw made his move. But by mid-August, Dreyfuss got wind of more than just the usual foul air.

With Clarke in Pittsburgh rehabilitating a spike wound, the Pirates played an exhibition in Atlantic City on August 15. Wagner handled the on-field duties and Dreyfuss was club chaperone. Following the game, Tannehill and reserve Jimmy Burke had a scuffle in the clubhouse that resulted in the diminutive left-hander's pitching shoulder being dislocated. In excruciating pain, Tannehill was shuttled to the local hospital, where the doctors administered ether to their patient while they popped the arm into its socket. While under the anesthetic, Tannehill spilled the beans to Dreyfuss about recent conversations with Ban Johnson. For good measure, Tannehill even dropped the names of the other Pirates involved, including Chesbro, Leach, Conroy, and ringleader Jack O'Connor. (For years, Pirate players who remembered the incident had a running joke anytime a player was summoned to Dreyfuss's office, calling out, "Don't let Barney put you under ether!")

Back in Pittsburgh and onto the scheme, Dreyfuss put one of his office boys on O'Connor's tail. On August 19, O'Connor met Johnson and Somers at the depot, and the three men hustled to the Lincoln Hotel where Somers registered under a fictitious name. Dreyfuss's sleuth reported the news, and the Pirate chief, along with first mate Pulliam, headed for the hotel. Versions of subsequent events vary by source, each story's owner claiming he got the best of the situation. Dreyfuss recalled staking out the room next door to his adversaries and after pressing his head against a ventilation grate to overhear the sales pitch, he was wise to what Johnson was offering. Johnson and Somers would not admit being caught and said that they escaped the hotel by a freight elevator before Dreyfuss arrived.

On August 20 at Tannehill's apartment, six Pirate players were promised a one-thousand-dollar bonus for jumping to the American League in 1903. The following day, O'Connor was released. In Dreyfuss's public statement on the episode he explained:

> If . . . any of our players at the expiration of their contracts choose to leave the Pittsburg club, well and good. But I will not stand for any treachery or disloyalty from anybody while in my employ. No player can be a stool pigeon for the American League and draw salary from the Pittsburg club at the same time.

Dreyfuss immediately attempted to line up his men for 1903. It became painfully clear that he could not salvage the entire squad when he asked the players to declare their intention for the next year and a few refused. At one point, Dreyfuss was so exasperated that he shoved a blank contract under Wagner's nose and invited the star to fill in his own figures. Balking because he and the other players had agreed not to do anything until they discussed it with one another, he finally signed. Dreyfuss voluntarily rewarded Wagner with a raise to five thousand dollars for 1903—a "wartime" salary but significantly less than the American League's offer.

◆ ◆ ◆

In September, with the team in the East and the pennant clinched, Clarke went to Kansas to celebrate his parents' golden wedding anniversary. He again left Wagner in charge. A few of the men asked the acting manager if he had any strategy for them prior to the first game, and Wagner responded, "Let's just beat 'em." That afternoon the Pirates were swept in a doubleheader for the only time in 1902. Wagner handled the team for seven games, going 4–3, but the trip was not a financial success, as the team did not even meet expenses. One four-game, three-day series in Philadelphia drew fewer than 1,200 fans. Phillie followers were disgruntled with the devastation of their squad in the war between the leagues and were either staying away from the ballpark altogether or switching allegiance across town to the front-running Athletics.

Wagner missed a pair of games when he suffered a broken bone in his thumb, but with the season winding down and the one-hundred-victory level in sight, he came back to finish out the year. An eight-game winning streak assured the century mark, and on October 4, the season's final day, the Pirates set a new major league high by winning game number 103, although in a rather tainted fashion.

Though the grounds were soggy, Dreyfuss was determined to give his troops a shot at the record and ordered the game played. The Reds were clearly in favor of canceling the contest and showed their displeasure by turning it into a travesty. Each Red tried a new position, including first baseman Jake Beckley taking the mound and pitcher Harry "Rube" Vickers going behind the plate. Vickers set a major league mark with six passed balls, and after each sailed by him he would leisurely stand up, take a handkerchief from his pocket, and blow his nose—to the delight of his teammates and disgust of Dreyfuss. Two Reds who recently made the jump back to the National League as part of the Baltimore insurrection—player-manager Joe Kelley and now full-time outfielder Cy Seymour—also had some fun. Seymour, playing third base, wore one of his stockings wrapped around his shoe; Kelley strolled to the plate in the first inning puffing on a lit cigarette. After the umpire's request to discard it went unheeded, Zimmer snatched the smoke dangling from Kelley's lips and threw it to the ground.

With the Reds playing less than inspired ball, the Pirates easily captured the game 11–2, but Dreyfuss was fuming. After a few innings, he announced that he would refund each patron's money and refused to pay the Cincinnati representative the Reds' guarantee. That evening, Dreyfuss fired off a scathing letter condemning the players' actions but enclosed the visitors' take of $110.44 to Reds president, August "Garry" Herrmann. Herrmann returned the check uncashed.

♦ ♦ ♦

Discussions had been held since June about scheduling a postseason series between the Pirates, a mortal lock for the title, and the winner of the American League. Dreyfuss was willing to wager five thousand dollars and let his players keep the receipts. He even offered to allow the other league to bolster its champion with other American Leaguers. The leaders of the contenders were favorable to the idea. Connie Mack took the opportunity to throw Dreyfuss a backhanded compliment, calling him one of the few National League magnates with sportsmanship and saying, "It is really a shame that [Pittsburgh] is not a member of the major league." But with the August raid on the Pirates and Johnson's conspicuous search for grounds in the Smoky City, it appeared as though any chance for a "world series" was over.

Johnson's vow to field a franchise in New York the following year, the recent enlistees from Pittsburgh, and obvious fan acceptance of the American League had more and more of the older circuit's magnates feeling that a fight to the death might be a losing battle. As the season wound down, Dreyfuss softened his stand and extended an olive branch by allowing a four-game series to be played between his Pirates and a picked team of "All-Americans."

On Tuesday, October 7, only 2,200 fans came out to rain-soaked Exposition Park to see Leever and the great Cy Young, winner of more than thirty games in each of his first two American League seasons. Pittsburgh scored two first-inning runs. Beaumont led off with a triple and scored on a Clarke double. A passed ball moved him to third, and after Leach popped out, Wagner brought home the second run with a ground out. Despite getting only one ball past the infield, the Pirates scored twice in the third inning in a driving rain. Wagner tallied one of the runs after legging out an infield roller, going from first to third on a wild pitch, and crossing the plate on a Bobby Wallace error. Leever gave up three in the ninth but held on for a 4–3 win.

The following day in front of 4,500 spectators, the Pirates did not have a hit through the first four innings off Addie Joss, a seventeen-game winner in his first year. In the fifth, Wagner reached first on an error, circled to third on an infield out, and scored on a Ritchey single. In the eighth, Wagner's second hit, a double, brought home the only other run of the game. Joss gave up two unearned runs, but Phillippe tossed a three-hit shutout and walked only one, winning 2–0.

The Pirates were working with just two pitchers in the series against the Americans. Doheny was out with a sprained ankle, and Dreyfuss knew that Tannehill, Chesbro, Davis, and Leach all had received bonuses with the stipulation that they jump to the American League. Prior to the first game, Dreyfuss paid Tannehill the remainder of his salary and said a terse goodbye. Chesbro seemed to be hedging in his commitment, but when he refused to take the mound in one of the postseason games, his teammates, who already questioned his gumption, voted unanimously to cut him out of any of the rewards. Chesbro's Pirate tenure was through. Davis, not an important loss, was allowed to walk.

Leach used a prior American League offer to attempt to negotiate a raise, and when Dreyfuss refused to up Leach's salary, the player told the president, "Well, don't come around bellyaching if I do [jump]." Leach was now thoroughly remorseful for having accepted the other league's terms and engaged Dreyfuss's help. The two returned the uncashed bonus check to Somers via registered mail with an explanation that Leach intended to stay put.

Most notable among the missing in the first two games of the series was Lajoie. In 1901, he made the leap across Philadelphia from the Phillies to the Athletics. In April 1902, the Pennsylvania Supreme Court issued an injunction barring Lajoie and the other Phillie jumpers from playing with any other team. The jurisdiction ended at the state line, however, and Johnson, Somers, and Mack agreed it was better to move Lajoie to another American League club than lose him back to the Nationals. Somers promised Lajoie a hefty four-year deal and even guaranteed the amount should a legal ruling prevent him from performing. He joined Somers' Cleveland club in June, but when his teammates traveled to Philadelphia for a series with the Athletics, Lajoie took a short sabbatical due to the Pennsylvania order. It also meant Lajoie and fellow Philadelphia defector Bill Bernhard, who went 17–5 with Cleveland in 1902, were prohibited from playing in the postseason games held in Pittsburgh.

On October 10, roughly three thousand people came to League Park in Cleveland, where they generally moaned about the foul-strike rule, which was in place for games one and three of the series but would not be adopted by the American League until 1903. Leever and Bernhard each gave up four singles in eleven innings before play was halted at a scoreless tie. Wallace and Wagner had two hits and two stolen bases apiece, but Wagner was caught trying to steal third, killing the Pirates' only threat. Young and Phillippe hooked up for six more scoreless innings on Saturday. In the seventh, two Pirate errors led to the only run of the game. Pittsburgh won two, lost one, and tied one in the exhibition. Pirate players were pursued by American League agents throughout the series, and the whole affair was a fiscal flop.

Lajoie went hitless in his seven at bats. Wagner finished 5 for 15 and played a fine shortstop, making only one error. Many of their statistics were strikingly similar over virtually parallel careers. Both provided extremely powerful bats and were considered among the best defensive players in the game, albeit with completely different styles. Lajoie, a fine second baseman, was smooth and graceful around the bag. Wagner was regarded as the best utility man ever seen and thought to be spectacular if unorthodox in the field. In 1902, both were reaching the pinnacle of their greatness as well as earning the love and respect of fans.

The suave and dapper Frenchman was becoming Cleveland's darling. By 1905, he was named manager, and the rooters voted to change the team's nickname from the Blues to the Naps in his honor. Pittsburghers were equally positive that the game's best player was Wagner, appreciating his unique combination of speed and strength and praising him as the driving force that brought the Pirates to the top of the baseball world. And amid the chaos of league-jumping, his allegiance was considered admirable. Dreyfuss made no bones about whom he preferred: "Wagner can beat Lajoie in any department *and* carry a rail." But when asked why he didn't actively promote his superstar to the public as the Cleveland club did with Lajoie, Dreyfuss explained that he felt "it's the team that draws, not one man."

As 1903 approached, the structure of baseball was about to shift into a more permanent state, and Wagner, in his sixth full season in the majors, was about to become the national game's preeminent player.

FIVE

"THE BOYS DESERVED IT"

Even in a day when fedoras, canes, and imported leather shoes were common male attire, Henry Clay "Harry" Pulliam was a dandy. But beyond his brightly colored waistcoats and outrageous wide-brimmed hats, the Pirate secretary was also a diplomat. He disliked confrontation and smoothed over many disagreements in the Pirate offices through his placid manner and levelheaded temperament. He even served a term in the legislature of his home state of Kentucky. Pulliam numbered his friends in the hundreds and had the trust and respect of several National League magnates—not an easy accomplishment considering the immense egos involved in the game even then. So, at the league meetings in December, when John Montgomery Ward, an attorney and former player, and William Temple, of Temple Cup fame, refused offers to assume the loop's presidency, Pulliam was nominated for the position. A majority of the owners supported the move but had to convince John Brush, now of the Giants, that Pulliam would show no favoritism toward Dreyfuss. Brush was eventually pacified, and Pulliam was unanimously elected National League president on his thirty-third birthday, December 12, 1902.

Most big league team owners now advocated an end to the league war and agreed to a peace conference. Animosity prevailed throughout the negotiations, but the two antagonists finally ratified a new National Agreement. The accord formally recognized both circuits as equal major leagues, protected territory, provided for uniform playing rules and complementary schedules, and reestablished a respect for the reserve clause in player contracts.

The agreement also created a three-man National Commission to preside over the two major leagues—as well as minor leagues seeking protection and rights under the umbrella of Organized Baseball. This governing body included league presidents Pulliam and Johnson and a chairman chosen by the club owners. The natural choice for chairman was Cincinnati Reds president Garry Herrmann, who although a National Leaguer was a longtime friend of Ban Johnson.

Not everyone was enthralled. The loudest objections were heard from John Brush, who screamed when the American League was permitted to move into New York in return for staying out of Pittsburgh. And while the leagues' power brokers agreed to an equitable division of disputed players, many more battles remained ahead. Though it was certainly not yet a tranquil peace in early 1903, the National Agreement made it possible for coexistence—an issue that until then had been in question—and was instrumental in solidifying the foundation of major league baseball.

◆ ◆ ◆

It was a new era for big league ball, but Wagner was self-absorbed. In February, he sent a concerned letter to Dreyfuss. Now that Wid Conroy was gone, it seemed to Wagner that the writing was on the wall for moving him to shortstop permanently. He expressed his dislike for the position and complained that it affected his batting eye. With Clarke and Beaumont manning left and center and with promising twenty-one-year-old Jimmy Sebring in right, Wagner's arguments were doomed.

In spite of puffing on his share of the two boxes of fine cigars Pulliam sent the Pirates for the trip south to spring training, Wagner moped all the way to Hot Springs. He usually had first choice of berths on the train, picking number thirteen, but this time, Dreyfuss took it and refused to swap. And Wagner had been rooming with Ritchey during spring training for the past few years, but the little second baseman ruined that arrangement by bringing his new wife on the trip. Wagner's pouting did not last long. He was the big winner at five-card draw, and the players were disgusted at his incredible luck when he broke a pair of aces and pulled two cards to a flush.

He also had his revenge on Dreyfuss a few days later when a practice was rained out and the squad gathered at a local poolroom and betting emporium. Dreyfuss was eager to exhibit his prowess at the ponies, giving the boys a few pointers and confidently announcing his selection for the first race. Wagner loudly dismissed the horse as an "old dog" and made his choices privately while the other players stuck with Dreyfuss. Over the card, Wagner outguessed his paymaster five winners to one, including a fifteen-to-one shot. The next morning Wagner emerged from his quarters with his nose proudly pointed skyward as Dreyfuss graciously, and quite facetiously, addressed him as "Mr. Wagner."

Throughout spring training, the Pirates basked in their success as two-time champions. Even Clarke was in noticeably lighter spirits than in previous years. The enjoyment culminated the night before heading north. Roommates Harry Smith, a notorious prankster, and Eddie Phelps started the ball rolling by disrupting the poker game in Phillippe's room. Wagner took off in hot pursuit with a pitcher of water, but the instigators ducked into their room. Bransfield and Wagner threatened from the hallway but retreated after being drenched by a stream of water delivered through the transom overhead. At that point, the entire squad was into the act—no one was safe. Leever, a boxing fan, was awakened and invited to take a look at the scrap taking place on the hotel lawn. But when he opened his window and stuck his head out, Wagner socked Leever's bald noggin with a pile of wet rags from the top of the building. The fun and games lasted most of the night, and few if any players or other guests got much sleep.

◆ ◆ ◆

Most agreed that the Pirates were not as strong as they had been in the previous three years, citing the defections of pitchers Tannehill and Chesbro—a combined loss of forty-eight wins from 1902. Phillippe, Leever, and Doheny provided a solid core, and the Pirates tried to fill out the staff with the unproven and ultimately unsuccessful combination of twenty-nine-year-old rookie Irvin "Kaiser" Wilhelm and youngsters Fred "Bucky" Veil and Fred "Cy" Falkenberg. Dreyfuss also signed veteran Bill Kennedy, who was referred to as both "Brickyard Bill" and "Roaring Bill," the latter because he conversed at the top of his lungs. Kennedy had won 174 games for Brooklyn in his first nine seasons but had chalked up only four victories over the last two years due to arm trouble.

Pitching worries did not suppress the enthusiasm of the fifty or so Pittsburgh rooters who came to Cincinnati for the opener on Thursday,

April 16. They paraded to the park in rented carriages, making a ruckus the entire way, and got a glimpse of the Pirates' new road duds—highlighted by a long-sleeved undershirt that matched their stockings, red stripes on a dark blue background. Phillippe made easy work of the Reds, pitching a two-hitter and walking one, winning 7–1. In the fourth, shortstop Wagner leaped up to intercept a Joe Kelley line drive headed for left-center. The ball smacked Wagner's mitt and ricocheted into the air. He landed on his feet and, concentrating on the ball's flight, snagged it with his bare hand before it hit the ground. He was treated to a standing round of applause from the twelve thousand partisan Reds fans as he ran off the field. Dreyfuss was not shy about expressing his contentment when the Pirates avenged the season-ending farce of 1902 by thumping the Reds in four straight games.

Dreyfuss considered the one hundred dollars awarded by the league to be insufficient for a suitable championship pennant, so he purchased a massive five-hundred-dollar flag. Pulliam witnessed the unfurling of the new banner at the Pirates' first home game on April 21, in front of an Exposition Park record twenty thousand supporters. Wagner's offer to write Pulliam's opening day address was declined, despite the president's appreciation for the conciseness it was sure to exhibit. Pulliam delivered a stirring tribute to his old friends and so impressed *The Pittsburg Dispatch* with his attire that the paper was "willing to bet that neither King Solomon nor the Queen of Sheba had anything on President Harry. . . ." Pulliam used the occasion to prod Beaumont into fulfilling a recent request to have a portrait produced for inclusion in the president's new National League "Hall of Fame," which would honor league batting champions.

Wagner was off to a fast start at the plate. On April 24, his three errors helped St. Louis to a 7–6, ninth-inning lead. But in the ninth, he tripled and scored the tying run on a Bransfield single. And with two outs in the eleventh, Wagner coaxed a walk, stole second on the first pitch, and scored on another Bransfield single. On the day, Wagner went 4 for 5, hit two triples, stole three bases, and scored four runs in helping to pull out an extra-inning, come-from-behind win. Of course, it was his poor fielding that led to the trouble in the first place.

Displeased about playing shortstop and performing poorly there so far, Honus was still considered the team's star utility man. With Zimmer having gone to Philadelphia to be catcher-manager of the Phillies and with backup catcher Smith home ill, Wagner was even put on notice that if first-string backstop Ed Phelps went down, Wagner would be expected

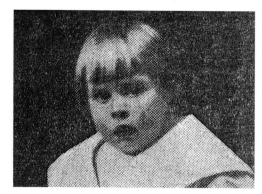

Wagner as a baby.

Wagner with his boyhood chums in Carnegie. *(The Political Gallery)*

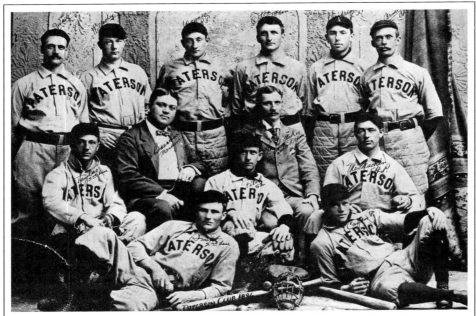

The 1896 Soby Cup Champion Club, Paterson, New Jersey. *Back row, left to right:* Lee Viau, Jack Killackey, Wagner, Bert Elton, Emmett Heidrick, Bill Armour. *Front row:* Jack Taylor, Ed Barrow, George Smith, Frank Fitch, Charles McKee, Dick Cogan, Sam McMackin. *(The Political Gallery)*

The 1902 runaway champion Pittsburgh Pirates. *Back row, left to right:* Chief Zimmer, Jimmy Sebring, Deacon Phillippe, George Merritt, Sam Leever, Eddie Phelps. *Middle row:* Jack Chesbro, Kitty Bransfield, Fred Clarke, Barney Dreyfuss, Wagner, Ginger Beaumont, Harry Smith. *Front row:* Jimmy Burke, Wid Conroy, Tommy Leach, Claude Ritchey, Warren McLaughlin. *(Pittsburgh Pirates)*

The 1908–1909 Hans Wagner basketball team. *Back row, left to right:* Robert Frye, Wagner, Wilbur Good. *Front row:* Raymond Artz and George Barum. *(National Baseball Library & Archive, Cooperstown, New York)*

Wagner prepares to take a rip at the Polo Grounds, 1908. The catcher is Roger Bresnahan, who invented shin guards a year earlier.

Rounding first base at Exposition Park, 1909.

A dapper bunch atop Monument Hill catches glimpses of the Pirates' final game at Exposition Park on June 29, 1909. *(The Carnegie Library of Pittsburgh)*

The Independence Day celebration at Forbes Field on Monday, July 5, 1909—just days after the park opened—included a doubleheader sweep of the Cincinnati Reds. *(The Carnegie Library of Pittsburgh)*

Wagner (*center*) and Ty Cobb compare their grips prior to Game One of the 1909 World Series, as Davy Jones looks on. *(The Carnegie Library of Pittsburgh)*

Batting in 1910.

Wagner clowning with his dog, Jason Weathersby, on Opening Day 1913, as Hall of Famers Fred Clarke (*far right*) and Max Carey (*center*) look on. *(Pittsburgh Pirates)*

Following Fred Clarke across home plate ahead of the throw to George Gibson at Hot Springs, Arkansas, in 1910. This photo is often misidentified as 1908, despite the fact that Wagner did not accompany the team to spring training that year. *(The Carnegie Library of Pittsburgh)*

Four heroes from the 1909 champion Pirates: Babe Adams, Fred Clarke, George Gibson, and Wagner. This photo was taken in 1915, their last season as a foursome. *(Pittsburgh Pirates)*

Sliding home safely in spring training action at Hot Springs. *(Pittsburgh Pirates)*

to go behind the mask. It would turn out to be the only position he never played in the major leagues. Right fielder Jimmy Sebring was off to a great start in his first full year with Pittsburgh, but when he became ill, Wagner moved to right field.

He immediately got back in the swing as a right fielder and drew notice for his wonderful catches. On May 5 at Exposition Park, he did not have a ball hit in his direction for eight innings and did nothing more than jog back and forth from the bench to right field. In the ninth, Chicago had two runners aboard and the tying run at the plate with two outs. Left-hand hitting Jimmy Slagle lined a ball down the right field line. *The Pittsburg Dispatch* observed that Wagner gave chase: "Running low to the ground to escape all possible resistance from the atmosphere, with his ears lying close against his head . . ." Sprinting toward the foul line he reached down, snatched the ball off the ground, and without breaking stride darted into the door of the Pirates' right field clubhouse as the crowd applauded his exit.

The win moved the Pirates into first place, but the next day, Phillippe blew a 4–2 lead over Chicago, giving up nine runs on nine hits in the ninth inning—the third time in eleven days that the Pirates lost to Jack Taylor. It would not be the same lopsided race as the year before. The competition in 1903 surprisingly came from the New York Giants, who had finished dead last in 1902, and Chicago, which in its first season as the Cubs the previous year had been a modest fifth at 68–69. New York and Chicago had righted their teams quickly, and not only would the three teams fight it out in 1903, but they were destined to battle for the next several years.

♦ ♦ ♦

When Sebring was healthy, Wagner moved back to shortstop. It was a much different stretch in the infield this time as he flawlessly handled thirteen chances, including a few tough stops, in his first game. The following day, he executed a difficult double play that had *The Pittsburg Post* stating that Wagner "shone out brightly" and that "his work at short simply teemed with brilliancy." In Boston, the fans cheered him when he robbed one of their own with a diving grab of a line drive.

On May 7, Clarke hit for the cycle and added a walk, a sacrifice, and a stolen base, but the Pirates wasted the effort, losing 11–8 to the Reds. More important, Wagner's attempted steal of second in the fifth inning cost the Pirates his services for the next few games: The throw beat him to the bag, and when he slid hard into Jack Morrissey, the second baseman charged. Wagner drew back his arm as if to throw a right but was clinched by base umpire Jim "Bug" Holliday. Pulliam suspended Wagner for three days for laying his hands on Holliday while trying to break free.

Within a few days, the players met to discuss Wagner's suspension. Clarke announced, "Today we decided to cut out all kicking. . . . As the present championship race promises to be a hot one, we will not risk having other players suspended. . . . In a close game any interested man is likely to forget all of his good resolutions and fly off the handle, but when one of the Pirates goes wrong the others will remind him of his obligations." It was a vow that the players adhered to with surprisingly few deviations. But since they did not make a provision to cease the taunting of opponents, trouble still found Clarke's men.

The Pirates started their first important series of 1903 on May 16 in New York. Pittsburgh was in third place, percentage points in back of Chicago and a half-game behind the Giants. What was argued to be the largest crowd ever to see a baseball game packed into the wooden Polo Grounds, necessitating ground rules for the first time in the ballpark's history. Many more New Yorkers sat atop Coogan's Bluff, peering in from a distance behind home plate. The Giants pounded Kennedy for thirteen hits in the opener, winning behind Mathewson 7–3.

The remainder of the series was marred with incident. Doheny defeated McGinnity in the second game but brought the wrath of the Giants and their fans. With a runner at first, Doheny popped up in front of the plate and tossed his bat in Frank Bowerman's direction as the big catcher circled under the ball. The crowd hissed and then grew indignant as Doheny took a long, sweeping bow toward the grandstand on his way back to the dugout.

Throughout the game, the Giants justifiably complained that the Pirates were playing dirty. Clarke was called out for interfering with Bowerman, and Wagner drew the ire of the Giants when he clotheslined McGinnity, preventing him from going from second to third. Doheny gave up only six hits and outpitched McGinnity for a 3–2 win. Not surprisingly, the Pirates had to be escorted to the clubhouse by police. For his part in starting the flare-up, Doheny was suspended for three days.

Leach was ejected in the third game of the series for arguing. Mathewson earned another win when he entered in the eighth and pitched two scoreless innings as the Giants rallied for two runs and a 4–3 victory. It was Mathewson for a full nine innings the next day, and his six-hit, 2–0 shutout knocked the Pirates to two and a half games back.

Pittsburgh exploded for thirty-five hits in two games in Brooklyn, with Wagner contributing a 4 for 4, three-stolen-base effort. Sebring, Ritchey, and Clarke also had four-hit games—Clarke's included three doubles. And Leach cracked two home runs in one of the contests. Brooklyn initially appeared to provide a tonic, but after dropping the next two, the Pirates were five games off the pace. With the team playing poorly and his men having trouble living up to their promise to stay out of trouble, Clarke was reported to be suffering a mental breakdown, though he emphasized that his only problem was a terribly sore back. Within a week, Dreyfuss ordered Clarke and his .365 average to Cambridge Springs, a health resort a few hours north of Pittsburgh, to recover.

◆ ◆ ◆

In Clarke's absence, Wagner served as acting manager. Beaumont remained in the leadoff spot, and everyone else moved up a notch, with Sebring, Wagner, and Bransfield rounding out the top four of the order. Wagner kept himself at shortstop and tried to patch left field with whomever he could from his skeleton crew. Veteran Otto "Oom Paul" Krueger, now the general utility man, saw a few games in left before moving to third when Leach headed home to attend to his sick young son. Outfielder-pitcher George Merritt played left for one game before a broken ankle ended his career. Hurlers Phillippe and Wilhelm were each in the pasture for a game, minor leaguer Romer "Reddy" Grey was loaned to the Pirates for one day, and even amateur Ernie Diehl played there one game. Thanks to fine pitching, Wagner's splendid hitting, and a pair of two-out, ninth-inning victories in a doubleheader with the Reds, the Pirates notched a 7–2 mark with Clarke on the shelf.

The most successful homestand in club annals began with a three-game series versus New York, and the Giants kicked throughout. Bowerman and Mathewson were both ejected and ordered from the grounds for arguing too strenuously, but Mathewson won the first game—his fourth win against Pittsburgh on the young season. In the final two games, Wagner's last as fill-in skipper, the Pirate pitching staff began a remarkable stretch. On June 2, Phillippe coasted to a 7–0 win, fanning eight and giving up eight hits and only one walk. The following day, Leever blanked the Giants 5–0 on six scattered singles and two walks. Clarke was back on June 4 and had a pair of singles from his familiar number-two slot in the order. Wagner played a superb shortstop and scored a run single-handedly when he singled, went from first to third on a bunt (which was becoming one of his favorite maneuvers), and tagged up and scored on a foul fly to the first baseman. For a third straight game, only one opponent reached third base as Wilhelm won a five-hitter, 5–0 over Boston.

Clarke went 5 for 5 and Beaumont 4 for 5 as the Pirates knocked out seventeen hits on June 5. Doheny became the fourth pitcher to join the whitewash brigade, and the Pirates, with their 9–0 defeat of Boston, became the first National League club ever to rack up four successive shutouts. Phillippe toed the rubber on June 6 and surrendered seven hits through six innings to the Beaneaters, but he received errorless support and four runs before the game was called in the seventh, a 4–0 Pirate win and a fifth consecutive shutout.

After an off Sunday, Leever faced Philadelphia and took a 2–0 lead into the ninth before tiring. John "Shad" Barry led off with a single for the Phillies and, after an out, moved to second on a single from William "Kid" Gleason. Frank Roth hit a screamer back to the mound that Leever knocked to the ground and relayed to first for the second out. With the tying runs on base, the Phillies sent big Bill "Klondike" Douglass up to pinch hit. He sent a liner toward left-center, seemingly tying the game and ending the shutout string, but Wagner leaped into the air and brought the ball down one-handed as the fans stood and wildly cheered his effort. The six consecutive shutouts is a mark still unequalled in major league history.

Wilhelm ran the scoreless-inning streak to fifty-six on June 9, before allowing a third-inning run, though he held on for the Pirates' seventh straight win. Doheny struggled through another victory the next day. Then on June 11, Phillippe tossed his third consecutive shutout, allowing just three hits and a walk. After two postponements, Phillippe was outdone by Leever, who gave up only a lone single in *his* third straight shutout.

The road to a franchise record eleven-game winning streak went through nemesis Jack Taylor, who had already defeated the Pirates three times in 1903. The Cubs jumped out to an early 3–0 lead, and the Pirates wasted Wagner's two stolen bases in the fourth. Seeking to preserve his shutout but risking a win, Taylor waved his infield to play in with the bases loaded and no outs in the fifth. Phillippe ruined the strategy by blooping a two-run single over the head of second baseman Johnny Evers, and Beaumont tied the game by scoring the third run on a deep fly ball.

Taylor was again mowing down Wagner, but after reaching on an infield error in the sixth, moving to second on a passed ball, and taking third on an out, Wagner scored the tie-breaking run on a Ritchey double. Frustrated at being hitless in his previous twelve at bats, including 0 for 3 in the game, Wagner batted against Taylor in the eighth. As he sometimes did in an attempt to end a slump, Wagner crossed over to hit left-handed. The fans were puzzled, but they erupted when Wagner hit a scorcher to center and legged the hit into a double. He scored an insurance run, and the Pirates added one more to down the Cubs 6–3 for an eleventh straight win.

The string was snapped at fifteen a few days later. Wagner had ten hits and a pair of home runs in the last three games of the streak, which moved the Pirates into first place for the first time in six weeks—a position they would maintain through the remainder of the year.

♦ ♦ ♦

Clarke was among the league's leading hitters, but his back continued to nag him and the medication for the problem made him ill. On June 25, he took a pitch in the stomach and laid on the ground several minutes before he could continue. His physical condition would get even worse the next morning.

On Friday, June 26, the Pirates entered New York riding a two-and-a-half-game lead over the Giants. The Polo Grounds, unlike many ballparks, provided dressing quarters for visiting players, so the Pirates arrived in their suits. Clarke, Giant secretary Fred Knowles, and new Pirate secretary William Locke approached the gate together and were met by several Giant players who exchanged a cordial greeting with the three.

Big Frank Bowerman, who was as surly as he was burly and a man whom Wagner said could take more physical punishment than anyone he ever saw, asked Clarke for a few minutes of his time. The two walked down the corridor with the Giants' Roger Bresnahan and Joe McGinnity closely behind. Bowerman led Clarke into a small ticket seller's booth as the two other players remained outside and the two secretaries peeled off into the team's general offices. Accusing Clarke of trying to stir up trouble between himself and teammate Jack Warner, Bowerman floored Clarke with a blow to the face, then buried a knee into Clarke's chest. With the Pirate manager wedged into a corner, Bowerman delivered several punches to the head of his victim.

Outside, Bresnahan prevented Locke and Knowles from entering the tiny room and even guarded the door after a policeman arrived, asking that the officer let the two fight. Bowerman eventually relented and walked out uninhibited by the police. Clarke, who had been unable to land a single blow, staggered down the hall in his ragged suit and mangled hat. It was several days before the visible evidence of the beating disappeared from his face, but later on the day of the attack, Clarke was in the lineup and went 1 for 4 at the plate. Mathewson won his fifth of the season over Pittsburgh and moved the Giants to within a game and a half of the lead.

A huge throng crammed into the Polo Grounds on Saturday, June 27. The Pirates crushed fifteen hits off McGinnity, including three singles and a double by Wagner, but could not wrap up a win until an eleventh-inning rally. A vengeful Clarke added a triple to the victory. Encounters with the Giants were getting rougher.

At Brooklyn on June 30, Wagner had a second consecutive four-hit game. He tripled, drove in five runs, scored three times, and his 450-foot home run over the center field fence was heralded as one of the longest ever hit at Washington Park. He homered again the following day, this one an opposite-field drive over the right field wall.

Wagner was on a tear in the East, and two of the fans who were enjoying his exploits were his sister and her new husband, Charles Gallagher. The newlyweds were using their honeymoon to see Honus in New York and Al, who was now playing for Providence, Rhode Island, in the Eastern League. Carrie was the second Wagner sibling to marry in 1903, brother Charley having tied the knot in February.

Wagner raised his average to .377, surpassing Clarke's .353 for the league lead. The Pirate manager suffered another setback on July 4 when he tumbled and separated his shoulder after making a shoestring catch. He was in the lineup for only one game in the next four and a half weeks, and while he rehabilitated away from the club, Wagner was again placed in charge of the troops.

The Pirates went 14–11 under Wagner, who played first base and shortstop while manipulating his lineup due to personnel shortages: Bransfield was hurt, Sebring went home to get married, and Doheny, who was 12–6, was AWOL. In the past, Doheny had exhibited odd behavior and had had altercations with teammates, but now he was acting very strangely, especially when he drank. Convinced that he was being followed by detectives, he was determined to give them the slip by returning to his home in Massachusetts. *The Pittsburg Post* announced his departure on July 29 with the unsympathetic headline HIS MIND IS

THOUGHT TO BE DERANGED. Wagner was itching to hand control back to Clarke.

Wagner, despite a badly swollen thumb and being spiked in the shoulder and on the arm during a single contest, remained in the lineup. The ailments did not hamper his performance as he maintained a steady clip at the plate and was playing marvelous defense. In one game, he leaped with his four limbs outstretched like the spokes of a wheel and snagged a line drive ticketed for left-center field with his bare right hand. He was praised for his range, particularly up the middle, as he was said to frequently produce outs on balls that no other shortstop could corral. In 1903, Wagner would play 111 of his 129 games at shortstop and lead the league in chances per game and in double plays.

The Sporting News ran a feature article acknowledging Wagner and Lajoie as the game's best players and drawing cards. Brooklyn manager Ned Hanlon went as far as to call Wagner "the greatest ballplayer who ever lived. . . . No ballplayer who ever lived or is living comes near him, and he don't know it." Back at home, the *Carnegie Union* assured the community that Wagner was still wearing the "same size hat [and] same smile."

Not all of the evaluations were favorable. One unidentified New York player commented that "[Wagner] should practice being as quiet and agreeable on the field as he is off." Unlike many others, Wagner was able to hold his own with the rough baseball being played but had the ability to turn off his aggressiveness when the game was over.

◆ ◆ ◆

Clarke was back in command on August 8 and did some lineup juggling of his own. Wagner even batted leadoff in one game (singling three times) before Clarke settled on his one-through-seven combination for the stretch run—Beaumont (who would finish 1903 a .341 hitter and the league leader in hits and runs), Clarke (.351, second only to Wagner and tied for the league lead in doubles at 32), Leach (.298 with 17 triples), Wagner (league leader in average at .355 and triples with 19), Bransfield (.265), Ritchey (.287), and Sebring (.277). Phelps and Smith were splitting time behind the plate. Phillippe and Leever were doing excellent mound work, but Kennedy and Bucky Veil were struggling to patch a thin staff that *The Sporting News* labeled a "bunch of misfits, has-beens and what-nots." They got a boost when Doheny returned on August 15; though outwardly morose, he pitched fairly well.

The Giants' last gasp to dethrone the two-time champion Pirates was a four-game set in two days in New York. Mathewson was on the mound for the opener of the August 20 twin bill. The Pirates, seemingly hexed each time they faced Mathewson that year, made a National League record six errors in the first inning, leading to seven Giant runs and an easy 13–7 New York win. Phillippe scattered five singles and a base on balls in the second game to win 4–1. The next day, Leever out-pitched McGinnity, winning 3–0. Mathewson, who made manager McGraw furious by refusing to take the mound in a contest versus Pittsburgh in July, agreed to work game two of the doubleheader on just twenty-four hours rest. He pulled his team back to within five games of first with a 9–5 win. In 1903, the Pirates would finish 10–10 with the Giants. Mathewson started and won seven of those games and picked up an eighth victory in relief.

The Giants' last charge fell short, but Mathewson and McGinnity combined for more than sixty wins during the year. McGinnity single-handedly pitched and won three doubleheaders in August. Their performance brought the Giants up from their spot in the cellar the previous year to this season's 84–55 record, good for second place.

A second long winning streak, fourteen games, propelled the Pirates well out in front of the pack. For the final weeks, their objectives were to stay out of trouble and keep enough players healthy to field a team. They managed to keep their collective noses clean, with a few transgressions. On August 28, Wagner was so frustrated over hitting a fly ball that he flipped his bat toward the mound. As he returned to the bench, Cardinal pitcher Charles "Chappie" McFarland yelled obscenities at Wagner, continuing his tough talk two innings later when Honus again approached the plate. Wagner thought he had the last laugh when he drilled a single to center, but McFarland picked him off first base, and crowed loudly as Wagner trudged off the diamond.

Trouble seemed to follow the Pirates, even if they were not always to blame. On September 6 in Chicago, when the regular umpire did not show up, Pirate Harry Smith and Cub John "Jock" Menefee split the officiating duties. In the fifth inning, Wagner was on third with the Cub infield playing in. Second baseman Johnny Evers fielded a roller and threw home ahead of Wagner, but a long slide got a safe call from the Cubs' own Menefee. His teammates protested and at the end of the game, Menefee was tormented by the crowd to the point that he offered to fight the entire mob—one at a time or in pairs.

With the Pirates obvious winners and a number of men nursing injuries, several new players saw late-season action, including twenty-one-year-old John "Hans" Lobert. Dreyfuss spotted Lobert while he was playing for the Pittsburgh Athletic Team in a game in Atlantic City and stunned him by offering him a tryout. Lobert lived in Beltzhoover, a suburb south of Pittsburgh, and like most of his young ball playing comrades, idolized Wagner. Lobert remembered Wagner offering the use of his locker and many years later recalled that "when he found out I lived near him and my name was John . . . the same as his, he started calling me Hans Number Two. Actually, we did look a little bit alike. Especially our noses! From then on he always called me Hans Number Two, for all the fifty years we knew each other. I've always been proud of that."

Not only did the two share names, similar backgrounds, and over-sized noses, Lobert even had the same bandy legs as Wagner. Lobert's debut of thirteen at bats in 1903 was memorable only for him, particularly when he took Wagner's place at shortstop in the seventh inning of a game. Two years later, Lobert resurfaced in the National League, where he put together a productive career over his next thirteen seasons. He earned a reputation not unlike his hero—off the field as a likable, easygoing fellow and on the field as a fleet-footed, base-stealing hustler who was willing to play anywhere.

◆ ◆ ◆

Dreyfuss considered taking his players on a junket to Hawaii and Australia as a reward for a third straight championship. Instead, in early August, he issued a challenge to Ban Johnson's circuit for an eleven-game championship series. In the American League, Boston had jumped into first place in late June and by September 1 had an insurmountable lead. (The Boston American League team, in 1903 called the Pilgrims or simply the Americans, would become the Red Sox a few years later.) Serious discussions about a postseason series began in early September when the Pilgrims' absentee owner, Milwaukee attorney Henry J. Killilea, came to Pittsburgh to meet with Dreyfuss.

While some owners still harbored grievances toward the other league, Killilea and Dreyfuss were eager to work out an agreement. Dreyfuss knew he had a great deal to lose if the league feud resumed. Killilea, in his first and ultimately last year of ownership of the Pilgrims, had not suffered through the war. He held little of the bitter feeling toward the Nationals and felt that even if his team lost, the American League would gain credibility in a postseason series with the elder circuit. League presidents Johnson and Pulliam were not only interested in preserving peace through the event; each was anxious to prove superiority by winning an unquestioned "World's Championship."

In mid-September, Dreyfuss and Killilea hammered out a wonderfully simple one-page agreement for a best-of-nine-game series to begin on October 1. The two refused to consider any neutral site offers—a feature of a few of the World Series held in the mid-1880s, which pitted the National League champion against the American Association winner. The first three games would be played in Boston, the next four in Pittsburgh, and if necessary the remaining two in Boston. Only players on the squad as of September 1 would be eligible.

With less than three weeks left in the season, Pirate injuries were mounting. In a day when trainers did little more than rub sore limbs, the Pirates relied on John D. Reese, of Youngstown, Ohio, for rapid cures. Nicknamed Bonesetter, Reese was part chiropractor and part masseur, treating injuries he diagnosed as wrenched tendons and displaced muscles; he was pronounced a miracle worker after he treated Leach for a leg ailment the previous year. In late 1903, Sebring and Bransfield were hobbling on bad legs, and Wagner, still troubled by a sore thumb, suffered an injury to his right leg that kept him out of nine games and had the club fearing an operation might be necessary. The three sought Reese's assistance in Youngstown on the same September day. Wagner later recalled that he was skeptical, saying at one point he thought Reese was trying to hypnotize him, but Wagner said that he was able to run after only thirty minutes with Bonesetter. With only three games remaining, Clarke hastily set an appointment with Reese when he himself twisted an ankle on an inside-the-park home run.

But the two most tragic losses were Krueger and Doheny. On September 19, Krueger, who had done such a fine job filling in at several positions, was struck in the temple by a Bill Reidy pitch and was carried from the field and hospitalized for the next week. Doheny, a sixteen-game winner for the second straight year, continued to be paranoid and irrational. On September 22, with his sanity in question, he was escorted to his home in Andover, Massachusetts, by his clergyman brother.

In the final days of September, Dreyfuss considered cancelling the championship series. With Krueger, the team's only utility man, still suffering from the beaning, the Pirates faced the prospect of using a pitcher in the field if Clarke or Wagner was not fully recovered. Even well-respected Francis C. Richter agreed: "Under the circumstances Pittsburg would . . . have been amply justified in declining the engagement, owing to the improbability of an equal contest." In the end, Dreyfuss decided to play. His men were under contract until mid-October, and he agreed to give them 50 percent of the club's take.

In Boston, the Pilgrim players protested that their contracts expired on October 1 and demanded a consideration from Killilea for their extra work. He offered them the choice of either a two-week contract extension or 25 percent of the receipts, but they rejected the proposal and threatened to strike. Killilea appeased them on September 25, six days before the Series was to begin, by agreeing to the same arrangement that Dreyfuss had with the Pittsburgh players.

◆ ◆ ◆

The Pirates headed north from the Pittsburgh & Lake Erie Station in Pittsburgh at 11:30 P.M. on September 28. In tow were fifteen players from the team that finished 91–49: five right-handed pitchers—staff aces Phillippe (24–7) and Leever (25–7 with seven shutouts), Kennedy (9–6 but used sparingly in the last month), Veil (5–4), and Gus Thompson (2–3 since his debut in late August); catchers Phelps, Smith, and Fred Carisch, who had appeared in just five games; infielders Wagner, Leach, Ritchey, and Bransfield; and outfielders Clarke, Beaumont, and Sebring. No position-playing substitute was available. Krueger was still suffering with ringing in his ears, and though he would suit up for the games in Pittsburgh, Clarke would hesitate to use him. Another concern was Leever's right arm, which was giving him problems once again—due in part to aggravating it in a recent trapshooting competition. The twenty-five-man Pittsburgh contingent also included diehard followers Robert Kennedy of Uniontown and Wagner's Carnegie friend Jim Orris, several newspapermen, a few of Pittsburgh's high-rolling gamblers, and Bonesetter Reese—hired by Dreyfuss for a two-week engagement at a cost of five hundred dollars.

Stopping in Buffalo for one last tune-up game, the Pirates crushed the locals on September 29 by a score of 9–1. Wagner had three hits, blasting two triples, while Bransfield had two singles and two doubles. But Leach's ailing right-hand finger became so swollen it needed to be lanced. The beat-up squad arrived at Boston's Hotel Vendome on the morning of September 30. A headline in *The Pittsburg Post* declared PITTSBURG MONEY SCARES BOSTON, and a subhead explained, "President Dreyfuss and Party From Smoky City With a $30,000 Roll Quickly Hammer Beantown Betting Odds Down to Even Money." Dreyfuss was very active in backing his team with his wallet, and one of Pittsburgh's "sports" was said to have carried a grip containing ten thousand dollars for placing bets on the Pirates that no Pittsburgh bookie would accept. Boston bettors soon backed off their morning line of ten-to-eight odds on the home team. Clarke advised his men that placing wagers on the Series might preoccupy them and affect their play. It was counsel most of them, but not all, took to heart. Odds quoting was everywhere, and even *The Sporting News* recommended, "If Wagner does not play, bet your money at 2 to 1 on Boston, but if he does play, place your money at 2 to 1 on Pittsburg."

Within a decade, this Pittsburgh-Boston matchup would be recognized as the first modern World Series. But in 1903, outside of the Pittsburgh and Boston dailies it was treated little differently than previous postseason competitions. Most sources that had an opinion agreed on three things: Pittsburgh was superior in batting and infield play, thanks primarily to Wagner; both outfields were strong; and Boston had far superior pitching. Led by future Hall of Fame player-manager Jimmy Collins, the Pilgrims had finished at 91–47, fourteen and a half games ahead of Philadelphia. Besides Collins, recognized as one of the greatest third baseman of his time, the Pilgrims' infield consisted of Freddy Parent, a tiny but talented shortstop who hit over .300 with seventeen triples in 1903, light-hitting second baseman Hobe Ferris, and dour first base veteran Candy LaChance.

Boston's fly-chasing corps featured three hard hitters: Chick Stahl, who along with Collins was with the Boston National League champions of 1897 and 1898, handled center field; Buck Freeman, one of the era's best power hitters and the 1903 American League leader in home runs and runs batted in, played right field; and Patsy Dougherty, a .331 hitter and league leader in runs and hits in only his second big league season, manned left.

Cy Young, now thirty-six years old, annually added a few dozen wins to his impressive ledger and several pounds to his massive frame. During the 1903 season, he passed Pud Galvin on the all-time wins list and finished the year with 379. Over the next eight seasons he would put the figure out of reach with a career total of 511. (He also easily holds the top spot on the all-time list with 316 losses, 7,356 innings, and 750 complete games.) In 1903, he had led his league with a 28–9 mark, 341 innings, and seven shutouts. "Big Bill" Dinneen, at 21–13, and "Long Tom" Hughes, at 20–7, gave Boston a trio of tall right-handed twenty-game winners. Catcher Lou Criger (rhymes with "trigger"), who followed Young from team to team, was thought to be superior to any Pirate backstop despite hitting only .192. Criger's most significant contribution to the postseason event would not come to light until years later, when he revealed that gamblers had offered him twelve thousand dollars to throw the Series to the Pirates.

◆ ◆ ◆

Hordes of eager spectators converged on Huntington Avenue Grounds well in advance of game time on Thursday, October 1. Grandstand seats were bumped from fifty cents to one dollar and no twenty-five-cent admissions were sold, as even standing room was charged at fifty cents. Killilea refused to listen to free-pass requests, and Dreyfuss himself had to purchase a block of tickets for the Pirate entourage.

Separated from their National League neighbor's home of South End Grounds by only a railroad yard, the Americans' ballpark was not as claustrophobic as that of their counterparts. In fact, an estimated eight thousand fans took their places for the first game standing up, many behind ropes stretched across the cavernous outfield. A gong sounded, and the enthusiastic record Huntington Avenue turnout of 16,242 grew silent. The two umpires, Hank O'Day from the National League and Tommy Connolly of the American, met Clarke and Collins at home plate. The four agreed to a ground rule that any ball bounding into the roped-off crowd would result in a triple—a rule that would see plenty of usage in the Series. The fans roared as the four men parted ways. Clarke returned to the Pirate bench, Collins took his position, O'Day jogged onto the diamond to ump the bases, and Connolly moved in behind the catcher.

Young was greeted to a thunderous welcome, and the din continued as he induced Beaumont to fly to center and Clarke to pop a foul to Criger. Leach skipped a ball into the right field crowd for his first of two triples on the day. Wagner lined a single to left for the first run of the game and of modern World Series history, then stole second and moved to third when Ferris muffed Bransfield's ground ball. Bransfield also swiped second, and on Criger's wild throw into center, Wagner scored and Bransfield reached third. Ritchey walked and stole second, and Sebring dropped a single into left to score two runs. *The Pittsburg Post* stated that the only voices heard were the Pirate rooters, "including Barney Dreyfuss . . . indulging in the wildest kind of antics, while all around them was dense silence."

The Pirates went on to bat around in the first, scoring four times on three hits and three stolen bases. It was all Phillippe needed. After allowing a harmless single in the first, Phillippe stunned the Boston faithful by striking out the side in order in the second. The Pirates added single runs in the third and fourth innings, and in the seventh, Sebring pounded a deep drive over center fielder Stahl's head for a home run—Sebring's third hit and fourth run batted in. Down 7–0, Boston scored twice in the seventh and added another run in the ninth, thanks in part to Wagner booting a ground ball.

Phillippe struck out each of the Boston starting nine at least once with the exception of Freeman and had his highest one-game strikeout total for 1903 with ten. He allowed just six hits, one hit batsman, and no walks and was given sharp defensive support. Clarke made a fine running catch of a deep line drive, and Beaumont made a pair of running grabs. Young was rocked for twelve hits, including three of the game's five triples. He gave up just one single to Wagner but worked around him in the sixth and eighth, walking him each time. The Pirates had a surprisingly easy 7–3 win in the opener.

◆ ◆ ◆

Threatening weather and dampened hopes kept Friday's attendance down to 9,415. Bill Dinneen, the hard-throwing right-hander, had the mound honors for Boston. Leever assured everyone that the pain in his arm was no worse than usual, but he had a rough first inning. Leadoff hitter Dougherty sent a drive into the far reaches of center field, where fans had roamed the day before, and circled the bases for a quick 1–0 lead. Leever gave up another run and was pulled after just one inning. Bucky Veil came on to do an admirable job; he received excellent defensive support and was touched for only one run in seven innings—a Dougherty drive over the left field fence.

In the fourth, Beaumont walked and Clarke picked up Pittsburgh's first hit on a single to center. Leach dropped a bunt in front of the plate, moving the tying runs into scoring position for Wagner, who smashed a line drive toward right-center, but Ferris nabbed it and raced Clarke to second base to complete a double play. Dinneen gave up only three singles, one apiece by Clarke, Sebring, and Ritchey, and allowed only one other ball out of the infield. He struck out eleven and walked two, and his backing was errorless as the Pilgrims evened the Series with a 3–0 victory.

That evening, as his teammates took in the play *Fools of Nature* starring actress Julia Marlowe, Leever stayed at the hotel and soaked his arm in hot water. Defying the criticism of outsiders that he had a "weak heart," he vowed to pitch better if given another chance in the Series.

◆ ◆ ◆

The third game on Saturday, October 3, brought Boston rooters out in force—more than ten thousand were turned away at the gate. Police on the scene were unable to handle the multitude, and an order was sent out for reinforcements. Official attendance was announced as 18,801, but at least a thousand people climbed the walls or broke through locked entrances; some sources estimated that twenty-five thousand were within the grounds that day. Unrestricted fans covered the field prior to the contest, and one urchin made off with second base before being subdued by a policeman. The crowd circled the field and was within forty feet of home plate. Clarke and Collins concurred that with the outfield fans encroaching to within two hundred feet of the plate, balls hit into the overflow, even on a fly, would be doubles.

Boston trotted Tom Hughes to the box, and the Pirates countered with Phillippe, winner of Game One forty-eight hours earlier. Just as with Leever the day before, the soundness of Hughes's arm was questioned, but he retired the first five men he faced on harmless ground balls. Ritchey and Phelps accounted for the first run of the game in the second inning with two-out doubles into the mob in center field—two of five doubles the Pirates would hit into the crowd.

In the third, Beaumont walked and Clarke doubled into the left field overflow. Leach pulled a single into left to score Beaumont and move Clarke to third. With Wagner coming up, Collins began to stall for time by carrying on a conversation with his pitcher and then umpire Connolly. Within a few minutes, the humanity in front of the grandstand parted, and Cy Young emerged from the field-level wooden shack that served as a players' bench and walked to the center of the diamond. Amid the ovation for Young, Hughes departed from what proved to be his only World Series appearance.

Young carried his own ball to the rubber, though Connolly asked to take a look and discarded it in preference to the one already in play. Young nailed Wagner in the upper back with a pitch to load the bases, but Bransfield popped up and Ritchey hit a roller to third that Collins tossed home for a force out on Clarke. With two outs, Young appeared to be out of trouble when Sebring bounced to shortstop, but Parent booted it and Leach crossed the plate for run number three. As the ball skittered away from Parent, Wagner also tried to score but was gunned down.

With the score 3–1 in the eighth, the Pirates added a run. Wagner doubled, hitting a shot into right field that smacked a spectator in the leg, and after moving to third on a bunt, Honus scored on Ritchey's infield single. In the bottom half, Young led off by bouncing a ball to the right of the mound. Wagner seized it fifteen feet on the first-base side of second base and whipped it to Bransfield for the out. The Boston partisans appreciated the greatness of the play and applauded. The out took on more significance later in the inning when Collins doubled and Stahl singled. Had Young reached, the tying run would have been on base with one out. As it was, Freeman's ground ball ended the inning, and the Pilgrims' rally was thwarted. Phillippe finished off the 4–2 win and was again the center of attention, having given up only four hits and three walks in his second victory.

A special car for the Pirates was attached to the Washington Express, and the entire party enjoyed the twenty-three-hour train ride back to Pittsburgh. Many travelers remained up until the late hours, playing practical jokes or simply congratulating each other—the players for winning two games on enemy grounds, the gamblers for winning thousands and for wisely betting only lightly on sore-armed Leever in the second game.

Arriving back from the East at Union Station on the evening of October 4, Clarke expressed confidence to the two thousand or so fans who gathered at the depot. Each player was cheered as he stepped from the Pullman car, but Wagner, seeing a train departing toward Carnegie, dashed across the platform and was pulled aboard by the brakeman. He waved at the crowd as Clarke told the throng that Wagner's work was an "eye-opener" to Bostonians: Wagner had just a single, double, and one stolen base in the three games but was commended for his work at shortstop. In Carnegie, Hans Wagner badges were the fashion rage for a recently formed fan club, already numbering two hundred members.

◆ ◆ ◆

Dreyfuss was determined not to suffer the embarrassment that occurred in Boston a few days earlier and prepared for an immense turnout for the first game in Pittsburgh. He also had carpenters construct a makeshift set of bleachers behind home plate and in front of the grandstand to accommodate another two thousand people. Trying to cover himself on all fronts, Dreyfuss, who was ordinarily tight-fisted with free passes, even sent a complimentary ticket to the local weatherman, but as a downpour ensued, *The Pittsburg Dispatch* wondered if the forecaster was "holding out for a box."

The Pilgrims and roughly one hundred loyal followers, who called themselves the Royal Rooters, rolled into Pittsburgh on the rainy morning of Monday, October 5, just five hours before the 3:00 P.M. game was to begin. By noon, the field was soaked and the game was postponed for a day. Many players from both teams spent the evening as guests of the Duquesne Theater for a musical. Clarke was asked many times about who would pitch Game Four and was spared making a last-minute decision between Kennedy and Veil. The day of rain enabled Phillippe to take the mound again on Tuesday.

Bad weather held Tuesday's attendance down to a disappointing but manageable 7,600. The constant drizzle did not bother Boston's Royal Rooters who, along with the brass band they had hired, made a perpetual racket throughout the contest.

The Pilgrims went one-two-three in the top of the first. In the bottom, Beaumont singled to center, his first hit of the Series. Wagner and Bransfield hit two-out singles to net a run, but Wagner was thrown out trying to go from first to third on Bransfield's hit. Criger tied the game for Boston in the fifth with a single. Phillippe struck out to open the Pirate half of the inning, but Beaumont drove a ball to deep straight-away center that landed for a triple when Stahl misjudged it. Clarke popped up for the second out, but Leach hit a liner to first that LaChance could not handle cleanly, and Beaumont scored to break the tie. When Dinneen caught Wagner looking to end the inning, Honus disgustedly dropped the head of the bat to the ground and drew a line in the dirt several inches inside the plate, indicating where he thought the ball had passed.

With a 2–1 lead in the seventh, Phillippe led off with a single to left and reached second as Dougherty juggled the ball. Beaumont laid down a perfect bunt toward first base and beat it out. After Clarke flied out, Leach hit a two-run triple down the right field line. Wagner capped the three-run inning with a single to center, his third hit of the game. As Bransfield struck out for the third time, Wagner set sail for second. His slide in the sloppy conditions carried him past his target but he reached back with his arm and grabbed the bag. Wagner thought he had pulled off the stunt and was upset when base umpire Connolly signaled "out."

After holding a 5–1 lead in the eighth, having given up four hits and no walks, Phillippe wavered in the ninth. Boston bunched three singles for one run, and a force out scored another. Two more singles loaded the bases and had the Pirates on the edge. A fly ball brought home a run and pulled Boston within one, but pinch hitter Jack O'Brien popped up to Ritchey to end the game, 5–4 Pittsburgh.

Phillippe had won his third, giving Pittsburgh a three-to-one lead in games. The fans were jubilant, streaming onto the field and carrying Phillippe around on their shoulders. After delivering him to the clubhouse, many fans insisted on congratulating him personally for his wonderful effort. For the next half hour, Phillippe stood in the rain, shaking hands and taking backslaps from hundreds of admirers.

◆ ◆ ◆

With Tom Hughes still having arm problems, Boston would go with Young and Dinneen the rest of the way. Clarke was also strapped for pitching, and he took a gamble in starting Bill Kennedy in the fifth game on Wednesday, October 7. Several of Kennedy's hometown friends from Bellaire, Ohio, were on hand to see him pitch on this his thirty-sixth birthday. Many of the 12,322 in attendance—a much larger turnout than the previous day—circled the outfield. It was decided that for the remainder of the Series, any ball reaching the crowd would be a triple even if it was in the air.

Collins tripled in the first inning, but when he tried to score on a ground ball, Wagner threw him out at the plate. Collins was stranded in the third after he singled and stole second, colliding with Wagner's outstretched left arm on a tough slide. The limb would bother Wagner for the balance of the Series.

Through five innings, Kennedy and Young battled in a scoreless tie, but the Pirates came unraveled in the sixth. Clarke dropped a short fly in left while trying to avoid a collision with Wagner. Freeman followed with a single. Parent bunted to Leach, who wheeled and threw to Wagner covering third base in time for the force out, but Wagner inexplicably dropped the ball. With the sacks full and nobody out, Kennedy walked in a run. Ferris grounded to Wagner, and in an attempt at a force out, Honus tossed the ball over Leach's head, allowing another run. A third Pilgrim scored on Criger's bunt, Young drove in two more with a triple into the left field crowd, and Dougherty's three-bagger capped the frame. The Pirates committed three errors in the inning, two by Wagner, and when the dust settled found themselves down 6–0 on six unearned runs.

Boston added four more tallies in the seventh. It was Kennedy's final big league inning. The Pilgrims knocked five triples into the overflow, and Young cruised to a six-hit, 11–2 win. Boston still trailed three games to two.

◆ ◆ ◆

Leever took the slab again on Thursday, October 8, in front of 11,556 fans. He went the distance, but his support was ragged. Leach muffed a ground ball to allow a run. Wagner was 0 for 3 on the day without a ball out of the infield, and his bad relay throw gave Boston another run.

Dinneen scattered ten hits and three walks for his second win of the Series as Boston prevailed 6–3. The Royal Rooters went crazy throughout the game. Many of the gang were postseason veterans, having followed the Boston Nationals during their 1890s Temple Cup play. The group was led by loyal-to-the-core Boston fans Mike Regan, Charles Lavis, and a chunky Boston saloon keeper named Mike "Nuf Ced" Mc-Greevey, who earned his nickname by abruptly ending discussions with the phrase, " 'nough said!"—a rather common expression of the day. They blew tin horns, sang ditties, and ran up and down the aisles twirling the colorful umbrellas they were given as gag gifts by Pirate fans. While the Pilgrims were rallying for three runs in the third, the Royal Rooters were in the middle of crooning the popular song "Tessie." Fans being no less superstitious than ballplayers, the band of merry men continued the tune throughout the contest. (The singer of the 1903 hit "Tessie," Billy Murray, had another success five years later when he released a version of "Take Me Out to the Ball Game.")

The Royal Rooters took a few liberties with "Tessie," creating lyrics of their own. Lines like "Tessie, you make me feel so badly," would be adapted to serenade the Pilgrims or roast their opponents, with a particular fondness for the refrain:

> *Honus, why do you hit so badly,*
> *Take a back seat and sit down.*
> *Honus, at bat you look so sadly,*
> *Hey, why don't you get out of town!*

◆ ◆ ◆

The Series was locked at three games apiece. It was the home team's prerogative to cancel games due to weather or field conditions, and Friday's contest was postponed unusually early. While the day was cold and windy, most people felt Dreyfuss and Clarke had a twofold reason for the decision: A much larger crowd would attend a Saturday game, and it gave their only dependable pitcher, Phillippe, an extra day of rest. It also allowed more time for scuttlebutt to surface, and the most ludicrous story making the rounds was that Wagner had been shot by a Boston rooter.

There *was* one legitimate news item that leaked out of secretary Locke's office. In September, Dreyfuss had decided that if the Pirates won, he would take only expenses from the receipts and allow the players to divvy up the club's entire share of the take. When approached about the idea prior to the Series, Clarke asked Dreyfuss to keep the proposal under his hat so that the players would be thinking only of the pride of the championship. Now it was known to all that there was a lot at stake in the remaining games.

Prior to the last home game, Pirate enthusiasts, who felt they were being outdone by the visitors from New England, staged a parade from downtown Pittsburgh across the bridge to Allegheny. Each participant wore a red-white-and-blue Champion Rooter badge and was well versed in the official yell—"Phil, Phil, Phillippe, Phil! He can win, and you bet he will!" They also hired the services of the Second Brigade Band and gave the members specific orders that each time their opposite numbers struck up "Tessie," the counter was to be "Hail, Hail, the Gang's All Here" or another recognizable popular melody—played loudly. It was a tame one-upmanship, however, and the two parties joined together in singing "My Country 'Tis of Thee."

The masses began arriving early Saturday morning, October 10, and the park was full by 1:00 P.M., two hours before the first pitch. The official head count numbered 17,038, exceeded only by the Pirates' 1903 home opener, and thousands were turned away for lack of space. As with prior games in the Series, hundreds of onlookers sat atop nearby Monument Hill, which provided a partial view of the field, and dozens more took in the game from the summit of Mt. Washington. Although this vantage point from across the wide expanse of the Ohio River gave a panoramic view of the entire cities of Pittsburgh and Allegheny, it would have been like trying to watch a present-day game from a blimp.

Clarke could only rely on one pitcher, but until Game Seven, at least his position players remained healthy. However, in pregame warm-ups, Bransfield let a bat slip out of his hands and it struck Clarke squarely in the leg, knocking him to the ground. He took the field but limped through the entire contest. Phillippe went to the mound for his fourth start and was opposed by Young, in his third start and fourth appearance. The newly formed Champion Rooters brigade, situated behind the Pittsburgh bench, gave Phillippe a lusty welcome. The cheer was short-lived, and "Tessie" was soon in the air again. After Dougherty bounced to second for an out, Collins tripled into the crowd in left and scored when Stahl found the fans on the right field side for three bases. Freeman grounded to Ritchey, who threw to the plate to head off the runner, and while Phelps had the ball for a moment, Stahl's jarring slide knocked the ball loose for an error and a run.

In the bottom half of the first, Beaumont secured his fifth hit in his last six trips to the plate by placing a bunt down the third base line. LaChance bobbled Clarke's roller at first base, giving the Pirates two runners. The Pirate rooters were back in full swing momentarily, but Leach bounced into a double play and Wagner struck out to end the inning. In the third, Phillippe came to the plate and play was stopped as a fan presented him with a diamond horseshoe stickpin. He responded with a single and Clarke reached on an error, but Leach whiffed for the third out.

Boston stretched its lead to 4–0 in the fourth before the Pirates scored their first run in the bottom half. After Wagner was out trying to bunt his way on, Bransfield tripled down the left field line and scored on Ritchey's high chop. The Pilgrims added two runs in the sixth to lead 6–1. Clarke made it a 6–2 game in the inning when he tripled and scored on Wagner's comebacker. Young fielded the ball cleanly and looked Clarke back to the bag before tossing to first. Clarke raced for the plate and LaChance fired to Criger to head off the charge, but Clarke slid in with his spikes high and got a safe call from umpire Connolly. Criger protested, saying the runner never reached the plate, and the next day's accounts led readers to believe that Clarke had yet to actually touch home.

Young breezed into the ninth with the lead and faced the bottom third of the Pirate order. Sebring beat out a roller to short, and Phelps singled to center. Phillippe was a good-hitting pitcher, and he batted for himself in the crucial situation. He singled to center for a run, and the Pirates had the top of the order coming up with two on and nobody out. But Young stomped the screaming fans' hopes by getting Beaumont on a pop up, Clarke on a fly to left, and Leach, who had already struck out three times in the game, on a harmless ground ball.

The Pirates stranded nine men for the second straight day. Young yielded ten hits and one walk in winning his second game of the Series, and he handed his team a four-games-to-three advantage. Phillippe was beaten for the first time after three wins. He gave up eleven hits and in typical fashion did not issue a base on balls. But five of the hits reached the crowd in the outfield for triples, and he had made a costly error and wild pitch. Wagner, who was on deck at the end of the contest, was hitless for a third straight game and made his fifth error in seven games. *The Pittsburg Post* summed up his effort in the 7–3 loss by explaining, "Stars of the Wagner magnitude did not twinkle as much as was desired." But the *Pittsburgh Chronicle Telegraph* was more understanding, stating, "Wagner was the main offender, but the Carnegie giant has few lapses and the crowd forgave him."

The Pirates would now have to win two games in Boston to capture the "World's Championship," and their spirits were noticeably glum as they headed north out of Pittsburgh on Saturday night. The two teams swapped yarns together as they shared accommodations from Albany, New York, to Boston. That evening after checking into their quarters at the Vendome, Wagner and Phillippe found a pointed gift from an anonymous Boston joker—complimentary copies of *American Undertaker* magazine.

On Sunday, October 11, word came from Andover, Massachusetts, just north of Boston, that Doheny had been committed to the Danvers Insane Asylum. A week earlier, hoping to cheer him up, the club had sent him his uniform. But because he believed he could still pitch, the club's gesture confused him, worsening his condition. When he read about Boston's fourth victory, Doheny went completely berserk, striking his male nurse, Oberlin Howarth, in the head with a cast-iron stove leg and knocking him unconscious. Stories surfaced that Doheny held officers at bay for more than an hour but his wife denied the tales, saying that her husband quickly realized he needed help and cooperated as he was led quietly away.

The weather on Monday was terrible and the postponement of the eighth game allowed Clarke to visit Mrs. Doheny in Andover. That evening, he returned to the Vendome with tears in his eyes and an envelope, which he handed to Ritchey. Inside were two one-dollar bills and a letter from Mrs. Doheny explaining that as her husband was being taken away, he told her, "I owe only two dollars, and that to Claude Ritchey. Won't you pay him?"

◆ ◆ ◆

Monday's rainout gave the Pirates a much-needed day to lick their wounds. Clarke hedged on his pitcher for the do-or-die eighth game, at different times announcing Veil or Leever as the starter. Ritchey's throwing hand was swollen due to an infected sore. He was unfit to play on Monday, and Clarke had prepared to play second base himself and station Kennedy in left field. Wagner was worn out. His arms were giving him so much pain that he told John H. Gruber, a Pittsburgh sportswriter and the Pirates' official scorekeeper, that he was tired of baseball and considering retirement. In his column on the morning of the eighth game, Gruber dutifully noted Wagner's feelings with *The Pittsburg Post* headline WAGNER THREATENS TO QUIT GAME. But on Tuesday afternoon, October 13, Ritchey, Wagner, and Clarke were all in their familiar spots, and Phillippe got the assignment at the center of the diamond for a fifth time.

Amid rain and reports of scorecard overcharging and a ticket-speculation scandal involving Pilgrim management, only 7,455 fans found their way to Huntington Avenue Grounds to see a pitcher's duel between Phillippe and Dinneen. Dinneen retired the first eleven men he faced before walking Leach in the fourth inning. Wagner singled to left for the Pirates' first hit, and Leach reached third. With Bransfield at the plate and two outs, Wagner broke for second on a delayed steal attempt. Catcher Criger did not bite and instead faked a throw to second and snapped the ball to third, nipping Leach off the bag.

Phillippe gave up two hits and no runs through the first three innings but was touched for two runs in the fourth and another in the sixth. Dinneen was outstanding. With two outs in the ninth, he caught a disgusted Wagner looking at a called third strike, and Boston was big league baseball's undisputed World Champion. Dinneen gave up only four hits—none after the sixth inning—and received errorless support in throwing his second shutout. The fans poured onto the field after the 3–0 victory, capturing the Pilgrims one by one and carrying them aloft for several minutes.

Dinneen and Young proved too much for Phillippe to fight single-handedly. Dreyfuss and Clarke each congratulated Jimmy Collins and his Boston club and had praise for their own. Dreyfuss commented, "The Boston Club has won the World's Championship squarely, playing the cleanest kind of baseball. . . . My confidence in my team remains unshaken, for no one knows better than I what a game fight my players put up under most distressing conditions. . . . Next year I hope it will be our good fortune to engage in a similar series with a different result."

The World Series was a success, bringing positive attention to baseball and relatively little scandal. Francis Richter proclaimed that "the public is bound to hail both teams as the very best exemplars of the one great, clean and honest national sport. In all respects has the great world's series been a credit to and good thing for the game of base ball."

◆ ◆ ◆

On the evening of the decisive game, the two teams attended a performance at the Colonial Theater, where they were roundly cheered. Dreyfuss provided an informal banquet at the Vendome for his players and the Pittsburgh newspapermen, praising his team's brave fight and announcing that even though the team had lost, the players would receive the club's share of the Series' proceeds. This news was met enthusiastically by his men and made for a pleasurable trip home, although all were of one mind that "Tessie" would not be sung as part of the merriment on the train.

The club arrived in Pittsburgh on Thursday morning, October 15, and that afternoon, the players gathered at the club offices to split the receipts into shares of $1,316.25 apiece. Since Killilea had not matched his counterpart's benevolence, the losing Pirates took home more than the winning Boston players, who each received checks for $1,182. Krueger and secretary Locke were each given full shares, and partial shares were awarded to trainer Ed LaForce, groundskeeper John Murphy, newcomers Thompson and Carisch, and Doheny—money that was forwarded to his wife. In fact, each married player's check was made payable to the spouse, a move that did not make Dreyfuss popular at the moment. But the players reciprocated his previous gesture, presenting him with a split-second stopwatch engraved with each player's name, and they burst into song, belting out, "For He's a Jolly, Good Fellow." They also gave Clarke a watch chain and charm.

Within a few weeks, Dreyfuss rewarded Clarke with an undisclosed cut of the club profits and signed the player-manager to a new three-year contract worth $7,500 per season—50 percent more than the $5,000 one-year deals Wagner would earn for four more years. It made Clarke one of the most well-paid men in the history of the game. He was now a very wealthy man.

Dreyfuss could afford to be generous. The Pirates had a record-setting year at the gate, drawing more than 326,000 fans, up more than 80,000 from 1902. It led to a profit of $60,000—second only to the Giants' estimated $100,000. But Dreyfuss had lost a little of the luster from his championships, not to mention $7,000 in wagers on the Series—much less than the losses of others, which were reportedly as high as Shad Gwilliam's $29,000. When asked why he had done such a noble and unforeseen good deed in turning over the receipts to his men, Dreyfuss said it was his way of showing his thanks for three pennants and for the loyalty of the players who stuck by him in the league war. He simply said, "The boys deserved it."

◆ ◆ ◆

The Pirates were clearly outplayed in the Series. Young won twice and Dinneen three times as they combined to pitch all but two of the innings in the entire Series. Dinneen threw three- and four-hit shutouts and tossed four complete games. Phillippe pitched forty-four innings, walked only three batters over five complete games, and notched all three of the Pirates' victories. (His innings total, hits and runs allowed, and five decisions remain World Series records.) The staid, thirty-one-year-old gentleman received considerable attention for his wonderful effort. Sporting publications and several of the nation's newspapers published profiles detailing the rags-to-riches story of how he went on to big league glory after getting his first professional experience in Mankato, Minnesota, where he plopped off a hay wagon. Even crusty Ban Johnson complimented Phillippe for his World Series achievement. Dreyfuss showed his appreciation by awarding Phillippe ten shares of stock in the Philadelphia Traction Company, which operated many of the Pittsburgh trolley lines.

Batting was light in the Series, with only Stahl and Sebring breaking .300. Ritchey hit .111 and Bransfield barely cracked .200, but by far the most disappointing performance was by the Pirates' and the National League's reigning star, Honus Wagner. He won his second batting crown in 1903, but in eight games against Boston, he collected just six hits in twenty-seven at bats and went 1 for 14 in the last three games—among the position players of both teams, only Ritchey had fewer hits in the Series. Wagner drove in more than a hundred runs on the year but only three in the postseason. With the confining conditions, Boston managed to hit sixteen triples to Pittsburgh's nine—none by league-leader Wagner, who mustered only one extra-base hit. Worse yet, after playing such a brilliant shortstop throughout the year, he made a Series-high six errors and had a hand in several unearned Boston runs.

Some people hounded him for his poor play. Following the games, under *The Sporting News* headline HANS WAGNER'S SHOWING IN WORLD'S SERIES A BLOT ON THE GREAT PLAYER'S RECORD, the Boston correspondent expressed the opinion that "while Wagner is a fast, gingery player he is not a wonder as regards courage." His report continued by implying that Wagner was not a clutch performer, adding, "I am half inclined to think that old Honus has some yellow in him."

In Pittsburgh the press was gentler, but Wagner still shouldered much of the blame. Frank B. McQuiston of *The Pittsburg Dispatch* wrote, "What would have happened if Wagner had batted at his usual clip in these games? We would have beaten them even though we had but one pitcher. But Wagner didn't."

For years Wagner carried the stigma of playing "yellow" in the 1903 World Series. In his ghostwritten 1912 book *Pitching in a Pinch*, Christy Mathewson described Wagner's feelings by explaining, "This grieved the Dutchman deeply, for I don't know a ball player [who exhibits] less quit to the ton than Wagner. . . . This was the real tragedy in Wagner's career. Not-withstanding [*sic*] his stolid appearance, he is a sensitive player, and this hurt him more than anything else in his life ever has."

Respected veteran baseball writer Hugh S. Fullerton recalled that after the decisive game, Wagner's concern was for his fallen comrades when he said, "I wouldn't mind it for myself—but the boys deserved to win." Wagner was distraught, feeling a personal responsibility for the loss. It was to be a slow recovery.

The following spring, Wagner was asked if he had forwarded his portrait to the National League for Harry Pulliam's "Hall of Fame" of batting champions. Wagner dolefully responded, "I was too bum last year. I was a joke in that Boston-Pittsburgh Series. What does it profit a man to hammer along and make a few hits when they are not needed only to fall down when it comes to a pinch? I would be ashamed to have my picture up now."

SIX

"THE GREATEST EVERYTHING EVER"

During the baseball season, Wagner frequently rode a ten-cent trolley from Carnegie to Pittsburgh and then changed cars to complete the trip to Exposition Park. He was an attraction along the entire route. Swarmed by children and adults alike, he was pumped for stories of games or the Pirates' outlook. Wagner, still uneasy around strangers, answered politely but with little embellishment.

At other times, he rode his horse-drawn buggy to and from the ballpark. He would bring a favorite dog or be accompanied by his father, who was employed by the Pirates as an all-important "grandstand watcher," on the lookout for fires underneath the wooden structure. After crossing the covered Union Bridge into Allegheny City, Wagner was usually met on the other side by a group of kids who ran alongside his coach for the remaining few blocks. Pulling up outside the clubhouse entrance down the right field line, he would sometimes give his glove or spikes to a youth and have him carry the gear into the park—the duty earning the boy free admission. Now and then, Wagner merely held the gate open for a handful of the kids to follow him. John Daley, a Carnegie teenager at the time and a man who made it to big leagues for a cup of coffee in 1912, remembered scuffling with other kids for the right to carry something, anything, of Wagner's into the ballpark.

Once inside, the boys saw what was clearly an American sports giant and the man Tommy Leach referred to in Lawrence Ritter's *The Glory of Their Times* as "The greatest shortstop ever. The greatest *everything* ever." Batting, baserunning, and fielding—Wagner was recognized as a master of all three.

He typically downplayed his technique, and in later years, when asked for the secret of batting success, he would respond with something trifling such as, "Slam any that looks good," or "I always tried to hit the ball square on the nose." One of his customary lines was, "There ain't much to being a ballplayer if you're a ballplayer." But he took his game, his craft, very seriously and readily told youngsters that it was hard work and extra batting practice rather than natural-born ability that led to success in baseball.

Like many of the great hitters, he doted over his bats and experimented often with different styles, models, and brands. He still made trips to Louisville, and Bud Hillerich came to Pittsburgh once in a while. The friendship led to Wagner generally using Hillerich bats—particularly after he became the first player to have his signature, a flowery "J. Hans Wagner," branded into a Louisville Slugger in September 1905. The endorsement, followed in a few months by Lajoie and in two years by Ty Cobb, earned no money for Wagner and received surprisingly little notice at the time, but it is likely that Wagner no longer paid for any Hillerich bats.

In a 1914 letter to the Hillerich factory, Wagner claimed to have been using its bats exclusively since 1909 and wrote that they were "perfectly balanced" and made of the "best driving wood." The J. F. Hillerich & Son bats were primarily made of ash, as they are now under the Hillerich & Bradsby name. An expensive Cuban wood called majaqua was used every so often, and Wagner did order a shipment of majaqua bats at least once. He liked a thirty-five-inch bat, longer than average, but would alter weights, between thirty-four and a half ounces and a hefty thirty-eight ounces, according to who was on the mound. He reasoned, "For a pitcher who serves slow ones and uses his head I use a lighter bat, but when a pitcher relies mainly on speed I find a heavy bat more serviceable." The weight could vary an ounce without causing a problem. In an unusual exhibition of vanity, he preferred that his Hillerich bats be produced with a deep red finish.

Wagner approached the plate in a manner that some described as confident and others said was cocky. He believed that a batter's grip was critical. Usually choking up a little, sometimes he would split his hands a few inches. Although not uncommon for the day, this split-hand style would often be referred to in later years as the Wagner-Cobb or Cobb-Wagner grip, as confirmation of their influence. At other times, Wagner would keep his hands together, changing their position depending on the pitcher (junk or fastball thrower), the situation (bunt, hit and run, or swing away), or even between pitches (swinging for maximum power with his hands together early in the count and splitting his grip to concentrate on contact and placement once he had two strikes).

Wagner believed that one of the most important ingredients in hitting was the stride. Discounting the stance, he said the main thing was to just feel natural in the batter's box. If he was in a slump, he would shift his feet to find a more comfortable position. He patterned himself after slugger Cap Anson, standing very deep in the box in order to fully extend his long arms. Crouching, in his words, "like a big gorilla" with his weight on his back foot, he would stride to meet the ball wherever it was pitched.

Wagner said, "The batter who is particular about getting the ball just right will not make many hits," and he earned a well-deserved reputation as a bad-ball hitter. He felt that if he was fooled, he was sure to see the same pitch in a similar location and he prepared to drive it, even if it was outside the strike zone. In fact, years later, Clarke insisted that Wagner would let pitchers "think he was dumb" by intentionally looking bad on a swing in order to induce a hurler to throw the same pitch again. Clarke declared that once Wagner swung and missed, he would sit on the next delivery, knowing that "vanity caused the pitcher to think he had found the spot where Honus was not hitting 'em that day." In July 1901, New York moundsman Bill Phyle laughed at Wagner when he cut and missed, purposefully or not, at a ball that was more than a foot outside. Moments later, when Phyle threw another in the same spot, Wagner pulled a double down the left field line.

Mathewson described Wagner as a "free-swinger," unlike so many hitters of the day who just tried to make contact. Mathewson, considered by Wagner to be the best pitcher he ever faced, said the only weakness he could find with Wagner was a high and tight fastball but confessed, "He will not bite on it unless he is unusually eager. . . ." Wagner admitted that the toughest pitch for him to hit was a moving fastball, remarking that even if the batter knows what is coming, "the ball is liable to jump differently each time." However, in seventeen years and more than three hundred career at bats, often in the heat of a pennant race with the Giants, Wagner treated Mathewson's high, tight fastballs rather rudely, hitting better than .300. There were a number of jokes that centered around advising young pitchers on how to deal with Wagner, but perhaps McGraw summed it up best when he said, "Just throw the ball and pray."

At shortstop, Wagner excelled in every aspect of fielding his position. Using the tiny, rigid mitts of the time, he would cut the entire palm out and stitch around the opening himself. This modification allowed him to manipulate the glove—and the ball—more effectively. Paraphrasing Wee Willie Keeler's famous line, "Hit 'em where they ain't," *Sporting Life*'s recommendation for batting against Pittsburgh was, "Hit 'em where Wagner ain't." But that was easier said than done.

McGraw credited Wagner with having a "sixth sense of baseball." Wagner prided himself on knowing opposing hitters' tendencies and picking up the catcher's signal to anticipate where the ball might be hit. Playing exceptionally deep, often complaining that the "skin" of the infield was cut too shallow, he could corral balls from any number of awkward positions and use his tremendous throwing arm to get an out. He was proud of his large hands, calling them "scoops," and actually did use them like shovels. On grounders to short, he had a reputation for digging up chunks of infield along with the ball, and first baseman Bransfield enjoyed saying that he just caught the largest object flying his way. Judging a runner's speed down the baseline, Wagner invariably got the ball to the bag just in time—a trick that both umpire Hank O'Day and his high-strung manager found particularly annoying. But Wagner told Clarke, "Well, let 'em run 'em out. When I miss 'em, I'll quit." As a result of Wagner's preparation and natural athletic ability, he led the league's shortstops in double plays four times despite working behind a pitching staff that allowed few baserunners compared with the opposition.

Wagner was a daring, sometimes reckless baserunner who liked to take the offensive. The Pirates were frequent practitioners of the hit-and-run play. Taking his lead at first, Wagner would often signal to the batter that he should swing away at the next pitch because Wagner was heading to second. In stealing, he prided himself on getting a long lead, and he would slide either head or feet first to avoid a tag. He boasted that he could detect the slightest flaw in a pitcher's motion that would indicate if he was going to the plate or to the base with a pickoff, and he would exploit it until the pitcher corrected the weakness.

In addition to using his head, Wagner was a very fast man—a speed that defied his size and shape. It was his baserunning prowess during this decade that induced a sportswriter to begin calling him The Flying Dutchman, a name originally given to a legendary ship whose captain's punishment for a crime was to sail forever without coming into port. In the 1840s, Richard Wagner composed a famous opera by the same name based on the folk story. Honus Wagner would share this handle with a horse, race car, and pinwheel toy, and he was not even the first ballplayer to be referred to by this name. In the 1890s, it was also infrequently applied to Herman Long, another speedy shortstop of German descent. However, to millions of people, The Flying Dutchman was and is only Honus Wagner.

◆ ◆ ◆

Wagner was destined to play his peak years during a tough time for hitters. The baseballs did not carry well. They remained in the game indefinitely and were retrieved, forcibly if necessary, whenever they were fouled into the stands. Until 1908, the pitcher was permitted to soil a new ball by grinding it into the dirt. Often by the end of the first inning, the ball was so dark and mushy, it would not be considered usable by the kids on today's sandlots.

In 1904, baseball was entering the height—or the depth—of the "dead ball" era. The foul-strike rule, adopted by the National League in 1901 and the American League in 1903, took a toll on batters early in the century. Now hitters had to contend with yet another setback. Pitchers had been experimenting with doctored deliveries for years, and now some were mastering a spitball. Moistened with any number of foreign substances, including slippery elm, sweat, plain saliva, or a fortified version with licorice or tobacco juice, the ball looked like a fastball as it approached the plate but then took a nasty break straight down.

In 1897, Wagner's first year with Louisville, the entire National League batted .292. In 1903, the league batted .269 and that dropped a full twenty points in 1904—to .249. Although not a recognized statistic at the time, the ERA for the National League during the six-year span from 1904 to 1909 averaged out to a stingy 2.63. Batting futility was big news in this period, and there were calls for rule changes to help the hitters. Many baseball people, some as well-respected as Henry Chadwick and Francis Richter, wanted a repeal of the foul-strike rule. Others argued that the spitball should be outlawed—for sanitary reasons if nothing else. Still others offered solutions as zany as having a man assigned to bat for the pitcher. A Detroit sportswriter, poking fun at some of the suggestions, proposed tying the outfielders to posts with a limited length of chain.

Wagner was asked for his opinion and, as most any slugger would, offered some ideas that were not in a pitcher's best interest. He not only favored the abolishment of the foul-strike rule and legislation against the spitball, he wanted the pitcher moved back three feet and a reduction to three balls for a walk. Luckily for moundsmen, Wagner had no control over the rules of the game. As it was, he was doing just fine. In 1904, as he turned thirty years old, he was entering his prime and about to begin a period of staggering success. His shining batting statistics take on even greater luster when it is understood that he spent his most distinguished seasons in a time when pitching dominated the game.

◆ ◆ ◆

Following the 1903 World Series, Wagner worked as an instructor at the Carnegie Gymnasium, added new birds to his henhouse, and was beginning to dabble in more speculative investments—purchasing stock in a local startup brewery and buying a few empty lots in his neighborhood.

Honus and Al, inseparable during the winter months, engaged in an active basketball season. The Pittsburg Big Five basketball squad was just that—big. The team featured the Wagners—Honus who was never small and Al who was adding a few extra pounds each year—plus a few other burly basketball hotshots. Under Honus's direction, they won more than they lost, a few against professional competition from teams of the Western Pennsylvania Basketball League and, a few years later, the Central Basketball League. Over the years, his teams often played to packed houses throughout the tri-state area. The attraction was always Honus. On one occasion, the team provided its services for no charge when a benefit game was held for sufferers of a tragic mine disaster in the Pittsburgh suburb of Cheswick.

Knowing the value of a second drawing card, Wagner publicized that Phillippe, now a local celebrity, would join the Big Five for a hoops tour of all the major league baseball towns. Unfortunately, Phillippe was informed after the announcement was made and, sensing the embarrassment of having to learn the game on the fly, turned the offer down. The outfit remained in the area, and Phillippe signed on as secretary-treasurer.

The Pirate squad that headed to Hot Springs one month after Wagner's birthday was very similar to the one that secured the last three league titles. Pitching jobs were up for grabs in 1904, and several candidates would get a trial. Dreyfuss tried to secure genuine pitching help but turned up very little. Thinking the Detroit Tigers of the American League, who were on the sale block, might be willing to part with hard-throwing workhorse "Wild Bill" Donovan, Dreyfuss offered $10,000. Ed Barrow, after his first season as Tiger manager, ridiculed the proposal by countering with identical bids for either Wagner or Leach. *The Pittsburg Dispatch*, taking the offers much too seriously, thought Dreyfuss would make a good move by trading Leach for Donovan but commented, "Detroit could not get Wagner for Donovan and all the relations he has, as well as those he hopes to get. . . ."

Al, now thirty-two years old, accompanied the Pirates to Hot Springs in preparation for yet another season in the Eastern League. During an intra-squad game, he was chasing a foul fly and slammed into a tree, but the natural padding he now carried cushioned the blow and he came through unscathed. He performed well, and prior to breaking camp, Al was told that if he wanted to play with the Pirates in 1904, Dreyfuss would try to buy him from Providence. Although the offer was reportedly worth twice his Providence salary of $1,200, Al declined.

Clarke was not surprised, saying, "To my mind, Al is one of the very best ballplayers in the country today, and I wish we had him on the Pittsburgh team. However, he prefers the minors, and nothing can induce him to tie up with a National League club." *The Pittsburg Dispatch* reasoned that Al turned down the offer because the contract would enforce a "strict compliance to club rules" and, giving Al the benefit of the doubt, continued, "Now, Al is not a rowdy, neither is he a heavy drinker, but he likes his freedom and objects to being tied down by any hard and fast rules." Sportswriter Alfred Cratty was not as kind, revealing that Al "is out for a life of joy. He does not think that work is the only thing a man should do." It was still a far more positive amateur analysis than that offered by Barrow, who once went as far as calling Al "an anarchist."

Al's season ended prematurely once again when he returned to Carnegie from Providence in early September with a badly injured knee. The following spring, with Dreyfuss's assistance, Al appealed to Garry Herrmann and the National Commission for $250 in unpaid salary from Providence for the 1904 season.

His minor league career would last a few more years in the Eastern League, and his knee would trouble him throughout. For the next decade though, he would make the trip to Hot Springs most every year, playing with the second team, or Yannigans, as well as running special errands for Dreyfuss.

The Pirate president pointed out that "yes, Albert is a fine ballplayer; one of the best if he only had the disposition. He is out for a good time more than fame and success on the diamond." Al was simply indifferent to playing baseball and lacked the dedication and discipline it demanded. In the Wagners' hometown, legend still has it today that Al was actually the better ball-playing brother, but it was his distaste for wearing a baseball uniform that short-circuited his career.

◆ ◆ ◆

Many of the so-called experts now felt New York was the National League's best team. Dreyfuss eagerly wanted "his boys," as he liked to call them, to become the first National League team to hoist four straight pennants. He was confident and willing to wager on its chances. Ban Johnson trumpeted the Pirates as the class of the National League, scoffing at the notion that the New York Giants could dethrone the champions "because Pittsburgh has by far the best team in the league. [It] has very fast baserunners, hard hitters, a first-class manager and fine team work. . . . The club owner, too, is a man for whom the players like to work." Taking every possible opportunity to insult John McGraw and John Brush, his mortal enemies from the league war days, Johnson asserted, "New York has none of these advantages."

Dreyfuss speculated that the New York Highlanders (to be renamed the Yankees in 1913) would land the American League pennant and claimed Johnson would do anything in his power to make the New York team a winner. In January, a petty tiff over the 1904 schedule flared between Johnson and Dreyfuss, who as usual was on his league's schedule committee. The two swapped charges of incompetency and of jeopardizing the peace agreement, but by spring, each league was satisfied with an expanded one hundred fifty-four-game docket. This format would remain intact until 1961, with the wartime exceptions of 1918 and 1919.

Despite Johnson's lofty predictions and Phillippe's third consecutive opening-day victory, the Pirates dropped eight and a half games back in the first month of play. The pitching staff was in shambles. Bucky Veil and Phillippe were both battling illnesses, and Leever was on the shelf at the outset with his bad arm and made the situation worse when he was ejected and suspended in his first start of the season. On April 24, in only his second inning of work, he protested a balk call so vigorously that he was suspended for a week. The thirty-two-year-old Leever, newly married to a woman ten years his junior, got no sympathy from his bride, who agreed that he had balked.

Dreyfuss penned an estimated $11,000 in checks during 1904 on players he felt would improve his club. Most of his money was wasted. However, on Wagner's suggestion, he spent $750 to purchase the release of Patsy Flaherty from the Chicago White Sox in June. Flaherty had a great pickoff move, a jerky rapid-fire delivery, a variety of junk pitches, and the knowhow of working a batter; today, he would be considered a "crafty left-hander." Since his release in early 1901 by Pittsburgh, he had bounced around the minors for a few years and resurfaced with Chicago's American League club in 1903, where he led the league in losses, going 11–25. The Pirates would use thirteen pitchers in 1904, more than any other team. With Leever off to a slow start and Phillippe's illness lasting much of the year, Flaherty emerged as the staff ace, and would finish at 19–9.

◆ ◆ ◆

As prospects for a successful 1904 season hit the gutter early, the team began to bicker, and the entire summer was one of turmoil, injury, and controversy. Dreyfuss was upset at his players' performance, particularly when they arrived at a game in Chicago without their bats. At one point, after watching "his boys" go scoreless for fourteen consecutive innings in a doubleheader, Dreyfuss stormed out in disgust.

Factions developed early. During spring training, Veil and Leach exchanged blows, with Leach getting the worst of it. Veil was released after just one regular-season appearance, ending his big league tenure. Bransfield was barely breaking .200, and when Clarke cursed him for advancing only one base on a single, hard feelings were said to exist between the two.

Jimmy Sebring became moody after his friend Veil was dropped. Then in late July, when Wagner chastised Sebring for a poor throw, the outfielder confronted Wagner outside the dugout—certainly not a good career move for any young Pirate. The two were said to be at odds for days, and *The Pittsburg Post* knew a change loomed, commenting, "Well, between Wagner and Sebring, it will not be a hard matter to choose the most meritorious."

On July 31 in Cincinnati, the sulking Sebring badly twisted his right ankle and told Dreyfuss that he would prefer to rehabilitate at home rather than travel with the team. After having challenged the franchise player in full view of the fans, Sebring was in no position to ask for favors, and Dreyfuss was in no mood to grant any. When Sebring reiterated his feelings at the depot prior to the team's departure on August 1, words between the two men became heated. A series of unfortunate events followed in which Dreyfuss suspended his player for "desertion," and Sebring said he merely obliged when ordered to quit. Within a few days, Dreyfuss traded the talented but temperamental outfielder.

Injuries decimated the Pirates. Phillippe's problems began on Memorial Day when he became ill after getting pounded 13–0 in a pouring rain; soon, he was hospitalized with what was described as a cold that had settled in his eye. In mid-June, Krueger was knocked unconscious from another beaning, and Phelps was hit in the head less than a month later. Smith underwent late-season elbow surgery that would cause him to miss almost all of the next two seasons. Carisch was hospitalized with typhoid fever. And a violent carriage accident en route to the ballpark in Philadelphia injured Roscoe Miller's pitching arm so severely that it ended his big league career.

The most serious health concern was for Clarke. Playing great ball and hitting over .300 in mid-July, he went down with a gruesome spike wound in his left leg. Two weeks later, he underwent surgery for blood poisoning—a life-threatening condition in the days before antibiotics. He was confined to bed for a month and was on crutches for weeks afterward. Over the last three months of the season, he could only pinch hit twice, and he did not return to manage until September 5. After four years of filling the role as Clarke's lieutenant, Wagner declined to take charge of the problem children. Dreyfuss had a long discussion with Leach and convinced the little third baseman to assume responsibility as acting manager. Leach's term was temporarily interrupted by a groin injury, with Smith and then Bransfield each handling the duties for a brief time.

In August, *Sporting Life* commented, "In its present condition the Pittsburg team would not present a very formidable front if it were not for the great and versatile Wagner." Throughout the entire chaotic 1904 season, Wagner's individual performance was exceptional. Despite the fact that he often created havoc, he was regularly applauded by the fans in rival cities when he approached the plate for his first at bat. In Brooklyn, he let a pop-up drop in the infield when he saw the batter barely out of the batter's box and turned it into a double play. The fans hooted the umpire's call, not understanding completely what had happened, but by the time Wagner trotted off the field, he was loudly cheered.

The skill that brought him the most acclaim was his hitting. On June 10 in front of 2,500 Ladies' Day Boston fans, Flaherty made his first start since being reacquired. The *Boston American* claimed, "The day could have been more aptly christened Wagner Day instead of Ladies' Day, as there was far more Wagner than there were ladies." He supported his buddy with a 4 for 5 day that included three doubles, three runs, and two stolen bases. The next two games were also at Boston, and Wagner made them productive, banging out six hits, including three more doubles and a home run.

He was the center of attention at the Hotel Vendome in Boston, where *The Pittsburg Post* correspondent caught up to him, describing him as "modest and retiring" but in a "happy frame of mind." In a rare retrospective interview from the middle of his career, he shared, "The game is very much changed from what it was when I first broke into big company," and, showing some frustration with the Pirates' dreary performance, added, "We were at it hammer and tongs all the time, and there wasn't a let-up from one end of the season to the other."

Moving on to Philadelphia, Honus collected five hits in two days and threw in three more doubles, giving him fifteen hits in five games with nine doubles and a homer. Two days later he crushed a double and home run, driving in four runs. In the middle of his hottest stretch of the year, he was saluted by an enthusiastic Independence Day Exposition Park crowd of more than twelve thousand. They fired off pistols and firecrackers each time he came to the plate. In the first game of a doubleheader sweep, he doubled three times—twice in one inning. In the second game, he hit a single, double, triple, and stole a base as the crowd cheered his every move.

Plaudits were being showered upon him. In New York, *The Sun* maintained, "It is unlikely that professional baseball has ever before had as good a player as Hans Wagner." Brooklyn's Ned Hanlon was once again said to be after Wagner via trade, but if it was difficult to make a deal for him five years ago, it would have been next to impossible in 1904.

At the end of July, Wagner's arm was ailing from a spike wound. In one game, he switched positions with Ritchey in order to have an easier toss to first. Wagner remained at shortstop for the most part, but with his arm continuing to bother him, he played a few games at first base, a couple in left, and a handful in center during the season's last two months. Offensively, the injury did not slow him down. He doubled and stole a base in four consecutive games and tripled home a ninth-inning game winner. On August 29, after striking out twice against former teammate William "Doc" Scanlan, Wagner batted left-handed and bounced out. In the tenth, he switched back to the right side and won the game with a single.

By mid-September, his arm and back were both troubling him, and he missed the last seventeen games. He won his third batting title by a twenty-point margin, and his .349 mark was a full one hundred points higher than the league average. He led the league in doubles with forty-four (sixteen more than his closest competitor), total bases, slugging average, and stolen bases, finishing second in triples and runs.

As the team finished off its dreadful season, Wagner headed to Mt. Clemens, Michigan, to recuperate. Through it all, he was praised for his "gameness" for staying in the lineup as long as he did, and when a story circulated that he asked to have his salary stopped since he couldn't play, he was lauded for his unselfishness.

◆ ◆ ◆

New York, Chicago, and Cincinnati each took brief turns at the top in 1904, but thanks to an eighteen-game winning streak, the Giants were a runaway, finishing at 106–47. The Pirates never got closer than ten games after July 1 and ended a discouraging fourth, at 87–66, nineteen games behind New York.

In the American League, the race came down to a final-day doubleheader between the defending champion Boston club and Dreyfuss's forecast, the New York Highlanders. Needing a sweep in front of their home crowd, the Highlanders sent former Pirate Jack Chesbro to the slab for the first game. Although he had won twenty games in each of the previous three years, his new spitball propelled him to new highs in 1904, including an astonishing 455 innings, forty-eight complete games, and a record of 41–12. With the score knotted at 2–2 in the ninth, Boston had Lou Criger at third with two outs. The Highlanders' pennant went up in smoke when Chesbro uncorked a wild pitch. Boston was the American League champ again.

Well before the season ended, Brush and McGraw made it quite clear that they had no intention of playing a series against their "inferiors." Brush was still disturbed that the Americans were treading on his sacred New York ground, and McGraw and Ban Johnson were at odds over the manager's turbulent stint in the American League and jump to the New York Giants—an issue that the two would hold grudges about for the rest of their lives. Brush and McGraw stuck to their guns and were no doubt heaving sighs of relief that their crosstown rivals did not win the American League pennant, knowing it would have caused enormous public pressure for a postseason series.

In the spring, Dreyfuss could never have imagined his team would finish fourth, so he consented to play a series with the corresponding finisher of the other league. Many expected him to beg off these games because of the poor health of his club. But Dreyfuss believed that McGraw and Brush were doing the game a disservice by refusing to play a World Series and went through with the anticlimactic series with Cleveland. Even with nothing at stake, Wagner and Clarke played, but Clarke was said to look so emaciated from his ordeal that there was some question whether he would ever recover.

◆ ◆ ◆

Bookmaker Shad Gwilliam predicted that President Teddy Roosevelt would easily win another term in the fall of 1904. Even Gwilliam underestimated the incumbent's political clout, as Roosevelt won by an unprecedented margin on his "square deal" platform. As a property owner and recent Elks Club recruit, Wagner was involved in everything from minstrel shows to euchre tournaments. He was now socializing with some of the more influential members of Carnegie society, but the election held little interest for him. A more important forecast, as far as Wagner was concerned, was that even Gwilliam favored the New York Giants as repeaters for the National League crown in 1905.

Embarrassed over the fourth-place finish, Dreyfuss sent the troops to Hot Springs earlier than he had in prior years. Sparing no expense, he even sent his Exposition Park groundskeeper to the southern resort a few weeks in advance to prepare the Whittington Park diamond and picked up the entire tab for the players except for uniforms. Wagner was at the station to see the team depart on March 12 but, to Dreyfuss's chagrin, remained behind. Wagner was concerned for his father, who for the last few weeks had been bedridden with pneumonia. And answering a local call for men of money to invest in housing, Wagner was finalizing the letting of a contract for the construction of four homes on additional properties he had purchased that winter. By midsummer, each of the newly constructed units would rent for thirty dollars per month. His first occupants were his sister Carrie and her husband.

With Peter Wagner recovering and the contract in the hands of a local man, Wagner joined his mates ten days later. There were many new faces. Catcher Eddie Phelps was traded to Cincinnati for Henry "Heinie" Peitz. The veteran catcher fit right into the Pirate game plan with his leather-lunged base coaching—a routine that in 1906 led to an on-field fistfight with Joe McGinnity at Exposition Park. First baseman Bransfield hit just .223 in 1904 and was sent to Philadelphia for promising first baseman Del Howard. Dreyfuss fancied Howard, but many believed it was a Bransfield-Wagner feud that led to the popular first baseman's departure. The accusation became so widespread that both players wrote letters to the local press explaining that they were friends and there was nothing behind the "false and malicious" statements.

The trade began a revolving door at first base that lasted several years, and although other positions also saw rapid turnover for the Pirates, many claimed there seemed to be a curse on Pittsburgh first basemen after Bransfield's departure. Bransfield was not unlike several other Dreyfuss high-priced minor league acquisitions. Some were not ready for the big leagues when Dreyfuss bought them, and others wore off their welcome due to a poor performance or a spat with the president or manager.

College players were becoming more common and more accepted in big league baseball. In the spring of 1905, Pittsburgh had its share of scholars in camp. Mike Lynch, a law student at Brown University, had done admirable mound work for the Pirates the previous year, finishing 15–11. There were also a couple of Princeton men now with the Pirates—reserve Arthur "Dutch" Meier and left-handed catcher Homer Hillebrand, whose arm proved so strong in camp that he was moved to the mound, though shoulder problems constantly dogged him.

Even a few from the old guard were getting into the academic spirit as Flaherty was taking coursework in the offseason and Clarke had spent a week coaching the Princeton Tigers baseball team the previous spring. Clarke came back from his brief tenure with glowing reports of the players' ability and poise. He was not, however, impressed with their practice of pitching without a cap or their affinity for cigarettes—a habit that Clarke despised. Campus life held no attraction for Wagner, and while their ways were still foreign to him, he was adapting. During one practice, he took the field capless and when Clarke jokingly asked the shortstop what college he had played for, Wagner retorted, "Carnegie Institute, Cap. I took a course in coal mining."

◆ ◆ ◆

In their first series of 1905, the Pirates took three of four in Cincinnati but could not get through the games without incident. Umpire Bill Klem, destined to be one of the most well-respected and famous arbiters in baseball history, was overseeing his first regulation big league action. He had umpired the Cleveland-Pittsburgh series the previous fall, and the Pirates complained throughout. They picked up where they left off and in only the second game of the year, Clarke was ordered from the field—his first ejection in three seasons. Years later, Klem gave Clarke credit for not harboring resentment like his contemporaries, McGraw of the Giants and Frank Chance, who would take control of the Chicago Cubs later in 1905.

Early on, Wagner missed a few games when he was spiked in the left hand on a headfirst slide into third base. He returned with a bandage covering the wound. Despite some pain while swinging, he smashed what was noted as the longest home run in Philadelphia Baker Bowl's ten-year history when he bounced a ball into an open door of the center field clubhouse. (Until 1931 in the major leagues, fair balls that bounced over or through the outfield fence were home runs.) Cheers greeted him in Brooklyn and Boston, and when the Pirates met New York for the first important head-to-head series, even Giant fans forced him to "lift his lid." He was the only Pirate afforded such pleasantries in New York as the series quickly deteriorated into a mess.

On Thursday, May 18, at the Polo Grounds, McGraw, now virtually a full-time manager, lit into a contingent of Pittsburgh fans stationed behind third base for rooting as the Pirates rattled Mathewson for ten hits and a 7–2 win. The next afternoon, McGraw berated Dreyfuss within earshot of many spectators as the Giants pulled even in the series.

More than twenty thousand Saturday patrons witnessed McGraw and Mathewson take up the third and first base coaches' boxes and begin to harass Pirate pitcher Mike Lynch in the first inning. The verbal onslaught continued when Lynch was sitting on the bench in the second, and after hearing an inning and a half of the two Giants' obscenities, Clarke appealed to umpire Jim Johnstone to halt the display. McGraw overheard the request and rushed out of the dugout. As he and Clarke began to square off at the plate, Johnstone intervened and ordered Mathewson to the bench and McGraw to the clubhouse in deep center field. As he often did after his numerous banishments, McGraw circled back under the grandstand. He positioned himself in the second deck where he began a barrage of insults directed at Dreyfuss, who was seated below. McGraw yelled, "Hey Barney! Hey Barney!" and loudly accused Dreyfuss of not picking up his gambling markers and controlling umpires through his friend, President Pulliam. Dreyfuss sat quietly and seethed as McGraw's tirade degenerated into a name-calling fit that included, according to Dreyfuss, "all the vile names he could lay his tongue to."

Proclaiming "McGraw's vile epithets are still ringing in my ears and I propose to see if an owner of a National League club must submit to such treatment at the hands of a thug," Dreyfuss formally protested McGraw's conduct to Pulliam, who quickly tossed the hot issue into the lap of the National League board. But McGraw called Pulliam to harangue him anyway, to which Pulliam responded by fining the manager a whopping $150 and suspending him for fifteen days.

Dreyfuss was sure that the league would finally put a stop to McGraw's brash and childish behavior, but over the next two weeks, the board not only exonerated the Giant manager of any wrongdoing, it even chastised Dreyfuss for "the undignified course of . . . indulging in an open controversy. . . ." Further expressing its displeasure with Dreyfuss, the board stated, "It sincerely hopes that no other club owner, in a moment of excitement, will so far forget the dignity that attaches to the presidency of a National League ball club." Brush and McGraw were even successful in getting the fine and suspension repealed through legal channels.

The ruling gave McGraw carte blanche to continue his tantrums. Flush with the success of his 1904 championship, McGraw was not content to merely flaunt his title. In 1905, it was as if he were attempting to alienate as many opponents, umpires, reporters, and club owners as possible and notch each of them on his ever-expanding belt. Dreyfuss could only look on contemptuously and stew about how to unseat the champions.

The Pirates and Giants were in a two-way fight for the pennant most of the summer. In June, a four-game split in Pittsburgh was played in surprisingly tame fashion. However, there were a few postgame confrontations. Following one game, the Giants' carriage was bombarded with an assortment of fruits and vegetables as it passed the farmers' market en route to the team's quarters, the Monongahela House at

Smithfield and Water Streets. Some players retaliated, others took whatever cover they could find. Shortstop Bill Dahlen was the only one hurt in the salvo when a well-aimed cantaloupe found his head.

Dreyfuss pouted through the remainder of the 1905 campaign. Brush approached Dreyfuss after one contest, but the Pirate president refused to shake hands, and *Sporting Life* noted that he "gave [Brush] one withering look of contempt and promptly told [him] to go to a place where snow balls are unknown." Dreyfuss even gave his old friend Pulliam the cold shoulder when he came to town. But the most unpleasant hour of the summer came when a priest, Father Walsh, wandered into Dreyfuss's private booth at the ballpark. Dreyfuss was certainly not a man prone to violence, but when he threatened to push the clergyman out of the area, Father Walsh decked him. Within a few days, the local bishop instructed his priests that they were no longer to attend games at Exposition Park.

◆ ◆ ◆

The Pirates were clinging to second place, seven games behind the Giants, when they opened a four-game series at the Polo Grounds on July 15. New York fans serenaded Dreyfuss to choruses of "Hey Barney," a cry he would become familiar with around the league. The Pirates rallied for five seventh-inning runs, but the Giants tallied two in the ninth to win 8–7. In game two, another Bowerman-Clarke bout was barely avoided. Phillippe, on his way to twenty-two wins after a poor 1904 season, threw a four-hitter and had a 1–0 lead in the eighth when Wagner's two-run homer onto the elevated railway tracks beyond the left field bleachers secured a 3–0 win. The following day, six Giants were tossed out of the coaching box, and Clarke barreled over Mathewson on a play at first base. It took Mathewson a few minutes to recover, but he remained in the game and lost 2–1.

On July 19, the Pirates pulled to within five games of first by overcoming a 5–2 deficit and winning 8–5. Umpire Klem was once again in the middle of the affair. After tossing Dan McGann and Mike Donlin out of the game for abusive behavior, Klem needed to dodge a shower of beer glasses and bottles hurled from the stands. *The Pittsburg Dispatch* printed: "There were at least a dozen policemen in the immediate vicinity, but they took no steps to protect Klem. He stood his ground, and in a few minutes the crowd in the bleachers ran out of ammunition, and the attack ended."

Wagner was having another fabulous year, but he also had his share of run-ins with umpires. After being ejected from one game, he trudged off the field holding his nose—a display that cost him a three-day suspension and thirty-dollar fine. On August 2, when the Giants came to Pittsburgh riding a twelve-game winning streak, Wagner was at the center of a storm in the first matchup. In the fourth inning, he tapped a two-out roller to the first baseman, and Mathewson was slow to cover the bag. The play at first was described as everything from extremely close to Wagner being out by two steps, and base umpire George Bausewine signaled "out." Wagner protested the call and continued to snort his disapproval as he took his position.

As the ball was being tossed around the infield, Wagner wound up and threw a bullet over first baseman Del Howard's head that landed five feet from Bausewine. The umpire, feeling Wagner's poor aim was deliberate, ordered him off the grounds. The Pirate players protested that the ball just got away from Wagner, but as Honus left the premises, fans who were already keyed up for the important series became belligerent. One man was dragged from the stands after launching a bottle in Bausewine's direction, and a howl went up when Wagner's replacement, Tommy Leach, sent yet another practice throw over Howard's head a few moments later.

The Giants held on for their thirteenth straight win and pushed the Pirates ten and a half games back. But Pittsburgh won the next two, and in the final game of the series on August 5, tempers exploded. With the score 5–5 in the bottom of the ninth, Ritchey led off with a double. Mathewson fielded a bunt in front of the plate and tried to nab Ritchey at third with a throw. Bausewine ruled Ritchey safe and the Giants went into an uproar. A few Giants jostled Bausewine before the umpire pulled a watch from his pocket and gave them one minute to resume play. McGraw threatened Bausewine, Mathewson tried to knock the watch from the umpire's hand, and the players carried on until Bausewine declared the game a forfeit.

By now, several hundred of the overflow crowd of at least eighteen thousand were on the field, screaming "Quitters!" and much worse at McGraw's men. A police detail and several Pirate players set up a line of protection around the Giants as they were slowly led from the park to their carriages. Yellow blankets proclaiming NEW YORK CHAMPIONS were ripped from the horses' backs, and stones and chunks of mud cascaded on top of the vehicles until the team was across the bridge into Pittsburgh.

◆ ◆ ◆

Appalled that he was accused of such a "cowardly act," Wagner prepared a case for a hearing on his errant throw. Clarke, of course, came to the defense of his shortstop, saying that if Wagner had "tried to hit the umpire, Bausewine would have more than his own imagination to show for the deed now." Pulliam suspended Wagner for three days and fined him forty dollars. While he watched, his teammates were hardly on their best behavior. At one point, the entire Pirate bench was ejected for mocking Klem's flamboyant style of signaling balls and strikes. It cost each offender ten dollars.

Nine games out in late August, the Pirates began a furious rush. Wagner went on a tear at the plate that led the Pirates to twenty wins in twenty-three games—with three tough defeats. Riding an eleven-game winning streak, the Pirates lost on September 3. Phillippe and the Cubs' Bob Wicker held a scoreless duel for eleven innings, allowing just three hits apiece before the Cubs pushed a run across. Five days later, the Pirates slammed fifteen hits and received eight walks from Cincinnati pitching but left a still-standing National League record eighteen men on base, losing 8–3. And on September 12, the Cardinals Harry Arndt stole home in the ninth inning to beat the Pirates 2–1. Jack Taylor, now a Cardinal, surrendered just three hits—all were Wagner singles. It was one of three times in his career that Honus spoiled an opponent's no-hitter—the others coming on May 27, 1911, versus Art Fromme, and on October 2, 1914, versus Phil Douglas.

The three-week stretch pulled the Pirates to within five of first, but it was not enough. Sluggers Mike Donlin, Dan McGann, and Sam Mertes braced a Giants' offense that led the league in runs, batting average, and stolen bases. Led by Mathewson at 31–8, the pitching staff had four other pitchers in double-figure wins: McGinnity had twenty-one, Leon "Red" Ames had twenty-two, and both Hooks Wiltse and Dummy Taylor chipped in with fifteen. New York finished 105–48 and waltzed home nine games ahead of the Pirates, at a commendable 96–57.

Wagner and Cincinnati's Cy Seymour, the pitcher turned outfielder, battled for the batting crown the entire summer. Both hitters increased their averages and performed well in seven head-to-head matchups in the last month of the season. On the final day in Cincinnati, Seymour was all but assured of the title, and the two combatants met at home plate, shaking hands amid the cheers of the Reds' fans. Seymour drove out four hits in a doubleheader to dethrone Wagner, .377 to .363. In by far his best big league year, Seymour not only snatched Wagner's batting title but led the league in slugging average, hits, doubles, triples, and total bases. Wagner had to settle for finishing second or third in seven different offensive categories. His crown as the king of National League batsmen was under no serious challenge, but he would answer any questions by winning the next four batting championships.

◆　◆　◆

In 1905, the National Commission set up guidelines for a best-of-seven World Series, preventing the McGraw and Brush postseason shenanigans of the previous year. The Giants and Connie Mack's American League champion Philadelphia Athletics squared off in mid-October. The Athletics did little to quiet McGraw's boasts of superiority, losing four games to one.

Dreyfuss was in much better spirits after the season. It had been another profitable summer, and the future of his team—and all of big league baseball for that matter—appeared promising. He recently had moved the Pirate administration office to the prestigious Farmers Bank Building—at twenty-four stories, the tallest building in the city. (Pittsburgh was among the leaders in the steel frame "revolution" and was now home to several structures of skyscraper height. The Pittsburgh *Bulletin* applauded, "Let them multiply," adding, "There is no sky in the world which needs scraping more than that which arches over the Iron City.") At the winter meetings, Dreyfuss would nominate Pulliam for reelection and in October even allowed the Pirate players to keep all the revenue from their barnstorming trip.

Wagner was managing the Pirate troupe, and after the World Series, he challenged the champion Giants to a showdown and invited the Athletics to play for the championship of Pennsylvania. His proposals were not taken very seriously, and the barnstormers disbanded in mid-month.

◆　◆　◆

Wagner had a true love for animals. His dogs often ran loose and their owner made them newsworthy. When one of his non-pedigrees, named Patsy, was seen begging at a local restaurant, it was thought to be cute. Local papers reported the losses of prized dogs, such as when his imported Irish terrier was hit by a train and when his foxhound was poisoned—a crime for which Wagner offered a hundred-dollar reward for the arrest of the culprit.

He also kept a few horses at his residence and dabbled in ownership of harness-racing pacers. He purchased a fine "fast stepper" to pull his rig—a sleigh in the winter and buggy in the summer. When it paraded through a lemonade stand at the county fair, the proprietors refused to accept any compensation for the damages, saying it was an honor to have Wagner's horse "pay them a visit."

A Carnegie band leader wrote and performed a march and two-step called "Husky Hans," dedicated to "the greatest of all players." Twenty-five-cent sheet music featuring a photograph and facsimile autograph of the subject was available for purchase through the *Carnegie Union,* and soon most every community concert around the Pittsburgh area included a rendition of the number. Even John Philip Sousa, the renowned March King, added the tune to his repertoire for his Pittsburgh performances.

Wagner was such an attraction that some claimed his presence would guarantee an additional one hundred admissions to *any* event. At exhibitions in rural cities and towns where residents could only read about big league baseball, many people turned out just to get a glimpse of Wagner. He was coerced into field events competitions and obligated to make an appearance when the train made a whistle stop. Some town teams scheduled games with the Pirates under the condition that Wagner would have to play in order for the Pirates to get their money. If Wagner was hurt or chose to sit out, fans sometimes became testy. At one exhibition game in Newark, Ohio, when Wagner was a no-show due to treatment for an injury, one man screamed, "Where is Wagner? We paid our money and we want to see him!"

Most fans wanted him to crush the ball as they had heard or read about, but they would cheer excitely if a local hotshot could strike out Wagner. Around the National League circuit, opposing teams' followers had much the same reaction—wanting to see the great Wagner perform as they knew he could and gushing with joy when he struck out at the hands of one of their own.

Uncomfortable and occasionally complaining about intrusions into his privacy, Wagner mostly accepted his fate. Now and then during barnstorming exhibitions, he would have some fun playing to the crowds, acting, as Leach depicted, like a "big boy." Wagner might take the field without his glove and amaze by stopping sharp grounders anyway. Once, when he was hit in the foot with a ground ball, he delighted the fans by removing his glove and slipping it over his toes. He was always much more at ease with this type of on-field fun than the required formal social functions.

Though regarded as amicable, Wagner got along best with people who expected little more from him than baseball brilliance. It was a fact that both Dreyfuss and Clarke understood, and they rarely placed too many demands on their star.

In the spring of 1906, Al and Honus were early arrivals to Hot Springs. By now, the younger Wagner was pretty much on his own as far as workouts and was only required to join the others when there was a game or for the daily team meeting in Clarke's room—year after year, fittingly, in Room 101. It was a privilege Clarke afforded the respected veterans, like Wagner and Leach. Most of the training regimen was mundane anyway. Clarke tried to toss in a few activities without success. Leapfrog lasted just one day and football just one play when Wagner ran ninety-five yards for a touchdown, knocking a few teammates flat along the way.

Wagner liked to have some fun hazing the younger players. On the field, one of his favorites was to catch a recruit in a seemingly endless rundown. Wagner and a few teammates would toss the ball back and forth with no tag until the runner's tongue was practically hanging to the ground. In the hotels, Wagner's standby caper—which caught more than one unsuspecting greenhorn—was to pen a flowery and perfumed letter with the signature of "Miss Sadie," asking for an encounter with the youngster. Wagner and his cronies would then gather at the meeting spot and, if their victim swallowed the bait, laugh unmercifully at his expense.

◆ ◆ ◆

Pittsburgh franchise attendance records were shattered in April 1906 as most fans envisioned another Pirates-Giants pennant race. Prior to one game, the two adversaries buried the hatchet long enough to have some moving pictures filmed, including one interesting scene in which Clarke feigned a steal of home against Bowerman. However, the rivalry with New York continued as fierce as ever. The Giants arrived in Pittsburgh for the first time on Wednesday, May 16, sporting their all-black road uniforms that had the local fans referring to them as "undertakers" and "blackbirds." The Pirates won handily, 11–0, ripping fifteen hits, including four Leach singles. Sinkerballing right-hander Vic Willis, obtained from Boston in December 1905 for a trio of players including Del Howard, threw his first of three straight shutouts. It began a stretch in which the staff would blank opponents in six of the next nine games on the way to a still-standing club-record twenty-six shutouts in one season.

The next afternoon, Leever faced just twenty-seven batters and allowed only three baserunners as he bested the Giants 3–0. As the visiting players headed from Exposition Park into Pittsburgh over the Sixth Street Bridge, a number of boys followed alongside in a wagon, teasing the Giants about their defeat. McGraw snatched the carriage driver's whip and slapped thirteen-year-old Earl Brady across the face. He was knocked out of the vehicle and run over by the rear wheels of the wagon. The boy was not hurt badly and his father, after filing charges against McGraw, settled for the manager's agreement to pay for the boy's doctor bill.

In the Friday, May 18 contest, Wagner paced a fourteen-hit attack with two singles and a triple as the Pirates beat Mathewson, who was suffering from diphtheria early in the season. The Giants were trailing 7–6 but had the winning runs on base in the eighth as Wagner nonchalantly strolled past second base and caught Bill Dahlen off the bag with the hidden ball trick. McGraw fined Dahlen a stiff one hundred dollars for ruining the rally by falling for Wagner's chicanery—a penalty McGraw later rescinded.

Clarke missed the series with an injured right shoulder and managed the first three games—three Pirate wins—from the bench before leaving town for treatment. Wagner took charge for Saturday's contest, and the Pirates lost 5–1 in front of more than sixteen thousand fans. But they had taken three of four from the Giants and moved to within five and a half games of the leading Chicago Cubs.

◆ ◆ ◆

Under a rapidly darkening sky in Philadelphia on June 9, umpire Klem insisted that the objecting Phillies take the field for the eighth inning with a 1–0 lead. As the Pirates began to rally, the Phillies stalled, refusing to make any attempt to put the baserunners out and hoping the rain clouds would open so the score would revert to that of the seventh inning. The Pirates tallied seven runs, five of them virtually uncontested, before Klem declared a forfeit to Pittsburgh for the defensive players' inaction. The fans were incensed, and target practice ensued at Klem's expense. The following day, Philadelphia columnist Charles Dryden reported that "valiant and eagle-eyed Wagner" rushed to the umpire's side and began "blazing away at bottles and cushions with his trusty bat. Being a great hitter, Hans never missed."

Four decades later, Klem recalled, "I can still see a wild-eyed Philadelphia fan poised on the edge of a box preparing to jump on me. . . .

As he coiled for the spring a ballplayer, bat in hand, stepped beside me and yelled, 'If you jump, mister, I'll knock your head off with this bat.' " Klem continued, "My protector was Hans Wagner, as great a man as he was a ballplayer. He was the best I ever saw—and I saw them all in the last sixty years."

With Wagner as his escort, Klem was ushered to safety. The fans then turned their wrath to the Pirate players, pummeling their carriage as it exited the park. Clarke was outraged that his blameless squad was subjected to the bombardment. Within two weeks, the National League directors instructed all clubs to provide dressing quarters for opponents in order to discourage this type of violence, although some of the accommodations were so primitive that the players still chose to dress at their hotel. Clarke had his own method of retaliation: Two days after the incident, he stroked five hits and scored the winning run in the tenth inning on Wagner's double. (Clarke's 5 for 5 performance was one of nine five-hit games in his career, placing him among the all-time leaders.)

In addition to saving Klem from the vicious onslaught, Wagner had a tremendous spurt in June that moved him into the batting lead at .342. Beaumont, suffering with a recurring leg injury, returned early in the month and hit .347 in eighteen games despite being terribly overweight from inactivity. Leach brought his average up to .321, fifth best in the circuit. Pittsburgh now led the league in batting and, combined with a number of fine pitching performances, particularly a one-hitter by Albert "Lefty" Leifield, it put the Pirates at 42–20, only two games behind the Chicago Cubs at the end of June.

Though Chicago had played over .600 baseball and won more than ninety games in each of the past two seasons, finishing second in 1904 and third in 1905, Clarke remained unimpressed. He insisted the race for the National League flag was between Pittsburgh and New York, saying, "Chicago has shot its bolt and we are not afraid of them." But within a few days, after the Cubs bombed the Giants by scores of 19–0, 6–0, and 11–3, it was beginning to become clear that Chicago was a powerhouse in 1906.

In the middle of the previous season, Cub manager Frank Selee, ill with tuberculosis, turned over the leadership of the developing squad to talented first baseman Frank Chance. Chance inherited a young keystone combination in shortstop Joe Tinker and tiny, feisty second baseman Johnny Evers, fine outfielders Jimmy Slagle and Frank "Wildfire"

Schulte, one of the game's premier catchers in Johnny Kling, and a marvelous pitching staff led by Mordecai Brown.

Brown was referred to both as Miner, due to his coal mining experience, and as Three-Finger, because of the missing index finger and mangled third digit of his right hand from a farm accident as a youth. Not only overcoming but capitalizing on the disfigurement of his pitching hand to throw a sharp curveball, Brown was now in his fourth big league season of a wonderful Hall of Fame career. In 1906 he was dominant, tossing ten shutouts on his way to a 26–6 mark, allowing an amazingly few 1.04 earned runs per game.

The Cubs decisively swept a four-game series from the Pirates in September and ended the season with a 16–5 mark against Pittsburgh. Brown hurled a one-hitter, and the Cubs' staff held Pittsburgh to fourteen hits over the four games. By the end of the year, the Cubs made believers out of most everybody. At 116–36, Chicago's 1906 winning percentage of .763 is a twentieth-century record. Finishing twenty games ahead of New York and twenty-three and a half out in front of Pittsburgh, the mighty Cubs were stunned in the World Series as their American League and crosstown rivals, the underdog White Sox, triumphed four games to two.

Wagner won his fourth batting title at .339, ninety-five points above the league average. He also led the circuit in doubles with 38, total bases with 237, runs with 103 and finished among the leaders in slugging, hits, and steals. A series of ailments, including a painful hip and sore back diagnosed as rheumatism, hampered Wagner down the stretch.

At Dreyfuss's urging, Wagner headed for Hot Springs to recuperate in the mineral baths. In one of his most lengthy voluntary trips away from Carnegie, Wagner remained in Arkansas for almost two months, accompanied by his brother Al and a few friends. Despite nothing more strenuous than strolling through the carnival district of the active resort community and tramping through the woods of the Ouachita Mountains in search of birds, Honus was said to be walking like "an old woman with corns and bunions on both feet" when he returned home in December.

◆ ◆ ◆

After three years of looking up at his arch rivals from New York, Dreyfuss thought his team had too many "capitalists" who no longer needed baseball as a means to make a living. In December, he pulled the trigger on a blockbuster trade, sending Ritchey, Beaumont, and the rights to Flaherty to Boston for infielder Ed Abbaticchio.

In 1906, Ritchey had led the league in fielding percentage for the fourth time in the last five years and was his usual steady if unspectacular self. But Dreyfuss questioned the second baseman's work habits and wondered how much longer he would desire to play since his oil wells were producing substantial personal wealth. Beaumont, whose name was not revealed as part of the deal until the following spring, was also said to be financially comfortable from an expanding dairy business in his home state of Wisconsin. He had played in every inning of the 1903 season and led the league in at bats and hits in 1903 and 1904. But leg injuries cut into his last two campaigns, and since he could not run regularly, he gained weight on an already pudgy physique. When he returned to the lineup in the second half of 1906, the ordinarily speedy Beaumont stole just a single base, and Dreyfuss outwardly criticized the outfielder's lack of hustle. Flaherty, who spent 1906 in minor league Columbus, Ohio, would win twelve games for Boston in each of the next two years before settling into a long career as a minor league manager and major league scout.

Ed Abbaticchio was the first notable Italian American major leaguer, a characteristic that would not have been lost on the growing segment of Italian immigrants in Pittsburgh. At the age of twenty-nine, he was a veteran of three undistinguished full seasons. Since Pennsylvania law forbade absentee ownership of a liquor license, he sat out the entire 1906 season in order to oversee his lucrative hotel and restaurant business in Latrobe, Pennsylvania, roughly thirty-five miles from Pittsburgh. Abbaticchio let it be known that the only team he would agree to play for was Pittsburgh, and despite seemingly holding all the cards, Dreyfuss forked over quite a price to secure a less than star-caliber player. The deal had some people thinking that Dreyfuss was trying to help out his old friends from back in Paducah, Kentucky, George and John Dovey, who were now owners of the Boston National League team.

With the coming of the new year, Wagner was feeling much better, and after participating in a reduced basketball schedule, he pronounced himself fit. In February, a new 250-egg incubator arrived and on March 5, he filled it with White Wyandotte eggs. After carefully explaining the temperature controls and procedures to his father, Wagner and his brother joined the Pirates in Hot Springs seven days late. Worried that something would go wrong during the three-week incubation period, Wagner was relieved to hear from his father that more than a hundred chicks had hatched and more were arriving by the hour. On road trips for the next few years, it was common for Wagner to receive news from Carnegie about the activity of his chickens.

Perhaps preoccupied with his new investment, he made four errors over the first two games of the season and was off to a slow start at the plate. With the Giants and Cubs both off to fine starts, the Pirates found themselves eight games out by mid-May.

Wagner soon righted himself. He had a pair of 5 for 5 games, one of which included a double, homer, and two stolen bases. Showing no regard for his friends, he hit two of his season total of six home runs off Flaherty and, on another day, ruined his shutout with a ninth-inning triple. Wagner also went 4 for 5 with a homer off Ed Karger, who during his brief stay with the Pirates the previous year boarded with Wagner's sister and brother-in-law. Later in the summer, Karger etched his name in the record books in an otherwise unillustrious career by tossing a seven-inning perfect game for St. Louis.

Wagner saved an extra-inning game against New York in June by making a fine stop over the second base bag and then throwing a runner out while lying on his back. The following day, *The Pittsburg Dispatch* mentioned, "It now remains for Wagner to make a stop and throw while standing on his head. He has done nearly everything else."

On June 20, he smacked what some sources reported as the longest hit in Exposition Park history. Despite launching a line drive over the center fielder's head that stopped at the farthest reaches of the park, Wagner only made it to third. Veteran Kid Gleason, nearing the end of a fine career and playing first base for the Phillies that day, clipped Wagner as he passed the bag, and Honus limped to third before pulling up lame. His friend Harry Smith, after missing almost all of the previous two years, pinch ran, and although Smith's name was left out of the game's box score, he crossed the plate a moment later on a fly ball. The Phillies generously allowed Wagner to return to shortstop for the rest of the contest, but within a few days, his leg bothered him so badly that he could only serve as a vociferous coacher for three games.

◆ ◆ ◆

As a ninety-one-year-old gentleman in 1971, Homer Hillebrand looked back at his short career with the Pirates and related one special memory: He had provided Wagner with a buggy ride from Pittsburgh to Carnegie. Upon arriving at the Railroad Avenue address, Wagner admired Hillebrand's horse and challenged him to a race. Wagner pulled his rig

and pacer from a small stable and the contest was on. Hillebrand remembered that he had a buggy-length lead before he and Wagner had to
slow the horses down in order to cross an old single-lane bridge.

Wagner loved the speed and daring of racing his horse, and it was
only natural for him to turn his attention to the new hobby of "automobiling." In midsummer of 1907, he purchased a luxurious, five-passenger
Jackson model, which he decorated by hanging a squirrel tail from the
lantern, "just for luck." If he had a mind to obey the speed restrictions in
Carnegie, he would have kept busy with calculations. The rule read that
it was illegal to exceed a pace of one mile every six minutes inside the
city limits and one mile every three minutes outside the city limits.

Wagner had formed a friendship several years earlier with industrialist Henry Ford, who used to take Wagner on rides in the inventor's
contraptions through Central Park when the Pirates were in New York.
"He gave me the automobile bug," Wagner later recalled. "Henry used to
stand on the running board, adjusting the carburetor, and had me steer-
ing." Wagner's first car was a one-cylinder, "one-lunger" Cadillac, originally manufactured by the Henry Ford Company.

Automobiles were still considered an extravagance in 1907, although their popularity would begin to burgeon the following year with
Ford's introduction of the relatively affordable ($850) Model T. Wagner
was already a devotee, though his early driving was not without incident, including a collision with a railroad gate and an encounter in
which his auto spooked a horse over an embankment, spilling its buggy
and driver into a ditch. The news of these and similar events by other
players led to the chastising of the more affluent in baseball for flashing
their wealth and taking undue risk with automobiles. Despite the criticism and his otherwise modest lifestyle, Wagner's passion for cars would
become well known. His grand entrances in his auto at events around
Pittsburgh and his habit of renting or borrowing cars to tour Central
Park while in New York became the subject for many newspaper stories.
One contrived report had Wagner writing a $4,500 check for an auto on
a road trip, only to sell the car for $5,000 before leaving town. While not
all of the tales were true, his zeal for "automobiling" would endure.

◆　◆　◆

The Chicago Cubs were simply invincible again in 1907, running out to
an overwhelming lead by midyear. The Pirates had to settle for a fight
for the runner-up spot—a battle that took on added significance since it
was against New York. Dreyfuss offered each player a five-hundred-dol-

lar bonus for a second-place finish, and through most of the summer, the Giants and Pirates were neck and neck.

Wagner wrecked McGraw's team down the stretch. In a late-August series, he doubled and scored a tenth-inning run in one game, stroked a double and two triples off Mathewson in another, and the following day, in front of an appreciative New York audience, went 4 for 4 with another triple. Then, against New York on September 25, as Clarke stole four bases for the only time in his career, Wagner also collected four, including second, third, and home in the second inning.

A few days earlier, on September 20, Wagner had contributed to a historic moment in Pirate history. Twenty-year-old right-hander Nick Maddox was making only his third big league appearance since being acquired by the Pirates after tossing a pair of no-hitters for Wheeling's Central League club that summer. He held Brooklyn hitless for eight and two thirds when Wagner's stunning game-ending play on a short hop clinched the franchise's first nine-inning no-hitter.

The Giants' late-season swoon allowed the Phillies to slip into third. The Pirates easily secured second place with a 91–63 record, a full seventeen games behind Chicago, who this year convincingly swept four games in the World Series from the Detroit Tigers.

Much of the Pirates' success in 1907, not to mention their bonuses, was due to Wagner's individual work. His efforts and contributions to the Pittsburgh nine were certainly not lost on baseball men. Clarke, turning thirty-five years old after yet another fine season, called his shortstop "the best ballplayer that ever stood in shoes." Clarke also issued a challenge to back his opinion saying, "I will wager one thousand dollars on Hans to beat any player in the world in an all-round contest, to consist of anything which takes in running, throwing, bunting, fungo hitting, throwing for accuracy, catching grounders, throwing for distance, a run around the bases, or any other thing they might desire."

The Pirates' competitors also recognized what they were seeing. John McGraw rarely handed out praise of players, including his own, but he always thought highly of Wagner. On one 1907 visit to Pittsburgh, McGraw openly shared his opinions with a few of the local scribes, saying:

> Wagner is just in a class by himself, and that is all there is to it.
> . . . I have often thought that Hans has not been properly appreciated here in Pittsburgh, but the fans in other cities throw spasms every time he makes a play. And, what is more, every

ballplayer in the land, as well as every manager and club owner, knows the real value of such a player to a club, and they all take off their hats to the big German. . . . His equal has never been known. . . . Wagner is a whole team in himself.

McGraw's opinion of the man he battled so fiercely over the years never wavered. In the feisty manager's 1923 book *My Thirty Years in Baseball*, he pointed out that "Hans Wagner was also blessed with that peculiar thing which for a better name we call personality. There was something magnetic about him." McGraw predicted, "[He] will go down in baseball history as the greatest of all time."

Wagner had one of his finest seasons in 1907, winning his fifth batting title—his fourth in the last five years. In a season where only four hitters were in the .300 class, including Leach and former teammate Beaumont, Wagner's .350 was 107 points higher than the league average. He led the circuit in doubles, total bases, and slugging and was just off the pace in triples, runs, and hits. And his aggressive baserunning led to a career-high total of sixty-one stolen bases—fifteen more than the runner up.

Just as in the previous year, though, his season ended with an injury. On September 27, a Frank "Rube" Dessau pitch cracked two bones in Wagner's left hand, and Honus watched the last twelve games from the bench.

SEVEN

UNFULFILLED PROMISES

Concerned about how the broken bones in his left hand were mending, Wagner found himself in the disagreeable role of spectator and drawing card as the Pirates barnstormed over the last few weeks of October 1907. The only bright moment in this drudgery for him was the traditional game against the Fosters of Carnegie. He was presented with a solid-gold medal decorated with a finely cut diamond in recognition of his 1907 batting title. Wagner wore the citation all afternoon, and he and Al umpired the exhibition before the day's honoree, with his healthy right hand, capped off the event by pitching the final inning.

Wagner's bones did heal, but the emotional impact of the injury lingered. On Tuesday, December 10, 1907, various newspapers announced that the great shortstop had played his last game. The *New York American* concluded that "Wagner is almost crippled with the rheumatism, which has settled in his right arm and shoulder" and disclosed that his doctor recommended that he quit baseball. Wagner, expressing no regret, explained, "I'm comfortably fixed financially, and I'm ready to quit. My old friend, the M.D., settled it for me yesterday. I am out of professional baseball for good." The Pittsburgh papers treated this news lightly. "If Wagner is going to quit anything let him quit kidding," wrote *The Pittsburg Dispatch* sports editor.

That same day Wagner received a telegram from President Pulliam urging him to come to New York, where the league meetings were currently being held. Pulliam had booked this year's event for the Waldorf-Astoria to celebrate the most successful year financially in National League history—all eight teams had been profitable. Wagner dreaded the attention that surely would be brought on by his announced retirement. However, after much persuasion and unable to find a suitable excuse, he departed for New York accompanied by Al and friend James Orris. The next evening, Wagner found himself the esteemed guest at a dinner for the World Champion Cubs. His feat of becoming the first player ever to win five National League batting championships was rewarded with the presentation of a silver loving cup. When Wagner responded to the toast by expressing his intention to earn a sixth title in 1908, the retirement issue was forgotten—for the time being.

Two months later, just two days before his thirty-fourth birthday, *The Pittsburg Dispatch* ran the following item hidden among other baseball news: "A report has gained circulation in Carnegie, the home of Honus Wagner, that the famous shortstop will not play this year. . . . Wagner's reason for not wanting to play this year is said to be that he wishes to rest . . . and that he is going into the poultry business."

This news was again dismissed, and even the Pirates did not seem concerned. A March 2 article in *The Pittsburg Dispatch* with a subhead "Not Alarmed About Wagner" quoted Dreyfuss as saying, "Oh, I am not losing any sleep over the threats which it is claimed have emanated from the lips of the great player. . . . I have an idea that if he does not accompany the team when it leaves for [spring training] that he will be there a week later, and that when the season opens he will be found repeating his famous diamond stunts, clad in a Pittsburg uniform."

Hans Lobert, now an established big leaguer with the Reds, eloquently said, "When the 'all-aboard' is called, [Wagner] invariably is there with his telescope, valise, and bag full of doughnuts."

✦ ✦ ✦

Clarke arrived in Pittsburgh on March 12, allowing himself only two days prior to the team's departure for spring training to address a number of contract problems. He and Dreyfuss were faced with the retirements of first-string catcher George Gibson, who planned on moving to

Chicago to enter business with his cousin, and Honus Wagner, who wanted to rest and raise chickens.

In addition, Tommy Leach was a holdout. The Cincinnati Reds' Garry Herrmann, dissatisfied with back-to-back sixth-place finishes under Ned Hanlon, expressed an interest in placing Leach at the helm. One Pirate official declared that Leach "would make good as manager of any team." Buoyed by such praise, he seemed to fancy his own managerial talents. Primarily an outfielder in 1907 (111 of his 149 games), Leach continued to bounce around the diamond as needed, playing third, short, and second while achieving new career highs in games, hits, runs, and stolen bases. Dreyfuss, making it known that he wanted fair compensation if he let Leach become Cincinnati's manager, turned the negotiations over to Clarke, where they soon broke down.

Leach was already disgruntled that his "wartime" salary had been cut a few years earlier and, now realizing his value to the Pittsburgh club, wanted fair compensation himself—a 15 percent raise. At one point, he suggested that a panel of arbiters settle the salary difference and proposed to have three Pittsburgh businessmen decide the issue. Leach would pick one man, and Dreyfuss another, and the two arbiters would select a third man. This novel idea was politely declined by Dreyfuss and derided by the press as "unbusinesslike." (Sixty-five years later, salary arbitration would become a reality in major league baseball.) At a time when management dominated labor throughout industry and the average working man was feeling the effects of a 1907 economic downturn, Pittsburghers showed little sympathy for Leach's position. When Leach finally agreed to the terms offered him, he asked for assurance that he would not have to play third base. Lacking a viable alternative, Clarke would end up using him at the hot corner in all but two games.

With Leach in the fold, Pirate management turned its attention to the others. At Wagner's invitation, Clarke spent an evening in Carnegie. Evasive about the baseball discussed, Clarke would only share that "Wagner is just as fine an entertainer as he is a ballplayer, and that is saying a great deal." Perhaps Clarke's unwillingness to discuss the contract situation should have served as a warning, but it still came as a shock to the populace the next day when the front page of *The Pittsburg Dispatch* announced HANS WAGNER, GREATEST PLAYER, RETIRES FROM GAME. A letter from Wagner to Dreyfuss added a sense of formality and finality to the bulletin:

My Dear Barney,

I will not be with your team this season, but wish you a pennant winner and will always be plugging for Cap and the boys to win.

It is certainly hard for me to lay aside the uniform which I have been wearing since 1897, but every dog has his day, and the sport has become too strenuous for me.

I can look back and see that I was lucky in landing with you in Louisville, and that I made no mistake in staying with your Pittsburg team during war times. I was offered nearly double the amount I asked from you then, but I have been a gainer by it, as my salary has always remained the same. Besides, I have had the satisfaction of knowing that my boss appreciated the fact that I always gave the club the best I had.

I wish to thank you for your treatment of me while a member of your team, and assure you that I highly appreciate the same. Again, wishing you success, I am

Very truly yours,
John H. Wagner

Dreyfuss clung to the hope he could dissuade Wagner from retirement but was humbled by the tone of his letter, saying, "He could have gained temporary financial advancement by being disloyal. He stated in his letter to me that he did not lose anything by sticking to the Pittsburgh club. His appreciation of that fact gives me a great deal of satisfaction."

Wagner was at Union Station to wish the team well as it departed on Saturday evening, March 14. As Dreyfuss and Clarke boarded, they were now convinced of Wagner's sincere intentions, having exhausted all attempts to induce him to play. The proposals they made to him included the option to forego spring training and a lavish annual salary of ten thousand dollars for each of the next three years, which would make him the highest paid player in the major leagues. As he declined these offers, letters and propositions arrived daily from around the country. Correspondences from friends and strangers pleading with him to get back into the game, promoting business opportunities, and promising surefire rheumatism cures were arriving in such great quantities that the local mail carrier claimed to be working overtime. The only overture that Wagner pursued was to visit the campus of Carnegie Technical Institute and discuss the finer points of baseball with its college nine.

Not happy with Wagner's given reasons for sitting out, the press began searching for the real motive, or a scapegoat. Many "in the know" attributed his refusal to play to the roasting he received by the multitude of gamblers who populated the stands at Exposition Park. Another theory had Wagner to be married shortly after Easter to an "estimable Carnegie lady" and taking a one-year honeymoon. Frank Chance, submitting his definitive reason, contended that Wagner and Clarke were engaged in a bitter feud. In answer to these charges and to queries about whether he would return, Wagner's only response was that the game had become too strenuous for him and he wanted to rest. Throughout what the *Carnegie Union* described as the Wagnerian Period, no one seemed to feel, or would publicly state, that Wagner's goal was purely more money.

◆ ◆ ◆

Dreyfuss was back in Pittsburgh, ostensibly for personal business. While home,he found Gibson willing to relent and sign his contract. Fans were pleased to hear of this development and overjoyed when the news broke that Wagner, although still not under contract, was to join the team at Winfield, Kansas. Insisting that he planned to rest for the year, Wagner only acknowledged that he had agreed to visit Clarke's "Little Pirate Ranch" for a few days of fun, entertainment, and Clarke family hospitality. In the public's eyes, Wagner was as good as signed.

Before daybreak on April 5, the Pirate players were awakened in their berths by a series of Indian war whoops. The "attack" on their Pullman car in the Wichita, Kansas, station had them facing the outstretched hands of Wagner and Gibson. Nobody seemed to mind, but perhaps the violent wake-up call was responsible for the team dropping a 9–6 decision to Western Association Wichita as Dreyfuss and Wagner looked on. There were more unsuccessful attempts to convince him to return that evening and throughout the next day as the two spectators watched the Pirates impressively avenge their loss.

Tuesday, April 7, was a memorable day for the people of Winfield, Kansas, and the surrounding Walnut River Valley. A storm of cyclone proportions had blown through the previous night, but this day was treated as a grand festival. Stores and banks closed early, schools declared the afternoon a holiday, and the hotels were filled to capacity. The reason for the locals' celebration was that their neighbor, Fred Clarke, brought his major leaguers to town. The players were in high spirits as well, happy to be free from their cramped Pullman quarters for a few nights while they stayed in a Winfield hotel.

That morning, the players were seated on their hotel veranda when a horse-drawn surrey sped toward them, its occupants howling at the top of their lungs. The driver and his companion were fully attired in rough corduroy suits, broad-brimmed white hats, and high boots, with shooting irons strapped to their hips. It wasn't until the cowpunchers swaggered down from their rig that they were recognized as Cap and Dutch. As one player recalled, "It was a very spectacular entrance."

The severe weather the previous night kept the crowd from reaching the anticipated three thousand, but those attending the exhibition at the local fairgrounds provided an ovation for Clarke and Wagner. The team displayed pennant-contending form despite the sloppy conditions, and in his first game action of the spring, Wagner went 3 for 4 with a double and a stolen base. After the game, the Elks of Winfield made the Pirates their guests and provided a sumptuous banquet, there being no evidence that Kansas was a prohibition state.

The following day, the players boarded buggies and journeyed a few miles from Winfield to the Little Pirate Ranch, where a hunting expedition ensued, complete with a pack of hounds. Dreyfuss took the first shot of the day, missing a jackrabbit, but throughout the morning, ducks, quail, and rabbits fell victim to the posse, which returned to the ranch both hungry and proud of its accomplishments. Wagner bagged several wild ducks and was also the brunt of a practical joke set up by his host. Encouraged to shoot a "coyote" in the brush, Wagner had to face Mrs. Clarke's feigned disgust after realizing he had shot a pig. The embarrassed Wagner offered to lay aside his gun for the remainder of the visit before a burst of laughter let him know the event had been prearranged.

Following a feast served in the loft of the Clarkes' spacious new barn, the team was treated to Western-style entertainment. Clarke demonstrated his riding and lassoing skills and was followed by rope-handling experts whom he had invited in for the occasion. Even a few of the players got in on the act, with Abbaticchio and pitcher Howard Camnitz showing off their riding abilities and rookie Owen "Chief" Wilson proving his Texas heritage by skillfully handling a lariat, greatly impressing his manager. The remainder of the afternoon was spent looking over the farm and livestock, including the mules branded L.P.R. Lavish praise was heaped on the host and hostess as the group departed.

The season opener in St. Louis was now only five days away, and it seemed that the entire squad would arrive in good spirits. But Wagner baffled everyone by reiterating that he was in no condition to play and was determined to sit out the coming season as he headed east. When it was pointed out that his performance in the game at Winfield did not support this contention, Wagner responded, "Just accidents that I hit and fielded well. I never felt sorer in my life. . . ."

Unwilling to give up hope that Wagner would yield, the *Carnegie Union* attributed his return to "his solemn promise to be home for the primaries" to be held on Saturday, April 11. His interest and influence in politics, especially Republican party issues, was increasing, and political nominees were now asking for his endorsement throughout Pennsylvania, a non-suffrage state until Amendment 19 became law in 1920. For the 1908 primary election, Wagner was advocating the reelection of U.S. Senator Boies Penrose, a wealthy Philadelphian and boss of the Pennsylvania Republican Organization. Wagner was even encouraged to become a candidate for any number of political posts in Carnegie. In Pittsburgh, the transition from ball field to public office was becoming more common. Of note were two former pitchers, Ad Gumbert, sheriff of Allegheny County, and John Tener, who would win a congressional seat this very year and eventually become Pennsylvania's governor. It was proof that, while baseball was still far from refined, its practitioners were at least held in higher regard than they had been only a few years earlier.

◆ ◆ ◆

On Monday, April 13, the day before the Pirates' season was to open, news hounds found Wagner and his friend and former teammate Harry Smith relaxing in Cambridge Springs. Asked if he would play in 1908, Wagner—probably just as upset about his fishing hole being discovered as he was about being found himself—replied, "I don't know whether I will or not. Perhaps I will, perhaps I won't. Holy smoke, I came up here to get away from you fellows. I thought I was safe here, but here you light on me when I was not expecting anything of the kind. . . . Now I'm going to get a string of fish."

Tuesday's scheduled opener in St. Louis was prevented by rain. If the dismal weather and the absence of his brightest star did not spread enough gloom over manager Clarke, surely the telegram from Dreyfuss didn't help, referring to the team as the "crippled Pirates" and wishing

Clarke good luck despite the situation. The Pirates inaugurated what would prove to be a tumultuous and historical season with a three-game sweep of the Cardinals. But the news of Leever's fine three-hit shutout in the third game of the series was buried in *The Gazette Times* of Pittsburgh on April 18, whose front-page banner headline rejoiced MIGHTY HANS PLAYS BALL.

Wagner had expected to relax in Cambridge Springs but instead found himself on pins and needles. He knew that his former mates were in action in St. Louis but was unable to get scores or details while in the isolated community. His curiosity became unbearable, and he hustled back to Pittsburgh on April 16. The following afternoon at the club offices, he met with Dreyfuss and Pulliam, who had made a special trip from New York with the purpose of persuading the reigning batting champion to sign. They impressed upon Wagner how much the Pirates needed him and emphasized his responsibility to his friends and to the National League. Wagner finally caved in, agreeing to just a one-year deal at ten thousand dollars, leaving the door open for retirement the following year.

Wagner and Dreyfuss would field questions for months about the motives behind the shortstop's brief retirement and how the issue was ultimately resolved. Both would insist that salary was never an issue. Dreyfuss said that Wagner "simply made up his mind that he would rather play than not, and there was no question—no argument whatever—about the figures in his contract." Wagner declared, "I have been convinced that the team needs my services and decided to get back into the game, and that is all there is to it. There was no financial trouble or any other misunderstanding between the club and myself. I simply thought I was tired of the game and wanted to rest, but I guess I was wrong."

At the time, the press duly reported the public positions of Dreyfuss and Wagner and ignored any evidence that the issue was financially motivated. However, forty years later, veteran baseball reporter Fred Lieb wrote in his book *The Pittsburgh Pirates* that Wagner had been advised by his friend James Orris that there was money to be gained by stalling. Throughout his life, Wagner maintained that his promise to retire in 1908 was sincere and not a ploy for a raise. Nevertheless, the ten thousand dollars—a 100 percent increase over his already considerable 1907 salary and almost twenty times what the average American worker earned—made him one of the highest paid players in the history of the game.

◆ ◆ ◆

Just as the season opener had been postponed a day by rain in St. Louis, Wagner's opener also had to wait an extra day because of foul weather. On April 19, the Easter Sunday crowd of sixteen thousand fans in Cincinnati saw the Reds win their first game in four attempts and gave Wagner a welcoming cheer upon his return. For the first game, he was in the unfamiliar fifth spot in the lineup, singling once in four trips to the plate, scoring twice, and playing errorless ball at shortstop as the Pirates lost 4–3. The team lost the next two in Cincinnati to even its record at 3–3, with Wagner going 0 for 8 in the two games.

The Pirates' home debut was to be the first major league game ever played within the Pittsburgh city limits. Allegheny City, home of Exposition Park and its predecessors, Recreation and Union Parks, had been annexed by Pittsburgh in December 1907. The Pittsburgh city fathers, eyeing additional tax revenue, land mass, and prestige, finally won a bitter forty-year battle to absorb their reluctant neighbor across the Allegheny River. The annexation gave Pittsburgh a population in excess of six hundred thousand and made it the nation's sixth-largest city.

Club owners were beginning to believe that the game had become big enough on its own merit and, according to Dreyfuss, "red fire" advertising tactics were no longer needed. So, for the first time since 1882, no opening-day parade was held, but the omission was hardly noticed as more than thirteen thousand people were on hand. The players showed off their new uniforms, which included an interlocking P-B-C monogram on the left sleeve signifying Pittsburg Baseball Club. The repeating maroon bands from the championship years of 1901, 1902, and 1903 made a comeback on their blue stockings. "I am not superstitious, but . . ." was Clarke's only response when asked about the return of this pennant-winning pattern.

The fans enjoyed the band's selection of "I Was Only Teasing You" when Wagner came to the plate in the first inning, but he popped out in the middle of a two-run rally. After a third-inning bounce out, he hit a two-out double to right-center in the fifth to score two runs. The Pirates eased to a 5–1 win and Pulliam, visiting from New York, breathed a sigh of relief for the National League that Wagner was back.

◆ ◆ ◆

With the conduciveness to spring flooding at Exposition Park, Dreyfuss was happy to open the season on the road in exchange for an additional holiday date in Pittsburgh. But the weather in the spring of 1908 was unpleasant for much of the nation—at least major league baseball country stretching from Boston to St. Louis. The Pirates would have a total of fifteen games rescheduled due to rain and cold in just the first five and a half weeks. Between April 26 and May 9, the team would play only three times and have ten games postponed.

The severe weather gave rise to Dreyfuss purchasing a tarpaulin of brown paraffined duck from the Pittsburgh Waterproof Company for two thousand dollars. It was alternately referred to as a "protector," "canvas tent," and "raincoat for baseball diamonds." If necessary, the tarpaulin could be stretched across the infield in a matter of minutes. However, as *Sporting Life* wisely noted, "It will keep off the rain, but not the Ohio River."

◆ ◆ ◆

Frank Chance's 1908 Cubs were virtually identical to the 1906–07 juggernaut that rolled to consecutive National League championships. They were off to a quick start again and already held first place when the Pirates went to Chicago for a four-game series starting on April 26. Only the last of the four could be played, and that in chilling winds. Down 1–0 after eight, the Pirates began the ninth quietly with two pop outs, and many fans began heading home. Beals Becker grounded sharply to first baseman Chance, and they both raced for the bag. One description had Chance beating Becker by two steps, but umpire John Rudderham called Becker safe.

After a long uproar in which Chance was ejected, Leach worked Jack Pfiester for a walk, bringing up Clarke with an opportunity to pull the Pirates to within a half game of first place. Instead of Clarke, the fans saw rookie Paddy O'Connor, in only his second major league appearance, coming toward the plate. Clarke, the man Wagner said was the best left-handed hitter against left-handed pitching he ever saw, was sending up the inexperienced but right-handed O'Connor in his place. If O'Connor failed, the move would have made Clarke look "like a monkey of the ape-like pattern," wrote the imaginative W. A. Phelon of *Sporting Life*. O'Connor proved worthy of his manager's faith by singling to center to score Becker with the tying run. Wagner then capped the inning and ultimately the win with a bloop single to score Leach. For O'Connor, his hit was to be one of only three, his run driven in one of only two for the entire season.

A few days later, Dreyfuss was in Louisville for the thirty-fourth running of the Kentucky Derby. He had part ownership in Bill Heron, a horse that had been racing and winning in London, Ontario, and was to be ridden by Jimmy Lee, the most successful jockey of the season. But Lee was injured in an earlier race on Derby Day, and the best his replacement could do was seventh in an eight-horse field. No estimates were given of the amount of money lost by Dreyfuss and many of his players who backed Bill Heron.

◆ ◆ ◆

Coming off a fourth-place finish in 1907, McGraw made several changes to his Giants in the offseason and believed he was now ready to challenge again. One of the most significant additions to his team was thirty-six-year-old first baseman Fred Tenney, who would lead the league in runs in 1908. More important was the return of "Turkey Mike" Donlin after a hiatus of almost two years. He had left the Giants in midseason of 1906, after marrying stage star Mabel Hite, to devote himself to a career in vaudeville. McGraw persuaded him to bring his fine defensive work and .300 lifetime batting average back to the Giants by offering him a four-thousand-dollar salary and a five-hundred-dollar bonus for serving as team captain. The fun-loving Donlin was convinced, even though it meant signing a no-alcohol clause. In spite of being away from the big leagues for well over a year, he soon became a fan idol and made a serious run at Wagner's domain—the National League batting crown.

As the crowd filed out of Exposition Park after the first Pirates-Giants clash on May 11, one rooter was overheard proclaiming, "It was five to two in favor of Hans Wagner." His day included a triple, two walks, two runs, and two knocked in, and his delayed break toward second allowed Clarke to score the fifth run on the front end of a double steal.

The Pirates were able to close to second, only two games behind the leading Cubs, by taking three of four at Chicago. After dropping the first game of a May 31 twin bill to Pfiester 6–3, the Pirates exploded for thirty-three runs over the last three games of the series. Leach and Wagner supplied much of the offense with Leach hitting a triple, homer, and two singles and scoring four runs in the third contest. Wagner was 8 for 18 in the series, and in the finale, he hit a two-run homer in the first inning, added two doubles, scored three times and drove in six runs, all part of a 12–6 romp. The Pirate offense that had been next to last in team batting average at the end of May woke up against the wonderful Cubs' pitching staff. And in a pattern established early in the season, the

Pirates would play mediocre ball at home but be torrid on the road. They were actually outscored at home in 1908 but finished 42–35. On the road, they had the major league's best mark at 56–21.

Wagner continued his batting tear in the East, hitting triples in three successive games versus the Phillies in early June. During one seven-game stretch, he had five doubles and three home runs, one a tenth-inning game-winner. During a series with the Giants, William F. Kirk of the *New York American* recalled, "The wonderful Teuton was everywhere, choking off sure hits and encouraging his comrades . . . and his large paws, the fingers of which seemed like tentacles of a devil fish, raked in everything that came within a mile of them. Oh, Honus, how could you do it?" The *Sporting Life* assessment was that "Honus was always in the way—that is, in the way of the Giants winning." The accolades continued throughout the trip with former Pirate player-manager Patsy Donovan, who was now with Brooklyn, grumbling, "Clarke, Wagner, and Tommy Leach are a team in themselves."

◆   ◆   ◆

On June 22, in the initial game after returning to Pittsburgh, play was halted in the top of the first inning when Wagner was struck in the finger with a line drive. His misplay would lead to the Reds' winning runs, but the crowd applauded as he chose to remain in the contest. His badly swollen finger did not prevent him from picking up his two-thousandth major league hit in the eighth inning, with a single past the shortstop off the Reds' Jake Weimer. It had taken him only six years to reach one thousand hits and another six to reach this mark. His career batting average now stood at an extraordinary .347. Two days later, he had a home run and a double, his eighth-inning single broke a 3–3 tie, and his steal of home capped the scoring in a 5–3 win. The finger remained inflamed throughout the next four weeks, but he stayed in the lineup.

With the coming of July, the Pirates and Cubs were locked in a battle of percentage points, with the Giants only a few games off the pace. Additional ticket offices were set up and portable benches were placed in front of the grandstand and bleachers to increase capacity at Exposition Park. Five games in three days in Pittsburgh, which included a July 4 morning-afternoon doubleheader, drew more than fifty thousand fans. During the series, the Pirates pounded Pfiester and Orval Overall for two lopsided wins, including Willis's eighth in a row. But the Cubs unloaded on Camnitz and Leever for a blowout of their own, and Mordecai Brown continued his mastery over Clarke's men by tossing a six-hit shutout and, following one day of rest, a two-hit shutout. Of the team's eight hits in eighteen innings off Brown, Wagner had three, including two doubles.

Returning to Chicago for a Sunday game, the Pirates broke open a 2–2 tie in the fifth by scoring three times after the inning seemed to be over. Roy Thomas, the center fielder and leadoff hitter recently acquired from Philadelphia, had doubled and moved to third on a fly out. Clarke walked and immediately darted for second. Tinker cut off the catcher's throw, returning it toward home as Thomas charged the plate. Umpire Jim Johnstone called Thomas out, and as the Cubs headed to the bench, Wagner pleaded for a safe call by drawing a diagram in the dirt around home plate. He must have made a good case for a few moments later, Johnstone astonishingly reversed his decision. The change did not meet with the approval of the Cubs or the sixteen thousand fans in attendance, and they made their own case—loudly. But the verdict stood and before the side was out, two more runs had tallied. The Pirates held on for the win, and the six-game split left the two teams neck and neck.

Gamblers were out in force on July 8 and giving ten-to-six odds on the home team as it faced the Phillies. Despite five hits in the doubleheader by Wagner, the Pirates dropped both games. They lost three of four in the series, and many "sports" suffered as well. As Alfred Cratty of *Sporting Life* described it, "One man applied a miserable epithet to Wagner. [Abbaticchio] was derided almost to desperation. It was all Clarke could do to keep the incensed athletes from clambering into the stands after their traducers." By the fourth game, the City of Pittsburgh dispatched plainclothesmen to police the crowd for open gambling. Worse yet was the loss of Phillippe. A shoulder problem had limited him to only a handful of games, and when Phillie Charles "Red" Dooin's line drive caromed off his hand, breaking a finger, Phillippe was done for the year.

The Giants, very much alive in the pennant race with a record of 43–30, came to Pittsburgh on July 10 and appeared to be off and running when they scored four runs in the opening inning of the first game. The Pirates chipped away on back-to-back triples by Clarke and Wagner, and after eighth- and ninth-inning leads disappeared, Leach led off the bottom of the ninth by hammering a home run to deep center. The next day, Willis shackled the Giants on only one hit, a Donlin triple, and the Pirates looked to be in the driver's seat.

In the midst of another outstanding season in which he would pitch 390 innings over fifty-six games and amass thirty-seven victories, Mathewson made quick work of the Pirates with a three-hitter. The Giants cruised to a 7–0 win and completed a doubleheader sweep with a 7–4 victory, a game in which home runs by Wagner, Wilson, and Alan Storke were wasted.

Following the four-game split, the Giants traveled to Chicago and pounded three Cub pitchers for an 11–0 win on July 15. That same day, the Pirates scraped a two-out run in the ninth against Boston and then scored the game-winner in the tenth when Clarke was hit by a pitch with the bases loaded. The combination of the Cubs' loss and the Pirates' come-from-behind win nudged Pittsburgh into first place by a slim one-half game. They would maintain the top spot until August 24 by going 20–10 but would never be able to expand their lead to more than two and a half games.

◆ ◆ ◆

July 16 had been set aside well in advance as Wagner Day and would include a special pregame tribute. As *Sporting Life* cheerfully reported, "After steadfastly refusing for years to allow any streets or babies to be named for him, J. Hans Wagner is to be made the victim of Wagner Day. . . . Hans can't help himself." A fund was set up for individual donations of one dollar (a significant sum for 1908), with each supporter having his name printed in the newspaper. The sports editors of the seven Pittsburgh dailies, headed by C. B. Power of *The Pittsburg Dispatch*, were to choose an appropriate gift. The first dollar was contributed by Sammy Dreyfuss, Barney's thirteen-year-old son, and many more followed from around the country. At Wagner's request, the day was pushed back to July 17 so it would not interfere with attendance at the annual benefit picnic for orphans. This news made the coffers swell as people congratulated him for such a fine gesture.

With hundreds of Wagner's Carnegie friends on hand, players from both teams gathered around home plate. He was presented with a gold watch and chain valued at six hundred dollars and the $97.22 in cash remaining from the fund. His brothers of the Carnegie Lodge of Elks added a beautiful charm, and a small boy pulled a more practical gift from a box, a rooster that he claimed "could lick anything." The *Carnegie Union* divulged that "his friends were probably more pleased than Wagner. Not that Honus does not appreciate the gifts, but he has no hankering to be in the limelight of publicity, and that is another good thing to be said about Honus." The day capped a week full of adulation, which included his younger sister Carrie, now Mrs. Gallagher, naming her newborn son John, nicknamed Hans.

◆ ◆ ◆

If there was any doubt that this was a season like no other in baseball history, the feeling was quickly put to rest on July 24 when the Pirates arrived in New York with a two-game lead over the Giants. A good-natured Friday crowd of more than twenty thousand greeted each of the Giant players with an ovation, applauded Wagner when he first stepped onto the field, and shouted when the band turned "The Star Spangled Banner" into "There'll Be a Hot Time in the Old Town Tonight." Wagner responded with two hits and a stolen base, and his bare-handed grab of a bunted pop allowed him to turn a double play. He inched closer to the batting lead as Mike Donlin went hitless, but the Giants pulled to within a game of the Pirates with a win and had the mighty Mathewson going to the mound the following day.

It was not John Brush's policy to announce official attendance figures, and estimates of turnouts at the Polo Grounds varied wildly. For the Saturday contest, the guesses of writers ranged from twenty-six thousand to an exaggerated thirty-five thousand. All agreed that it was the largest number of people to date to witness a baseball game. Ticket speculators were demanding and receiving five and six dollars for a sixty-five-cent reserved seat, and all were taken an hour before the game.

Ropes circled the outfield but the crowd quickly invaded, reducing the playing dimensions. In front of the grandstand, it was necessary for special police and a group of players to control those filling the area around the infield. By game time, the populace had overtaken the players' benches and was within a few yards of fair territory, requiring the players to sit on the grass along the baselines. Order would need to be restored during the game as, according to *The Pittsburgh Post*, "Time after time the fans, overjoyed at some play, rushed upon the field and held a frenzied carnival." It would be on this cramped little stage, in a critical game, and in front of an immense assemblage that Wagner would have one of his most memorable days.

After a scoreless first inning, Wagner opened up the second with a double into the overflow in left field, and as a pitch skipped a few feet away from Bresnahan, Wagner headed for third. The catcher recovered quickly, and his throw to Art Devlin was in time and on target, leaving Wagner no choice but to improvise. W. W. Aulick of *The New York Times* described the scene: "But what does Hans do but jump about sixteen feet in the air, clean over the outstretched hands of Devlin, and make the base. There's something you never saw before, did you?" Abbaticchio followed the acrobatics with another ground-rule double, and Wagner trotted home with the only run of the first four frames.

A rain began to soak the trapped spectators as the Giants came to bat in the bottom of the fifth. Lefty Leifield walked Al Bridwell to open the inning, and after Mathewson lined a single off Abbaticchio's glove, Tenney bunted the runners into scoring position. The crowd was anxious for Larry Doyle to do something before the rain caused the game to be called. Doyle shot a liner to left scoring Bridwell, and when Clarke bobbled it momentarily, Mathewson crossed the plate to give the Giants a 2–1 lead. The rain subsided during the several minutes that it took to push the celebrating fans back to their previous boundary.

The 2–1 score survived the sixth, which included Wagner's third hit of the day, but the seventh would prove to be Mathewson's and Doyle's downfall. Wilson singled sharply to left, Harry Swacina—the Pirates' latest first baseman of the month—coaxed a walk, and Gibson doubled down the left field line to score the tying run. Doyle booted Leifield's ground ball into right field, allowing two runs, and after two outs were recorded, Doyle misplayed Clarke's grounder for a run. Wagner singled, his fourth hit, and Abbaticchio followed closely with a single, scoring Clarke to complete the five-run inning. It was plenty for Leifield, but Wagner drove in another run in the ninth with his fifth hit of the day, making the final 7–2.

After pregame taunts by Donlin in the direction of the Pirate pitchers, he went hitless for a second consecutive game. Meanwhile, Wagner vaulted over him in the batting race by going 5 for 5 and sending a mocking message of his own. After his third, fourth, and fifth hits, Wagner rounded first base and held up the appropriate number of fingers toward a fuming Donlin in right field. (Long after his retirement, Wagner recalled with pleasure this day in New York when an incensed Donlin dove into the overflow crowd after being heckled about losing his grip on the batting lead. "All you could see was Mike's feet," Wagner laughed.)

Wagner's boastful display was uncharacteristic, as were the actions of the New York Giants' fans in the moments following the game. As thousands of people swarmed onto the diamond to head for the exit beyond the left field wall, many surrounded a surprised Wagner, intending to show their admiration. In his only failed attempt all day, he was unsuccessful in convincing the fans not to carry him from the field. Clarke, Paddy O'Connor, and Jimmy Kane came to Wagner's rescue, but not before Honus's cap was one fan's souvenir and his jersey had been shredded by the adoring mass.

Following a day of rest on the Sabbath, an unprecedented Monday crowd of more than fourteen thousand gathered at Coogan's Bluff on July 27. Attired in a new cap and shirt rushed in from Pittsburgh, Wagner smacked the first pitch of the top of the second down the left field line for a double and scored the game's first run on a Wilson double. In the fourth with the score 1–1, Clarke hit a leadoff double and Wagner electrified the crowd by hitting his second double to left field, his seventh consecutive hit. Wilson followed with a triple and then scored the fourth and final Pirate run on Gibson's infield single.

Nick Maddox gave up four singles, walked six, and hit two batters. In the eighth, with Giants at first and third, Donlin stole second and collided with his batting rival. Wagner limped around the bag for a few minutes and Clarke and Donlin exchanged terse words. When the dust settled, Irv Young, now sufficiently warmed up, emerged ready to take the place of the struggling Maddox. Wagner, his stalling mission completed, gave up his act. Young hit two batters, but the Pirates held on for a 4–3 win.

A Tuesday crowd of more than sixteen thousand came to see the series finale and cheered Wagner each time he approached the plate. Wiltse and Willis dueled for sixteen innings, the last ten scoreless, before the game was called because of darkness with the score 2–2. Wagner went hitless in six at bats but did drive in one of the runs with a newly termed "sacrifice fly." The Pittsburgh Pirates left the Polo Grounds with their slim first-place margin intact and with one of the fattest checks ever for a visitor's share of the gate. It would take only two weeks before these unheard-of attendance figures would be matched—when the Chicago Cubs would visit New York.

♦ ♦ ♦

The Pirate offense hit a horrendous slump in mid-August. In the middle of a stretch in which they would manage just fifteen runs over eleven games, they had back-to-back four-hitters tossed at them by Brooklyn's Kaiser Wilhelm (the former Pirate) and Harry McIntire, both of whom were well on their way to twenty-loss seasons for the 100-loss club. After

Brooklyn exploded for fifteen hits off three Pirate pitchers in McIntire's four-hitter on August 20, Clarke's men found themselves in a first-place tie with New York.

The next day, Maddox pushed the Pirates back out to a half-game lead by driving in both runs in a 2–1 victory. He had accounted for five of the Pirates last seven wins, was on a personal eight-game winning streak, and his record now stood at 15–5. Combined with his five victories from 1907, Maddox's total of twenty major league wins had come in only thirty appearances, making him the quickest twenty-game winner ever. (It is a mark since equalled, never passed, by Russ Ford of the New York Yankees in 1910, David "Boo" Ferriss of the Boston Red Sox in 1945, and Cal Eldred of the Milwaukee Brewers in 1993.)

The Giants came to town for four games trailing by that narrow half-game margin and with differing opinions on who would provide their competition for the stretch run. Two weeks earlier, with the Pirates a game and a half in front, the *New York American* quoted Wiltse as saying, "I see but one team with a chance to beat us, Pittsburgh. . . . [The Pirates] may be a one-man team, but that man is a 'dilly.' " Mathewson, sharing his thoughts in the same publication, disagreed: "Chicago, in my mind, is the one team we have to beat. . . . the Pirates are more or less a one-man aggregation. Without Hans Wagner, Pittsburgh would have a hard time to get into the first division." The two Giant hurlers convincingly swept the first two games of the series-opening doubleheader on Monday, August 24. The next day, even Maddox couldn't stop the Giants as the Pirates lost 5–3. And on Wednesday, the Giants erased a deficit with one run in the eighth and two in the ninth, giving Mathewson another victory as he held on to a 4–3 lead for what today would be termed a save.

The four straight wins in Pittsburgh gave the Giants an eight-game winning streak and had McGraw's players practically counting their World Series shares. In three days, they had lifted themselves from a half game back to three and a half games ahead of both Pittsburgh and Chicago. McGraw pronounced the Pirates dead as his team boarded for Chicago for a three-game series that would close out August.

◆ ◆ ◆

On August 30, the Cubs' ninth-straight win finished off a three-game sweep of the Giants. The Cubs were now only a half game out of the lead and helped the Pirates pull back to within a game of first. The Pirates pounded the Reds' pitchers in sweeping a five-game series in early September but could only inch a half game closer as New York was in the middle of a seven-game winning streak. If Pittsburgh gamblers were any indication of Pirate pennant hopes, the team was through. Although earlier series brought odds of ten to six on the home club, the opener of the two-game series with Chicago was bringing overwhelming five-to-one odds on the visiting Cubs. The Pirates had just won seven of eight and had Willis going to the mound with his nifty 17–8 mark, but there were not many takers on September 4. The locals had seen what Mordecai Brown could do, and they wanted no part of it. So far in 1908, Brown had dominated the Pirates, winning four games without a loss.

Willis was in and out of trouble for the first three innings. He allowed two walks in the opening frame, two singles in the second, and two walks again in the third, but neither team could push a runner across. In the ninth, after Tinker's two-out double, Willis chose to walk Johnny Kling intentionally. As Gibson moved out to take a wide one, Kling stepped up and drove the ball down the right field line. The surprised Pirates watched as it dropped just inches foul. Willis completed the walk, with pitches a little further from the plate, and induced Brown to strike out on three curveballs. The crowd of 8,300 was shaken but relieved.

Brown, true to form, allowed only four scattered singles through nine, and the game entered the tenth scoreless. The Cubs went quietly in the top half, but Clarke led off the bottom with an infield single. Leach laid down a sacrifice, and Wagner's second single of the game moved Clarke to third. Warren Gill was plunked by a Brown curveball to load the bases, and Abbaticchio struck out for the second out. Wilson lined Brown's first pitch into center, and Clarke headed home with the winning run, as everybody else headed for the clubhouse.

Gill, who was on first, ran toward second until he saw the ball land safely in the outfield, then he joined the parade to the dressing quarters. Leach later recalled hearing Tinker and Evers "jabbering" around second base and calling for Jimmy Slagle, the center fielder, to throw them the ball. Slagle retrieved it and threw to Evers who stepped on the second base bag and declared a force out. Umpire Hank O'Day, in the custom of the time, had waited to see Clarke touch the plate and hightailed it himself. The keystone combination tracked down the umpire to describe the happenings, but O'Day, insisting that Clarke had scored, refused to hear their arguments.

Cub president Charles W. Murphy dictated a telegram to Pulliam that stated, "Chicago protests today's game. . . . Chicago claims Gill should have touched second base before he ran to the clubhouse, and will prove by affidavits of a number of persons that he failed to do so." Murphy publicly said that he expected to lose his case, and he did. A few days later, Pulliam rejected Murphy's argument and supported his umpire, contending, "I think the baseball public prefers to see games settled on the field and not in this office."

Gill's action on the controversial play was like that of many others in similar game-winning situations over the years. Despite the "letter of the law," it was commonly assumed that, regardless of the movement of the other baserunners, the game was over when no play was made on the runner crossing the plate with the winning run. It was so much taken for granted that the press coverage of Murphy's protest was nominal in Chicago and Pittsburgh and almost nonexistent in New York. But Evers and his teammates had discovered that the custom did not conform with the rule book. O'Day later agreed with their logic and resolved to be on the lookout for the situation in the future.

The Cubs' Ed Reulbach allowed only four singles the day after the Gill incident in an 11–0 blowout, and the two teams headed to Chicago for a doubleheader. More than twenty-two thousand fans saw Maddox pitch a four-hitter in game one, a 3–0 Pirate win. In game two, the Cubs scrambled to hang on 8–7, as Brown was called on in the ninth to stifle a four-run Pirate rally and assure a split.

Pittsburgh returned home on Labor Day, trailing New York by a game and a half but leading Chicago by a half game. The Pirates took six of seven on the homestand—Wagner was on fire, going 15 for 23 and at times appearing unstoppable. He was 6 for 7 with three extra-base hits in the holiday doubleheader sweep and the next day drove home the only two runs of a 2–0 win. In another victory, he accounted for two of the Pirates' four hits with a double and a game-winning homer. And in the loss, he contributed two of only three Pirate hits with a triple and a single.

When the Pirates arrived in New York on Friday, September 18, they were three full games behind the red-hot Giants. The New Yorkers had won nine straight and sixteen of seventeen, and John Brush was preparing for a World Series he felt sure was coming to the metropolis. New stands were added during a recent Giant road trip, increasing the Polo Grounds' capacity by two thousand, and Brush contracted for the construction of four thousand more grandstand seats in the final days of the season. In addition, he optimistically arranged for World Series tickets to be printed.

In anticipation of an enormous crowd for the series-opening doubleheader, some two hundred policemen lined the field. The gates were to open at noon, hours before the scheduled start, and lines began forming at the entrances at 10:00 A.M. By game time, the additional seating proved woefully inadequate and the fans encircled the playing field. Paid admissions were recorded at thirty-two thousand, and thousands more were turned away.

Mathewson was in the middle of a six-game winning streak and had already won thirty games. In the opener, he did not allow a base on balls and was touched for only five hits, one by Abbaticchio and two each by Clarke and Wagner. The Giants coasted to a 7–0 win and then collected eighteen hits for a 12–7 rout in the second game. The mood of the Pirate squad was expectedly glum, but Clarke had not given up despite the five-game deficit. He demonstrated a quiet confidence, saying there was still hope if his troops could take the last two in the series.

On Saturday, an estimated forty thousand fans approached the park, and approximately thirty thousand found their way to seats, with the remainder rebuffed. With the Giants comfortably in first place, it was a genial gathering, and the crowd applauded the efforts of both sides with equal enthusiasm. Leifield was shaky and required a seventh-inning visit from left field by his manager but pitched out of bases-loaded jams in the seventh and ninth and took a 2–2 tie into the tenth. The Pirates scored four in the top of the inning, and Leifield made it stand with a one-two-three bottom half.

Rather than sightseeing in New York, the players atypically spent their off Sunday wasting time and playing cards at the Hotel Somerset. They knew they would face Mathewson again on Monday. The Pirates countered with Vic Willis, who along with Maddox had accumulated twenty wins. In front of fifteen thousand, Mathewson was brilliant once again. He faced only thirty batters, and just three reached base. But the three—Wilson, Gibson, and Clarke—bunched hits in the third inning, leading to two runs. Willis gave up a lone run on two hits, a hit batsman, and a walk. Only seven men reached base on the day, and the game was played in a blistering one hour and twenty minutes.

The Pirates remained in New York City to start a three-game series with Brooklyn the next day. In better spirits, back to within three of the lead, the team joined the Giants as guests at a Manhattan theater performance that night. The Cubs, only two games out, sped toward New York for four critical contests with the Giants. Twenty-four hours later, the entire complexion of the race had changed. The Pirates squeezed out a

3–2 win in eleven innings to stand at 88–54 (.620), and the Cubs took two one-run decisions from New York to pull within percentage points of the lead with a record of 90–53 (.629), compared with the Giants' mark of 87–50 (.635).

◆ ◆ ◆

The hotly contested, three-way race was one of the most exciting in years. The stage was set for the most analyzed, most controversial, and perhaps the messiest ballgame in baseball history. News of the Pirates' 2–1 win over Brooklyn on September 23 was overshadowed in *The Pittsburgh Post* by the front-page headline CHICAGO AND GIANTS MIX UP IN THE NINTH. The caption continued with other sordid teasers about swarming crowds, protests, and police, while the accompanying article tried its best to explain the confusion in New York.

Another huge weekday crowd was at the Polo Grounds, and the mood was electric as the game entered the bottom of the ninth tied at one apiece. After an out, the Giants' Art Devlin singled to center, but Harry "Moose" McCormick's ground ball forced him at second base for out number two. The next batter was nineteen-year-old Fred Merkle. Merkle, a friendly, likable youngster, had been pressed into action as the Giants' first baseman due to Fred Tenney's severe lumbago attack—the only game Tenney missed in 1908. Merkle temporarily endeared himself to the home crowd with a line single to right that moved McCormick, the potential winning run, to third. Al Bridwell wasted no time and lined Mordecai Brown's first offering, a fastball, into right-center for a single as McCormick scampered home. The fans, believing the game was over, began to leave, with many streaming onto the field as they headed for the left field exit. Just as Warren Gill had done nineteen days earlier for Pittsburgh, Merkle saw the winning run cross the plate and sought shelter before completing his trip to second base.

The Cubs were ready. Center fielder Arthur "Solly" Hofman tracked down the hit and, in returning it to the infield, threw it over Johnny Evers's head. By now, the fans outnumbered the players on the field, and the scene turned into a circus. McGinnity, onto the Cubs' scheme, fielded the overthrow and, unsuccessful at dodging the oncoming infielders, heaved the ball into the multitude of fans behind third base. The Cubs gave chase. Tinker emerged with a ball—of questionable origin—and tossed it to Evers, who was standing on the keystone sack. Two umpires had been assigned for the important game, but base umpire Bob Emslie had not seen the action around second base. That left Hank

O'Day—the same Hank O'Day that was in Pittsburgh for the identical situation a few weeks earlier—as the umpire the Cubs turned to for a decision.

This time O'Day had not retreated to the dressing room so quickly. He had come out from behind the plate and was now reaching second base himself. A throng of spectators surrounded the Cubs and the umpire at the bag and, sensing their "evil" intention, became belligerent. An ugly mob scene ensued with the Cubs' players and O'Day being the object of punches and projectiles. It took dozens of New York policemen to escort the umpire and players to safety and break up the crowd, but not before O'Day had sustained several body blows.

Pursued by a horde of reporters, O'Day explained that Merkle had been forced out at second base and therefore the game was still tied. Dissatisfied, the scribes tracked down President Pulliam at home and pressed him for a ruling. His only response was that until his umpire briefed him on the matter, no decision need be made.

The stage of flying fists was now over and was replaced by that of flying paperwork. O'Day reported to Pulliam that the game had ended in a tie as a result of Merkle's incomplete journey to second and the inability to continue the contest because of the crowd. Pulliam again supported his umpire's judgment. John Brush fiercely disagreed with this decision, vowing to protest and fight in court if necessary. The Cubs were not completely satisfied, either. They submitted a protest to Pulliam calling for the game to be theirs by forfeit. They claimed that if the game was a tie as O'Day had ruled, it should have been continued at that point. Since the riot made this impossible, the Cubs deemed the game should have been awarded to them. The following day, they filed a second protest, again claiming the game by forfeit. They contended that if the game was to be replayed, it could only be done as part of a doubleheader that day since it was the Cubs' last scheduled afternoon in New York. The Cubs argued that they were at the ballpark ready to play an early game, but since the Giants were not, it should be credited as a Cubs win.

Over the course of the following week, Pulliam would receive and reject each team's protests. It was not until October 2 that Pulliam would hand down a final ruling that the game had ended in a tie and the Cubs had no grounds for a forfeit. He went on to explain that any further appeals would be handled by the National League Board of Directors.

The Giants won the last game of their series with the Cubs on September 24 as the visitors were jeered throughout. The Pirates, behind Wagner's four hits, completed a sweep of lowly Brooklyn and were now tied with Chicago, a single game out of first place. Unbelievably, the race would get even tighter the next day, as the three teams would be separated by a mere .006 in the percentage column. The Pirates split their doubleheader in Boston to stand at .623, the Cubs handily defeated Brooklyn in a single contest to stand at .628, and the Giants were upset twice at the hands of Cincinnati to end the day at .629.

Pitching would be the story on September 26. The Pirates' Willis threw a six-hit shutout at Boston, and after Mathewson defeated Cincinnati in game one of their doubleheader, Red Ames followed with a four-hitter to complete the sweep. These were fine pitching performances in the pinch, but on this day they paled in comparison to Ed Reulbach's effort for the Cubs. Reulbach allowed only five baserunners on five singles in posting a 5–0 shutout in the first game of a doubleheader at Brooklyn. Seeming fresh and unhittable, Reulbach was manager Chance's choice to take the mound for game two. This time, Reulbach allowed just three singles and one walk, and it took him only one hour and twelve minutes to post his second shutout of the day in a 3–0 win. It was one of the greatest pitching feats in baseball, and to this day, Reulbach stands as the lone pitcher in major league history to throw two shutouts in one day.

In the final week of the Pirates' season, which would culminate in a head-to-head matchup with the Cubs the following Sunday, each of the three contenders would have a fleeting hold on first place.

◆ ◆ ◆

The Pirates closed out the home portion of their schedule by rebounding from a 5–0 deficit to beat the Cardinals 7–5 behind Leach's home run and three runs knocked in. Wagner made a mad dash home from second base on a passed ball, and Leever pitched six shutout innings of relief during the Pirates' comeback. After the game, both teams headed for St. Louis for three more, and the canvas tarp was loaded for a trip to Chicago. At Cub president Murphy's request, Dreyfuss had agreed to ship the "protector" to West Side Grounds to increase the likelihood of playing the final game on Sunday, which would ensure a huge turnout.

More than thirty loyal fans joined the Pirates on their final four-game trip and were rewarded with a doubleheader sweep on October 2. In the opener, Clarke had three hits and Wagner broke open the game with a bases-loaded double to score three. In the second game, Gibson tied the score with a solo homer in the seventh, and Wagner's ninth-inning home run gave the Pirates a 2–1 win. They were now in the lead, but the separation between the three teams was being tracked to a fourth decimal place.

Clarke was indecisive about how to use his pitchers in the last two games. Though they lacked a dominant hurler, like the Cubs' Brown or the Giants' Mathewson, the Pirate staff featured five pitchers who would win fifteen or more games that year, led by Maddox (23–8) and Willis (23–11), followed by Camnitz (16–9), Leever (15–7), and Leifield (15–14). Clarke decided he would use Maddox in the last game of the St. Louis series and save Willis, who had defeated the Cubs and Brown in the ten-inning, 1–0 Gill game, for the season finale in Chicago. Maddox came through with a five-hitter and chipped in two hits, including a triple in a 3–2 victory. For the second consecutive year, the Pirates had taken twenty of twenty-two from St. Louis, which lost 105 games by scoring a mere 371 runs. Meanwhile, the Cubs were bombarding the Reds in Cincinnati, and the Giants were losing at Philadelphia.

The Pirates, since dropping the first two of their series back in New York, had won thirteen of fourteen and were riding a season-high, eight-game winning streak. As they headed to Chicago for their regular season wrap-up on Sunday, October 4, the Pirates led the Cubs by a slim .003. The Giants found themselves a game and a half back after dropping three of their last eight but had three games remaining in the coming week. The tightness of the race, combined with the meeting of the board of directors scheduled for October 5 to analyze the Merkle game, made for what seemed an infinite number of outcomes to the race. Would the board decide to uphold Pulliam's decision and order the game replayed? Would a three-game playoff be necessary? Would the board overturn the decision and give the win to the Giants—or to the Cubs, for that matter? What would the Giants do in those last three games against Boston? One thing was certain. Both the Pirates and Cubs felt a win in this Sunday matchup was vital to a chance at the title. The winner would almost certainly be assured at least a share of first place; the loser would have no hope.

The unprecedented interest in baseball during the summer of 1908 had editorialists carping that the pennant races were more important to the public than the presidential race, which pitted William Jennings Bryan against William Howard Taft. During the stretch run, a few of

Pittsburgh's major newspapers had placed bulletin boards in front of their offices to post inning-by-inning scores. For this final game in Chicago, men with megaphones were stationed on top of the buildings to announce the telegraphed bulletins to waiting crowds below. Hours before the first pitch, the assembly had begun, and by midday an estimated fifty thousand people were in the streets of Pittsburgh, shutting down traffic on several of the city's major arteries. In New York, 3,500 Giants fans gathered at the Polo Grounds to watch a depiction of the game between their two rivals on electric boards positioned in front of the grandstand.

West Side Grounds in Chicago was the home of the Chicago National Leaguers from 1893 to 1915 and played host to eleven championship games over four World Series, but it never held a larger turnout than the 30,247 who crammed its barriers on October 4, 1908. Spectators began arriving at 9:00 A.M., two hours prior to the opening of the ticket windows and a full six hours prior to game time. Charles Dryden of the *Chicago Tribune* likened the rush when the gates opened to "a run of sockeye salmon struggling to get into fresh water. . . ." By 1:00 P.M., the crowd filled the stands and had already begun to encroach on the field and foul territory.

The Pirates' only route to the flag was straight through their nemesis, Mordecai Brown. Only Mathewson's stunning season would outshine Brown's 29–9 mark. But the Pirates were hoping for better results this time, since Brown was working his third game in six days and Willis was well rested, having only pitched four innings in the previous week. Besides, the Pirates were an excellent road team and had already won their season series with the Cubs.

The Cubs struck for a run in their half of the first. In the fifth inning, Wagner made a running, one-handed stop of a ground ball up the middle by Evers. It was a sure infield single, but Wagner came up throwing, and his ill-advised toss sailed into the crowd sitting behind first base. The error gave Evers an extra bag and allowed him to score on a Wildfire Schulte single.

Brown breezed into the sixth with a three-hitter and a 2–0 lead, but Thomas singled and moved to second on Brown's errant pickoff throw. Clarke popped out, and Leach hit a grounder for the second out, as Thomas moved to third. Wagner swung at and missed two curveballs but managed to pull an outside fastball just inside the third base bag for a double and a run. He moved to third on a wild pitch and scored on

Abbaticchio's single to center. A deafening roar erupted in the streets of Pittsburgh as the tying run was announced.

The exuberance was short-lived, as Tinker clouted a two-out double into the right field crowd in the bottom half of the sixth. Willis intentionally walked Kling to get to the opposing pitcher, but Brown singled to right to break the tie. It was precisely at this exciting moment that an unpaid patron entered the scene. In the midst of the masses in center field, a woman gave birth to a child. She fell forward and the fans, sensing she had fainted, pulled back to give her air. She confided to someone what had happened and was whisked away with the baby to the clubhouse and presumably to Cook County Hospital across the street. The *Chicago Tribune* coverage of the contest included two separate references to the "baseball baby" and "infant phenom" but reported: "The woman refused to give her name, and the west side hospitals last night denied that any such case had been brought to their attention."

In the seventh, the Cubs scored an insurance run as Wagner, who according to *The Pittsburgh Post* "played the field all afternoon much like a cheese sandwich without mustard," misplayed a ground ball for a second costly error. And in the eighth, Brown accounted for another run by singling and scoring on an Evers double. Down 5–2 in the ninth, and with Brown showing no signs of tiring, the Pirates looked doomed.

Wagner led off with a single, and Abbaticchio drove an 0–2 pitch down the right field line into the crowd for an apparent double. The two umpires assigned to the game differed in opinion, with base umpire Cy Rigler indicating fair and Hank O'Day, seemingly magnetized to controversy, calling foul. O'Day, as plate umpire, had the final say, and the Pirates were livid. The entire team joined in a fruitless argument that lasted for several minutes. Abbaticchio's return trip to the plate was brief, as he took a called third strike. A pair of fielder's choices followed, ending the game and the Pirates' season.

Enormous crowds in three faraway cities dispersed from different venues. In Chicago, thousands of fans were festive as they left the park convinced that the pennant was theirs. At the Polo Grounds in New York, the Cub-rooters-for-a-day had seen what they wanted. Their Giants only had to sweep the three remaining games from sixth-place Boston to end the season in a tie with Chicago. And in Pittsburgh, the disenchanted onlookers headed home for Sunday dinner. The thrilling pennant race ended for them with the posting of a zero on a bulletin board on a city street.

Wagner remembered that the players sat "dazed in the clubhouse," but Dreyfuss, perhaps clutching his check for the club's share of the gate receipts, was in unusually cheerful spirits for having just lost the pennant. He proposed to President Murphy that if a three-game playoff series was required to break a tie between Chicago and New York, it be played in Pittsburgh. A noncommittal Murphy expressed his interest in seeing the results of the Giants' three games with Boston, then paid Dreyfuss what he must have thought was a high compliment when he said, "You are a better loser than I am. . . . You are the best loser in the league."

During the next two days, while the Giants were easily beating the Boston Doves in the first two games of their series, the National League Board of Directors was deliberating the September 23 Merkle game. The five-man board was reduced to three voting members as both Murphy and Dreyfuss, despite his objections, were judged too involved in the events to be objective. After two days and an evening of listening to testimony and examining evidence, Garry Herrmann read the decision to an anxious audience. The board conceded, "The game should have been won for the New York club had it not been for the reckless, careless, inexcusable blunder of one of its players—namely Merkle." But the board upheld President Pulliam in his earlier judgments by saying that the rule governing the situation was "plain" and "explicit," and that "while other clubs may not have taken advantage of its provisions in the past under similar conditions . . . it did not deprive the Chicago club of the right to do so. . . ."

Refusing the two teams' protests, the board ruled that the game was a tie and would have to be replayed on Thursday, October 8. Since a three-game playoff would not be necessary, the possibility now existed for a three-way tie at the end of the regular season. If the Giants lost the last game of their series with Boston on Wednesday and then defeated the Cubs on Thursday, it would leave all three contenders with identical 98–56 records and necessitate a three-team, nine-day playoff. By now, those Pirates who were not participating in the team's postseason tour were scattered across the country, convinced their season was over. Team management began scuffling to contact the players. The Pirates took heart on Wednesday as the Doves scored two first-inning runs in New York, but the Giants rolled to a 7–2 win, and the Pirates were officially done.

It was a one-game showdown in the Polo Grounds for the National

League pennant. After the Giants and John Brush had considered both refusing to play and taking legal action to prevent the game, they consented. The Cubs traveled overnight from Chicago and were subjected to jeers, taunts, and even death threats from the time they entered New York to the time they left. The new grandstands that had been added were still insufficient to handle the crowds. People tried to climb to any thinkable vantage point no matter how insecure, leading to one fatality and several serious injuries.

The Giants had four men reach base in the first and had already scored a run when manager Chance replaced Pfiester with his ace, Brown. He not only snuffed the rally, he allowed only four hits and one run the rest of the way. Mathewson, New York's obvious choice for the critical contest, was subpar, allowing four runs in the third inning and taking the loss.

Giant players would always recount how they had the pennant taken from them after they had it rightfully won. McGraw and his players refused to forgive those they felt responsible for the thievery. Among the targets of their criticism were Hank O'Day for lying in wait of the play on Merkle and Pulliam for upholding O'Day's decision. As for young Merkle, the events had taken their toll. An intense feeling of guilt left him despondent and losing weight throughout the final days of the season. He received admirable support from his teammates and McGraw. Merkle would become a mainstay on McGraw's Giants for years, and the manager would always maintain that it was unfair to blame Merkle for the lost pennant. But fans and writers were not as understanding and saddled him with the moniker Bonehead, which would follow him not only for the remainder of his career but for the rest of his life and into the annals of history.

The Pirates and Giants, both having lost their final head-to-head matchups against the Cubs, finished 98–56, one game behind the Cubs' 99–55. While the 1908 National League campaign proved to be one of the most thrilling in history, it was rivaled in every way by the American League's four-way race, which lasted until September and was played out in front of equally impressive crowds of enthusiasts before Detroit won its second straight title on the final day.

The rematch of the previous year's champions in the 1908 World Series proved a lackluster affair as the Cubs won decisively. After the wonderful races, the attendance for the final game in Detroit was only 6,200, the smallest turnout in history to witness a World Series game.

But the turnstiles had clicked at a record rate for almost every team during the season, and the number of fans attending big league games had doubled in just seven years. Many baseball people marveled at the increasing importance of the game to the American public.

◆   ◆   ◆

Wagner had another sensational year in 1908, easily maintaining his status as the premier player of the game. Defensively, he was already recognized as the greatest shortstop the game had ever seen. Ironically, this was the first year that he had played all of his games at shortstop. He led or was runner-up in almost every offensive category in the National League. In a year when only five men in the circuit with more than three hundred at bats reached the .300 mark in batting average, Wagner easily outdistanced Donlin's .334 by hitting .354 for a sixth batting title. His slugging percentage surpassed second-place Donlin by a full ninety points, thanks to league-leading totals of 201 hits, thirty-nine doubles, and nineteen triples, and Wagner led the league in stolen bases for a fifth time with fifty-three. Only Fred Tenney, with 101 runs, scored more than Wagner's 100, and only Brooklyn first baseman Tim Jordan, with twelve homers, surpassed Wagner's total of ten.

It had not been enough for the Pirates. The offense was solid, finishing third in runs. Five regulars, including Wagner, surpassed the league batting average of .239, lowest in twenty years. Clarke's average slumped to a new career low of .265, and Leach hit just .259, but the figures were the second and third highest on the club. Gibson caught a whopping 140 games and established himself as one of the better backstops in the league, behind Kling and Bresnahan. Wilson, in his rookie year, was already gaining notice for his fine defensive work and outstanding throwing arm.

Despite the fine individual efforts of many, the Pirates were still regarded as a one-man show. The recap of the season in the following year's *Spalding Guide* called the work of Wagner "little short of miraculous." Francis Richter, in a *Sporting Life* editorial entitled "Without a Peer," wrote, "Wagner has set new marks for succeeding 'wonders' to shoot at with scant hope of success; and has once more proven himself the greatest player of this or any other generation, whose like may never again be seen in base ball. . . . [There] is now none past or present, to dispute his honors or share his glory as the world's greatest ball player."

Wagner was not satisfied. He was still carrying the stigma from the 1903 World Series, accusing him of playing "yellow" ball in the pinches, and he had disappointed again. *Baseball Magazine*, despite the compliment to Wagner, asked its readers, "A weakener, eh? What would not clubs give to have such a weakener!" His Herculean effort down the stretch had the Pirates in the hunt until the end, but both his errors in the final game had contributed to runs and left him hanging his head. Wagner would always feel the responsibility for his team falling just short in 1908.

Believing he may have blown his and Clarke's last chance for a World Series title, Wagner referred to his manager and uttered, "If ever there was a man that deserved to win, it was Fred. That fellow has things awful hard at times, but he never lost heart and he kept us all going. . . ." At an inquiry about his batting title, he exploded, "Bosh with those hits and all that stuff, what does it all amount to when we didn't win that game at Chicago?"

However, it had been a lucrative year for Wagner. The accolades and awards had flooded in, enhancing his already lofty reputation. He continued to receive the respect—indeed the reverence—of fans throughout the country, and he was becoming a wealthy man. But a second consecutive season had ended on a down note and had him looking forward to getting away from baseball for a while. Perhaps a bustling offseason, filled with fun, activities, enterprises, and investments, would raise his spirits. He had both the inkling and the money to do whatever came along.

EIGHT

THE CIRCUS COMES
TO PITTSBURGH

It was a downright hectic offseason for Honus Wagner and many of those around him. Patsy Flaherty, after spending his second season with the Boston Doves, headed for the Orient with a barnstorming troupe. Fred Clarke collected his final check for 1908 and penned a new contract with a three-thousand-dollar raise, giving him the fantastic 1909 stipend of twelve thousand dollars. It was also a profitable year for the Little Pirate Ranch—not only was wheat fetching a good price, but oil was discovered on the property.

In addition, Clarke kept himself busy by puttering with his inventions. He had introduced a new design for players' sliding pads a few years earlier, an idea which was patented in 1912, and now he had a couple of other projects under way. Among his products that would eventually be patented was a small equipment bag that would supplant the players' custom of rolling up their uniforms to carry them. But his most promising work this winter was on a roll-up version of the new tarpaulin. An elaborate system of ropes, ratchets, and winches, Clarke's new Diamond Cover could be operated by as few as four men and without the aid of a truck. During the 1909 season, he leased an office just down the hall from the Pirate headquarters on the ninth floor of the

Farmers Bank Building and put his older brother, William, in charge of selling the tarps to other ball clubs.

There was some bad news during the winter as well. Tommy Leach's wife of ten years passed away at their Cleveland home in November 1908 after a bout with pneumonia. Harry Pulliam was being besieged with criticism over the Merkle affair, as well as most every other decision he ever made, and the strain on the sensitive Pulliam was becoming evident. At a public affair in December, he was described as morose. Then, during a squabble at his office in New York, Pulliam ushered his old friend Dreyfuss and Brooklyn Dodgers president Charles Ebbets to the door in a huff. In February 1909 at a league function in Chicago, Pulliam delivered a particularly bleak message to the magnates, saying, "My days as a baseball man are numbered. The National League doesn't want me as president anymore. It longs to go back to the days of dealing from the bottom of the deck, hiding the cards under the table, and to the days when the trademark was the gum shoe. . . ." The following day, apparently on the verge of suffering a nervous breakdown, he requested and was granted an indefinite leave of absence.

Despite the continued sluggishness of the Pittsburgh economy, the Pirate organization had enjoyed a financial bonanza in 1908, and Dreyfuss was upbeat about the seemingly rebounding economic situation and baseball's burgeoning popularity. Many existing ballparks had been bursting at the seams during the excitingly tight pennant races in both leagues, and club owners lamented the lost revenue from turning thousands away. According to *The Sporting News*, "Base ball clubs of the country are not yet ready for the great prosperity that is coming their way." Clarke remarked that the crowds of ten thousand that once were thought to be so substantial were being surpassed routinely, and if the stands were big enough, turnouts as large as fifty thousand might one day be possible.

In Chicago, White Sox owner Charles Comiskey was said to be negotiating for land, and in Philadelphia, the American League Athletics would open the 1909 season in state-of-the-art Shibe Park. Dreyfuss had been dissatisfied with Exposition Park for years. He felt it was situated too close to Allegheny City's red-light district, which kept away upstanding female patrons. Twice the grandstand roof had been blown off by high winds. The Baltimore & Ohio Railroad, owner of the land, frequently dropped hints that it might want the grounds to expand its railroad yard. But the two most prominent concerns were fire and water.

Flooding was a problem most every year, and Dreyfuss was wary of potential devastation due to collapse from rot or fire. In Philadelphia in 1903, the third base stands of the Baker Bowl had collapsed during a contest, killing twelve people and injuring hundreds. And remembering how League Park had burned to the ground in Louisville and seeing a number of calamities averted when small fires were quickly extinguished at Exposition Park, Dreyfuss knew a fireproof facility was necessary.

During 1908, the situation worsened. Since the acquisition of Allegheny City, Pittsburgh now saw the Pirates as a revenue source of their own, and when Dreyfuss cut back on the free pass privileges to local officials, the City Council made his life miserable. The council attempted to establish a fee of up to seventy-five dollars for each game played at Exposition Park, but as the theaters were only levied an eighty-cent charge per day, Dreyfuss won that fight. A threat to increase water fees was dropped when it was learned that the railroad paid for the utilities as part of the lease. One faction of city government tried to shut down the Pirates completely, proposing an ordinance for the immediate extension of Kilbuck Street, which would have meant paving right through the opening between the third base grandstand and the left field bleachers, over Wagner's shortstop position and on through right-center field.

Dreyfuss successfully navigated through the turmoil and, in typical fashion, armed himself with a plan. As early as February 1908, it was announced that Dreyfuss and a few of the strongest financial men in Pittsburgh had their eye on property in Oakland, three miles east of Pittsburgh's downtown. At the time, Oakland was a fashionable residential district that some envisioned as the city's center of arts and culture. A few members of Oakland's Board of Trade were said to "gasp with chagrin" at the news that the Pirates might move there. In October, the purchase of a seven-acre parcel of the plush Schenley family estate was finalized through its three trustees, including Pittsburgh's most influential man, Andrew Carnegie. Dreyfuss spent the rest of the winter awarding contracts and tracking the progress of his new ballpark, which would be ready for baseball by mid-1909.

◆ ◆ ◆

Wagner, though, had the most active offseason of them all. He declined just about every social offer, including Mike Donlin and Mabel Hite's request for him to be their guest at their Pittsburgh engagement of *Stealing Home*. Wagner could not be coerced to New York for the league meetings, and even George "Honey Boy" Evans, minstrel entertainer and sponsor of a $550 cup for the major league's top hitter, could not track down the winner to give him the award.

In addition to his typical winter agenda, Wagner was involved in several new ventures. He was rumored, along with Sam Leever, to be interested in buying the minor league club in Grand Rapids, Michigan. That deal never materialized, but Wagner did purchase a few more tracts of Carnegie real estate. He was providing a much-needed service by building houses on the lots, and he continued to expand his holdings, eventually owning an entire plan between Sixth and Seventh Avenues in Carnegie.

In November, oil began flowing from wells near Wellsburg, in the northern panhandle of West Virginia. As a partial investor in the drilling, Wagner was in the headlines as having latched onto a potential fortune, although by January it was evident that the financial gains would be modest at best.

Wagner struck a partnership with local businessman J. Joe Feicht, and the two opened an automobile garage on Mary Street, just off Carnegie's Main Street. The Wagner & Feicht Auto Company became the sole western Pennsylvania agent for the Regal automobile. The two models, the runabout and the five-passenger touring car, each sold for $1,250, and the new dealership had an exhibit at the now-annual Pittsburgh auto show. Five Regals were on display at the garage, and Feicht made numerous trips to the Detroit factory to replenish the local supply. Wagner was more than happy to give any interested party a personal demonstration of either model. The partnership would dissolve in November 1909, but Wagner, as local distributor of the forty-horsepower Cutting "Forty," continued to sell autos out of the Mary Street garage for the next few years.

But by far the most intriguing Wagner enterprise in the offseason of 1908–09 was unveiled in December, when a stock solicitation was announced to capitalize the Hans Wagner and Brothers' Circus and Congress of Athletes. Incorporated under New Jersey law, the operation was run out of an address on Main Street in Carnegie. With a par value of ten dollars each, 7,500 shares were offered in order to raise $75,000 in backing. J. Hans Wagner, listed on the prospectus as World's Greatest Baseball Player, was president of the organization and one of the corporation's three officers and seven directors.

The Motor Wagon Circus was to operate under the name of Wagner Brothers' Circus and, as the literature explained, was designed to compete with traveling acts such as Ringling Brothers, Buffalo Bill Cody, and P. T. Barnum. Plans called for the hiring of roughly sixty performers and laborers, as well as a main show tent to seat three thousand people at an average of thirty cents per head. Although it lacked an animal menagerie, the Wagner Brothers' Circus included a few unique features. First, it intended targeting cities with a population of fewer than fifty thousand, figuring that smaller locales were ignored by bigger shows. It also offered "the novelty of a circus parade composed entirely of motor wagons, which should prove as great a drawing power in parade as a herd of elephants."

However, the prospectus left no doubt about the venture's most salable item, saying, "Hans Wagner, of baseball fame—the man whose name is known to every hearthstone of the remotest country settlement, whose name is a magic drawing card amongst the high and the lowly—a man now in the very heighth [sic] of his professional career—a man, the use of whose name is the strongest asset this Company would have from a box-office-sales point of view." *Baseball Magazine*, a monthly publication begun in mid-1908, agreed with the assessment, offering, "Wagner is an attraction, circus or no circus; in fact he's a circus all by himself on the ball field."

With stock sales less than inspiring in January 1909, Wagner resigned his presidency in order to spend more time with his autos, and Al took his place on the board of directors. In February, a seven-man act from Japan and the Brothers Laurenz trapeze artists were signed to contracts. Unfortunately, the whole affair was postponed for one year and then completely folded before the Brothers Laurenz could get off the ground.

Wagner's outlay in the ill-fated undertaking was wasted. The only good to come out of the fiasco was that a three-ton truck purchased for the failed circus was pressed into service and took the local fire company's hose cart to the scene of a fire "in record-breaking time."

◆ ◆ ◆

With all of Wagner's activities, many people anticipated there would be a problem signing him for the 1909 season. And when the club headed south without him, the press was up in arms about another holdout, retirement, and/or salary dispute. Wagner assured those who would listen that he had no complaint whatsoever but was just entirely too busy for spring training. Dreyfuss was not concerned in the least, saying that he knew the shortstop would play and was sure to be in fine condition.

In fact, Dreyfuss and Wagner had already agreed to another year at a ten-thousand-dollar salary. Ultimately, Wagner joined his teammates earlier than he had in 1908, although he cut it a little closer than some may have wanted, arriving two days prior to the opener in Cincinnati.

All seemed fine when Wagner and Clarke walked out arm-in-arm for the opening day festivities on a beautiful day in front of twenty-two thousand fans in Cincinnati. Camnitz ushered in the season by firing a shutout to begin the year, but the Pirates dropped the next three to Cincinnati before beating Mordecai Brown 1–0 in a twelve-inning nail-biter in Chicago.

On the way to Exposition Park for the home opener, Wagner was caught speeding down Grant Avenue in Pittsburgh. The magistrate being a baseball fan, Wagner was permitted to continue on his way with the understanding that he would report to the courthouse the following day. On the field, things weren't much better. The Pirates dropped two of their first three home games and had their only win protested when, during an intentional walk, Wagner headed to first while Reds pitcher Harry Gaspar's 3–0 delivery was still on its way to the plate.

Ten days into the season, Pittsburgh stood at 3–5, and although the team was only three games out of first, its record was the worst in the league—the first time in ten years that the club had been in last place at any point in the season. Clarke was already tinkering with the lineup, seeking the combination that could finally head off the three-time-champion Cubs. Center fielder Roy Thomas, on a leave of absence to complete his coaching duties for the Penn University team, was released by the Pirates before reporting for duty. In early May, Clarke moved Leach back to center field and batted him second behind the team's new third baseman, tiny, 140-pound William "Jap" Barbeau. Clarke and Wagner batted third and fourth, followed by the latest first base experiment, Bill Abstein. Abbaticchio, Wilson, Gibson, and the pitcher rounded out the batting order, but the most decisive early move Clarke made was benching his veteran second baseman.

Abbaticchio had been a disappointment the previous year. He had contributed only twenty-four extra-base hits, and while he led the league in fielding percentage for his position in 1908, he got to fewer balls than almost every other second baseman. When Abbaticchio committed six errors in the first four games of the season, Clarke called on twenty-two-year-old rookie John Miller.

Miller was an enthusiastic, hustling shortstop in the minor leagues, and after splitting most of the previous summer between the Atlantic

League and the Pittsburgh-area McKeesport club, he had worked out with the Pirates late in the season. With Wagner missing all of spring practice, Miller cut such a figure as the number one shortstop that his teammates began referring to him as Hans. Once he got his chance in 1909, Miller was superb. He preserved the 1–0 victory over Brown and the Cubs with a fine unassisted double play. He did not make an error at second base until his seventieth chance and committed only two errors in his first six weeks. Throughout the year, he would consistently drive in runs from the number five and six spots in the order.

The youngster had a personal baseball tutor in Wagner, and the two were becoming inseparable friends. Miller also had a new nickname thanks to Wagner. When a reporter asked who the new kid was at second base, Wagner blurted, "That's Miller." The writer misunderstood and wrote the newcomer's first name as "Dots"—although not because Wagner spoke with a German accent as some have claimed. The name stuck, and while he would still be called Hans and Hans Number Two, Miller was most commonly referred to as Dots.

◆　◆　◆

Playing better ball, the Pirates began a four-game series in Chicago with a doubleheader on May 2. Johnny Kling, the Cubs' star defensive catcher, had won the world championship in pocket billiards that off-season and attempted to use his pool-shooting talent as leverage for a pay raise. When his ploy failed, he decided to skip the 1909 baseball season in order to devote his time to billiards. The Cubs had to split the catching duties between veteran Pat Moran and unproven Jimmy Archer. The weakness would plague the Cubs throughout the year, and Pittsburgh immediately took advantage of it. In game one of the doubleheader in enemy territory, the Pirates stole two bases in a 5–2 win. They put the second game away by pilfering six bases in the first inning, including Wagner steals of second, third, and home.

The following day, Wagner paced the Pirates to their third straight win over the Cubs by going 5 for 6 and, for the second consecutive game, stealing three bases, including home. The Pirates completed the four-game sweep on May 4 by pushing across the game's only run in the eleventh on singles by the three old standbys, Leach, Clarke, and Wagner, plus another single by the new addition, Dots Miller. It was the second time in the first three weeks of the season that they defeated Brown 1–0 in extra innings, and they had convincingly swept four from the champions in Chicago. More importantly for the Cubs, Chance injured his shoulder in a jarring home-plate collision with Gibson. The shoulder troubled Chance for the rest of the season, and he would eventually have his arm placed in a plaster cast when a break was discovered.

On May 5, with Wagner's batting average approaching .430, the Pirates moved into the lead for the first time and, as it would turn out, to stay. A few weeks later at the Polo Grounds, Miller was given a diamond pin from his hometown admirers of nearby Kearny, New Jersey. That same day, Honey Boy Evans finally pinned down Wagner and presented the 1908 batting champion with a silver cup.

◆ ◆ ◆

President Theodore Roosevelt's successor in the election of 1908 was fifty-one-year-old Republican William Howard Taft. On Saturday, May 29, a few months after his inauguration, Taft joined fourteen thousand other fans at Exposition Park to see a matchup of Lefty Leifield and Mordecai Brown.

In the bottom of the first, Clarke walked and Wagner pounded a ball toward the flagpole in center field. He circled the bases, but the ball shot past the temporary ropes in the outfield, so the umpires sent Wagner back to second and Clarke back to third; Clarke unsuccessfully protested the game on the grounds that, because the overflow crowd was confined to the corners and there were no fans in center field, a homer should have been allowed. The Cubs scored three in the sixth to overcome a 2–0 Pirate lead. Wagner made a leaping catch of a line drive, walked, stole a base, and tied the game by driving in a run in the seventh. But the Cubs broke the game open with a five-run eleventh to move within percentage points of Pittsburgh.

Taft was America's first chief executive to take a special interest in the national game and the first to witness a game in Pittsburgh. He loved the extra-inning contest he saw and made it clear that he disliked the bunt play and that in his opinion, Wagner should have been given a home run. (The following spring in Washington, D.C., Taft would begin the well-known custom we know today of the president tossing out the first ball at a season opener. On a return visit to Pittsburgh in May 1910, he insisted on seats with a good view of Wagner, and when Taft stood up during the seventh inning to stretch his portly body, many in the crowd, believing the president was departing, arose as well. While the practice was actually much older, this episode is sometimes cited as the origin of the seventh-inning stretch.)

Following the extra-inning game, the two teams immediately departed for Chicago to square off in a Sunday, May 30 doubleheader. In front of twenty-five thousand Cub fans, the Pirates came from behind to win the opener 5–4. The second game was tied 2–2 when the Pirates loaded the bases with two outs in the top half of the ninth. Wagner worked the count to 3 and 2 before knocking a Jack Pfiester pitch against the left field fence for two runs and the win. The Pirates now held a two-game lead. For most of the next week, the players were buzzing about their second doubleheader sweep in Chicago and Wagner's ninth-inning, two-out, full-count heroics.

The Pirates remained hot for the next few weeks and were getting contributions from everyone. Charles "Babe" Adams, a right-hander, had brief and uninspiring big league trials in 1906 with St. Louis and 1907 with Pittsburgh. The Pirates farmed him to Louisville for 1908, where Adams won twenty-two games and earned a ticket to Hot Springs for 1909. A strikingly handsome man, Adams was tagged with the nickname Babe by female fans in Louisville, who crooned, "Oh, you babe" when they saw him. The label stuck and he became the first Babe of note in baseball—to be followed in a few years by George Herman Ruth. Adams had won the eleven-inning game against the Cubs on May 4 and on the last day of May won both ends of a doubleheader, one in relief.

Robert Hamilton "Ham" Hyatt, a new utility man, was a dreadfully slow runner. He was said to play defense with the ferocity of a cigar-store Indian, but early in 1909, he became a pinch-hitting phenomenon. Referred to as Clarke's "disappearing gun," Hyatt was hitting .437 in limited duty. He was also, along with teammate Miller, sharing quarters with the Wagner men at Railroad Avenue.

Clarke had yet another 5 for 5 game that included a double, triple, and two stolen bases and, at .330, was among the league leaders in batting average. Gibson was surpassing his durable performance of the previous year by catching almost every game and, for the first time in his career, hitting the ball consistently well.

Wagner continued to amaze. On June 3, he clubbed a grand slam, and his five runs driven in led Pittsburgh to a 9–8 win. In mid-June, Wagner was at .405, sixty points ahead of his nearest challenger. The Pirates won fourteen straight before Mathewson defeated them on June 16—a loss they would avenge later in the season by ending Mathewson's personal thirteen-game winning streak. The June 16 contest ended a stretch of eighteen victories in nineteen games, with the only loss coming in front of President Taft. But six consecutive wins followed, and the Pirates had their first breathing room with a five-game lead.

Wagner relaxes in a favorite position while he chats with John McGraw in 1915. *(Pittsburgh Pirates)*

Choosing a weapon. *(Pittsburgh Pirates)*

Wagner enjoying one of his favorite hobbies. *(Pittsburgh Pirates)*

Taking a few minutes during spring training to fish while in Dawson Springs, Kentucky, in March 1915. *(National Baseball Library & Archive, Cooperstown, New York)*

At Hot Springs, Arkansas, with Fred Clarke (*center*) and brother Al Wagner (*right*). *(Pittsburgh Pirates)*

Pittsburgh's Big Three: Fred Clarke, Tommy Leach, and Wagner. *(The Allegheny Club)*

Managers Wagner and Eddie Collins vie for first pick in the choose-up game at the Hall of Fame dedication, June 12, 1939. *(National Baseball Library & Archive, Cooperstown, New York)*

An overflow crowd watches
newly elected National League
president Harry Pulliam (*second
from left*) address the Pittsburgh
and St. Louis clubs at the Pirates'
1903 home opener. *From left to
right, facing the camera:* Barney
Dreyfuss, Fred Clarke (holding
Pulliam's coat and cane),
Cy Falkenberg, Deacon Phillippe,
Kitty Bransfield, and Wagner
(visible between the Cardinals'
vice president and players facing
away from the camera).
(Pittsburgh Pirates)

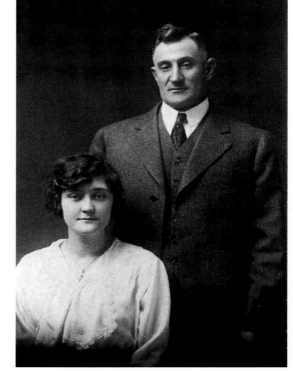

Honus and Bessie shortly
before their wedding.
(John Burk)

Wagner shares a drink, a smoke, and a joke with Bill Benswanger, Herbert Hoover, and Babe Ruth, at the New York Baseball Writers' dinner at the Commodore Hotel on February 4, 1940.

Betty (*far left*), Ginny, and Bessie (*far right*) celebrate the opening of one of Wagner's sporting goods stores. *(National Baseball Library & Archive, Cooperstown, New York)*

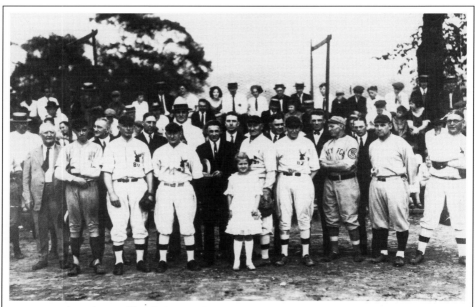

Ginny stands in front of her father as they pose with his Carnegie Elks sandlot team.
(Pittsburgh Pirates)

Wagner is happy to sign
another coaching contract
with Pirate president
Bill Benswanger.
(Pittsburgh Pirates)

Ten of the "eleven immortals" at the dedication of Baseball's Hall of Fame on June 12, 1939. *Back row, left to right:* Wagner, Grover Alexander, Tris Speaker, Nap Lajoie, George Sisler, Walter Johnson. *Front row:* Eddie Collins, Babe Ruth, Connie Mack, Cy Young. Ty Cobb was a late arrival, missing the photo session. *(National Baseball Library & Archive, Cooperstown, New York)*

Enjoying a chaw in 1948. *(Pittsburgh Pirates)*

Wagner's Hall of Fame plaque.
(National Baseball Library &
Archive, Cooperstown, New York)

HONUS WAGNER
LOUISVILLE, N.L.,1897–1899.
PITTSBURGH, N.L.,1900–1917.
THE GREATEST SHORTSTOP IN BASEBALL
HISTORY. BORN CARNEGIE, PA., FEB.24,1874
KNOWN TO FAME AS "HONUS", "HANS" AND
"THE FLYING DUTCHMAN" RETIRED IN 1917,
HAVING SCORED MORE RUNS, MADE MORE
HITS AND STOLEN MORE BASES THAN
ANY OTHER PLAYER IN THE HISTORY
OF HIS LEAGUE

Wagner's Spalding glove.
He altered it for greater control by
cutting out the palm and
stitching around the opening.
(Pittsburgh Pirates)

◆ ◆ ◆

The midsummer of 1909 was an emotional period for those associated with the Pittsburgh Pirates. First, the National League board passed down its ruling on the protested game with Cincinnati, declaring that Wagner should have been called out for crossing the plate and that the game would have to be replayed. Clarke and Dreyfuss were extremely critical of the decision, particularly toward Cubs president Charles Murphy, who they felt should have excused himself from voting because his team was in the race. Dreyfuss went as far as calling Murphy a "rat," and Clarke's comments were so strong that there was concern he might draw a suspension. He ultimately apologized.

Later in June, Dreyfuss's old friend George Dovey passed away on a train en route to Cincinnati from Pittsburgh. The National League postponed its complement of games for the June 22 funeral in which Dreyfuss and Secretary Locke were honorary pallbearers. On the brighter side, Pulliam now seemed to be recovering and was preparing to resume his duties as league president.

Then on June 29, the Pirates played their last game at Exposition Park, home to the National League team since 1891. In front of 5,545 fans, the home team jumped on Chicago's Brown for four first-inning runs. Wagner had two hits, and his plays at shortstop were characterized as "sensational in the extreme" by *The Pittsburgh Post*. Gibson doubled in the eighth for the ballpark's final hit, and the Pirates cruised to an 8–1 win. As Leifield threw a third strike past Jimmy Archer for the last out, local musician Charles Zeig played "Taps" on his cornet.

Throughout the first half of 1909, Dreyfuss had been overseeing the design and construction of his team's new playground. He asked the public to suggest names, and after seriously considering Schenley Stadium, Schenley Field, and Dexter Park (for a famous trotter that once ran on a racetrack at the site), Dreyfuss chose the name Forbes Field. (In 1758, British General John Forbes had led a force to capture strategic Fort Duquesne from the French during the French and Indian War. The French retreated and burned the garrison, but the British erected Fort Pitt nearby—where Pittsburgh later arose.)

While Shibe Park in Philadelphia had opened earlier in 1909 and was the first of the major league concrete-and-steel parks, it was no rival in size or grandeur with Forbes Field. Pre-opening reviews were mixed. Thousands of people flocked to see the structure, and Pulliam as well as the New York Giants' contingent of Brush, Knowles, and Mathewson raved when they got their first glimpse in mid-June. But former big league manager Ned Hanlon told Dreyfuss he spent too much money and that the park was way too big. Some even called it Dreyfuss's Folly.

Dreyfuss was confident that the park would appeal to a higher class of customer and that Pittsburgh was growing eastward. He responded to any unfavorable comments calmly and said he was trying to "give the people something they deserve, and build for the future." The new grandstand was twice as long and twice as high as that of Exposition Park and would seat more than eighteen thousand people. A concrete bleacher down the left field line had room for roughly six thousand fans, bringing the seating capacity close to an unmatched twenty-five thousand. And of course, a few thousand more could be herded behind outfield ropes when necessary. Player and patron comforts were well–thought out, including spacious clubhouses complete with laundry facilities, ramps rather than stairs for ease in moving from one level to another, telephones, and even ladies' rest rooms.

Including land, design, and construction, Forbes Field was an incredible $1 million proposition. Wednesday, June 30, 1909, was to be its grand unveiling. A strike of local trolley workers threatened to put a damper on the occasion, but the conflict was settled on the morning of the game. Many local businesses closed at noon, and the typical scad of city officials was on hand so that each could be seen with his good friend Barney Dreyfuss, the man of the hour. Dreyfuss carefully orchestrated every detail of the historic day. He thoughtfully located many of the old-time baseball players from the area, and they paraded prior to the game. Ferns and palms decorated the broad corridors, and small stickpins in the shape of a ball-and-glove were given to first-game attendees.

A massive turnout of 30,338, a full five thousand more than could be seated, came out for the civic event, and the only down note for the partisans was the game's outcome. Johnny Evers, the first batter, was hit by a Willis pitch and scored on the first hit in the new ballyard, a single by Frank Chance. Gibson garnered Pittsburgh's first hit with a second-inning single, but the score remained 1–0 until the sixth, when Wagner led off with a single to left and later scored on Miller's hit. In the seventh, Wagner made a fine one-handed stop on a ball up the middle and threw the runner out. The record-setting crowd cheered, wanting Wagner to doff his cap, but he walked over to Barbeau and lifted and replaced the third baseman's cap instead.

The Pirates collected only five hits off Reulbach, two each by Miller and Wagner and one by Gibson, losing 3–2. Despite the loss, Dreyfuss was extremely pleased. His Forbes Field was a success from the very start. The first five dates for the Pirates at their new home drew an overwhelming ninety-eight thousand fans, including more than forty-one thousand for a July 5, morning-afternoon doubleheader. Most every baseball and sporting publication praised Dreyfuss for his bold vision and raved about the park's comfort and beauty.

Forbes Field began a new era for ballparks. Over the next few years, it was followed by others, including Chicago's Comiskey Park, Cleveland's League Park, Cincinnati's Crosley Field, Boston's Fenway Park, and a new Polo Grounds in New York. In 1923, they would all be dwarfed by Yankee Stadium—dubbed The House That Ruth Built. Years later, William Benswanger, Dreyfuss's son-in-law and himself president of the Pirates from 1932 to 1946, would refer to Forbes Field as The House That Wagner Built and say, "He was as much the Pirates as Ruth was the Yankees."

◆ ◆ ◆

The drama continued in July. In New York, more than ninety thousand fans came out to an enlarged but still primarily wooden Polo Grounds to see the Pirates and Giants play six games in four days. Victorious in four, the Pirates pushed their lead to seven over the Cubs and ten over the Giants. Camnitz chipped in with his second one-hitter of the year, the only hit a sixth-inning bunt single by pitcher Richard "Rube" Marquard.

Wagner went into his first prolonged slump in the East. Despite dropping fifty points in July, he was still well out in front for the batting lead. He was also able to maintain his sense of humor during the downturn. When he received an ovation for a leaping grab of a line drive, he comically slid his cap to the side of his head. In Philadelphia, he laid a successful bunt down the first base line that was fielded cleanly by Kitty Bransfield, who ran up to tag Wagner. But Wagner turned and headed back where he came from, playfully sliding into home plate in a cloud of dust to the delight of the Philadelphia fans. He ended his weeklong drought and 0 for 19 stretch by singling—left-handed.

Back in front of the home crowd on July 28, Wagner pulled a muscle in his left rib cage while avoiding a tag at the plate. The next day, his side ached but his mind was elsewhere.

When Harry Pulliam returned to his post, the Philadelphia *Public Ledger* welcomed him back, proclaiming, "Long may Pulliam live and rule," and *Baseball Magazine* wrote, "It is to be hoped that Mr. Pulliam will be able to retain for a long time to come his grasp upon affairs." In one of his first official acts, he cracked down on Clarke's bad habit of letting the bat slip out of his hands by instituting an automatic ejection for the offense. Despite initially functioning well, the thirty-nine-year-old Pulliam was still quite obviously despondent. On the evening of July 28, he returned to his boarding room on the third floor of the New York Athletic Club, opposite Central Park, and fired a pistol shot through his temple. He was found within an hour, lying in a pool of blood, but did not die until the next morning.

Clarke, Dreyfuss, Leever, several other Pirate personnel, and many Pittsburgh figures boarded a train for Louisville to attend Pulliam's funeral on Sunday, August 1. Wagner was missing. His side injury was feared to be a broken rib or even heart trouble, and his examining physicians refused to let him ride a train. His teammates had some difficulty convincing him that he could not go, but Wagner remained in Pittsburgh where, according to *Sporting Life*, he "could not be consoled."

◆ ◆ ◆

Within a few days, it was concluded that Wagner's injury was not serious, although the *Carnegie Item* attested that "the bare thought of it makes the universe quiver." He missed nine games, and while Abbaticchio filled in admirably at shortstop, at one point the team's lead was whittled to two and a half games. Wagner was back to full-time duty on August 12. Two days earlier, he had served as a twelfth-inning replacement in left field after Clarke was ejected. The only action Wagner saw in his one inning of work was a fly ball lifted to shallow left-center field. He lost the ball in the sun for a moment, ripped off his smoked glasses and tossed them aside, but Leach gathered in the fly without a problem. Unlike Exposition Park where the sun set over right field, in Forbes Field it dropped behind the first base grandstand, which meant both the left and center fielders had to battle the late afternoon sun. Clarke had missed a fly ball a week earlier and was now diligently working on his idea of mounting a pair of smoked glasses to the bill of a cap to assist an outfielder playing the sun field. Clarke's "sun-shields" would be granted a patent within a few years.

Players had other beefs about Forbes Field. For one, the distance from home plate to the backstop was more than one hundred feet, creating an immense amount of acreage for a catcher to cover. Clarke soon took advantage of this feature by scoring from second on a wild pitch to win an extra-inning game. The infield dirt was extremely rough, causing baseballs to be worn fuzzy within a few innings. And due to an error in the original grading, the infield was built too high, meaning that the batter could not be seen from the knees down by the outfielders. Originally, the skin of the infield was a quirky "heart-shaped" or "camel-back" design; regrading in the offseason to lower the infield eliminated this feature.

Fans registered complaints about Dreyfuss's obvious intention to appeal to wealthier patrons. Not only was the park less accessible to downtown workers, but grandstand ticket sales were withdrawn from the primary business district altogether and prices were higher. Along with larger crowds, Dreyfuss had a keen interest in increasing the profit per admission.

Christy Mathewson made light of the swanky clientele, saying that it was easy to lose a fly ball in the glint off the diamonds in the stands, and he commented that in order not to lose social caste, one of his teammates would have a manicure before taking the field. Further evidence that Forbes Field was different was as close as the back cover of the nickel program, which featured a full-page advertisement for homes in beautiful Schenley Farms, priced at an outrageous sixteen thousand dollars. Looking back, Wagner admitted the move into Forbes Field in 1909 was a transition, observing, "Things were changing fast by that time. Women were beginning to come to the ballparks. We hadda stop cussin'."

◆ ◆ ◆

Wagner paced Pittsburgh to two come-from-behind wins on August 18, one clinched with a ninth-inning sacrifice fly and the other tied with his first Forbes Field home run in the sixth and won in the ninth with his run-scoring double. His homer cleared the left field wall and was grabbed by a youngster in Schenley Park. A security guard gave chase but was no match for the youth who, as *The Pittsburgh Post* described, escaped "with one of the choicest prizes known to kidhood."

Clarke's 1909 lineup was about as set as any he ever managed. In mid-August, he put the final piece in place for the stretch run. Barbeau, who had cooled off considerably after a decent start, was sent to St. Louis along with little-used first baseman Alan Storke. In return, Pittsburgh picked up twenty-four-year-old third baseman Bobby Byrne, who was struggling at the plate for the Cardinals. Leadoff batter Byrne played the hot corner and made just two errors in forty-six games as a Pirate.

Pittsburgh remained comfortably ahead of Chicago through most of August. The Cubs' last significant chance came in a five-game set in early September. In the opener, twenty-nine thousand fans filled West Side Grounds. Clarke made a number of sparkling catches and the game was tied 1–1 after ten innings, but Pittsburgh exploded for four runs in the eleventh to win for the eighth time in eight tries in Chicago. It was also Brown's fourth loss against the Pirates in 1909, his third in extra innings. The two teams raced for Pittsburgh for a morning-afternoon Labor Day doubleheader the next day. In front of a combined forty-five thousand fans, the Pirates dropped both ends and watched their lead shrink to five games.

The following day, the Pirates pegged Brown with another loss, this one in relief, but he tossed a four-hitter in the last game of the set. The Cubs picked up just one game in the standings, and Brown had been beaten twice. In yet another of his great years, Brown would finish 27–9 with a 1.31 ERA and lead the league in wins, games, and innings. But five of his nine losses would come at the hands of Pittsburgh.

With Kling out of baseball in 1909 and Bresnahan giving himself less playing time in his first year as catcher-manager of the St. Louis Cardinals, Gibson was now the best catcher in the National League. He was called Moon and Mooney because of his full round face, and Wagner slapped the nickname Hack on him because his burly build resembled that of professional wrestler George Hackenschmidt, known as The Russian Lion. Gibson had a reputation for recognizing batters' faults and working well with pitchers as well as umpires, and the right-handed hitter was enjoying his best year yet at the plate. On September 9, he set a record by receiving in his 112th consecutive game, surpassing Chief Zimmer's big league mark set in 1890. The same afternoon, the Pirates began a sixteen-game winning streak that sewed up the National League title.

On September 18, in the middle of the Pirates' streak, Vic Willis came within a lone hit of firing the first no-hitter at Forbes Field. Brooklyn rookie Zack Wheat swung and tapped a roller out in front of the plate in the third. Willis and Gibson converged, but the two got their signals crossed and Wheat beat out the bleeder for a single—Brooklyn's only hit of the afternoon. It was the second one-hitter in the ballpark's brief history—Hooks Wiltse had one in late July—and with the vast area of foul ground behind the plate, which turned many foul pops into outs, it seemed just a matter of time before a no-hitter would be tossed. But in sixty-one years of big league ball at Forbes Field, not one no-hitter was thrown.

A few days later on lucky September 22, the Pirates stroked thirteen hits and won their thirteenth straight game in front of just over 1,300 fans. It gave them a record of 103–36, identical to that of the 1902 champions. Three more wins followed as Pittsburgh set a still-standing franchise record with sixteen consecutive wins. Prior to play on September 28, Clarke was awarded more than six hundred dollars in gold by Pittsburgh mayor William A. Magee as a token of appreciation from the manager's admirers. After a rather lengthy speech, Clarke walked and scored, then took himself out of the game. Wagner doubled twice and singled, but the Pirates were drubbed 13–9 by the Giants. Nonetheless, the flag was clinched that day as the Cubs lost to the Phillies.

Clarke wanted to prevent his players from going "stale" before the World Series, which would match them against either the Detroit Tigers or the Philadelphia Athletics, who were fighting it out in the season's final days. Except for Wagner, who missed the last seven games with an ankle sprain, Clarke went with his regular lineup over the final week. But the Pirates lost six of their last ten to finish at 110–42, six and a half ahead of Chicago, eighteen and a half over third-place New York, and more than thirty games out in front of the rest of the pack. (The 1909 Cubs, 1942 Brooklyn Dodgers, and 1993 Atlanta Braves are the only three teams to win 104 games but fall short of the World Series.)

Just as in the previous year, the Pirates played over .700 ball on the road, but in 1909, they improved their home record to a league-best 56–21, including a 20–5 mark before departing Exposition Park. They blew apart the weaker members of the National League—going 18–4 with Brooklyn and 18–3 with St. Louis. Even more notable was their 20–1 record against Boston, 108-game losers in 1909, including fifty-four losses apiece for their two managers, Harry Smith and Frank Bowerman.

The 1909 Pirates were one of baseball's greatest teams. Their .724 winning percentage has been surpassed in this century only by the 1902 Pirates (.741) and the 1906 Chicago Cubs (.763). In its review of the 1909 season, the 1910 *Spalding Guide* referred to the Pirate squad as "a solidly built and compact one" and explained, "They played good, sound, orthodox base ball with occasional flashes of brilliancy excelled by none."

Surely it was a well balanced team. Pittsburgh led in most offensive categories including team batting average, doubles, triples, slugging, and most importantly, runs—with Leach, Clarke, and Wagner ranking one-two-three in the league. The defense committed the fewest errors and led in fielding percentage, thanks to league-leading marks by Miller, Gibson, and Clarke, who set a new major league record for most putouts in a season by a left fielder and tied the mark for fielding percentage, which he had established a few years earlier.

However, even the *Spalding Guide* seemed a bit giddy over Wagner's individual performance maintaining, "Wagner, of course, is a player of the type who seems to come only as new stars are discovered at rare intervals in the skies. . . . [There] were moments when Wagner seemed superhuman and stopped batted balls that one would almost believe out of the range of man's feeble possibilities." At .339, he outhit the league average by .095 in winning his seventh batting title, was the only player to drive in one hundred runs, and led in doubles, slugging, and total bases. Clarke told him not to take chances on the base paths down the stretch, leading to Wagner's lowest stolen base total since 1898. Still, his thirty-five steals in 1909 would top any of his single-season stolen base marks for the remainder of his career.

◆ ◆ ◆

In 1903, the World's Championship Series was primarily the brainchild of Barney Dreyfuss and Henry Killilea and loosely sanctioned by their respective league presidents. By 1909, the World Series was a thriving, popular, and respected annual event under the auspices of the National Commission. While in 1903, a best-of-nine-game format was used, subsequent Series have all been the best-of-seven setup we know today—except in 1919, 1920, and 1921, when a best-of-nine was greedily staged. By 1909, the media had embraced the World Series, and there was no shortage of analysis on how the Pirates stacked up against the Tigers, who at 98–54 had edged out the Athletics by three and a half games for a third straight American League title.

Tiger manager Hughie Jennings, the ex–Oriole shortstop, was now well known to the baseball world for his unusual antics in the coaches' box that featured a grass-pulling, fist-pumping, foot-stomping routine accompanied by screeches of "Ee-yaah!"

Just like the Pirates in the National League, the Tigers led their league in runs and team batting average. They also stole a league-high 280 bases. Good-natured veteran Bill Donovan, whose control problems earned him the nickname Wild Bill, suffered with a bad shoulder in 1909 and slipped to 8–7. But led by George Mullin, who had an eleven-game win streak on his way to a league-best 29–8 mark, Detroit's pitching was still solid. A trio of Eds—Ed Willett at 21–10, Ed Summers at 19–9, and Ed Killian at 11–9—rounded out the staff. Catching was a perennial weakness. Oscar Stanage and Charles "Boss" Schmidt, one of Detroit's goats in its previous two World Series losses, shared the work behind the plate almost evenly during the year. Neither provided any offense whatsoever in 1909 and both were suspect defensively.

During the season, Jennings rebuilt the defending champions' infield. In the spring, he handed the shortstop position to twenty-one-year-old Donie Bush. Then in midyear, Jennings moved George Moriarty, an offseason purchase from the Highlanders, from first to third base and traded for first baseman Tom Jones and veteran second baseman Jim Delahanty (one of five Delahanty brothers to play in the big leagues, including Hall of Famer Ed).

The combination was hardly one to be feared, and prominent baseball writer Hugh Fullerton thought the Pirates had a resounding advantage in the infield. He favored Moriarty over Byrne by a slight margin at third base but gave the Pirates the nod at first, where he believed Bill Abstein was "more dangerous" than the experienced Jones, and at second, where Fullerton considered Miller "the sensation of the season at his position." Referring to Bush as "a magnificent player" as well as "brilliant, heady, and fast," Fullerton clarified that "he does not at all compare with the Flying Dutchman."

Detroit's strength was its all-left-hand-hitting outfield. Matty McIntyre and Davy Jones split time in left field, combining to exceed one hundred runs. Center fielder Sam Crawford, now in the eleventh year of his Hall of Fame career, was the club's productive cleanup hitter. But the Tigers' three-year run of championships was easily linked to one factor—Ty Cobb's rapid ascension to the top of the game.

The extremely talented and highly volatile Cobb led the American League in almost everything in 1909. In the days before the Triple Crown was an acknowledged achievement, Cobb led his league in batting at .377, home runs, and runs driven in, and for good measure he threw in league-high totals in stolen bases, hits, runs, slugging, and total bases. Still a few months shy of his twenty-third birthday and in only his fifth year of big league ball, the young Georgian was already a superstar and recognized as a dominant player. He was also crowding Honus Wagner for sports-page headlines as the game's best.

Cobb also had a propensity for making front-page news for other reasons. With his insufferably abrasive personality, he alienated most everyone equally—strangers, opponents, and teammates. In 1909, Cobb was involved in two of his ugliest affairs. In Philadelphia, he spiked Athletics third baseman Frank Baker; Connie Mack and his players charged that the act was deliberate, and Cobb became the object of condemnation and even death threats in Philadelphia. Late in the season, the racist Cobb became entangled in a controversy with a black hotel night-watchman in Cleveland. The incident escalated into a brawl, and Cobb pulled a knife before being clubbed in the head a few times with a nightstick.

Only three World Series have ever pitted the batting champions head to head. (In addition to 1909, the others were Al Simmons and Chick Hafey in 1931, and Willie Mays and Bobby Avila in 1954.) In 1909, the matchup took on added meaning. Not only were Wagner and Cobb batting champions, they were clearly the best players of their respective leagues and were recognized even at the time as two of the greatest players ever. This Series was not simply the Tigers against the Pirates or the city of Pittsburgh versus the city of Detroit—it was also generally considered Cobb versus Wagner. The young upstart Cobb, with a seemingly unlimited future, who in 1909 had one of the greatest seasons on record for a baseball player, was pitted against Wagner, the thirty-five-year-old veteran who posted yet another stellar year at the plate and in the field.

Everyone had an opinion on the outcome of the Series as well as on which star would get the upper hand. There was active betting on both items, with the Pirates favored by most to capture the title and an estimated ten thousand dollars evenly split on the Cobb-Wagner battle. Clarke, as usual, refused to speculate on his team's chances, saying, "Pennants are not won by managerial hot air or by newspapers. Championships are won on the grass."

On the beautiful Friday afternoon of October 8, all functional streetcars were pressed into service as tens of thousands of people converged on the Pittsburgh community of Oakland. Pirate fans displayed their pride in any number of ways. Many people wore badges with insipid messages such as YOU MIGHT TY COBB, BUT YOU CAN'T TIE WAGNER and I LOVE MY WIFE, BUT OH YOU HANS WAGNER. One local clothier went as far as placing a real skull-and-crossbones in his store window.

Despite prices ranging from one to two dollars, the entire lot of reserved seat tickets was sold well in advance of the first two games. Additional wooden bleacher seats had been erected in the brand-new park's outfield, and a short, two-foot-high wooden fence was placed in front to avoid the ground-rule confusion of ropes and posts. Directly behind these new seats was the permanent concrete outfield wall—wrapped in barbed wire ribbons for the affair. This jagged welcome mat proved an insufficient deterrent to many youngsters, who resorted to stacking three or four morning newspapers for self-styled seat cushions. A half-dozen more young fans climbed a telegraph pole behind the left field wall, and still more sat atop the Carnegie Library or on the hillside of Schenley Park in the distance.

In front of an unheard-of World Series crowd of 29,264, the Pirates and Tigers warmed up on the diamond below. Amid batting practice and the general milling around, left fielder Davy Jones tried his new sunglasses, a last-minute purchase he made after the previous day's practice session. A pair of photographs, snapped during the pregame, perfectly sum up the approach of two of the greatest hitters to ever swing a bat. In one shot, a left-handed, lithe Ty Cobb is shown uncurling in a picturesque follow-through—most likely stroking a hit. In the other photo, Wagner's back foot is completely off the ground as he finishes his swing off-balance—with the result, no doubt, an equally stinging line drive.

Wagner, rugged and by now leather-faced, spotted his tall, slender, fair-haired rival near the plate and approached. The two shook hands, compared their split-hand grips, and even made plans to enjoy an off-season hunting trip together in Georgia. As the two great figures of the game spent a few minutes talking, an astute media man with an early-model motion picture camera recorded the moment for posterity.

◆ ◆ ◆

Manager Clarke had a stable of quality pitchers to choose from for Game One. Howie Camnitz was the staff ace in 1909 with a 25–6 record—identical to Mathewson's and good for the league's best winning percentage. But Camnitz was ill in early October. Some reports had him suffering from tonsillitis or quinsy, a painful inflammation of the throat, while others attributed his late-season affliction to falling off the wagon. Vic Willis was 22–11, Nick Maddox finished 13–8, and the staff's only southpaw, Lefty Leifield, went 19–8. The two thirty-seven-year-old veterans remaining from the 1903 staff, Leever and Phillippe, saw limited action but both chipped in. Leever finished 8–1 while Phillippe rebounded from a winless 1908 for an 8–3 mark. But Clarke surprised some self-styled experts by choosing rookie Babe Adams to pitch the first game.

Famed baseball writer Fred Lieb later connected the choice of Adams to a recommendation made by new National League president John Heydler. According to Lieb, Heydler had seen Washington pitcher William "Dolly" Gray stifle Detroit earlier in the season and, detecting a style similarity between Gray and Adams, encouraged Clarke to start his right-hander, Adams. It is true that in July 1909, Gray threw eight and a third scoreless innings against Detroit in an eighteen-inning, 0–0 tie— still the longest scoreless game in American League history. Clarke probably would have considered this advice (if it were given at all) more credible if thirty-year-old rookie Gray had not set a major league record by walking seven consecutive batters in an August contest, if he had compiled anything better than a deplorable 5–19 mark for last-place Washington, or if Gray had even been right-handed instead of a lefty.

More likely, Clarke based his decision on the eye-popping performance of Adams over the last half of the season. Clarke, as he would often do with rookie pitchers, protected Adams by using him sparingly and mostly in relief until he got his feet wet. But in August, Adams became Clarke's most reliable hurler. During the Pirates' sixteen-game winning streak, Adams contributed a pair of three-hitters and a four-hitter and took one of the games into the seventh before surrendering a safety.

In the final two months, Adams was even better than his 7–2 mark would indicate, losing one game by a 1–0 score and dropping the other in ten innings due in part to Clarke misjudging a fly ball in the nasty Forbes Field sun. In the extra-inning loss, Adams fanned six batters in a row and logged a franchise-high twelve strikeouts. (The mark remained a Pirate record for 55 years, tied by Bob Veale in 1964 and surpassed by Veale in 1965 with sixteen.) On the 1909 season, Adams finished 12–3, including a perfect 6–0 in relief, and compiled a microscopic 1.11 ERA. Always very calm and composed, and perhaps aided by the infield surface, which roughed up baseballs and helped put a little extra break on his best pitch, a sharp curveball, he was nearly unbeatable at new Forbes Field.

Adams was surely not a dark horse for the Game One start and, in fact, he and past World Series hero Phillippe were selected by a local newspaper to write a running commentary during the Series. Clarke still had a few reservations. Leach remembered that the manager approached a few of the veterans prior to the opener and asked if they thought Adams could do the job. Leach and his teammates knew what fine work the pitcher had done down the stretch and, citing Adams's control, the influence of catcher Gibson, and the immense grounds that helped outfielders shag many mistakes, concurred with Clarke.

Clarke expected that even the unexcitable Adams would be a bit nervous, but he felt confident that if Adams could get through the first inning, he would settle down and pitch a good game. The twenty-seven-year-old right-hander did little to ease his manager's worries when he almost beaned the leadoff hitter, Davy Jones, on the first pitch and then walked him on four straight. Bush, celebrating his twenty-second birthday, dropped down a sacrifice bunt, and Cobb, after a warm welcome by the Pittsburgh fans, walked. Adams seemed back in control when he got Crawford to bounce back hard to the mound for a force out at third, but Delahanty ripped a single to left and Cobb crossed the plate with the first run of the Series. Adams and the Pirates got a break when Moriarty's bouncer hit Delahanty in the leg to end the inning with just a single run across.

Mullin, the hard-throwing right-hander, was Jennings's obvious first-game choice and responded by facing the minimum over the first three innings, although he did walk and then pick off Abstein in the second. Adams allowed at least one baserunner in each of the first four frames, but the game entered the bottom of the fourth with Detroit ahead just 1–0. Mullin retired the first two in the inning as Byrne bounced back to the mound and Leach lost his bat flailing at a third strike, but Clarke chalked up the first Pirate hit and run with a home run drive over the temporary fence in right field.

The bench jockeys of both teams were active from the first pitch of the game, and Clarke's homer heated the already tense atmosphere. Wagner, whose first at bat amid thunderous applause resulted in a ground out, now followed Clarke to the plate after the home run. He knew what to expect and took up a spot in the very rear of the batter's box, but when Mullin drilled him in the ribs with a fastball, the war was on. Before the Series was over, six players would be fined for violent protests, six inflicted with spike wounds, and two more carried off the grounds with injuries.

In the top half of the fifth inning, Davy Jones singled to right and was forced at second by Bush. Bush was erased on a force out by Cobb, who quickly stole second. This steal by Cobb brought about the single most talked-about, most widely referenced, most embellished scenario of Wagner's great career.

Gibson's throw was in the dirt, but it was a close play at the second base bag as Wagner one-handed the throw on a short hop and in the same motion, made a sweeping tag on Cobb. *The Detroit Free Press* referred to Wagner's effort as a "neat pick-up" and a "difficult play." A few Pittsburgh sources had Cobb out by anywhere from two feet to a yard, but more objective onlookers agreed that Cobb was safe thanks to a long feet-first slide. In the only dispute of the day, Wagner and his teammates ranted to American League umpire Silk O'Loughlin that the tag was in time.

Over the years, this play took on a life of its own and the scene was painted in any number of ways in order to epitomize the two characters—the aggressive Cobb and the stalwart Wagner. The incredible legend that has evolved from this simple stolen base usually begins with Cobb's outlandish boast and warning from first base in the direction of his rival: "I'm coming down on the next pitch, Krauthead!" Wagner's alleged reaction to Cobb's foolhardiness varies, from silent indifference to a daring proclamation of "I'll be ready, Rebel!" And the story continues with Cobb churning down the baseline with flashing spikes and Wagner slamming a rough tag to the baserunner's head, resulting in— again depending on the source—anywhere from a few teeth loosened or lost, three stitches to the lip, and on up to near decapitation.

As the men at the pinnacle of the game, their every move and action was news. At the time, the only importance placed on the play was that of an extra ninety feet for the Tiger baserunner and the resulting argument by the Pirates, who disagreed with the call. The contrived details of the "Krauthead incident" hold virtually no plausibility since the slur "Kraut" was not even applied to those of German descent until World War I, and the derogatory term "Krauthead" did not surface until World War II. But the mere fact that such an extraordinary fabrication was conceived decades after the play is testimony to the figures involved.

Wagner would often relate how his respect for Cobb grew over the course of the Series, saying that Cobb played a "shrewd, heady game." In his later years, though, Wagner would occasionally give credence to the story in one of his many tall-tale sessions. Cobb usually fervently denied the confrontation completely, and in his autobiography, *My Life in Baseball*, he referred to Wagner as "a block of granite" and expressed, "Spike Honus Wagner? It would have taken quite a foolhardy man." Cobb recalled that they struck up a mutual admiration for each other during the Series, but as Cobb conveyed, "You can't fill sport-page space with simple good fellowship."

The Tigers self-destructed in the bottom half of the fifth inning. Abstein hit a hot shot past Delahanty for an error, although several accounts stated that it should have been ruled a hit, and when Cobb kicked the ball, Abstein made it all the way to third. Wilson fanned, but Gibson, after fouling off several pitches, doubled to bring in the tie-breaking run. Bush muffed Adams's ground ball, and Byrne stumbled to first after being hit in the head with a pitch to load the bases. Leach hit a sacrifice fly to left to make it 3–1 Pittsburgh, and the Pirates added another run in the sixth on Wagner's leadoff double to left, an errant pickoff throw by catcher Schmidt, and an infield out.

After two outs in the Tigers' seventh, Davy Jones singled and Bush walked. Jennings shifted his coaching routine into a higher gear. The Forbes Field grass was cut too short to pull out of the ground, but shadowboxing and shrieking, Jennings was trying his best to rattle Adams. Cobb swung and missed at two curveballs but stroked a third to deep center. Had Cobb pulled the ball to right, it would have had the distance for a home run, but Leach made the defensive play of the game when he sprinted back and hauled down the drive to end the inning and Detroit's final threat.

Cobb was hitless in three at bats but walked, stole a base, and scored. Wagner went 1 for 3 with a double and a run. In his final at bat of the day, he was hit with an off-speed pitch. Umpire Jim Johnstone ruled that since Wagner did not attempt to get out of the way, he was not entitled to a base. Wagner then bounced back to the mound for an out. The Tigers made four miscues, and the Pirates played errorless ball. The flawless infield was described as "machine-like" by Francis Richter, who served as one of two official scorers for the Series. Adams, saying he fed the Tigers a steady diet of low curves, gave up just six singles and retired the Tigers in order over the last two innings for a 4–1 complete game and a 1–0 lead for the Pirates.

The two teams spent the evening at the Grand Opera House, and the entire Pirate organization was on hand with the exception of Wagner, who sought the solitude of Carnegie. Mobs of fans descended into downtown Pittsburgh to celebrate the opening-game victory. The Friday-night festivities were "pleasantly civilized" and lasted until the late hours. *The Sporting News* described what must have been a beautiful scene with "The whole city was intoxicated with joy," adding, "Everybody was on the streets, and you heard nothing, saw nothing, felt nothing, thought nothing but base ball."

♦ ♦ ♦

An Indian summer afternoon greeted yet another record gathering in excess of thirty thousand people for Game Two of the Series on Saturday, October 9. Both managers made a late decision on their starters. Jennings had both Summers and Donovan warming up but opted for Donovan, feeling that the warmer weather would allow the veteran to get his sore right arm "lubricated." Clarke chose a seemingly recovering Camnitz—recently accused of being "well-oiled" himself.

The Pirates mounted a first-inning rally as Byrne led off with a walk and Leach doubled him home for a 1–0 lead. Clarke sacrificed Leach to third, and Wagner approached the plate. He tried a few useless antics to rattle Donovan but ended up wasting an easy chance for a run by striking out. With two outs and Leach at third, Miller stroked a fair line drive down the right field line, and the fans went crazy as he circled the bases for what seemed to be a two-run homer. But the ball had bounced into the crowd, and Miller was sent back to second, where he was stranded when Abstein struck out.

Detroit tied the score at two in the second. Then in the third, Davy Jones reached safely on a bunt when first baseman Abstein dropped Byrne's throw. Camnitz fell apart. He gave up a single to Bush, a walk to Cobb, and a two-run double to Delahanty. The Tigers now had a 4–2 lead, and Cobb was standing on third. Clarke had seen enough and summoned Willis to the mound. Following a few warm-up tosses, as Willis toed the rubber and went into his windup to deliver his first pitch, Cobb sprinted down the line and slid feet-first under Gibson's tag for a thrilling steal of home plate.

Ahead 5–2, Detroit tacked on two more runs in the fifth. Donovan, after an unsteady first, breezed through the remainder of the game. He struck out seven, including Abstein three times, and surrendered just three more hits—another Leach double in the third, an Abstein single in the fourth, and a Wagner single in the ninth. The Tigers had an easy 7–2 win and a tie at one game apiece in the Series.

As far as the head-to-head matchup, Wagner went 1 for 4 and Cobb had his first hit in the Series, going 1 for 3 and losing another hit on a great play by Abstein. Each star stole a base, although Cobb's steal of home had a far greater impact than Wagner's uncontested steal of second in the ninth inning. Each was a bit overaggressive on the base paths as well. Cobb was thrown out oversliding the bag when he went from first to third on a ground out, and Wagner was gunned down stealing third. Game Two went to Detroit; round two went to Cobb.

◆ ◆ ◆

The decisive games of the 1907 and 1908 World Series had both been staged in Detroit, and attendance at the two contests was wretched. But if Tiger fans were becoming bored or disillusioned with the event, it was not apparent at the first game held in Detroit in the 1909 Series. On Monday, October 11, an overflow gathering of 18,277 packed old wooden Bennett Park, which one Pittsburgh correspondent likened to an Allegheny County League ball field. Several thousand other fans found a vantage point from surrounding rooftops or homemade bleachers erected behind the outfield wall. And while the tightfisted president of the Tigers, Frank Navin, tried to obstruct the view of these unauthorized seats by having long strips of canvas stretched above the fence, it was still a better spot for watching the game than that afforded the two official scorers; Francis Richter of *Sporting Life* and Joseph Flanner of *The Sporting News* were stationed behind a post.

Roughly three thousand Pirate rooters made the trip to Detroit, but they left behind the beautiful weather the players and fans had enjoyed for the first two games in Pittsburgh. Low-hanging dark clouds made for a gloomy, gray day, and intermittent icy showers as well as chilling winds made conditions worse.

Nineteen-game winner Ed Summers, a knuckleballer, took the hill for the Tigers but faced only six men and recorded just a lone out before being driven from the mound in preference to Ed Willett. The Pirates amassed five first-inning runs by batting around on four hits, a walk, and three Detroit miscues in the sloppy conditions. After a quick bottom of the first that included a Cobb strikeout, the Pirates added another run in the second. Leach was hit in the hand by a pitch, Clarke took one in the knee, and after Wagner forced Clarke at second, Wagner and Leach tried a double steal from the corners. The play seemed to fail as Leach was caught in a rundown, but when Willett dropped the ball, Leach scored to make it 6–0 Pittsburgh.

Although he had both pitchers warm up before the game, Clarke chose Maddox over Leifield, and the right-hander defended the big lead by allowing four scattered hits and walking no one through the first six innings. But Detroit mounted a comeback in the seventh; Delahanty opened the inning with his second double of the game, and Moriarty reached when Abstein missed Miller's throw.

Clarke ran into the infield and led an argument that Abstein was interfered with by Moriarty as he crossed the bag. Several Pirates stormed around complaining about the call, and Clarke went as far as to imply that they were getting the worst of American League umpire Johnstone's calls. Following the game, Clarke and a few others would be fined twenty-five dollars for umpire-baiting, but on the field, play finally resumed, with Moriarty on first. Tom Jones singled in Detroit's first run, and after two outs, Davy Jones beat out a bunt to fill the bases. Bush singled over Wagner's head to drive in a pair of runs, and Cobb singled to center for another, but Crawford popped out to end the inning. Detroit still trailed 6–4.

A cold rain streamed down in the ninth as the Pirates expanded their lead off rookie reliever Ralph Works. Byrne singled, Leach doubled into the crowd in left, and Clarke hit a sacrifice fly to drive in Byrne. Wagner followed with a run-scoring single, his third single of the game, and then stole second for the third time before Cobb made a tumbling catch of Miller's sinking liner to end the inning.

With the Pirates ahead 8–4 in the ninth, Maddox struggled to nail down the victory. After an out, Wagner made a terrific stop of Davy Jones's grounder, but Abstein once again dropped a throw, his third error of the Series. Bush followed with an infield hit and Cobb doubled into the overflow in right field. It would have been a home run under normal conditions, but Cobb had to settle for a ground-rule double. Crawford came to the plate representing the tying run but could only ground to Wagner as Bush scored to make it 8–6 Pittsburgh. Detroit was down to its last out and had Delahanty, 3 for 4 so far on the day, coming to the plate, but he lined to Clarke to end the game. Maddox had dodged a bullet, and his teammates left the field dodging the now-forming puddles in the diamond.

Wagner was the focal point of Game Three. *The New York Times* called it "Wagner Day, with an uppercase W and a capital D" and explained, "The Flying Dutchman had on his batting clothes, and he also had rubbed mercury on his feet for the occasion." He went 3 for 5, scored once, drove in two runs, and stole three bases in four attempts. And his performance was thought to be even better at the time due to several of the next day's game accounts crediting him with both a fourth single and a fourth stolen base—saying that he reached in the first inning on a hit rather than an error and giving him credit for a steal on the busted double-steal attempt in the second. During the coming offseason, Hugh Fullerton referenced this game as the contest in which Wagner finally shed the "yellow ball" blemish that some people still saw. He pointed out two plays in which Wagner ranged, in Fullerton's estimation, thirty-seven feet and forty feet to flag down ground balls, turning them into outs.

◆ ◆ ◆

The weather for Game Four on Tuesday, October 12, was more wintery than the previous day, and many expected the bitter wind to blow in snow at any moment. Another difficulty for many fans was that, by Michigan law, the saloons were closed for the Columbus Day holiday. *The Pittsburgh Post* remarked, "The wise ones fortified themselves last night" but added that some "neglected to lay in a day's rations, and these fellows are almost famished." Despite the nasty conditions, another surplus turnout of 17,036 appeared at Bennett Park. The expected matchup was Mullin and Adams, the first game's starters, but Clarke decided to send his left-hander to the mound. Leifield was not sharp, giving up five runs in only four innings of work, but it made little difference as Mullin's fastball proved almost unhittable in the dark surroundings.

In the bottom of the first, Cobb was stranded on second after being hit by a pitch and moving up on an error. In the second, Wagner walked and, following several unsuccessful attempts to pick him off, advanced when Abstein legged out a bouncer. The Pirates had two on with only one out but did not score as Mullin retired the next two batters on comebackers.

The Tigers broke through in the second on a two-run single by Oscar Stanage, and another Pirate rally fell short in the third. Leifield struck out to begin the inning, but Byrne doubled into left and Leach walked. A running commentary began between batter Clarke and pitcher Mullin. As each pitch passed the plate, the two tried to get under each other's skin with, most likely, colorful and well-timed verbal barrages. Mullin asked whether Clarke was looking for a base on balls when he let the first wide one go by; Clarke responded with his observation that the pitcher seemed to be losing his control. The volley continued, but after fouling off a pair of 3–2 pitches, Clarke struck out. As Clarke fanned, the two runners moved into scoring position on a double steal, but Wagner was caught looking at a third strike to end the inning. As the Tiger fans roared, Wagner waved his hands in front of umpire Klem's face in disgust at the call. Mullin had struck out the side in thwarting the last Pirate push of the day.

Pirate highlights were few. Wagner went hitless in three at bats and, just as in the opening game, was refused a base when it was judged that he purposely stepped in front of a pitch. Miller was fined for pounding his bat into the ground in a heated argument with Klem after being called out on strikes. The second baseman was also spiked in the arm on a high slide by Davy Jones. The Pirates did not get a runner to third base after the third inning, and they made six errors—two more by Abstein at first base and two each by Miller and Phillippe. Phillippe, the workhorse of the 1903 Series, provided the only bright spot for Pittsburgh fans by pitching one-hit shutout ball over the last four innings.

Mullin struck out ten and gave up only five hits as his 5–0 shutout evened the Series at two games apiece. For the Tigers, it was the first time in three World Series that they had won a game on their home grounds and the first time they had managed two wins in the same Series.

As the Pirates stopped off at the Pontchartrain Hotel to collect their belongings, they were subjected to quite an amount of good-natured ribbing. Much of it was directed at Wagner, including a huge jack-o-lantern with a placard inscribed HANS WAGNER—PUNKIN-HEAD. The team raced to the station to join the Tigers and the members of the National Commission on a special train of a baggage car and six sleepers bound for Pittsburgh on the Lake Shore Railroad.

Ty Cobb was noticeably missing from the precious World Series cargo that made its way across Ohio along the southern shore of Lake Erie. Cobb, accompanied by his wife and mother, rode eastward across Ontario to Buffalo, then down through the western tip of New York and western Pennsylvania. The circuitous route to Pittsburgh, as well as the return trip, was necessary in order to bypass Ohio, where an indictment had been secured for Cobb's arrest on charges of felonious assault for the Cleveland hotel incident.

◆ ◆ ◆

It was a clear but cold and windy afternoon in Pittsburgh, and attendance dropped with the thermometer as 21,706 people gathered for the fifth game on Wednesday, October 13. Ticket speculators who had been receiving twenty dollars for a Forbes Field reserved seat a few days earlier were now hard-pressed to get face value for their pasteboards. The temporary center field stands were completely unnecessary, although the short fence in front of them became an important part of the day's play.

Clarke sent Game One phenom Babe Adams to the mound, and just as in his prior start, he had first-inning trouble. Leadoff hitter Davy Jones lifted a ball over Leach's head that bounded over the short new fence for a home run and an immediate 1–0 lead. Bush walked on five pitches, and Cobb, knowing Adams was in a bind, tried to rile the Pirate hurler by making faces at him. Adams seemed unperturbed. After Cobb swung at and missed one ball and complained about a called strike, he harmlessly flied to center for the first out of the inning. Crawford kept the rally alive by singling Bush to third on a hit-and-run, but Adams retired Delahanty on strikes and got Moriarty to pop up to end the inning with just one run across.

Manager Jennings bypassed his warm-weather pitcher, Bill Donovan, instead calling upon Ed Summers. Summers had lasted just one third of an inning two days earlier and looked no sharper in the early going of this contest as the Pirates answered with a run in the bottom half of the first. Byrne singled to left, and after Leach beat out a bunt, Clarke laid down a two-strike sacrifice to move the runners into scoring position. Wagner was intentionally passed to load the bases, and it looked as though Summers might wriggle off the hook when he struck out Miller. But Abstein walked to force in the tying run before Wilson's strikeout ended the inning.

While Adams struck out six and held Detroit scoreless over the next four innings, Summers continued to be generous. In the second, his wild pitch cost the Tigers a run, and in the third, he started the inning by walking Clarke, who came around to score on Wagner's hit-and-run single and Miller's ground out.

Trailing 3–1, Detroit struck in the sixth. Cobb hit a one-out single and scored on Crawford's gapper into left-center that almost skipped over the low fence for a homer. Wagner fielded Delahanty's grounder but threw wildly as Crawford tallied to tie the score before Adams retired the next two batters.

Summers settled down and through the middle innings allowed only an infield single to Clarke, just the skipper's second hit since his homer in the opening game. In the seventh, the Pirates reached the knuckleballer to break the 3–3 tie. A pair of one-out singles by Byrne and Leach put runners on the corners for Clarke. He had connected for just three home runs during the entire 1909 regular season and only ten in the past six years but hit his second in five games of the World Series by bouncing a ball over the left–center field fence. Having given the Pirates a 6–3 lead, he circled the bases to as deafening a roar as twenty thousand human beings can make.

Just as in his appearance after Clarke had homered in Game One, Wagner was subsequently drilled with a fastball. This one caught him in the back, dropping him to the ground in a heap. His teammates sprinted from the bench to his aid, and the fans who had been so exuberant a few moments earlier were now still and silent. After a few minutes' delay and a rubdown from the trainer, Wagner jogged to first base. Showing no lasting effects from being hit, he tried to rile Summers by gyrating like a "circus clown"—and then stole second. Continuing with an act described by *The Pittsburgh Post* as "a combination hornpipe, reel, and jig between second and third," Wagner stole third and delightedly headed home as Schmidt's wild throw landed in left field.

The teams traded eighth-inning runs. Crawford hit a high drive to center that landed for the game's third home run. Leach raced back, unaware that he was nearing the temporary barrier, and crashed into the boards. He tumbled over the wall and lay on the ground out of sight of most fans. As Clarke and Wilson converged on the scene, a dazed Leach emerged and climbed back over the planks he had just broken to resume his position in center field.

A Wilson double and a Gibson run-scoring single made it an 8–4 final, and while Adams was touched for four runs, he struck out eight in notching his second victory. The fans descended onto the field. A few took turns on the mound, imitating the delivery of Adams. Others surveyed the ground between second and third, pointing to Wagner's and Bush's spike marks and scooping up handfuls of dirt from the sacred spot. It was the last contest to be played in Pittsburgh in 1909. The Pirates were one win from the title, a game they would have to win in Detroit. The two teams gathered at the Pittsburgh & Lake Erie Station at 11:00 P.M. and boarded their special train bound for Michigan.

◆ ◆ ◆

Mullin, with a win and a loss to show for a pair of five-hitters in the Series, was Detroit's sixth-game starter on a clear but cold Thursday, October 14. The Pirates went to work on him in the top of the first in front of only 10,535 Tiger fans. Byrne singled to left and moved up when Jones could not corral Leach's hard-hit ball. Clarke, once referred to by Wagner as the best hit-and-run man he ever saw, knocked in a run with a hit-and-run single to right. Wagner lined a double to deep left for two runs. With a 3–0 lead before Mullin could record an out, the Pirates looked well on their way to their first world championship.

Willis was shaky in his first Series start. He almost managed to get through the first inning unscathed when he caught Cobb looking at a third strike, but Crawford's two-out double put Detroit on the board. In the fourth, Willis was touched for two runs on three hits to tie the score 3–3.

Wagner starred in the field, ranging far from his position and twice registering putouts at third base. But he contributed to Detroit's tie-breaking run in the fifth when he muffed a hot line drive off Crawford's bat and recorded only a single out on what could have been an easy double play. It was a ball that Wagner admitted should have been caught. A double play would have ended the inning, preventing the go-ahead run from scoring moments later on Delahanty's double.

Camnitz relieved in the sixth and surrendered a run on a ground-rule double by Cobb—a three-run home run under regular-season ground rules. The Tigers clawed out of the hole and into a 5–3 lead. Meanwhile, Mullin settled down after the three-run first, allowing just two hits from the second through the eighth.

The ninth inning was furious—and brutal. Miller and Abstein singled, and the left-hand hitting Wilson, trying to bunt the tying runs into scoring position, tapped the ball in front of the plate. Schmidt pounced on the roller. First baseman Tom Jones bent down to scoop the low throw and Wilson slammed into him, knocking the ball away as Miller scored to make it a 5–4 game. Several minutes passed before an unconscious Jones was carted from the grounds on a stretcher.

Play resumed with Crawford playing first base and Pirate runners at the corners with no outs. Gibson's grounder found the new first baseman, and Crawford fired home. Francis Richter noted that Abstein, representing the tying run at third with nobody out, "stupidly tried to score." He was dead at the plate, and he severely spiked Schmidt in the right leg on the play. Schmidt, like his counterpart Gibson, did not let his disdain for shin guards preclude him from blocking the plate. Though badly hobbled, the gritty Tiger catcher remained in the game.

With one out and Wilson now at second, Abbaticchio pinch hit. Making his first and only appearance of the Series, he fouled off several pitches before striking out. On strike three, Wilson tried to steal third. Notwithstanding the gash in his leg, Schmidt made a perfect peg. Wilson's hard slide into Moriarty's left knee leveled the third baseman, and the two flailed at each other with their spikes a few times before being separated. The contest ended on an out call, and Detroit held on to what *The Sporting News* labeled "the most exciting World's Series game ever perpetrated."

Detroit ensured a do-or-die seventh game with the 5–4 win, but with three Tigers wounded in the final inning of Game Six, fans and players were testy. As Leach sat alone in the Pirate dugout after the game, he sensed trouble when a gimpy Moriarty approached. Outweighed by the Detroit third sacker by thirty-five pounds, Leach prepared to protect himself. He was surprised to see Cobb stop Moriarty on the way across the diamond and berate him for picking on the smallest player he could find. Leach knew Cobb loved a good rumble and counted several teammates among his enemies but gave him credit for breaking up this confrontation before it started.

◆ ◆ ◆

A few days earlier, on the afternoon of the fifth game, members of the National Commission had gathered at the Schenley Hotel. After nixing the idea of a neutral game site, they tossed a coin to determine whether Pittsburgh or Detroit would host a potential seventh game. National League President John Heydler's "tails" call was a loser, and his American League counterpart, Ban Johnson, thumbing his nose at the additional receipts that could be realized in larger Forbes Field, unhesitatingly named Detroit as the venue. Dreyfuss was completely confident at the time that this was unnecessary, saying, "I think the Pirates will put an end to the Series on Thursday but, of course, the Commission had to provide for emergencies." But now, for the first time in the event's short history, a seventh game was necessary to determine the world champion.

An off day was scheduled for Friday to give Tiger management some additional time for ticket sales, a situation that, *Sporting Life* pointed out, "would have been obviated if the Detroit Club had had the foresight to print tickets for a full series." Clarke determined that his team needed rest more than practice, and while some of the Pirates relaxed at the Pontchartrain or headed across the border to a racetrack in Windsor, Ontario, others took advantage of Wagner's company connections to take rides in complimentary Regal automobiles.

The Pittsburg Press ran a front-page article claiming that Bill Abstein had played his last game as a Pirate. Clarke was said to be taking such drastic action due to Abstein's bonehead baserunning and poor performance in the clutch. The story contended that he was sure to be re-placed in the final game by Ham Hyatt at first base and traded or released in the offseason. While some intentions seemed well known, the pitching matchup for the final game was not. In time-honored fashion, each manager coyly kept his starting pitcher a secret until the after-noon of Saturday, October 16—coincidentally, Dreyfuss's fifteenth wedding anniversary.

Clarke had three pitchers warm up. One was Maddox, winner of Game Three. Another was Phillippe, who had pitched so well in two relief appearances and was begging for a chance to overcome his disap-pointment of 1903. But to the surprise of few, Clarke chose two-time winner Adams despite the fact that the hurler was battling a slight cold. Jennings passed over Willett, coming off two successful relief stints, and Killian, the left-hander who had yet to pitch in the Series. Feeling his ace, Mullin, would not be completely rested after pitching his second complete game of the Series just two days earlier, Jennings selected Donovan, who threw so well in the second game.

It was a decision that left Jennings open to second-guessing because the temperature, while improving to the upper forties, was certainly not ideal for Donovan. In front of a rejuvenated Tiger throng of 17,562 that filled the tiny stands and spilled into the outfield, Donovan looked like he was trying to live up to his Wild Bill label. He hit leadoff hitter Byrne in the shoulder with a pitch. After a sacrifice, Byrne was called out stealing third and collided with third baseman Moriarty so fiercely that both men needed medical attention. Moriarty stayed in the game despite a badly injured leg, but Byrne's ankle was so severely hurt that he was carried off the field by his teammates. Donovan walked the next two hitters, Clarke and Wagner, but when Miller bounced into a fielder's choice, the inning ended without a run.

With Byrne gone, Clarke moved Leach in to play third and hoped no balls would be hit to Leach's old stomping grounds, where Hyatt now patrolled a small patch of center field. When Gibson nailed Bush on a steal attempt, the catcher received a cheer from his hometown friends visiting from nearby London, Ontario. It helped Adams pitch his first scoreless opening inning in three starts.

Donovan put himself in trouble again in the second. Abstein led off with a walk, stole second on Schmidt's high throw, and beat the catcher's throw to third on Wilson's bunt. Gibson popped up for the first out but Adams, a ridiculously bad hitter in his first big league season, walked to load the bases. Hyatt, batting in Byrne's leadoff spot, hit a deep fly ball to center to score the first run of the game. Leach walked to fill the bases again, and Clarke pushed a run across with yet another base on balls. Cobb's grab of Wagner's hard drive prevented further damage. Pittsburgh was hitless but had a 2–0 lead thanks to four walks, a steal, a late throw, and a sacrifice fly.

In the bottom half of the second, Delahanty drew a one-out walk and moved to third on a double into the overflow crowd in right field by Moriarty, who painfully limped into second and had to be replaced. But Adams got Tom Jones, who was not as seriously injured in the previous contest as had been feared, to pop up in the infield, and when Schmidt dribbled a ball in front of the plate, Detroit remained scoreless.

Miller singled to open the third, and Abstein doubled to put two runners aboard. But on Wilson's grounder to short, Abstein made another baserunning mistake by heading to third, forcing Miller toward the plate, where he was nailed. Abstein was thrown out trying to retreat to second for a strange double play. Donovan had escaped yet another jam but was through for the day, having given up two hits, a hit batsman, and six walks in three innings. Despite his struggles, he had allowed only two runs, and Detroit was very much alive as Mullin took over the mound duties in the fourth.

Mullin had already pitched twenty-six innings over three Series games and immediately justified his manager's fears of overwork by walking Hyatt and giving up a bloop single to Leach. Clarke bunted the runners up, Wagner was intentionally passed to load the bases, and Miller punched a two-run single to right for a 4–0, fourth-inning lead. The frame ended with Abstein's ninth strikeout of the Series, a feat that along with his five errors and poor baserunnning, had *The Reach Official American League Guide* describing his performance as "being exceedingly mortifying to himself and painful to his friends."

All the while, despite giving up at least one baserunner in each of the first four innings, Adams was in control. In the sixth, the Pirates essentially socked away the championship on the work of their three veterans. Leach doubled into the crowd in left on a 2–0 pitch and Clarke walked. Unlike the 1903 World Series, which featured an astounding twenty-five triples, the 1909 Series had yet to see a three-bagger until Wagner tripled into the left field corner for two runs, and when he continued home as Davy Jones's throw back to the infield skipped away, it was 7–0 Pittsburgh. Wagner would often cite this hit as his most gratifying moment. The Tigers were dead. The Pirates added another in the eighth as Clarke walked for the fourth time in the game, stole his second base of the day—Pittsburgh's eighteenth in the Series—and scored on a dropped fly ball. With two outs in the bottom of the eighth, Cobb virtually conceded defeat when he batted in his warm-up sweater and flied to left.

Adams surrendered just six hits, one hit batsman, and one walk in pitching his third six-hitter of the Series, and his teammates offered perfect support behind him in the 8–0 victory—the third successive year that the World Series ended with Detroit being shut out in front of its home crowd. When Tom Jones's lazy fly landed in Clarke's glove for the final out, the baseball world had a new idol in the quiet, good-looking Babe Adams. He had defeated the American League champions three times in nine days and held Ty Cobb to one single in eleven at bats.

Hundreds of Pirate fans hustled from Bennett Park to the Pontchartrain ahead of the team. They hoisted each of the players overhead and carried them one by one into the hotel. Within a few hours, the players and their fans reunited at the station for a joyous yet surprisingly subdued journey home. Anticipating the fun in store upon their return, Wagner successfully persuaded his teammates not to overindulge on the train and to postpone their festivities for the proper time.

In the streets of Pittsburgh, the celebration lasted well past midnight. Many storefronts displayed pictures of Adams. Spontaneous, disorganized parades of people, some honking or banging on musical instruments, marched down the city's major thoroughfares. After a relatively calm and particularly satisfying Sabbath, the entire wild scene was replayed on Monday, although in a much more formal fashion.

Dreyfuss dipped into his pool of fifty thousand dollars' worth of Series receipts and dined his champions at the Fort Pitt Hotel. Wagner, a late arrival, ducked out before the speeches could commence. Mayor William A. Magee encouraged the citizens to decorate their homes and establishments, and he authorized a 7:30 P.M. street parade of youth baseball teams, civic figures, and military regiments from downtown to Forbes Field, where the day would culminate with a ceremony for the winners. A procession of dozens of autos shuttled to the ballpark as an estimated 150,000 people lined the streets and paid homage. To ensure a quick escape later, Wagner drove his own car, and hundreds of children followed him the entire three-mile length of a roped-off Fifth Avenue to Oakland.

Upwards of twenty thousand fans ignored a drizzle to be on hand at Forbes Field. Each player was called to the podium and presented with a winner's-share check of over $1,800 (for those still around from the 1903 Series, it was only about $500 more than their loser's share, which had included Dreyfuss's receipts). The crowd showed its appreciation for Bobby Byrne as he made his way on crutches, and every player was cheered, even Bill Abstein. Gibson, who had handled such a load during the season and outplayed the Tiger catchers by a wide margin in the Series, was moved enough to share his feelings with the crowd through a megaphone.

Leach followed; with a Series average over .300, a club-best eight runs, and errorless defense, he received a special greeting. Then came Clarke, who drove in seven runs and hit the only two Pirate homers of the Series. Like Gibson and Leach before him, he tried to express his happiness to the audience. Wagner put the clinching game on ice with a two-run triple, batted .333 to Cobb's .231, stole six bases, and played sparkling defense throughout the Series. Although a little more accustomed to being the center of attention, he was still described as "bashful as a blushing schoolgirl" and had to be forcibly led to the podium. He most likely would have forfeited his check rather than follow his teammates' lead with the megaphone, and he responded to cries of "Speech, speech" by darting back across the small stage and hook-sliding toward his chair—and receiving twenty thousand "safe" calls.

The loudest reception was saved for Adams. He was not only presented with his winner's check but was handed the additional reward of $1,264—the amount from a fund drive begun on the return trip from Detroit that included five hundred dollars' worth of contributions from teammates.

Of course, there was no way of knowing that it would be Wagner's final World Series and, although Cobb's career would span another nineteen years, it proved to be his last Series as well. In fact, the only member of the 1909 champions who would ever represent the Pirates again in a World Series was Adams—in 1925 at the ripe old age of forty-three.

◆ ◆ ◆

Wagner's amazing yearlong—indeed career-long—ride peaked with the World Series victory. Up to his elbows in business interests, he was as involved with off-field activities as he would ever be. While his career continued, as a baseball man the 1909 season would be impossible to match. His grand performance in helping to bring a world championship to Pittsburgh helped cast off whatever personal baggage he still carried. Adding to his enjoyment was that at various games of the Series, such friends as Claude Ritchey, Ed Barrow, George Moreland, and even Rolla Taylor from Adrian, Michigan, were in attendance. The only significant influential person from Wagner's early years who had been missing was Harry Pulliam.

Wagner was the most distinguished player of the best team of the national pastime. He was playing on—and, in part, responsible for—the most beautiful grounds yet devised for the game. He represented a large and vital city. Even President Taft sang his praises. In early-twentieth-century America, a robust period in industry, politics, and sport, Wagner was one of the most recognizable men in the country.

N I N E

STILL FIRST DIVISION

Just as it does today, fame in the early 1900s meant product endorsements, and Wagner had his share. His face or figure in likeness, photograph, or caricature was featured on packages or promotional items for chewing gum, candy, ice cream, baseball sweaters and gear, Budweiser beer, gun powder, and just about any item an enterprising businessman would want to hawk to the public. On behalf of Coca-Cola, Wagner asserted that the soft drink "assisted my mental and physical activity." While there is no evidence that a player ever had a limb blown off by using the wrong ointment, Wagner and Bonesetter Reese provided testimonials for a "non-explosive" analgesic balm that was a surefire cure for ailments ranging from a sore throat to lumbago.

By 1909, Wagner was quite a popular property in a less-than-sophisticated advertising world. Promoters paid their subjects little or nothing, and some did not even bother to ask for Wagner's consent. Advertising was certainly not a lucrative arena for Wagner, and he seemed indifferent to the products bearing his name or even the claims attributed to him in print. But there was a point where he drew the line.

From 1909 to 1911, baseball cards measuring one-and-one-half by two-and-one-half inches were produced by the American Tobacco Company for inclusion in packages of Sweet Caporal, Sovereign, and Piedmont, its five-cent cigarette brands. Hundreds of players were included. In 1909, the company offered John Gruber, a local sportswriter and the well-respected, longtime official scorekeeper of the Pirates, ten dollars to secure Wagner's written permission for the use of his likeness in this set of cards. Gruber sent the letter to Wagner, who wrote back that he didn't want his picture in cigarettes but enclosed a check for ten dollars so Gruber would not miss out on the opportunity. Gruber saved the check and framed it.

There has been much speculation about what possessed Wagner to reject this offer when he had accepted many others. Some people assumed that he must have had a disdain for tobacco, but he was an avid cigar smoker and more often than not had a chaw in his mouth. Just as in Louisville a decade earlier, he was the subject of a cigar in Pittsburgh—this one by a local stogie maker who featured Wagner's bust on a box lid. And throughout the 1909 World Series, a New York firm ran a steady stream of ads in Pittsburgh newspapers for Murad cigarettes featuring a Wagner action pose and the obligatory trite, baseball-related slogan, "A Hit Every Time."

However, until World War I, cigarettes were held in much lower esteem than cigars, which were often viewed as a symbol of self-assured manhood. Dreyfuss and Clarke despised the use of cigarettes, and the Pirate manager often credited his boss for breaking him of the nightlife and "coffin nail" habits early in their time together in Louisville. Dreyfuss was even wary about procuring players who smoked and for that reason missed out on signing Hall of Famer Tris Speaker as a youngster.

At the time of Wagner's decision, many politicians were being asked to take action on smoking by minors. In 1910, Pennsylvania passed a law prohibiting the sale of cigarettes to boys under age twenty-one. Concerning adults smoking, Wagner said, "Tobacco may shorten a man's life and interfere with his baseball career. . . ." But he also had to admit, "I have noticed that where a player starts to quit hitting, it will shorten his career a good deal quicker than tobacco." He was certainly not self-righteous, but now the issue was the welfare of kids. In his mind, no doubt, were some of the boys in knee britches that he held a gate for at the ballpark or played ball with in a vacant lot. He simply did not want these youths to be lured into purchasing cigarettes just to get his picture card.

At least a portion of the planned Wagner cards were printed, and an unspecified number made their way into circulation in packs of American Tobacco cigarettes. In 1991 hockey great Wayne Gretzky and Los Angeles Kings owner Bruce McNall made international news when they forked over $451,000 to obtain one of the cards. According to Rita Reif of The New York Times News Service, "The purchase, at Sotheby's in New York, represented the highest price paid at auction for sporting memorabilia, about four times the previous record, set in 1989 for another Honus Wagner card." Recapping the sale, Reif described the audience's reaction as the bidding escalated past the $300,000 mark and when the auctioneer's gavel came down on the final bid: Thirty-five years after his death, Wagner was still generating cheers and applause.

A few dozen of the cards, now catalogued as the T-206, are known to exist today. Every couple of years, a story circulates about how another one has been found in someone's basement or attic. There are certainly rarer baseball cards and even scarcer Wagner cards, but this particular item has become one of the most famous, most prized, and expensive treasures in the baseball card hobby—and perhaps of all memorabilia collecting. It is safe to say that a less significant figure could not have fueled such mystique.

In what today seems like an extremely ironic understatement, half-page ads for American Tobacco that appeared in sporting publications during 1909 prophesied that these "handsomely" printed pictures would "make a valuable collection."

◆ ◆ ◆

While Wagner was squeamish about the amount of attention he received, one individual was becoming outraged. Andrew Carnegie was usually a good sport about sharing with Wagner his billing as Pittsburgh's leading citizen. The industrialist did not protest even when a group of businessmen toured the Midwest by train promoting the city with a "Made in Pittsburgh" exhibit and chose Wagner's picture to display as the "Greatest Man in Our Town." But when the time of a conclave at which Carnegie was to be a featured speaker was changed so the guests could attend a ball game and cheer Wagner, Carnegie had had enough. Peeved at what he perceived as an unappreciative public, or at least one with twisted priorities, Carnegie threatened to cut off his outpouring of millions of dollars in philanthropy to western Pennsylvania.

Fortunately, Carnegie's jealous tantrum was brief, and libraries, schools, and playgrounds continued to spring up from his generous gifts. Grantland Rice, a twenty-nine-year-old scribe in 1910 and the man who would become known as the Dean of American Sports Writers, gave Carnegie appropriate credit for his benevolence but attempted to explain public sentiment by penning the following:

> *He passed the city coin enough to overload a mint;*
> *He gave it parks and palaces and playgrounds without stint;*
> *He scattered countless shekels all along the Smoky shore—*
>   *BUT—*
> *He never soused a triple when a hit would tie the score.*
>
> *Oh, Andy, Andy, Andy—though you stand upon the street*
> *And shovel out a million unto every guy you meet;*
> *Though you blow a half a billion, you will never have the call,*
> *As the greatest man in Pittsburg while H. Wagner hits the ball.*

◆ ◆ ◆

Many of Wagner's contemporaries used the winter months to capitalize on their celebrity by writing newspaper columns or barnstorming in California or overseas. Traveling teams knew Wagner's involvement would mean more revenue, and he sometimes agreed to accompany a group, though he would eventually back out. Several of the most well-known names in baseball, including Christy Mathewson, Joe Tinker, and John McGraw, were cashing in on easy money by "acting" in vaudeville shows. In the winter following the 1909 season, Wagner turned down a five-hundred-dollar inducement for himself and two hundred dollars for his friend Dots Miller for a brief basketball sketch in a local show. Concerned that he would be laughed at or thought to have a "swelled head," Wagner declined every offer, regardless of the incentive.

While Wagner had no qualms about appearing in print for most any advertisement, he still shunned personal engagements or any activity that would intrude on his own business or fun. The press thought it was admirable that he was not a "money grabber," but some ballplayers resented him for hindering their opportunity to supplement their income.

Some people just considered him unreliable when he was off the diamond. In December 1909, Dreyfuss held a banquet in the ballroom of the Waldorf-Astoria in New York. The gala had a two-hundred-person guest list that read like a who's who of baseball notables. Setting past hostilities aside, McGraw and several New York Giants, as well as Johnny Evers and a few Chicago Cubs, were among those in attendance;

Wagner was a no-show. Later that winter, after he had agreed to accompany Dreyfuss to visit Clarke at the Little Pirate Ranch, he canceled at the last instant. And after actually making a trip to Macon, Georgia, with the intention of hunting with Georgians Ty Cobb and big league manager George Stallings, Wagner decided to turn around and come home before he fired a shot.

◆ ◆ ◆

Wagner's eyes lit up when Hugh Chalmers, president of the Chalmers Automobile Company, announced he would award a new automobile to big league baseball's top hitter for 1910. Proud possessor of the last four batting average titles in the National League and six of the last seven, Wagner was expected to battle Ty Cobb for the prize. Wagner expressed his enthusiasm by saying that an auto "has the usual medals and loving cups beaten by a mile."

Without the slightest hint of a holdout and determined to capture the automobile, Wagner, now thirty-six years old and rapidly graying around the temples, managed to navigate his way to Hot Springs for the first time since 1907. Both he and Clarke made it clear that they intended to defend their title. Clarke, in order to devote 100 percent of his time to baseball, leased his land to another rancher for the next two years and even auctioned off most of his farm equipment and animals, including his two mules, Deacon and Honus. It made for lively chatter back at Pirate headquarters when Clarke wired, "Have sold Honus for $190. Particulars later."

There were very few changes in the Pirates for 1910. Six different players, including Wagner, would see action at first base; to no one's surprise, Bill Abstein was released after his dismal World Series performance. Amid implications that Vic Willis (Hall of Fame, class of 1995) was a boozer and bad influence on the young pitchers, the Pirates sold to St. Louis the man who had won 239 big league games and was a twenty-game winner in each of his four Pittsburgh seasons. Willis would finish 9–12 with the Cardinals in what would be his last major league year. For the most part, though, the lineup that took the field for the opener at Robison Field in St. Louis on Thursday, April 14, was the same one that won the championship in 1909. Early results were similar as well, as Wagner tripled and singled, the perennial second-division Cardinals made five errors, and the Pirates beat their old teammate Willis 5–1.

Several bad omens marked the Pirate home opener one week later.

Biting winds and a threat of snow kept the fan count down to a mere 7,826. Worse yet, after a march to the center field flagpole, the National League championship banner was hoisted upside down. Then John Morin, Pittsburgh's director of public safety, took the mound for the ceremonial first pitch and hit the Cardinals' pint-sized leadoff man, Miller Huggins, in the right leg. All of this did little to dampen the optimism of the team's title defense. Adams won his first start of the year, Phillippe tossed three hitless innings, Miller banged out four hits, and the Pirates defeated Willis once again.

Although Wagner, Clarke, and Leach were each off to poor starts, the foreboding signs at the home opener were forgotten by early May, as the Pirates pushed out into the lead. But after May 21, when Halley's Comet became visible to Earth as it streaked across the night sky, the Pirates dropped six straight games. They would not recover.

By mid-June, the honeymoon following the world championship was over. With the team in fourth place, seven games out of first, local sportswriter David Davies was so disgusted with the poor pitching, he wrote, "Adams is fat; Camnitz is fat; Maddox hasn't been given enough work to enable him to locate the plate. . . . Phillippe and Leever can't stand the strain of pitching regularly . . ." Mound work *was* a problem: During one particularly nasty 18–0 beating, Clarke responded to the flak from the bleachers by offering to let any fan within earshot take a turn on the hill. An anemic offense was damaging, too. Clarke and Wilson were barely above the .200 barrier, which Gibson could not crack. Wagner and Leach were in the .240s, and Miller, after a good start, was dropping rapidly.

In an eventful final week of June, Wagner and Leach cost the team a win when they let an easy fly ball drop between them, and in another contest, Wagner was ejected for pushing umpire Augie Moran. But Wagner won one game with a three-run triple and on the week was 16 for 27. This included a 7 for 7 stretch over two games and 4 for 4 on the one-year anniversary of Forbes Field, the day the world championship banner was unfurled—right side up.

The hot streak pushed Wagner near .300. But after he had injured his shoulder in May on a hard slide into third base, he was stealing fewer bases and not getting nearly as many extra-base hits as he had in the past. His pull-hitting became so predictable that when he came to the plate during one contest, Cincinnati Reds manager Clark Griffith shifted center fielder George "Dode" Paskert toward left-center and right fielder Mike Mitchell into center.

◆ ◆ ◆

Late in the 1910 season, the cork-center baseball was introduced to the big leagues. Although still a far cry from the lively ball used today, the new ball was a bit more springy than the rubber-center one. For the first time, fans were treated to the crack of the bat, rather than the thud that resulted from what Wagner described as hitting "a chunk of mud." If there was any doubt that the cork-center ball would have an effect on the game, it was dispelled during an August homestand, as six homers were blasted over the Forbes Field wall in nine games—a feat accomplished just eight times in the previous year.

Wagner took an immediate liking to the new ball, and at Forbes Field on August 22, he registered one of his most unforgettable performances. In game one of a doubleheader sweep of the Phillies, Wagner singled twice, hit a sacrifice fly, and slammed a ball over the wall in left-center for what was considered the longest home run yet in the one-year-old ballpark. In game two, Wagner was even better, doubling three times and hitting another fence-clearing home run to left-center. His homer in the second game was one of three Pirate circuit clouts in one inning, including the only home run of Camnitz's career. On the day, Wagner was 7 for 7 with sixteen total bases.

For most of the summer, Pittsburgh bounced between second and third, trailing the first-place Cubs (with Johnny Kling back after his yearlong absence) and at times the Giants. Clarke and Wagner headed a resurgent offense that led an August charge, moving the Pirates to within five games of the lead. Pittsburgh fans were thinking pennant once again, but hopes soon faded as the Cubs ran away to their fourth title in five years and the Pirates tumbled to third, seventeen and a half games back.

The pitching fell apart. Adams finished at 18–9. Phillippe rebounded to 14–2, including a thirteen-game winning streak and a 7–1 mark in relief. But Camnitz slipped to 12–13. Dreyfuss, saying, "There is no room in major league baseball for sentiment," released flash-in-the-pan Maddox in September. The offense was still strong, but Miller, touted along with the great Tris Speaker as one of the best finds of 1909, suffered from what today would be called a sophomore jinx.

Clarke held his own at the plate despite a leg injury that kept him sidelined for some time. Shortly after his return, he hit two doubles, a triple, a single, and lined out in a fifth at bat. In another game, he remained prone and dazed for several minutes after being beaned, but when he heard that he was denied first base because he had swung at the pitch, he stepped back into the box and singled. During a five-game losing streak in late August that sealed the Pirates' also-ran fate, a few fans in the Forbes Field bleachers hissed and facetiously asked Clarke to send up a pinch hitter for himself—treatment that even John McGraw conceded was reprehensible. Clarke was stunned. One source said his "usual contemptuous smile" disappeared, but he was certainly resilient, striding to the plate and responding with a double.

There would be no Chalmers car for Wagner. The American League batting race—in 1910, held at a much superior level than the National League—ended in accusations and controversy. As a result, Mr. Chalmers presented autos to both Cobb and Lajoie but altered the basis for future prizes by allowing the top sportswriters to vote for each league's best player—a forerunner to today's Most Valuable Player Award. Wagner suffered another rib cage injury late in the season and after missing a few games played mostly first base when he returned. He led his league in hits, and after making a run at the batting title with a late-season surge to over .330, he dropped to .320—his lowest average since 1898. While most of his numbers were solid, although not league highs or Wagner standards, he had definitely slipped a bit, and many people were saying he was "all in."

His prestige did not suffer greatly. He was offered one thousand dollars for a ten-game exhibition tour following the season and three thousand to observe the World Series so that articles could be ghostwritten under his name. While some of his contemporaries accepted such assignments, Wagner declined, saying, "I ain't no writer and don't pretend to be. Reporters are paid for that kind of stuff, and it's not a ballplayer's job." Lajoie, with dollar signs in his eyes, enticed Wagner with a lucrative deal for a few minutes on a vaudeville stage doing a basketball skit. Honus brushed aside that proposition as well.

He certainly did not need the money. In fact, when the Boston National League franchise was on the block during the following season for what seemed like its annual sale, Wagner inquired about the asking price. Finding that it would require an investment in the six-figure range, he backed off but did not discount the possibility of getting into club ownership in the future, saying, "Well, maybe I'll have better luck the next time I try to buy a club."

✦ ✦ ✦

An official 1908 city publication summed up Pittsburgh's religious values by testifying:

> Probably in no city of its size in the United States is the Lord's Day better observed, but the observance is obviously deteriorating. We are free, however, on that day from professional baseball, open places of amusement, manifest commercialism and the open saloon. In contrast with such cities as Cincinnati, St. Louis and Chicago, we are almost Puritanic on Sunday. In contrast with New Orleans and San Francisco we are positively angelic.

Carrie Nation, the axe-wielding, saloon-busting temperance leader, viewed the city much differently. Arrested in Pittsburgh, she sent out a warning to the citizens, preaching, "You have a conspiracy against the gospel in this town. All the young men of this city are going to hell."

Alcohol consumption was hotly debated around the country. Dreyfuss blamed the lack of a 1910 pennant race as well as estimated league-wide losses of $100,000 on players who spent too much time drinking and carousing. He even charged that the Philadelphia Athletics' upset of the Chicago Cubs in the 1910 World Series was due to the Windy City players' appetite for nightlife.

Although not directly implicated by Dreyfuss, Wagner was accused by a few writers of enjoying "a bit too much foamy." His love for beer was no secret, but until now, no overindulgence had ever been brought to light. On one occasion, a reporter visited Wagner in his hotel room seeking an exclusive. After opening the door, Wagner turned and pointed to a bathtub full of beer and uttered, "Have all the beer you want but no interview." One opposing manager predicted that Wagner would not last much longer unless he checked his drinking habits. A few stories even surfaced that Wagner had been spotted after a game at a saloon across the street from the Polo Grounds while still in uniform!

Dreyfuss and Clarke were not teetotalers. They were both social drinkers—the Pirate president enjoying a drink or wine now and then, and Clarke believing that a few glasses of beer following a hard-fought contest would do no harm. But both jumped on the wagon to set a good example to their men, whose 1911 contracts included an abstinence clause. Soon, other teams were encouraged to add a similar provision, and Francis Richter of *Sporting Life* insisted that such a "drastic move" was necessary to abate the "demoralization in the major league ranks." Richter's editorial, ringing of sentiment that can be found today, attributed this "demoralization" to players having "too much idle time, too much hero worship, too much automobiling, too much 'joy-riding,' too much high living—all the result of the exceeding prosperity that has favored base ball in recent years to the great financial benefit of the players; a small, but potential, minority of whom have lacked the character and disposition to bear their honors meekly and to accept their good fortune with gratitude and discretion."

Stressing that it was critical for him to be on time this year for spring training and promising Carnegie Common Pleas Court judges John M. Kennedy and L. L. Davis that the Pirates would win the pennant, Wagner successfully wrangled his way out of jury duty in late February 1911. Upon arrival at Hot Springs, Wagner and each of his teammates were issued a copy of the team's written rules of behavior— featuring a midnight curfew and a no-alcohol, no-cigarette policy that was punishable by "a fine, a suspension, or both, according to the offense." These guidelines were met with the anticipated dismay, and they proved only marginally successful because manager Clarke infrequently enforced them.

◆ ◆ ◆

Despite obviously dwindling skills marked by a 6–5 record the previous year, the notoriously thrifty Sam Leever asked for a raise and refused to go south with the team in the spring of 1911. Dreyfuss was ordinarily indignant with players who were salary holdouts, and he often remained spiteful for years, but he was appreciative of Leever's contributions to the ball club over the last decade and offered him the entire proceeds of any sale to a minor league club. After their useful days as major leaguers were over, many men were satisfied to be sold or optioned to minor league teams. Although a step down, it did not have the stigma that is attached to it today, and it allowed players to continue to make a living at what they did best—play baseball.

Leever was offended, though, and asked for an outright release. Dreyfuss obliged and cut loose the man who had compiled one of the better winning percentages in big league history with a 194–101 lifetime record and was the last remaining Pirate from prior to the late-1899 Pittsburgh-Louisville deal. The release proved costly to Leever when he signed on with minor league Minneapolis later that summer after all.

Reunited with several former Pirate teammates, including Warren Gill and Rube Waddell, Leever went 7–4 to help Minneapolis win a second straight American Association championship.

When Phillippe, with an equally impressive 189–107 lifetime mark, followed Leever out the door by retiring after pitching in just three 1911 games, the only players left at all from the 1899 transaction were Wagner, Leach, and Clarke—a trio often referred to as Pittsburgh's Big Three. In 1911, the triumvirate was in its fourteenth season together, a rarity in baseball, and the three men had changed little. Wagner and Clarke were among the league's leading hitters, keeping the team in contention much of the summer, and there were more nasty squabbles with umpires. *The Pittsburgh Press* once observed that "there was no set of men who could make more trouble for the umpires than Clarke, Wagner and Leach. . . ."

In the opener, Pittsburgh bombed Cincinnati 14–0 on seventeen hits, including three by Wagner, four by Miller, and a 5 for 5, five RBI day by Byrne. It was a drubbing made even sweeter for Dreyfuss because some of the onslaught was at Jesse Tannehill's expense. Trying to come back after a one-year big league hiatus and pitching in his first National League game since his Pittsburgh career ended in 1902 when he jumped to the American League, Tannehill hung it up at the end of this game.

Pirate runners streamed across home plate for much of the summer, and run production was up across the board thanks to the new cork-center baseball. Wagner was pounding the new ball, muscling five home runs in a month and causing Bozeman Bulger of New York's *The World* to write, "[Wagner] is going back fast—and so are the other fellows he plays against—they are going back fast to the fence after drives he slams out there."

On the whole, though, the Pirates hated the new sphere. Dreyfuss felt the "cheap" home run detracted from the athleticism of the game, particularly baserunning and speedy outfield play. So his two-year-old concrete wall was knocked down at Forbes Field and a new deeper, wooden one slapped up, increasing the center field dimension to beyond five hundred feet. Incurring the wrath of the men in blue, the Pirates disobeyed the rules by soiling baseballs in order to make them more difficult to see. Wagner was ejected twice and fined once, and several other Pirates were tossed out of games during the season. Dreyfuss moaned that the umpires were deliberately against his team. Clarke, whom Jack Ryder in *The Cincinnati Enquirer* branded a "fancy protester," submitted three protests to the league office in the first half of the season. All were rejected.

✦ ✦ ✦

In midseason, as the Pirates remained close in a five-team chase, fate struck. Leach's second wife passed away after a long illness. Clarke missed time with a severe ankle sprain and was hit in the head with a pitch soon after his return. The beaning kept him out of the lineup for a month and even sparked a few rumors that he had died. Through the last ten days of July and into early August, the Pirates tore off a thirteen-game winning streak and won eighteen of nineteen to move into a half-game lead. It was short-lived. In a taut race, the Pirates started an eastern swing in Brooklyn on August 16, and in the first inning, Wagner suffered one of the most debilitating injuries of his career.

Wagner was leading the league in batting at over .350. He had been wearing a brace on a bad ankle, and for all of the acrobatics he performed, it finally gave out completely when he did nothing more than round the second base bag. The original diagnosis of a fracture proved false. The day after the injury, he returned to Pittsburgh in the care of Phillippe, now on the payroll as a Pirate scout, and George Aston, Wagner's friend and sidekick. Aston had been a maintenance man at Wagner's garage, and when Wagner sold the business, he convinced Dreyfuss to hire Aston as the team's assistant trainer (one of the two black trainers that Wagner defended from poor treatment). Although Aston did not drive, Wagner had introduced him at spring training as his chauffeur, earning him the lifelong nickname of Chauff. Wagner was pushed through Pittsburgh's Union Station in a wheelchair, holding a pair of crutches and pledging to concerned onlookers that he would return to duty within a week.

In their cleanup hitter's absence, the Pirates dropped eight of thirteen in the East. Wagner insisted on playing upon the team's return home and was placed at first base for one game, going hitless and striking out three times, before missing the next twelve games. Agitated by seeing New York creep into the lead and his Pirates drop out of contention, Dreyfuss went so far as to accuse Wagner of staying out too long.

Returning to the lineup in mid-September, Wagner played mostly first base and in his one outfield appearance dropped the only fly ball hit to him. Still not completely healthy and with the team's pennant hopes shot, he was trying to secure his lead in the batting race. But he struggled, getting very few extra-base hits and dropping almost twenty points in less than a month. In the end, the club finished third in 1911, fourteen and a half behind the Giants, though Wagner did hold onto the batting lead with a .334 average—just one point ahead of his nearest challenger. At 37 years of age in 1911, Wagner is still the oldest player ever to win the National League batting crown. Despite the honor of his eighth and final batting title, Wagner finished in just a three-way tie for third in the National League voting for Hugh Chalmers's automobile.

◆ ◆ ◆

Clarke was getting fed up fighting his leg injuries. Despite another fine year, finishing among the leaders in hitting and slugging, he decided to hang up his spikes and announced that he would be a bench manager in 1912 in order to give a few of the young outfielders a chance—particularly twenty-one-year-old Max "Scoops" Carey, who had looked promising in his first full major league season. Most people scoffed at this news and projected that the competitive Clarke would jump back into the fray the following spring. But Clarke bet each of his doubters a suit of clothes or a hat that he was sincere. By the end of 1912, Clarke had one of the most extensive wardrobes around.

He retired from active duty with more career games, putouts, and total chances than any previous big league left fielder. Amassing more than 2,600 hits, 500 stolen bases, a .312 career batting average, and still ranking seventh on the all-time triples list, he is one of very few men in baseball history whose credentials either as a player *or* as a manager warrant induction into the Hall of Fame. Except for twelve sporadic appearances over the next four seasons, Clarke would stick to the bench and the coaches' box.

For the most part, ballplayers' careers early in the century were not as long as they are today. Clarke's withdrawal from the diamond at the age of thirty-nine, coupled with Fred Tenney's retirement during the same offseason, left Wagner as the National League's oldest player for 1912 at the age of thirty-eight. Like Cap Anson before him and Connie Mack to follow, Wagner was honored by being referred to as the Grand Old Man of Baseball or simply "GOM." For 1912, he was once again slated to take his "old bones" out to play one of the game's most challenging defensive positions.

Offseason gossip, fueled no doubt by the Reds' Garry Herrmann hinting that a famous shortstop would take charge of the club, had Wagner going to Cincinnati to manage the Reds in 1912. But he was an early arrival to Hot Springs and was in excellent condition. He had maintained an active basketball schedule with one of the best independent teams of western Pennsylvania and took a bowling team to Paterson, New Jersey, for a national tournament.

Clarke now needed an on-field leader, and having considered Leach, Byrne, and even newly acquired former Giant Mike Donlin, he eventually named Wagner as team captain. It was a post many said Wagner was not "tempermentally fit" to hold. He accepted the appointment proudly and insisted that his mission was to "carry out Cap's orders" and told his teammates that "if anybody finds me getting all swelled up on myself, I hope he will bounce something off my head." Throughout spring training in 1912, he seemed to be showing uncommon zeal, and *Sporting Life* commented that he had "additional pepper" as well as "the chattering habit."

Clarke put all the blame for his team's rapid decline the previous year on the loss of Wagner. With Wagner's ankle now sound and with the additions of Donlin and Marty O'Toole, a prized minor league spitballer for whom Dreyfuss paid a then-record price of $22,500, the Pirates were once again optimistic. The team dropped its first four, though, and was never in the race. Donlin battled numerous ailments, including a broken toe. O'Toole was the subject of extraordinary buildup and expectation. Tagged as the Valuable One or the $22,500 Beauty, he had received endorsement offers and marriage proposals before he ever took the mound for the team. He was a complete washout, however, and seemed to be trying to walk a batter for each of the dollars that Dreyfuss had forked over for him.

To Dreyfuss, it was bad enough that by mid-April he lost front-page coverage, which for weeks was almost completely devoted to the horrifying news of the Titanic disaster, in which 1,500 perished. Disconcerting him even further in the spring was that he now had to share the sports page, once the Pirates' sole domain. The fledgling United States League seemed harmless enough. It adopted a hands-off policy to current big league players and merely staffed its squads with a hodgepodge of former major leaguers and semiprofessionals. Yet the eight-team outlaw circuit, operating outside of the National Commission, was constantly under a watchful eye because it was attempting to horn in on the protected territory of six major and two minor league teams.

Pittsburgh's entry, cleverly nicknamed the Filipinos for pitchermanager Deacon Phillippe, got underway on May 1 and opened its home season a week later at Exposition Park—just five weeks after Dreyfuss let the ballpark's lease expire. Claude Ritchey had spent parts of the last two seasons playing minor league ball, and it seemed as though his career was over when he broke an arm sliding into second base while with Louisville. But before he could retire to his oil wells and business interests in Emlenton, Pennsylvania, the popular second baseman was invited to play for the Filipinos. Ritchey booted four balls in the second game of the season and was gone within a week.

The Filipinos, in first place with a 16–8 record, were one of the last two teams to fold in June. Ultimately, the league proved little more than an inconvenience to Dreyfuss. In one acknowledgement to the presence of a competitor, though, he stopped releasing attendance figures in order to avoid any head-to-head comparison with the crosstown challenger. Magnates in the major and minor league cities where the United States League had tried to gain a foothold gloated that the attempted infringement was a total failure. However, a few of these same U.S. League officials would join a group of men with even deeper pockets the following year to try again. Under the name of the Federal League, the circuit would complete a full season in 1913 and gather steam as it was about to pose the next and, at least to this day, last serious threat to Organized Baseball.

◆ ◆ ◆

With his team languishing in fourth place early in 1912, Clarke attempted to shake up his charges. In a headline-grabbing swap of versatile veterans and young pitchers, the Pirates sent thirty-four-year-old Leach, who had struggled through an injury-plagued and unsuccessful 1911 season, and Leifield, who was off to a slow start in 1912 after a 16–16 mark the previous year, to Chicago. In return they received twenty-nine-year-old Solly Hofman and pitcher Leonard "King" Cole, who was a wonderful 40–13 in just over two years of big league experience.

The trade was a flop for Pittsburgh. Although Leifield would never regain the form that allowed him to win 103 games from 1906 to 1911, Leach proved a serviceable player for the Cubs over the next few years. But Hofman and Cole were worthless to Clarke. Hofman was a no-show after the trade and was said to be suffering from a nervous breakdown and even malaria—which may have been a sportswriting euphemism for venereal disease or an alcohol problem. He played in only seventeen games once he came around. While Cole reported promptly, he soon went AWOL, was suspended, and was eventually relegated to the minors.

The trade of Leach left Wagner as the only player remaining from the Pittsburgh-Louisville transaction. With differing interests off the field, Leach and Wagner were not close, although they always got along just fine. Some observers guessed that Leach's exit was due to hard feelings over Wagner's appointment to team captain or friction between the two over who would eventually succeed Clarke as manager. Wagner had never expressed an interest in the post, and when asked about managing, he responded, "I love my peace of mind too much to go out and hunt for trouble." He swore that not even $100,000 could tempt him to take the job.

It was public knowledge that Leach fashioned himself as a candidate to lead a ball club, and while he would never have his aspiration fulfilled at the big league level, he did manage in the minors. After being out of the major leagues for two years, Leach rounded out his playing career with a brief return to the Pirates in 1918 before eventually retiring to Florida.

♦ ♦ ♦

Hobbled with a charley horse in his left leg through the first few months of the season and hitting only in the .280s, Wagner seemed to be showing the signs of an inevitable downfall. But holding down the team's cleanup spot and playing exclusively at shortstop for only the second season of his career, his performance over the remainder of 1912 was spectacular.

With a spurt of seven consecutive multi-hit games in mid-June, including ten hits in four games in New York, he was over .320. In a three-game stretch in late July, he collected four singles, two doubles, and three triples, winning one contest with a ninth-inning single and contributing to another victory with a fourteenth-inning double. He once again had captured the sportswriters' attention. *The Pittsburgh Dispatch* asked, "Concerning this Wagner person; are there no means which could be employed to keep him from tearing things loose day after day? His fielding yesterday was wonderful; his batting was sensational." David Davies wrote, "It gets monotonous telling what Honus did at bat, and what he did in the field. Yesterday was no exception; look at the box score and convince yourself."

Yet, all this praise was prior to perhaps Wagner's two best performances of 1912. In Boston on July 31, he was walked three times with men on base but stole third and then home to tie the game in the seventh, and in the nineteenth inning, he singled home what proved to be the game-winning run. Then on August 22 in front of an estimated twenty thousand fans at Forbes Field, the Pirates faced the first-place Giants. In game one of a doubleheader, Wagner stroked two singles and a double, and in game two, he hit for the cycle off Rube Marquard. On his way to a twenty-six-win season and just recently having his personal 1912 winning streak snapped at nineteen, Marquard was now one of the league's top pitchers. He was no puzzle for Wagner, however, who battered Marquard all year long. Three of Wagner's seven home runs came off the Giant lefty, including two drives over the left field wall at Forbes Field—moved further back yet again for 1912.

Wagner's individual feats meant little to the pennant race as the Giants easily won for the second straight year. But thanks to a twelve-game winning streak in September and a near total collapse of the Cubs, Pittsburgh finished second, ten games off the pace. Although well behind the leader, Wagner finished among the league's best hitters at .324 and bettered many of his 1911 totals. In a very good offensive year (some sources credit him with leading the league in RBIs), he had more extra-base hits than in any of his seasons since 1908, including twenty triples—an impressive total but a far cry from that of teammate Chief Wilson, who sprayed a still-standing major *and* minor league single-season mark of thirty-six three-baggers.

In what *Sporting Life* stamped as "remarkable all-round work" and "one of his best seasons," Wagner also led National League shortstops in double plays and set a new league-high in fielding percentage. He missed out on the car again, however. The Chalmers Trophy Commission recognized his performance by ranking him runner-up but awarded the automobile to New York's Larry Doyle as the National League's best player.

◆ ◆ ◆

Over the years, Wagner began slowly accepting and understanding, although certainly not enjoying, his role as a public figure. He still considered cameras bad luck and slipped away when any conversation focused on him or even baseball in general. However, he no longer hid his hat under his chair at public functions for a quick getaway, and now if called upon to say a few words, he would at least stand up, red-faced, and mumble a few words about fishing or automobiles or deliver a brief recitation of what he titled "Umpires I Have Known." His attire was also a bit sharper these days. Partial to brown suits—"a nice quiet color"—he was also sporting a fur-lined overcoat, white linen shirts, and even a diamond stickpin through his tie.

At least some of the credit for his more dapper apparel could be attributed to the influence of Miss Bessie Baine Smith, Wagner's girl-friend for the past four years. With his relationship with Bessie now widely known and with his younger brother Bill getting married near his adopted home of Danville, Ohio, in June 1912, talk was ripe about Honus himself getting hitched. He dodged all questions on the subject, and Clarke assured those who were looking for a scoop that though Wagner was "of age," he would be sure to ask his manager for consent before rushing into anything.

Baseball news out of Hot Springs in March 1913 was minimal. Terrible flooding in much of the Midwest made it difficult for sportswriters to transmit their stories to Pittsburgh. Outside of the holdouts by Max Carey and Wagner's friend Claude Hendrix, the most significant news to come out of spring training was that Dreyfuss reversed his stance that the southern trip should not include exhibition games with other big league clubs and agreed to a series with the Boston Red Sox. He soon regretted his change of heart.

The Red Sox, led by center fielder Tris Speaker and right-hander "Smoky Joe" Wood, were the 1912 World Champions. At the age of twenty-two, Wood had used his tremendous fastball to rack up thirty-four victories and then defeated New York three times in the World Series. In the second preseason game between the two clubs, a Wood fastball struck Pirate Bobby Byrne behind the left ear. Knocked unconscious by the blow and remaining in serious condition overnight, Byrne managed to return to action within a week. The Pirates won twice and tied once in the six-game series with the Red Sox, but Wagner was also a casualty, severely spraining his right knee with less than two weeks until the opener.

When the season of 1913 rolled around, the Pirates were once again the center of attention in Pittsburgh. Even Agnes I. Wedgewood wrote her society column for *The Pittsburg Dispatch* from Forbes Field during the home opener in front of a crowd that to her eyes "was worse than a bargain sale." However, she took to the Pirates' blue-on-white pinstriped uniforms, which she described as "the darlingest things" with short sleeve "blouse fashion" shirts and trousers that were "made very full and gathered at the knees." Likening Babe Adams to a "matinee idol" and smitten with the "single, and oh so handsome" Hendrix, she made sure to mention to her audience that "ball players make lots of money—especially the Pittsburg ones." Trying to muster a compliment for Wagner, she had to confess he was "nobody's Apollo" and could only say that "he has the cutest little dog that follows him around."

While he certainly would have appreciated the kind words for his loyal pet, Jason Weathersby, Wagner had more pressing concerns. The pain in his knee was not subsiding. After missing the first four games of the season, he demanded to play shortstop in the home opener. Limping noticeably, he went 0 for 4 with an error. David Davies complained that "[Wagner] could neither run, hit nor field; and it is to be hoped that until such time as he has recovered his wonted agility and soundness of limb he will be given a chance to rest."

Staying in Pittsburgh while the team was in St. Louis for a series that saw Gibson break an ankle chasing a foul pop, Wagner missed the next fifteen games. His next action came in an exhibition game in Cleveland on May 5, but he did not play the entire game, and when he crushed a ball to the left field fence that should have been a home run, he loped to second and stayed put.

In the lineup the following day at Boston, he was 0 for 4 and made two errors. He rebounded with eighteen hits over the next nine games and, for the time being, silenced those who now seemed to be incessantly looking for signs that the other spiked shoe was about to drop. Even *Baseball Magazine* was on the lookout for "the dreaded chuting of Hans Wagner over the slope of Hasbeen Hill. . . ." As the Pirates headed to New York for the first time in mid-May, one New York scribe wrote, "Honus Wagner arrived in town today and will play the Giants a series of four games. Mr. Wagner is accompanied by the Pittsburgh baseball team." He lived up to all promotion by going 3 for 5 with a homer in the series opener.

By the third week of June, the Pirates were already eleven games back. Wagner was riding an average of .330, albeit with less power than he was accustomed to, but he wrenched his right knee again on June 23 and was used only as a pinch hitter for the next month.

Struggling upon his return in late July, it looked as if his string of .300 seasons might come to an end. He even had to endure some fan criticism, quieted somewhat when he went 12 for 22 in a mid-August series versus the Giants. In the game Mathewson started, Wagner was 4 for 5 with a three-run homer and was only retired when a pitch he attempted to dodge hit his bat and rolled into fair territory for an easy out.

Missing more action here and there in 1913, Wagner played in fewer games than in any season since 1897, when he joined Louisville in mid-year. He clung to the .300 level, finishing at an even .300. Although the Pirates maintained a first-division standing with a fourth-place finish, home attendance had dropped for the fourth consecutive year, and at 78–71, the team made its worst showing since the Louisville gang came to Pittsburgh in 1900. Having just completed such a miserable season, it was hard for anyone involved with the team to imagine that the immediate future of both the Pirates and Wagner would soon take a turn for the worse.

TEN

MANAGING CHANGE

Upon being asked what it felt like to turn forty in February 1914, Wagner snapped, "And how should I know? I've never been that old before." He was most likely thinking that it didn't feel all that great. The winter months following the 1913 season held little joy for Wagner. On November 12, 1913, at 10:30 A.M., seventy-five-year-old Peter Wagner passed away in the family home. He had been battling an illness for some time and had recently contracted pneumonia, but his death was still unexpected. It left the three bachelor brothers, Honus, Al, and Luke, in the Railroad Avenue house. For the next few years, they remained on their own, eating their meals at local Carnegie restaurants.

In addition to the loss of his father, there were disturbing developments of lesser significance in Wagner's offseason. He had to curtail his basketball because his knees troubled him, and with less activity than in previous winters, a few more pounds were showing.

On the last day of February, frantic that he would be late to comply with the March 1, 1914, deadline of President Woodrow Wilson's new federal income tax law, Wagner drove to the Pirate offices to engage Dreyfuss's assistance. (Ironically, the origin—or blame—of a direct tax on all incomes can be traced to William Pitt "The Younger," Britain's youngest prime minister and son of Pittsburgh's namesake.) Under the new law, the affluent were responsible for paying a 1 percent tax on income in excess of $3,000 for individuals or $4,000 for married couples. Wagner, still single and making his $10,000 annual stipend in baseball, was required to pay taxes on $7,000. Without comment, he anted up seventy dollars for Uncle Sam.

Known to keep a watchful eye on his pennies, Wagner was said to have long pockets when it came to buying rounds for his pals. He did play a few benefit basketball games over the years for needy friends or a worthy cause but was not overly generous outside of his immediate family. So it came as some surprise when Wagner proposed that each player should make an annual contribution to establish a home for former ballplayers who had become elderly or indigent. Wagner insisted that players were "ever willing to lend a helping hand," but disinclined to shoulder the responsibility for the cause himself, the idea went no further.

◆ ◆ ◆

Some of the principals from the ill-fated United States League of 1912 linked up with a few additional capitalists to try another league outside of Organized Baseball in 1913. The six-club Federal League had Phillippe at the helm of the Pittsburgh entry, Cy Young as manager in Cleveland, and Leever at the controls in Covington, Kentucky, a suburb of Cincinnati that would surrender its club to Kansas City in June. In addition, former pitcher Bill Phillips managed Indianapolis and Jack O'Connor, a thorn in Dreyfuss's side during the American League war, was the skipper in St. Louis. After fulfilling a 120-game schedule in 1913, Federal League moguls were overflowing both with the optimism and the financial resources necessary to withstand some serious setbacks en route.

Following the 1913 season, the powers of the Federal League began aggressively trying to establish it as a major league. Better ballparks were under construction, and current big league players were being pursued and signed. Veteran American League first baseman and manager George Stovall became the first notable to jump to the "Feds" in early November, and through the remainder of the offseason, *signing*, *reneging*, and *jumping* were catchwords for much of the baseball news. Another baseball war was at hand, and while few of the game's superstars made the move, Federal League rosters were dotted with recognizable names such as Howie Camnitz, Joe Tinker, Mordecai Brown, George Mullin, and Otto Knabe.

Wagner, no longer the number-one choice for a budding league that he once was, nonetheless would have been a plum. He was approached with a multiyear deal worth $15,000 annually to manage the Pittsburgh Feds. Since he had passed up the American League's lucrative offers years earlier, it was no surprise when he spurned this one as well, saying, "[The Feds] know there's no use talking to me."

Just as he had done when the American League tried to seduce his players years before, Dreyfuss was attempting to sign his men to contracts expeditiously. For the most part, this strategy once again proved successful, although by the beginning of the 1914 season, catcher Mike Simon and spitball pitcher Claude Hendrix were lost to the seemingly greener pastures of the Federal League.

The defections of primary catcher Simon (Gibson's injury sidelined him for much of 1913) and Hendrix, a twenty-four-game winner in 1912 and fourteen-game winner in 1913, were not the only changes to the Pirates over the winter. In their never-ending search for a first baseman, Dreyfuss and Clarke made an eight-player trade with the St. Louis Cardinals. Dots Miller, one of the 1909 heroes, may have accelerated his exit by being implicated in a Pittsburgh man's divorce suit as having had indiscretions with the man's wife. Also sent packing were fourteen-game winner Hank Robinson, late-1913 third base acquisition Albert "Cozy" Dolan, utility man Art Butler, and outfielder Chief Wilson, whose penchant for triples and great throwing arm, Clarke felt, were offset by a lack of assertiveness on the field. In return, the Pirates received pitcher Bob Harmon, third baseman Mike Mowrey, and first baseman Big Ed Konetchy, a man Clarke and Dreyfuss had coveted for years.

Typical banter over which team got the best of the deal followed, but with Konetchy and Miller both hinting that they might join the Federal League rather than report to their new clubs, no one knew quite what to make of the trade just yet. Miller, moved to first base in 1912, was hardly disenchanted to leave and glibly referred to himself as the latest victim of the Pirates' "old first base jinx." But his friend Wagner reacted with, "Knocks me off my feet. I can't say a thing. . . . Wonder why they don't throw me in the deal?" In fact, Clarke was so eager to secure Konetchy that he considered parting with Wagner, but Dreyfuss insisted that this not be done under any circumstances.

As though he welcomed the change from the turbulent winter and certainly in need of the workout, Wagner was part of the advance guard that gathered in Dawson Springs, Kentucky, on the way to Hot Springs. Perhaps no member of the party was happier than John Daley, a middle infielder who saw a little action for the St. Louis Browns in 1912 and had played minor league ball in Huntington, West Virginia, in 1913. Daley welcomed another shot at the big leagues and was thrilled to be alongside his childhood idol, Honus Wagner, the man who used to allow Daley and a few friends to pass through the gates at old Exposition Park.

Daley would not appear in a big league game again and was released to Columbus, Ohio, as the first of Clarke's roster moves in the spring, but Daley always looked back fondly at his few days in Dawson Springs. Until he died in 1988 at the age of 101, he was able to provide firsthand confirmation of how Wagner used to "excavate" ground balls. Daley recalled covering the second base bag in a drill, when Wagner scooped a ball out of the dirt and tossed it to him, showering him with dirt, pebbles, and one baseball.

◆ ◆ ◆

The 1914 season opened poorly for the Pirates on April 14. In St. Louis, Wilson and Miller each had a hand in the Cardinals' victory over Pittsburgh, and Gibson, after tentatively circling near the same bench where he had broken an ankle the previous April, dropped a foul pop. In Pittsburgh on the same day, the Federal League opener was replete with a street parade, a ceremonial first toss by Mayor Joseph G. Armstrong, and a crowd of twelve thousand people in Exposition Park. Since Phillippe had been released after a last-place finish in 1913, the renaming of the team was thrown open to the fans in March. With the new nickname Rebels, after their popular outfielder and soon-to-be-named manager, Ennis "Rebel" Oakes, the Pittsburgh Federals won their opener.

The new-look Pirates soon had the upper hand in the intra-city fight with the Feds as the National League club won a surprising fifteen of its first seventeen games. By late May, the Pirates were four games out in front, and Wagner was looking more like a twenty-year-old sensation than a forty-year-old fading star. But a ten-game losing streak started the team on a summerlong descent.

Wagner provided the only highlight in an otherwise dreadful road trip. On June 9 at the Baker Bowl in Philadelphia, he stepped into the box in the ninth inning and stroked his three-thousandth career hit—a double off the Phillies' Erskine Mayer. Only Cap Anson was thought to have achieved the mark previously. Becoming the all-time major league hit leader a few weeks later was one of Wagner's proudest moments.

The team continued its slide, and Wagner, bothered by a gash in his right hand from a flying spike, suffered through a horrific 0 for 19 slump and lost twenty points on his average in one week. By mid-July, only Boston, with second baseman Johnny Evers in his first year as a Brave, had a worse record than the struggling Pirates.

Attendance dropped along with the team's fortunes, with only an estimated four thousand on hand for a Friday, July 17 contest with the Giants at Forbes Field. The Pirates pushed across a run in the first off Rube Marquard, and New York touched Babe Adams for a third-inning run on a sacrifice fly. Neither pitcher would be scored upon again for the next three hours, and when the game entered its twenty-first inning, it became the longest contest in National League history to that date.

With a runner on base, Larry Doyle hit a two-out liner to center. Adams always claimed the ball should have been caught, but it not only dropped, it rolled past the Pirates' rookie center fielder, Joe Kelly, for a Doyle home run. Marquard gave up a single in the bottom half of the inning but easily held on for the win; he gave up fifteen hits and walked just two, one intentionally, in completing twenty-one innings. Adams surrendered twelve hits and, in setting a record that it is safe to say will never be broken, pitched the longest major league complete game without issuing a base on balls. Both pitchers suffered the effects of the marathon and had losing records the rest of the way, with Marquard enduring a twelve-game losing streak later in the year.

Wagner had three hits in the game and drove in the Pirates' first-inning run with a triple, but he also cost his club a promising rally with a controversial play. In the sixth inning, he hit a one-out single, and when Jimmy Viox followed with a single, Wagner slid into third ahead of the throw. As the puzzled Giant infielders feverishly searched for the ball, Wagner jumped to his feet and sprinted toward home. After separating himself from his opponents by several steps, he let the ball drop from his armpit and easily scored. But umpire Bill "Lord" Byron ruled Wagner out for interference and sent Viox back to second, where he was stranded.

Clarke argued passionately and was ejected. He protested the game on the grounds that since the play was not covered clearly in the rule book, Byron had no authority to call Wagner out. A written statement from Wagner, maintaining that the ball had gotten trapped in the folds of his uniform, was included in the paperwork sent to the desk of National League president John Tener. Tener, a former big league pitcher, was a busy man. Elected to the National League presidency the previous offseason, he concurrently served as Pennsylvania's governor for the year of 1914, a unique double duty that caused *The Courier-Journal* of Louisville to comment, "Now that the governor of Pennsylvania has been chosen for a baseball job, it's no use to tell a boy that he will be wasting his time if he devotes himself to politics when he grows up." In an official act as governor that spring, Tener had appointed his friend Wagner to the uncompensated post of adviser to the State Fishery Commission. And in an official act as league president in July, Tener flatly rejected the Pirates' grievance.

◆ ◆ ◆

Twelve consecutive losses by Pittsburgh in late September sealed a seventh-place finish—twenty-five and a half games out of first. Only a worse collapse of the Cincinnati Reds kept the Pirates out of the cellar. The Reds, in second place as late as July 19, lost nineteen in a row in September to drop to the bottom. Even more amazing than the Reds' breakdown was the Boston Braves' second-half revival. In the most dramatic comeback in baseball history, Boston went from last on July 18 all the way to a comfortable ten-and-a-half-game cushion over runner-up New York. Led by manager George Stallings and second baseman Evers, the Chalmers award winner in its final year, Boston completed its season by sweeping the heavily favored Philadelphia Athletics in the World Series.

The Pirates were a fine defensive club in 1914, but their offense was feeble—finishing dead last in runs and batting average during the year and getting shut out 1–0 a major league record ten times. Wagner's offensive numbers took a dramatic drop, and in by far his worst season in competitive baseball, he hit just .252 with a lone home run and fifteen doubles.

Dreyfuss pointed to the Federal League for the Pirates poor showing, saying, "Our players talked, played, and ate Feds." Indeed, his foes were persistent. At Hot Springs the previous March, Dreyfuss had to secure an injunction to keep former Pirate and recent jumper Howie Camnitz from actively recruiting Pittsburgh players in the lobby of the Hotel Eastman and even outside the gates to Whittington Park. The usually unopinionated Wagner called down Camnitz and told the "troublemaker" to stay away from the younger players. During the season, Fed agents were seen at Forbes Field, and first-year pirate Ed Konetchy was known to be talking contract with them in midyear.

Combined attendance in the National and American Leagues was its lowest in more than a decade, and Pittsburgh's figure was less than half of any of its totals since 1902. Many teams were in the red, and the Federal League, now a legitimate third major league, suffered financial losses as well. Yet still committed to their goal, the Feds continued to entice National and American League players with a promise of bigger paychecks and filed an antitrust suit against Organized Baseball.

Between the seasons of 1914 and 1915, Philadelphia Athletics pitchers Eddie Plank and Charles "Chief" Bender were signed by the youngest circuit, and the baseball ground shook when it was announced that the great Washington pitcher, Walter Johnson, had jumped—only to change his mind a few days later. Taking advantage of what was, at least for a brief time, a competitive marketplace, several players used the situation to their advantage by what Dreyfuss termed "a holdup." Pirate outfielder Max Carey, who never missed a chance to coax a little more money from his employer, received a new two-year deal with a raise.

After nibbling at previous Fed bait and certainly not overjoyed with his first season as a Pirate, Konetchy made an easy catch. No more happy with Konetchy than the first baseman was with the Pirates, Dreyfuss scoffed at a demand of a three-year contract at an annual $7,500. Shortly after the 1914 season, Dreyfuss and Clarke were once again on their never-ending hunt for a first baseman, as Konetchy joined the cross-town Rebels.

If Wagner had his choice, he would have been the Pirates' new first baseman. He was on record as having wanted to move there for years, but even though his skills were slowly eroding, he was still the best shortstop on the squad and led the league in fielding percentage at the position in 1914 and would again in 1915.

◆ ◆ ◆

Wagner was never fond of formal affairs and dinners, although some said it was more the following mornings he disliked. Over the next few years, he would get very used to ceremonial banquets. On the evening of February 24, 1915, roughly two hundred "Stove League" fans honored Wagner on his forty-first birthday at the Colonial Annex Hotel in Pittsburgh. John Tener was the primary speaker, and Clarke came from Kansas to deliver a short message. Many who were unable to attend sent letters of regret and congratulations. Ty Cobb wrote, "Down here in Georgia, I will be drinking a toast to the greatest ball player that ever lived. . . ." Connie Mack, Hughie Jennings, and Joe Tinker, now manager of the Chicago Federal League team, expressed similar sentiment. Johnny Evers admitted in his letter that he emulated Wagner but had "not been as modest or 'clean' . . . largely because of the impossible high standard set by . . . Wagner." Grasping his gift—a pair of fishing rods and a reel—and with Clarke whispering encouragement to him, Wagner slowly stood up to deliver a brief and humble thank-you to the guests.

Many people expected Wagner to announce he was quitting at any time. Retrospective articles published in the January 1915 issue of *Baseball Magazine* fanned the flames of Wagner's retirement talk. Included was a letter from Dreyfuss in which he called his star "the greatest of all time" and added, "Still with all the credit due him as a great ball player, I think that even greater credit is his for his high personal character, for he is not only one of the squarest and fairest of men, but one of the most modest and unassuming gentlemen I have ever had the pleasure of knowing."

Dreyfuss assured the public that the veteran would remain with the ball club in some capacity, saying, "There will be a lot of things to keep Honus useful in a Pirate uniform until one or the other of us is gone." Neither of them, however, wanted Wagner's playing career to end just yet. Wagner promised his employer not to retire until a replacement was ready, which had *The Sporting News* declaring, "If that is so, the Dutchman will go on playing forever"—a prediction that was beginning to seem not entirely farfetched. Once again, Al and Honus prepared for another spring in the South.

Al had been bouncing from one job to another, managing businesses or pool halls and coaching local ball clubs and never straying far from Carnegie except for a few weeks each March in Hot Springs. Under the condition that he would still be able to make his annual trip, he accepted a position as basketball and baseball coach for 1915 at the Carnegie Technical Institute in Pittsburgh (now Carnegie-Mellon University). Founded by Andrew Carnegie and opened in 1905, Carnegie Tech was a school of roughly three thousand two hundred students and was practically within sight of Forbes Field beyond the left field wall. Honus was to serve as Al's assistant when time allowed, and the two men set up an exercise routine for the prep athletes to follow while the brothers were in Arkansas. The Wagners' tutelage of the young men proved less than successful, as the basketball team lost seven of thirteen games and one of their baseball players decked an umpire.

In Hot Springs, Wagner wondered if he was being phased out of the Pirates' plans. Wally Gerber, seemingly Wagner's heir at shortstop, and Wheeler "Doc" Johnston, a first baseman purchased from Cleveland, were getting most of the action at their positions, and Wagner was relegated to coaching and playing first base for the Yannigans. But he played well, and after his charges defeated the Regulars in five of six games, a feat that came with Dreyfuss's age-old tradition of rewarding the Yannigans with a box of cigars, Wagner was once again in the picture.

He began the 1915 season nursing two bad fingers. Playing second base and pinch hitting for the first few weeks, Wagner was moved back to his old position when Gerber proved ineffective. Wagner played well in the field but was struggling in June to keep his average above a pathetic .200. He was, however, paid a tribute when Roger Bresnahan, now manager of the Cubs, ordered him intentionally walked with the bases empty.

The Pittsburgh team fluctuated around the .500 level for much of the summer, but with no team playing much better, modest but realistic pennant hopes survived until late August. Wagner enjoyed an excellent second half after bottoming out in June: Rebounding to an average of .274, he also had his best totals in several categories since 1912 and set a still-standing mark for players over age forty with seventeen triples. With twenty-two stolen bases, he topped the twenty mark for the eighteenth consecutive year—a string unmatched in baseball history. Perhaps even more intriguing was that for the first time since 1901 and at the age of forty-one, he played in every one of his team's games.

The Pirates finished fifth, and while only a half game out of the first division, they were also just three games up from the basement. Manager Clarke had considered retirement the previous winter but agreed to come back after some encouragement. This year, he meant to hang it up.

Clarke gave Dreyfuss substantial credit for setting him on the straight and narrow path twenty years earlier, as well as providing sound advice that helped him accumulate a sizable fortune. Estimates of Clarke's net worth varied, and while definitely substantial in 1915, it would increase dramatically over the coming years. The financial motivation to manage had disappeared long ago, so with a bad team on his hands and blossoming business interests, he walked away. Clarke left baseball in 1915 with four pennants in nineteen arduous years, having managed more games (2,829, including ties), more wins (1,602), and more losses (1,181) than any preceding manager. He still maintains the Pirate club record with 1,422 victories.

Prior to the game on September 23 at Forbes Field, the players and employees of the Pirates presented Clarke with a grandfather clock and a red leather binder filled with the names of thousands of Pittsburghers who wished him well. That afternoon, he put himself in the lineup for one last time. Playing left field for four innings, he did not receive a chance and in two trips to the plate, he lined out to left and singled to right. After reaching first base, he called for Max Carey, another future Hall of Famer, to take his place on the bag. Clarke walked off the field to thunderous applause. On October 3 in Cincinnati, after the Pirates closed out their season with a 5–3 win, Clarke hosted a dinner for himself and his players to celebrate his retirement from the diamond as well as his forty-third birthday.

◆ ◆ ◆

The next few months were filled with speculation as to who would become the next skipper. While popular names from the past, Tommy Leach and Harry Smith, were mentioned, most people felt the choice would be Wagner or Gibson. Wagner was the overwhelming fan choice in a local newspaper's straw poll. He repeatedly denied any managerial aspirations and said, "I would not be a manager, because I would not want to leave the ball field and take my worries and troubles home with me. Nor would I feel like going back to the barber shop." It was certainly his job if he wanted it. He made it clear that he didn't.

Dreyfuss surprised all guessers when he announced that the new Pirate manager was Jimmy Callahan. Born one month after Wagner and just as much an old warhorse, the forty-one-year-old Callahan was qualified and talented. He had twice won twenty games as a pitcher and played almost every position on the diamond successfully during a fine career. A respected baseball strategist, he had managed the Chicago White Sox for four full seasons and part of another. Dreyfuss cherished loyalty and was a proponent of player-managers. Since Callahan was through as a player, had jumped to the American League in its early days, and had spent several years playing, managing, and championing the cause of independent or "outlaw" clubs, he was a most unlikely choice.

He eagerly accepted a two-year deal to manage and expressed his pleasure that Wagner endorsed his appointment. Assuring everyone that Wagner would retain his team captaincy, Callahan added, "In my mind Wagner is the greatest of them all, and I expect to receive some valuable assistance from him. . . ."

President Ed Gwinner of the Pittsburgh Rebels challenged Dreyfuss to a city championship late in the 1915 season. It is doubtful that Gwinner received a reply. Confessing that the season had been "precarious" but feeling the Feds' demise was imminent, Dreyfuss was against any type of compromise. But with both Organized Baseball and the Federal League suffering staggering losses, the two made peace on December 22 in New York.

The Federal League withdrew its protracted antitrust suit and terminated operations, receiving substantial remuneration from Organized Baseball for doing so. Fed backers purchased controlling interest of the St. Louis Browns and Chicago Cubs, and each Fed team was permitted to sell its players—now absolved of any wrongdoing. The only remnant that survives from the last serious attempt to establish a third major league is Weeghman Park. The ballpark of the defunct Federal League's Chicago Whales and the Cubs' adopted home since 1916, it is known today as Wrigley Field.

◆ ◆ ◆

Peace was at hand in baseball, but a bitter and bloody war was raging in Europe. The ever-worsening situation was on many Americans' minds throughout 1916, as it became increasingly difficult for the United States to maintain its neutral position. In February, with better times presumably ahead for baseball, the National League held a gala at the Waldorf-Astoria to celebrate the circuit's fortieth anniversary. The special guest, former President Taft, searched the ballroom for Wagner asking, "Where is that bowlegged Dutchman that walks like me?" Despite assurance that he would not need to speak, Wagner stayed home with the grippe—today's common cold.

When Clarke was asked for a prediction on the pennant winner, he chirped, "Pittsburgh . . . of course. I'm a fan now . . . and I have a right to my opinion for the first time in eighteen years." Like most fans, he was overly optimistic. While Wagner was healthy by the season's onset, the Pirates were not. It was another long summer for Pittsburgh baseball followers in 1916. With play that *Baseball Magazine* characterized as "ragged, full of miscues and dumb stumblings," the team never broke .500 and suffered a club-record twenty-seven shutout losses.

On opening day, Wagner had three of the team's six hits in a 2–1 loss at St. Louis. Pitcher Erv "Kanty" Kantlehner, Wagner's friend and room-mate, was the tough-luck loser. Kanty was on his way to a 5–15 record after compiling a 5–12 mark the previous season—due in part to being on the short end of eight shutouts.

In the third inning of the next day's contest, a ball that Pirate second baseman Joe Schultz later admitted he should have caught squirted out of his glove and was ruled a base hit. It turned out to be the only Cardi-nal hit that day, and although Adams complained, most of the men in the press box agreed with the call. Adams settled for a one-hitter. He walked only one in the complete game shutout and seemed to be off to a great start. But then he mysteriously lost his curveball, winning just one more game in 1916, and was 2–9 with a 5.72 ERA when the Pirates released him in early August. After pitching in a minor league in 1917, Adams was re-signed by the Pirates to a World War I–ravaged roster in 1918. Adams spent parts of the next nine seasons with Pittsburgh and retired with a 194–140 lifetime record. Issuing just 1.29 walks per nine innings during his career, Adams is second only to Deacon Phillippe as the best control pitcher in big league history.

Although the Pirates were never contenders in 1916, Wagner was playing quite well and at .341 was second in the league in batting aver-age in mid-July. Philadelphia manager Pat Moran even afforded Wagner the unlikely honor of pulling the rope to lift the Phillies' 1915 National League pennant during a pregame ceremony at the Baker Bowl.

Then on August 5, Wagner split the webbing between the third and little fingers of his throwing hand. Four stitches closed the wound but it remained painful, and bothered by a bad hip and sore thumb as well, Wagner made five pinch-hitting appearances and played just twice in the field over the next month. Slumping horribly upon his return, he dropped to .287 and, other than his partial year of 1897, had career-low totals in hits, runs, RBIs, and stolen bases.

Pittsburgh dropped nineteen of its last twenty, including the final ten, to finish in sixth place. Callahan and Dreyfuss whined throughout the 1916 season: In Cincinnati, they asserted that the ushers planted balls in the stands and if a Pirate hit a foul into the crowd, an "old" ball was thrown back onto the field. The Brooklyn groundskeeper was said to be watering down the baselines, and Dreyfuss accused McGraw of trying to distract talented but impressionable Al Mamaux by comment-ing to newspapermen about how well the young Pirate pitching ace would fit in with the Giants. Dreyfuss had brought the wrath of many fans late in the season when, within a two-week span, he unceremoniously cast adrift both Adams and Gibson. And the Pirate president alienated all of his players in October by announcing that, unlike previous years, all of the proceeds of the squad's barnstorming tour would be retained by the club.

Dreyfuss felt he had been given the short end of a few important National Commission decisions. Prior to the 1912 season, he had lost his argument that slugger Clifford "Gavvy" Cravath was Pirate property, and in June 1916, the Commission ruled against Pittsburgh's claim on George Sisler. Despite strong evidence in his favor, Dreyfuss lost each case. He now called for dissolving the Commission entirely, and at the National League meetings in December, he proposed the ouster of chairman Garry Herrmann. Failing on both counts, Dreyfuss acknowledged that, for the right price, he would sell his franchise.

Notwithstanding the years of success and enormous profits, as well as the fact that the game once again seemed to be on a solid foundation, Dreyfuss clearly was not enjoying his position as a baseball club owner. It seemed that even Wagner was not immune to the president's disapproval. Hinting that he thought Wagner stayed out of the lineup too long with his injury the previous year, Dreyfuss revealed that a pay cut was in order for the veteran—now the only remaining member of the 1909 champions. Wagner admitted that the strain of playing shortstop was becoming too great. In the winter following the 1916 season, many wondered if he would return at all.

◆ ◆ ◆

On the last day of October 1916, the crushing news reached Carnegie that Charley Wagner had unexpectedly passed away that morning in Canonsburg, Pennsylvania, where he had resided for several years. The forty-six-year-old barber died after a short battle with pneumonia, leaving three young sons and his wife, Olive. Brighter moments were ahead for Honus.

In mid-December, the grapevine was humming about the ongoing courtship of Honus Wagner and Bessie Smith. After an eight-year relationship, it was apparent that a wedding was in the works. Miss Smith deflected all inquiries to Wagner who, of course, made no comment on the matter and, when pressed, changed the subject to the fray in Europe. With many of their movements under careful scrutiny, they managed to keep their intentions hidden. Carefully released information through intimate friends pointed to New Year's Day, but on the evening of Saturday, December 30, the forty-two-year-old Wagner donned his best brown suit, maroon tie, and brown hat to call on the twenty-seven-year-old Miss Smith at her home.

Driving into Pittsburgh, they were met after hours by the marriage license office chief clerk, Walter Nevin. Securing the last license issued in Allegheny County in 1916, the two sped to Carnegie ahead of many now-wise reporters. Shortly after 7:00 P.M., the two arrived at St. John's Lutheran Church, where Wagner's former teacher, the Reverend E. F. A. Dittmer, performed the ceremony in front of maid of honor Alice I. Downey, best man Al Wagner, and a few members of the immediate family.

Bessie, one of four children of John G. and Annie Smith, was a self-professed tomboy as a child and later a graduate of the Pittsburgh Conservatory of Music. Bessie's father had played ball for many years in and around Pittsburgh and years earlier had invited Wagner to dine in the Smith home in nearby Crafton. Bessie later remembered that she and Jay, as she always called him, "started to go around together and finally married," adding, "That is the story of my romance."

Immediately following the simple ceremony, the newlyweds hustled to Pittsburgh and departed under a shroud of secrecy. Heading west and intending to visit Erv Kantlehner in California, the two returned home within a few days when they learned that Bessie's mother was ill. They set up temporary housekeeping at an Eighth Avenue residence in Carnegie, but Wagner soon purchased two lots in the community's finer neighborhood of Beechwood Avenue. A brick home would be ready later in 1917, where the two would live for the rest of their years together.

◆ ◆ ◆

Wagner pledged in the past to stay single while an active player, and when he showed up at headquarters in February "as big as a battleship" (according to one report), it seemed as though his playing career might be over. War news flooded America, and with the nation's involvement in Europe on the horizon, baseball's owners were anticipating a lean 1917 season. *Retrenchment* was the byword around baseball, although Ralph Davis of *The Sporting News* charged that Dreyfuss "boasted of a cheap policy." Cutting player salaries was foremost in Dreyfuss's mind, and Wagner's salary would not be spared the knife. *Sporting Life* correspondent Alfred Cratty noted Dreyfuss was "a bit ticklish on the matter," and no doubt he must have cringed as the public chastised him for his callous treatment of his star. Even Clarke was outspoken that Wagner deserved a better fate at the hands of the Pirate president.

Conjecture of the salary offer made to Wagner varied from five to eight thousand dollars, which would still have classified him as the highest paid Pirate other than Callahan. Wagner was not sure if he wanted to play at all. He had seen many of his contemporaries leave the game: Christy Mathewson, Mordecai Brown, and Larry Lajoie all joined the list of former greats after the 1916 season. Wagner acknowledged that his wife's "good home-cooking" had taken its toll on him, and he questioned his own ability to get into proper condition. He halfheartedly mentioned that he was interested in scouting for the Pirates, though it did not fit his lifestyle, and he was informed that he could expect even less of a monetary reward for the duty.

Despite Dreyfuss and Wagner insisting that there was not a salary dispute, Wagner was on the list of holdouts since he did not return his contract to the club. Harry Keck of *The Pittsburgh Post* made a tongue-in-cheek prediction that "along about May or June, when the Pirates are all busted to pieces and down in eighth place, or maybe ninth, [Wagner is] going to be little Johnny on the spot, and go to their rescue and get sweet revenge on Barney. . . ."

On April 6, 1917, provoked by the sinking of numerous American merchant ships, the United States formally declared war on Germany. Baseball was considered a "non-essential" industry, making its players eligible for conscription. Since Wagner was well past draft age and he made no formal statement of his baseball intentions, he began to simply drift into retirement as Carnegie's leading citizen while the nation's attention turned to the war effort.

Over the first few months of the 1917 season, he went to Forbes Field to watch what was now a wretched Pirate team. He joined the team briefly during practice on June 2 and then watched from the grandstand as the Pirates, already trailing the pack, were dumped by a 9–1 score for a second straight day. Afterward, he and Callahan had a long meeting in the clubhouse. On June 6, at the Pirate headquarters in the Farmers Bank Building, Wagner and Dreyfuss agreed to a ten-thousand-dollar contract for 1917. Ever the sentimentalist, Dreyfuss welcomed Wagner back, saying, "He has been a fixture for so many years that he has come to be almost a part of the club, like the grandstand or the pitcher's box."

Despite a lack of spring training as well as looking overweight and older, Wagner wasted no time getting back in the lineup. On June 7, he received a stirring welcome from the four thousand in attendance when he walked onto the field, and he was cheered during batting practice as well as with each plate appearance. He bounced out to second three times. In the eighth inning, he stroked a run-scoring single but, representing the tying run, he was thrown out attempting to stretch the hit into a double. It was evident that his Flying Dutchman days were over.

With the Pirates on their way to finishing last, twenty and a half games out of seventh, the attraction for fans for the remainder of the summer was Honus Wagner as he made what is known today as a farewell tour. Kicking things off on Friday, June 22, an automobile parade snaked through Pittsburgh to Forbes Field with Wagner in the lead car. In front of ten thousand people at the ballpark, he was given a lifetime Elks Club membership and a silver loving cup. He armed himself with baseballs and, walking in front of the grandstand, tossed them to the soldiers and sailors in the crowd. Wagner Days followed in Cincinnati, Brooklyn, New York City, Boston, Paterson, and even Marion, Indiana. If he did not corner the silver market in the summer of 1917, he at least stockpiled a number of valuable loving cups.

◆ ◆ ◆

Wagner was playing both third base and first base, leading the club in hitting at .342, when Callahan was fired on June 29. With many Pirates griping about their salaries and Callahan unable to establish any authority, morale was abominable. There had been whisperings for weeks that he should be replaced by Wagner, and Dreyfuss, feeling the players might respond to "one of their own," pleaded with Wagner to take the job. He initially balked but finally agreed to "try it" as long as he was relieved of the team's business affairs.

Fans in Pittsburgh were ecstatic. Telegrams poured in congratulating him on his appointment, but Wagner stressed that it was "temporary." Meanwhile, Dreyfuss sent a dispatch to Hugo Bezdek, the team's West Coast scout, with instructions to report immediately to act as business manager of the ball club and to be on hand just in case.

Although he had filled in as manager for Clarke and Callahan many times, Wagner's first official game at the helm was on June 30, 1917. He was matched against Christy Mathewson, now in his first full year as manager of the Cincinnati Reds. Wagner tied the score with a two-run double in the sixth, and his team went on to win in his managerial debut 5–4. Three days and four losses later, he resigned, his self-doubt about managing confirmed. It was an awful team and a bad time to be in charge of it. He had said repeatedly that he never wanted the position and had to be coerced into accepting it temporarily. Still, his detractors chalked up Wagner's resignation to a lack of toughness or an inability to lead.

His replacement was Bezdek, a man whose qualifications to manage the Pirates were that he served as a scout for the club, was once a great college fullback playing under Amos Alonzo Stagg, and had built successful college football programs at the University of Arkansas and the University of Oregon. *Baseball Magazine* had to admit, in a story entitled WHO IS HUGO BEZDEK? that he was "a dark horse candidate for . . . manager of a crippled, disheartened ball club." (The volatile Bezdek's tenure with the Pirates would last only through 1919, and he is more widely remembered for being an inventive and able head football coach at Pennsylvania State University for twelve years.)

The entire Pirate organization was in tatters. Many people clamored for a new owner who would right the ship. According to *The Sporting News*, at a dinner held for Callahan by a growing anti-Dreyfuss faction, the deposed manager "eloquated on his handicaps and flooded the hall with his alibis." In a parting shot, he said, "If I were eager to wish a terrible fate upon the German Kaiser, I could think of nothing more awful than to have him sentenced . . . to come to Pittsburgh and manage the Pirates under Barney Dreyfuss."

◆ ◆ ◆

Wagner was still hitting well over .300 on July 14 when, Brooklyn outfielder Casey Stengel slid into first base and spiked Wagner's right foot. The wound was cleaned and dressed on the field, but the injury ruined Wagner's season. He missed several games and performed poorly when he did play. In his last career appearance at the Polo Grounds on August 29, as a treat to his faithful New York fans, he moved from first base to shortstop in the eighth inning for his only appearance at the position all year. He played infrequently over the next few weeks, securing just two more hits, and his playing career ended with three innings at second base on September 17. With his painful foot preventing him from batting, he was pinch hit for by teammate Bill Wagner, who struck out.

◆ ◆ ◆

At the age of forty-three, Wagner's career was over. He retired with major league record-setting totals for games played (2,789), at bats

(10,441), hits (3,418), runs (1,735), runs batted in (1,732), stolen bases (722), extra-base hits (996), and total bases (4,868). He had more singles (2,422), doubles (643), triples (252), and batting titles (eight), than any prior National Leaguer. Although the numbers gathered from accounts of the day differ slightly from those shown above, which are now generally accepted to be more accurate tabulations of his statistics, the fact remains that he established many new thresholds. In time, most of the marks were broken, with new major league records established by Ty Cobb and Mel Ott or Stan Musial later eclipsing Wagner's National League levels.

The numbers, though, were secondary to what Wagner meant to baseball. Perhaps Bozeman Bulger of *The World* summed it up most appropriately when he wrote in 1917, "Instead of trying to fix these figures in your head, just remember that he is the best hitter and the best infielder that the game has ever known and that will be sufficient. . . . The fans love Wagner because he loves baseball. . . . [Wagner is an] argument for the newly accepted theory that professional athletics and decency can go together."

ELEVEN

A BASEBALL MAN

Though many players received a cut in pay in 1918, Dreyfuss had learned his lesson the previous year and offered Wagner a contract for ten thousand dollars. But his career as a major league baseball player was over and Honus knew it. For a while, his name was on the list of players to be invited to spring training, but shortly before the team headed south, the Pittsburgh club asked for waivers on him—a necessary formality. He left major league baseball and entered into a comfortable retirement in his own way—quietly.

The construction cost of the Wagners' new house was reportedly ten thousand dollars, a huge amount for Carnegie at the time. A large, three-story, square building of yellow brick, it sported a broad front porch and was quite luxurious by the standards of the day. The home would be professionally decorated and filled with fine furniture, including Wagner's sizable trophy case. However in late 1917, construction delays repeatedly moved back the completion date. It looked as though they would barely be settled before a new family member joined them. Bessie was pregnant.

Knowing that their spacious house would be quite a job to keep up and with the baby on the way, the Wagners hired a day housekeeper—eighteen-year-old Mabel Aston, younger sister of Wagner's friend George

"Chauff" Aston. Mabel had the opportunity to prove her value to the Wagners almost immediately, supervising the entire move while Bessie spent the final weeks of her pregnancy in the hospital. On January 9, 1918, Bessie gave birth to a girl, but the child was stillborn. The Wagners named the infant Elva, after Bessie's older sister, and buried her in the family plot near Honus's parents and brother Charley.

Though the loss of the baby was heartbreaking, Wagner soon immersed himself in scores of activities. The nation's attention was focused on the war in Europe, and all Americans were encouraged to "do their bit for the boys over there." Pittsburghers were particularly proud of the role their mills played in providing the Allies with munitions as the city became known as the Arsenal of the World. Wagner did his part by becoming one of the thousands of citizens nationwide, referred to as "four-minute" men, who were responsible for making brief speeches on behalf of the Allied cause. Wagner encouraged young men to enlist in the armed services and sold Liberty bonds at moving-picture shows, schools, churches, and other public gatherings in and around Carnegie. His reputation for ducking the limelight still fresh in everyone's mind, the running joke was that a four-minute talk would be the longest of his life. His lack of oratory skills did not diminish people's admiration for him, and newspaper accounts often mentioned the large number of people in the audience.

As Wagner made several four-minute presentations each week and sometimes two or three in a day, he became more comfortable with public speaking. In February, the Pittsburgh Stove League held what had become an annual banquet for Wagner's birthday, this one his forty-fourth. Instead of muttering a few words and sitting down as quickly as possible, his previous custom, Wagner stood confidently and slowly addressed the crowd. He began by poking fun at himself, then thanked everyone for being there and expressed his appreciation for their kindness.

Wagner's instincts and reactions had served him well on the baseball diamond, but they were of no use at the podium. His little talks had shown Wagner that it was beneficial to rehearse a few pat lines. He collected a cache of silly stories, loosely based on incidents he was involved in or heard about during his playing days, and drew on them again and again.

He also supported the war effort by using some of his more natural talents. A benefit game was scheduled between the Superior Steel Company team of Carnegie and the 319th Infantry Regiment club from local

Camp Lee, with the proceeds used to buy tobacco for the soldiers. Cigarettes were in great demand during the war, and military men were constantly urging people to send them tobacco. Wagner played first base for Superior, providing a drawing card for the event, and more than one thousand people turned out to see the Regiment win 2–0. Wagner performed in his Pirate uniform, but two Carnegie boys on the soldiers' team competed with him for the fans' affections. The matchup raised more than four hundred dollars and was considered a huge success.

Coordinating a recycling program to raise money for the Red Cross, Wagner placed an iron rack at the end of his street where people could hang old tires and tubes. He then collected the scrap rubber and delivered it to a plant for processing. Al Wagner also got in on the act. When he heard that the troops at Camp Lee were looking for baseball suits that they could wear in their intramural games, he dug out one of his old uniforms and sent it along with his best wishes for Uncle Sam's boys.

◆ ◆ ◆

In the fall of 1918, Wagner became football coach at Carnegie High School and would later head up the basketball team. He was slated to coach baseball there in the spring of 1919 as well, but a bigger and better opportunity arose. In February, he was appointed physical director at Carnegie Technical Institute. Shortly after the announcement was made, Bessie became seriously ill and had to be hospitalized. A few months earlier, a flu epidemic had swept through Carnegie and a temporary infirmary was set up at the Elks Lodge; of the more than ninety patients admitted, nineteen died. By 1919, the worst was over and Bessie soon regained her health, allowing her husband to report to his new job.

The position of physical director was much different from that of today's athletic director. A school council handled the hiring of head coaches and fiscal management of the sports programs. Wagner's responsibilities included coaching baseball, assisting the coaches of other sports, helping out with intramural activities, and offering individual athletic instruction. His salary was not divulged but was reported in the local press as "substantial."

So many young men tried out for the baseball team that Wagner, who managed wearing his Pirate uniform, had to divide them into groups in order to handle them. He eventually pruned the throng down to a reasonable number, only to have his team decimated by injuries and poor grades. His squad got off to a good start, beating an all-star nine of former college and semipro players of the area and winning its first two regulation games. The team then lost eight in a row to finish 2–8. Even so, the school yearbook, *The Thistle*, suggested, "Too much credit cannot be given Coach Wagner, better known even to the girls as 'Hans,' for the wonderful work which he accomplished with the baseball team this year. He made stars out of recruits; not individual stars, but stars who sacrificed their own records for the welfare of the team."

Wagner was frustrated by typical college ball issues, such as some of the best talents being declared academically ineligible and a necessarily short season that precluded real player development, but he stuck with the job for two more years. In 1920, he was able to put together a winning combination with a record of 8–6 and one tie. The following season, Tech finished with an 11–9 record. Though the students seemed to flock to Wagner, for unexplained reasons his tenure at Carnegie Tech was limited to just three years.

◆ ◆ ◆

By 1919 World War I had ended, but Wagner's patriotic efforts continued. In February, he helped organize a successful benefit for a wounded soldiers' athletic fund at an area hospital and even played guard for the Hans Wagner Five in one basketball game.

He was already an active member of the Elks. In the spring when he joined the Masons, special arrangements had to be made to accommodate some seven hundred members who attended his induction, including three county judges, court officials, lawyers, doctors, bankers, preachers, and others from all over Pennsylvania and elsewhere.

In September, word spread that Wagner had signed a contract to "star" in four films to be made by a local company. One of the pictures was to be a two-reel comedy with a baseball finish; the others would be educational, dealing with hunting, fishing, and other aspects of outdoor life. The time-consuming process would take all of two weeks, with production beginning September 15 and a release date of October 1.

Little evidence remains of these projects. It is known that Wagner did play a part in a comedy, *Spring Fever*, which was produced in 1919 by a Pittsburgh-area company and ran in local theaters for several years. In addition to Wagner, two other notables performed in this movie— Moe and Shemp Howard, who would go on to Three Stooges fame. The *Three Stooges Scrapbook* states that Moe Howard and Wagner may have made as many as a dozen two-reel shorts together, but no record of these films endures.

Wagner was also featured in another picture, *The Corner Drug Store*, a few years later. In 1922, he expanded his entertainment repertoire by catching baseballs dropped from the top of the ten-story City-County building in Pittsburgh while hundreds of people watched and cameras rolled. Pittsburgh police superintendent and former professional ballplayer John C. Calhoun dropped three balls more than 150 feet to a waiting Wagner, who was able to snare the first and third "pitches." The film of the stunt was later shown at the Carnegie Theater as a prologue to *In the Name of the Law*.

In October 1919, Wagner's automobile was stolen, but it was located a few days later on a Pittsburgh wharf. The recovery was fortunate because he soon needed his car for daily trips into the city. Along with five business associates, he opened a store at 438 Wood Street in Pittsburgh. The Honus Wagner Sporting Goods Store carried guns, ammunition, automobile and bicycle tires, boxing gloves, golf clubs, fishing tackle— and, of course, baseball uniforms and equipment. Wagner was president and manager. The new establishment kept him busy and provided a great setting for "fanning" (chatting) with his friends, such as Deacon Phillippe, who was "working" there.

◆ ◆ ◆

After an untroubled second pregnancy, Bessie gave birth to a healthy girl on December 5, 1919. The new father explained that he could not come up with a name that was pretty enough but within a few days settled on Betty Baine in honor of her mother, the former Bessie Baine Smith.

Betty was Wagner's little darling. When she was old enough, he loved to take her out and show her off at events such as the Elks' annual corn roast. At the Pittsburgh Stove League's banquet for his forty-seventh birthday in 1921, Wagner was presented with a framed picture of the child, then just over a year old. Upon seeing the portrait, Wagner's eyes became watery and then tears streamed down his craggy face. "My friends," he said with a quivering voice, "this gift, simple as it may seem, has struck me a mighty blow. . . . My little daughter is the one thing which I now live for."

Another daughter, Virginia "Ginny" Mae, was born on May 3, 1922, completing the family. Wagner called his daughters "my two boys" and taught them to throw, catch, and hit a baseball. The tall and husky Ginny, whom Honus called "the fat one," was quite a tomboy and loved playing basketball with her dad. Betty, thinner and shorter than her younger sister, shared Bessie's interest in music.

The Wagners were in most ways typical Carnegie residents. Their yard was a popular playground for local children, and an empty lot behind their house served as the neighborhood ball field. Whenever Wagner would spot the kids getting up a game, he could not resist joining in the fun. He entertained them with tricks—one being to crouch down and sit astride his bat until the pitcher threw the ball, then spring up and hit it at the last second.

Wagner and Bessie were quite devoted to one another, and any disagreements they had usually centered around Wagner's dogs or his tobacco chewing. Ongoing spats occurred over where the animals would eat and sleep, but Bessie's pet peeve was when her husband missed his living-room spittoon and sprayed tobacco juice on the carpet. When his aim was errant one too many times, she shattered the cuspidor in the yard.

Bessie insisted that the family attend church regularly, and all four Wagners were usually present for Sunday services at St. John's. Wagner went along to make her happy but believed it was the wife's role to indoctrinate the children in religious matters. Though he grew up in a devout family, as a single man he was much more lax in worship, preferring to spend his Sundays hunting in the fields.

His businesses and other interests kept him occupied and, with all those women in the house, he frequently sought refuge at the Elks Club. There he could manage to get into a card game at almost any time and drink a few glasses of beer. Throughout Prohibition, from 1920 to 1933, Wagner had to be discreet about his watering holes. Like many otherwise upstanding citizens of the time, he managed to keep up to date on the places where alcohol could be found. During his playing career, Wagner consumed beer regularly and after retirement began drinking more heavily. More than once, the day after found him embarrassed about his behavior and apologetic to friends or neighbors.

◆ ◆ ◆

Baseball fans remembered Wagner fondly. Countless communities had Wagner Days. One of the more elaborate affairs brought 250 people out to celebrate his fifty-seventh birthday in Paterson, New Jersey. Wagner and Bessie were dined at the Lido Venice Club, on an island in the Passaic River, where he was presented with a radio set and the keys to the city.

Major league baseball had not forgotten Wagner, either. He threw out the first pitch of the Pirates' 1921 home opener. He served on the committee that organized a testimonial dinner for Dreyfuss's twenty-fifth anniversary as president of the Pittsburgh Baseball Club in October 1924. In addition, Cobb and Wagner were special guests at Game One of the 1925 World Series in Pittsburgh. He stayed in touch with many of his old baseball acquaintances, and modern players came to know Wagner through his frequent visits to Forbes Field. Often out-of-town players accompanied him back to Carnegie after games—a highlight of the trip, no doubt, being one of Wagner's favorite speak-easies.

Even when not invited by Wagner, some players who found themselves in the Carnegie area took a custom tour of his old stomping grounds courtesy of Chester Conboy, a *Pittsburgh Chronicle Telegraph* writer and area resident. Conboy liked to show the house on Railroad Avenue where Wagner grew up and the lots where he had played ball—some now obscured by manufacturing plants or other buildings. Note-worthy players who took the Wagner tour in 1921 included Walter "Rabbit" Maranville and Babe Ruth. Later that year, Wagner did his brothers at the Carnegie Elks Club a favor by inviting the latest baseball sensation, Ruth, to the lodge one evening.

Throughout the 1920s, Wagner was an enthusiastic supporter of all amateur sports. In 1920, he served as a member of the boxing commission of Pittsburgh, which supervised all matches in the city. Later, he helped organize a new basketball league in Carnegie and served as chairman of its board of directors. Sometimes, he would take to the court himself, and his Old-Timers Basketball Stars even challenged a team of high school seniors from a neighboring town.

Wagner gave even greater attention to baseball. In 1920, he helped promote both his store and youth baseball by offering a trophy to the winning team of the Allegheny County American Legion League. As president of a newly formed amateur loop, Wagner went before the Pittsburgh City Council in 1922 to condemn a proposed repeal of day-light savings time, which in an era without field lights would have drastically cut into after-work sports. "I represent no interests except boys in baseball infancy and men who, with me, have passed beyond baseball,"

Wagner explained. "All men should play baseball more for the exercise there is in it and we should encourage them to play." The city council eventually decided that daylight savings time should remain in effect.

Another Wagner effort as a booster of sandlot ball was Hans Wagner's All-Stars, a traveling outfit consisting of the area's best young players just out of high school. The boys were paid a share of the gate and had the thrill of playing for and sometimes with Honus Wagner, who would often take the field for an inning or two at shortstop.

It wasn't just men and boys that Wagner supported. He also helped promote the women's game. The Bloomer Girls were a big draw in themselves, but when Honus Wagner agreed to umpire one of their games in Carnegie in 1922, a huge crowd was guaranteed. Nearly two thousand people turned out to see the women play a local church team in a charity game.

Most of the postcareer games that Wagner played in were fund raisers, such as Cleveland's Amateur Day in 1925. Turning down a chance to play alongside Larry Lajoie and Elmer Flick in the old-timers' event, Wagner chose to represent the Carnegie Elks at first base in the final sandlot game of the day. He went 1 for 4 at the plate in the Elks' 8–2 victory. Wagner was able to put on a uniform and "line them out" when he was well past the age of fifty.

Perhaps Wagner's most memorable exhibition game was the 1925 matchup between the Pirates of 1901 and the current Bucs. The three-inning affair was a feature of the National League's Golden Jubilee Celebration. Included among the former champs were Wagner, Ginger Beaumont, Fred Clarke, Kitty Bransfield, Claude Ritchey, Tommy Leach, Chief Zimmer, Deacon Phillippe, and surprisingly, Jesse Tannehill and Jack Chesbro. The 1901 Pirates delighted the eighteen thousand fans by entering in an old-fashioned coach pulled by a team of horses, with Wagner and Bransfield making an entry in their own one-horse buggy. The game was more an amusement than a show of bygone talent, although the crowd rooted loudly for the 1901 champions. Wagner led the old-timers, going 2 for 2, but the 1925 Pirates won 5–3 behind still active forty-three-year-old pitcher Babe Adams.

Wagner also employed his diamond skills to promote his sporting goods store. One of his good friends and best customers was Jim Black, mining personnel director at the Pittsburgh Coal Company, which supported several teams. The firm's headquarters formed a squad that promoted goodwill by playing the mine teams throughout western

Pennsylvania. Black purchased baseball equipment for all of the squads from Wagner's store and, to keep the business as well as help his buddy, Wagner agreed to play first base for the main office in the late 1920s.

Thirty-three years after making an appearance on the Twin Cities (Ohio) team, Wagner was hired to be player-manager of the communities' 1927 entry in the Eastern Ohio League. He preferred to manage from the bench in this case, and after his team lost its first six games, he was replaced.

It was common for players of Wagner's day to round out their careers in the minor leagues or on the sandlots. Wagner sometimes played for pay on Pittsburgh-area teams such as the Otto Jordans. Most people cheered energetically whenever he stepped on the diamond, but there were those who cringed at the idea of seeing him on semipro teams, as they thought it demeaning. Many wondered whether Wagner needed the money. He didn't. He continued to play out of love for the game and because there was still an audience for him—and always frugal, he did not object to earning a little extra cash, whether or not he needed it. But it was a fact that at the end of the decade and into the Great Depression, Wagner's financial position became much more unstable.

♦ ♦ ♦

The Honus Wagner Sporting Goods Store remained in operation until the summer of 1928. Though not an original partner, Wagner's longtime friend Jim Orris had invested $26,000 a few years earlier and signed on as secretary and treasurer. When it became obvious that he was unlikely to recover any of his money through the store's profits, Orris filed an involuntary bankruptcy petition. The assets of the store were sold at auction, allowing Orris to recoup at least some of his outlay. Wagner's original investment in the venture was lost, but he was far from impoverished. Without the store, he needed another occupation. What he really wanted was to get back into major league baseball.

Knowing that the Brooklyn Dodgers organization was experiencing inner turmoil and might be for sale, he asked for information from John Heydler (once again, National League president) in September 1928— just weeks after the store's bankruptcy. Wagner wrote, "I personally would be interested in such a proposition if you should happen to know of any owners of a National League baseball club who desire to retire from the baseball business and who would be willing to sell their holdings at a reasonable figure." Perhaps already preparing for the National League to step into an increasingly divisive ownership situation in

Brooklyn, Heydler responded within a week that he knew of no teams that were available at the time. Baseball and Wagner would have to wait for a reunion.

Wagner's business setback was amplified by personal loss. Three days before Thanksgiving, Al died unexpectedly at age fifty-seven. Since his retirement from baseball, Al had held a variety of occupations and, like Luke, remained single. In 1928, Al lived and worked as a clerk at the Home Hotel in Pittsburgh. For several months, he had been having bouts with a minor but annoying bladder disorder that was certainly not considered life-threatening. On November 26, while in Dr. Robert McKenzie's office in downtown Pittsburgh, Al was stricken with apoplexy, a rupture or obstruction of an artery to the brain. Death followed quickly. Upon notification, Honus was said to be ill and unavailable for comment. Al's passing not only came as a shock but meant the loss of Honus's baseball mentor, biggest fan, and best friend.

With Luke's passing of pneumonia at age fifty-one five years earlier, Al's death left Honus and Bill as the only surviving Wagner brothers.

◆ ◆ ◆

As early as 1919, Wagner became interested in entering politics. Some of his cronies urged him to run as a candidate for Allegheny County commissioner, believing that his fame and popularity would help sweep him into office. Wagner eventually backed out but did not entirely give up the idea of a civic career. In 1925, he learned that his celebrity status *would not* guarantee a political victory when he mounted an unsuccessful campaign for Allegheny County sheriff.

Wagner never was elected to an office, but in January 1929 he was appointed assistant sergeant-at-arms for the Pennsylvania House of Representatives in Harrisburg. He had little responsibility but was paid seven dollars per day to be at the call of speaker Aaron B. Hess and keep order on the floor. Though higher than the national average of about twenty-seven dollars per week, Wagner's salary was paltry compared to what he had earned as a ballplayer. With the publicity surrounding his store's bankruptcy, and the fact that he accepted an unimportant and relatively low-paying job so far from Carnegie, many people speculated that Wagner was financially strapped.

Within two months, he resigned to take what *The New York Times* called "a better position" in Pittsburgh. The better position was with the new Honus Wagner Sporting Goods Store located at 813 Liberty Avenue. For one dollar and "other valuable considerations" set forth in a separate agreement, Wagner sold E. L. Braunstein "the *exclusive* right to use the name 'Honus Wagner,' and to print or publish in any manner the picture of Honus Wagner in advertisements in the public press, on stationery, in literature, or on merchandise. . . ." Wagner started working as a salesman for the store at a salary of sixty dollars per week. Telegrams inviting various dignitaries of the baseball world to the grand opening were sent out under his name, and he was present for all the festivities, personally welcoming thousands of potential customers as they stepped through the door. But within a few years, a dispute arose over the commissions he was to be paid.

Dissatisfied with the turn of events, Wagner started a competing establishment one block away. Needing a partner, he turned to his good friend and Pirates' star third baseman Harold "Pie" Traynor. The Wagner-Traynor Sporting Goods Store opened in 1931 at 709 Liberty Avenue, as the Depression deepened. Wagner's lack of business savvy and the fact that people had little money for essentials, let alone sports equipment, led to the store's bankruptcy in just two years. While Wagner and Traynor both lost their investments, they remained close friends.

The 1930s were tough times for millions of Americans, and though Wagner was nowhere near a bread line, he did take a financial beating. He had lost substantial sums of money in the sporting goods business on two separate occasions. To make matters worse, after selling off a number of his properties throughout the 1920s, what remained depreciated by roughly 20 percent during the initial years of the Depression.

Compounding his woes, Bessie was seriously injured in the spring of 1930 when the car she was driving collided with another automobile and slammed into an iron pole. She sustained two broken ribs, a bruised collar bone, torn ligaments, and head lacerations; she was hospitalized for two weeks.

◆ ◆ ◆

Big league baseball had become a much more offense-oriented game during the 1920s—thanks in part to the banning in 1920 of trick pitches such as the spitball, shine ball, and emery ball. The Pirates underwent a transformation as well. Between the organization's two most successful years of the decade—the World Championship of 1925 and the National League pennant of 1927—a terribly unfortunate incident occurred.

It had its inception when Fred Clarke returned to the Pirates as vice president in 1925. Rather than confine himself to the front office, he dressed in a uniform and took a place on the bench beside manager Bill

McKechnie. Clarke hadn't changed even though baseball had. By August 1926, some of the players tired of his criticism and felt he was usurping McKechnie's authority. Veteran players Max Carey, Babe Adams, and Carson Bigbee believed that they spoke on behalf of the majority of their teammates when they asked that Clarke be removed from the dugout. Within days, the regrettable affair culminated with the outright release of both Adams and Bigbee, ending their big league careers, and Carey was suspended without pay, then put on waivers and picked up by Brooklyn. At the end of the 1926 season, McKechnie was fired but continued his Hall of Fame managing career in St. Louis, Boston, and Cincinnati. Clarke resigned and sold his club stock but would make an unsuccessful request to come back to the team in 1944. He was the oldest living member of the Hall of Fame prior to his death in 1960 at the age of eighty-seven.

Barney Dreyfuss prepared for retirement by grooming his son Sammy to take over as president of the Pirates. The thirty-six-year-old Sammy was serving as vice president and treasurer when he died suddenly in February 1931 from pneumonia. His death crushed his father emotionally, and within months, Dreyfuss's own health was failing. Admitted to New York's Mount Sinai Hospital on December 14, 1931, he contracted pneumonia after the second of two prostate operations and died on February 5, 1932, just a few weeks before his sixty-seventh birthday. Wagner once described Dreyfuss as "just as rabid a fan as any rooter in the grandstand" and maintained, "All he asks of a player is to give him his best and obey the club rules. It is his belief that a ballplayer owes it to the public to give the fans a run for their money. If [the players] deliver the goods, they can depend upon Barney remembering them for their efforts." Upon learning of Dreyfuss's death, Wagner confided, "I lost a good friend."

Mrs. Dreyfuss turned over the presidency of the club to her son-in-law, Bill Benswanger. An insurance salesman and classical music lover, Benswanger liked the national pastime but was never able to match his father-in-law's baseball—or business—acumen.

♦ ♦ ♦

Although he most likely would never have been wealthy enough to afford a major league franchise, Wagner's business failures put a definite end to any such ambitions. Nonetheless, he was itching to get back into baseball. In October 1932, he journeyed downriver to apply for the job as manager of the Cincinnati Reds, though he lost out to Donie Bush,

Wagner's shortstop counterpart from the 1909 World Series and the man who had succeeded Bill McKechnie as Pirate manager a few years earlier.

Most industries suffered during the Depression, and baseball was no exception. Attendance was down and the owners initiated many cost-cutting measures. Salaries were sliced, and a few clubs pared down their coaching staffs. With all the cutbacks, Benswanger surprised the baseball world in February 1933 by announcing he had hired an additional coach—Honus Wagner. On February 2, 1933, Honus and Bessie drove to the Pirate offices where, after a sixteen-year absence, he affixed his signature to a baseball contract. Bessie was both elated and relieved, divulging that "He never should have been out of the game. After all, he knows more about baseball than anyone else. . . . That's the one place where no one else can tell him what to do. Even I wouldn't dream of giving him any suggestions."

Reaction to the news was immediate and positive. A *Pittsburgh Sun-Telegraph* headline proclaimed HONUS MAKES BASEBALL ITSELF AGAIN and went on to call the hiring "one of the most popular moves ever made by the local club." Honus was swamped with fan mail and invitations to speak at various functions. A few letter writers inquired whether he would be coaching first or third base so they could decide which seats to purchase for 1933 games. He responded, "I think I'll write and tell them that I'll coach at second so I won't be playing any favorites." He demonstrated his knowledge of the current Pirates by reviewing the entire lineup on WCAE radio's "Trained Seals" program, a sports talk show. He gave especially favorable marks to the current double-play combination of shortstop Joseph Floyd "Arky" Vaughan and second baseman Anthony Pietruszka, better known as Tony Piet.

The team was now under the leadership of Wagner's former teammate George Gibson. Gibson had managed the club for parts of three years in the early 1920s and was now in his second year of another term as Pirate skipper—he remains the only Canadian-born big league manager. On the lengthy trip to the team's spring training camp in Paso Robles, California, Wagner was the star attraction at every whistle stop. Seeming more at ease with the fans' adulation than he ever did during his playing career, he signed his name hundreds of times between junctions so that he could distribute more autographs and ensure that no one went home disappointed. Over the next few decades, he would tirelessly oblige admirers, explaining, "Nowadays some players seem to look upon the wild-eyed fans who follow the team around as some sort of pests. That's all wrong. Those are the fellows who made the game, who made our big salaries possible."

At Paso Robles, he took fielding practice at first base and received particular satisfaction from hitting some hard liners. He went swimming every day and even lost eight pounds during the first few weeks of practice. Commenting about his "rejuvenation," the sportswriters pestered Gibson to play Wagner in an exhibition game. At El Paso, Texas, on the return trip, the manager caved in to the clamoring fans. Wagner grounded to short and according to *The Sporting News* showed "that he is not a thoughtless entertainer" by heading toward third instead of first.

Wagner was not hired to play. He later asserted, "They wanted me to coach one man, nothing else. That's all I had to do. They said if I couldn't make a shortstop out of Arky Vaughan, nobody could." As a twenty-year-old rookie, Vaughan hit .318 in 1932, but his fielding was suspect. Wagner worked individually with Vaughan on charging slow-hit ground balls. When Gibson asked how the lessons were going, the young shortstop answered tentatively, "I'm not sure. When I asked Mr. Wagner what to do, he said, 'You just run in fast, grab the ball, and throw it to first base ahead of the runner.' But he didn't tell me how."

Perhaps he did leave something to be desired as an instructor, but Wagner could recognize talent when he saw it, and Vaughan quickly became his protégé. The two went on to room together for the next nine seasons—the rest of Vaughan's tenure with the Pirates. In 1935, Vaughan hit .385 to become only the second National League shortstop since 1900 to win the batting title. (In the twentieth century, the only men to win batting crowns at that position in the National League are all Pirates—Wagner, with seven of his eight titles coming as a shortstop; Vaughan; and Dick Groat.) Wagner later said of his pupil, "Of all the players I tried to help, he's the best and the one that went the farthest." Vaughan's Hall of Fame plaque supports Wagner's praise, reading, "Among Hall of Fame shortstops, his .318 lifetime batting average is second only to Honus Wagner's .329."

◆ ◆ ◆

Much of the idle chatter in spring training of 1933 centered around holdout Babe Ruth. Amused by Ruth's tactics, Wagner reckoned that the Yankees' offer "reads like a lot of money to me. But if he can get them to raise it, I say more power to him."

A popular pastime for retired ballplayers and many older fans has always been to belittle the present-day game and extol the virtues of the past. Many men from Wagner's playing era complained that the outlawing of trick pitches and a modified baseball had led to an offensive explosion that was detrimental to the game. When asked, Wagner noted that the game seemed to have become a little "too ladylike" and involve "too much handshaking," but he usually gave latter-day players credit for being "more scientific" than those of his own generation. While he did not question the hitting prowess of more recent players, every now and then he would blissfully admit that he wished he had "a crack" at that lively ball.

The Pirates opened the 1933 season in Cincinnati on a sunny April 12. Some twenty-five thousand Reds fans gave Wagner a warm welcome and presented him with a huge basket of flowers. He had enjoyed the entire western excursion. At various stops, he had been greeted by baseball luminaries and old friends such as Ty Cobb, Commissioner Landis, and Fred Clarke. Upon arriving home, Wagner could raise a toast to his new career as Pittsburghers celebrated the return of the legal sale of beer—although liquor and wine would not be available for a few more months, when Prohibition would be officially repealed on December 5, 1933.

Thirteen-year-old Betty Wagner decided to attend school on April 21, but Ginny, almost eleven, threw out the first pitch at her father's homecoming. Wagner was once aptly described as "a squat . . . man whose legs take off at the ankles in an outward and upward direction and join his torso at the belt with some element of surprise." Though he now seemed shorter, as well as substantially wider, those bowed legs instantly gave away his identity. As he lumbered to the first base coaches' box to assume his duties, many of the fifteen thousand or so fans surely noticed that for the first time, he wore a number on his jersey, 36. At the time, Gibson had number 33, and for much of the 1930s it was worn by coach Jewel Ens. Wagner stuck with 36 for seven years, then in 1940 was switched to his now-retired number, 33.

His first season as a Pirate coach resembled his last as a player in that Wagner Days were staged in city after city as the team made its way through the league. Paterson and Brooklyn tried to outdo one another in honoring him. At one point, Benswanger remarked, "I don't know whether Honus is traveling with the Pirates or the Pirates traveling with Honus, but it's a great feeling to have the Dutchman back in the uniform he loved so well."

When word of the celebrations in the East reached Pittsburgh, the

Carnegie Elks Club initiated a local event and was soon joined by the Pittsburgh Chamber of Commerce and Kiwanis, Rotary, and Lions Clubs, among other organizations. Albert K. "Rosey" Rowswell—an Elks member, longtime Pirate booster, and future radio announcer for the ball club—coordinated the groups' efforts.

Friday, June 9, was set aside as a half-day holiday by Pittsburgh mayor John S. Herron. At noon, more than six thousand people formed a two-mile-long procession that rode and marched out Fifth Avenue into Oakland, with Wagner riding at the front. Tens of thousands of people withstood ninety-two-degree heat to watch the parade, which included the 308th Cavalry, various baseball and political dignitaries, former ball-players, the current Pirates and Reds, dozens of bands, fifty-one Elks lodges, and several other groups.

At Forbes Field, Wagner and many of his contemporaries took part in an old-timers game. Afterward, he was presented with an array of gifts (when handed a large ham, he clowned that it was too heavy for him to hold), and he also received a check for $1,500 donated by fans.

The Depression had taken its toll on western Pennsylvania. Due to the diversity of Pittsburgh's industry, unemployment was not as wide-spread as elsewhere, but hunger marches, soup lines, and box cities were still to be found. Many people with steady work had lost their entire life's savings in failed banks. In light of the times, the tribute shown to Wagner in June 1933 was extraordinary.

With a decent coach's salary, Wagner's situation was considerably more secure than it had been just a few months earlier. Then in the summer of 1933, he filed suit for eight thousand dollars in unpaid commissions from E. L. Braunstein's Honus Wagner Sporting Goods Store and asked that his name be dropped from the establishment. Judge J. Gardner of the Allegheny Common Pleas Court wrote in his opinion that Braunstein had legally obtained exclusive right to the words *Honus Wagner* in the 1929 agreement but ruled that Wagner was entitled to a clear accounting of sales. The matter was settled out of court for an unspecified amount, and the two men patched up their differences, with Wagner continuing to promote the store through the remainder of the 1930s and into the 1940s. The Honus Wagner Company survives to this day in downtown Pittsburgh.

◆ ◆ ◆

Despite second-place finishes in each of the last two seasons and a winning record in June 1934, Gibson was fired in favor of Pie Traynor. The change did little to help the Pirates, who finished fifth with a record of 74–76, including 47–52 under Traynor. During one particularly brutal stretch, Traynor's wife mentioned to Wagner how dejected the new manager was over the team's poor play. Advising Mrs. Traynor to tell her husband not to worry, Wagner confided that during his playing days, the Pirates once lost seventy-two straight games on a road trip. Mrs. Traynor passed this consoling wisdom on to her troubled mate, and the normally soft-spoken Traynor blew up: "You stay away from that lying old coot," he ordered. Traynor managed the Pirates through 1939. Five more managers would come and go during Wagner's coaching career, for a total of seven—more than he played under in twenty-one big league seasons.

The year of 1933 began an extremely enjoyable and rewarding period of Wagner's life. He was an integral part of the Pirate coaching staff throughout the remainder of the decade, tutoring players during spring training, coaching on the baselines, running practice drills, and fulfilling other chores. Pirate great Paul Waner, in *The Glory of Their Times*, reminisced about Wagner taking fielding practice at shortstop during his early coaching days. Waner recalled that "a hush would come over the whole ball park, and every player on both teams would just stand there, like a bunch of little kids, and watch every move he made."

Wagner was still very much in the public eye. In 1936, he was paid a great tribute by being one of the first five men voted into the National Baseball Hall of Fame. And in 1939, he was a central figure in the original induction ceremonies and baseball centennial celebration in Cooperstown.

Wagner stayed active outside of major league baseball as well. In June 1936, he was named commissioner of the National Semi-Pro Baseball Congress, a position he held for two seasons. His duties included appointing people to various posts, and in 1937, he selected Fred Clarke as an executive. Wagner took a leave of absence from the Pirates to spend the entire month of July traveling from state to state, presiding over tournaments that qualified clubs for the national finals in Wichita, Kansas.

Wagner was also responsible for rule-making decisions. In 1937, he barred the spitball except in cases where the pitcher had been a member of Organized Baseball prior to 1926. Perhaps the toughest judgment Wagner had to pass down involved the semipro tournament eligibility of players considered "outlaws" from Organized Baseball. Wagner was initially sympathetic, explaining, "An outlaw player has already paid his penalty. If this player wants a job to play industrial ball, should the semipros prevent him from earning a livelihood in that manner? After an individual receives his punishment, I do not believe it is consistent to prevent him from getting a new start in life." However upon conferring with the hard-nosed Landis on the issue, Wagner toed the line and declared the players ineligible.

This job was perhaps more demanding than Wagner desired at this point in his life, and he resigned in March 1938 at the age of sixty-four. For the most part, Wagner had enjoyed the experience, professing, "I like to monkey around with youngsters. You get a kick out of seeing them develop. And don't let anybody tell you the youngsters aren't just as interested in baseball today as we were when we were kids. I know different."

He soon found a less strenuous way to help young ballplayers. He and former teammate Wilbur Cooper represented the Atlantic Refining Company in conducting seminars around Allegheny County as part of the firm's Atlantic Baseball School. Off and on for a few summers, the two visited different locales, offering instruction in the morning and overseeing games in the afternoon. Wagner would take the boys out to his old shortstop position where he demonstrated a few skills and advised them to run after a ball until it was past them because "it might just hit a stone and jump into your glove."

◆ ◆ ◆

Wagner's two most famous physical characteristics were now the very things that revealed his age. He limped noticeably on his crooked legs, and the huge hands that he was always so proud of were misshapen with the evidence of decades of ball playing. His role for the Pirates changed from that of a coach to more of a goodwill ambassador. In spring training of 1941, he was struck in the knee by a line drive, and it became so swollen that he was bedridden the next day. Pirate management began to worry that the now sixty-seven-year-old Wagner would get seriously hurt on the field. Before long, the players convinced him to remain in the dugout.

He hadn't driven an automobile for years and depended on the streetcars, his daughters, or friends for rides to and from the ballpark. But he continued to report daily to Forbes Field, spending his time telling outrageous lies to anyone who would listen. "How about *that?*" he liked to spit out after each of his yarns. Most fellows played along, asking the right questions on cue and snickering at the corny punch lines. If questioned about the authenticity of his anecdotes, he merely retorted,

"At least I never told you one you couldn't tell your mother." His sense of humor was not completely confined to his standby jokes: A few years later when Ralph Kiner kiddingly asked if Wagner had a woman in each road city, he answered, "Sure, but they're all dead now."

A chaw was ever-present in Wagner's toothless mouth, his dentures often tucked away in his back pocket. He seemed to never buy his own tobacco and patted players on the rump to find out if they were carrying any "scrap" in their back pockets. At the ballpark, Wagner chummed with everybody—stars, rookies, and lesser-known veterans. Forest "Tot" Pressnell, a knuckleball pitcher with an illustrious minor league career in Milwaukee and a couple of big league seasons with Chicago and Brooklyn, remembered bringing Wagner a particular brand of tobacco from Chicago. On several occasions, Wagner and Pressnell sat—as peers—with their backs against the Forbes Field outfield wall, chewing the fat along with Pressnell's special delivery.

Many players enjoyed a beer or several with Wagner after the games. He was habitually late getting home for supper and as often as not would bring one or more unexpected guests. Mabel learned to keep plenty of extra food in the house, especially Wagner's favorites— Limburger cheese, red cabbage, and just about any kind of pie. She didn't mind the additional work these visitors created because she routinely found a nice tip tucked under the guests' plates while clearing the table, although it usually wasn't a surprise after Wagner peeked under each place setting and clued her in about how much to expect. Paul and Lloyd Waner, Frankie Gustine, and Pie Traynor were among the frequent callers to the Wagner household.

Rather than run drills or help with batting practice, Wagner spent the hours before games conversing with fans and signing autographs. He also helped promote the team to the community as a popular speaker at banquets, or smokers, where he proved he had come a long way from the days when he panicked if he thought there was the slightest chance of being called on to say a few words. In his own drowsy manner, Wagner willingly told the same clean but ridiculous tales that he told to players, relatives, and neighborhood kids.

One fond "memory" Wagner loved to share with his audience was the time he charged a ground ball, fielded a rabbit by mistake, and threw it to first base. "Got the runner by a hare! How about *that?*" he would roar. He would describe how tough he had it in his first few National League years and said that once, after congratulating an opponent for hitting a home run, he was told to go to hell. "That was the first time any big leaguer ever spoke to me on the diamond," he said. Wagner also relayed that when he first arrived in Louisville, his new teammates refused to let him take batting practice. It was not until he waved his bat in the direction of one player's head, warning, "I'm gonna swing at somethin' and I don't much care what it is," that he was permitted to get in his work.

◆ ◆ ◆

In January 1942, Wagner was appointed a deputy sheriff in Allegheny County. For parts of the next two years, he took a leave of absence from this job during baseball season, but it's doubtful that his departure put much of a strain on the sheriff's department, as the position was largely honorary.

Wagner was hospitalized for an eye infection in May 1942 and remained there, denied all visitors except immediate family, for more than two months. Late in August, he returned to the Pirate bench, appearing gaunt and weak. He rebounded over the winter but in 1943 began to limit his travel with the team to spring training and just one or two road trips per year.

When the Pirates, or "my Bucs" as he called them, were on the road without him—as well as in the offseasons—Wagner whiled away his time by walking down to the Elks Club or the Carnegie taverns. He had a ritual of taking a dime out of his pocket, tapping it on the bar, and waiting for someone to recognize him and buy him a beer. Some of those old enough to remember drinking with him maintain that he carried the same dime around in his pocket for years. Others swear that the coin Wagner showed was not even legal tender but some type of commemorative piece. When he overindulged, he had no trouble getting a lift home from neighbors or friends. At this point in his life, he was a quiet drunk and no longer felt apologetic about coming home tipsy.

As the nations around the globe entered into the Second World War, people began to fret that it might mean the demise of baseball. Wagner, having been through it all before, remained unperturbed. "This will always be the game," he predicted. "Don't know of anything to take its place. It's wide open and not complicated. It's bound to go on improving. . . . When this mess is finished, just watch it grow."

In 1945, the Pirates planned yet another Wagner Day—only this time it was Wagner Night. The first night game at Forbes Field had taken place on June 4, 1940. Of the historic affair, Wagner deadpanned, "This is the first time in forty-five years that I found myself at the ball orchard when I ought to be in bed." The Wednesday, September 5, 1945, salute to Wagner was originally scheduled as an afternoon game, but the Pirates moved it to evening so that more fans could attend. Benswanger announced that in order to provide a cushion for Wagner's old age, he would present the part-time coach with all the event's gate receipts in excess of $12,000. Wagner netted $13,887—more than he had ever received for a season's pay as a player.

◆ ◆ ◆

Benswanger and Mrs. Dreyfuss put the Pirates up for sale in 1946. The team had not won a pennant in nineteen years and Forbes Field, once the crown jewel of ballparks, was in disrepair. The fans were disgusted, and players had grievances about manager Frankie Frisch and the club's second-rate hotel and travel accommodations. Robert Murphy, attempting to form a players' organization that he called the American Baseball Guild, found a receptive group in Pittsburgh, and in June, the players threatened to strike. Benswanger vowed to field a team "even if I have to use seventy-two-year-old Honus Wagner at shortstop." A popular story in western Pennsylvania was that after Benswanger made this proclamation, an elderly gentleman from South Carolina flew to Pittsburgh "just to see ol' Honus play shortstop once more." In some versions, the fan was from North Carolina and brought his grandson, but the tale always ends with Wagner signing a ball for the old guy. The players called off the strike at the last minute.

On August 10, 1946, a deal for the ball club was consummated. Soon, the Pittsburgh players voted against unionizing, but that did not mean that they immediately became good pals with the new management. There was a great deal of skepticism, and Wagner had his doubts, too—about whether or not the new Pirate owners would want him around. Feeling that Wagner was worth the money as an attraction, they reassured him that he had a job for as long as he wanted.

◆ ◆ ◆

Spring training of 1948 at Hollywood, California, was Wagner's last trip with the team. He became ill with the flu while there and returned home to recover. The following March, with the squad in the West without him, he sent a postcard to the Pirates' clubhouse attendant, reminding him, "Please don't forget to save me a locker at Forbes Field opening day." He began spending less and less time there, however, occasionally staying for the entire game and at other times leaving before the first pitch was thrown.

In the last few years of his life, Wagner's eyes watered constantly and his hands trembled with palsy. He needed help buttoning his Pirate jersey, trimmed in black and gold since 1948 instead of the familiar blue and red. As he prepared to leave the locker room at the end of the 1951 season, Wagner was asked what was running through his mind as he surveyed the surroundings. "I was thinking about the first time I came to this clubhouse in June of 1909. Things have changed since then, a lot of changes, but I thought this place and all of Forbes Field was beautiful then," he solemnly reflected. "I was thinking of Cap Clarke, Tommy Leach, George Gibson, Babe Adams, Chief Wilson, Mr. Dreyfuss, and the rest. We had fun in those days. That's all I've got left now in baseball, my memories, but they're worth a million bucks to me."

Prior to the 1952 season, Pirate general manager Branch Rickey halfheartedly offered Wagner another contract. Wagner declined, becoming baseball's first double pensioner, receiving income from both the players' and the coaches' retirement funds, the latter having been established in 1947. Rickey announced that no Pirate would ever wear the number 33 again. It was the first number retired by the organization.

Wagner attributed the best things in his life to opportunities afforded him by baseball, saying that without the game, he may never have left the coal mines, met his wife, had his two daughters, or earned fame and money. The things that Wagner appreciated most, though, were "rich, fine memories and true blue friends. In this respect, I'm a wealthy and contented man."

Though Rickey assured Wagner that he could have free run of Forbes Field, "as if you owned every share of stock in the Pittsburgh Baseball Club," Wagner could not enjoy the privilege. It was just too much for him to stray far from Carnegie. He spent most of his hours sitting on the front porch, smoking cigars or chewing tobacco and playing with his little granddaughter, Leslie. His daughter Betty had married Harry Blair in 1948, and less than two years later, Leslie was born.

When Bessie fell in 1951, breaking a hip, Betty and her family moved to the Wagner household so that she could help care for her parents. It was a full house, as Ginny and her friend Sally Motto were also living there. Wagner got a kick out of watching Leslie grow up. One day, as she raced with her little dog Winky, he remarked, "She puts you in mind of Scoops Carey the way she flies around the yard, and she touches all the bases. If she was a boy, we'd have to get spikes for her shoes." Leslie adored her grandfather, always referring to him as Buck Jay after seeing a picture taken of him out West, sporting a ten-gallon hat.

In 1953, major league baseball celebrated the fiftieth anniversary of the first World Series. Wagner was in no condition to attend the Fall Classic but perked up considerably when he heard that his old friends Fred Clarke, Tommy Leach, Otto Krueger, Cy Young, Bill Dinneen, and Fred Parent were reunited in New York for the golden jubilee festivities.

Wagner celebrated his eightieth birthday at home on February 24, 1954. Letters of congratulations from current and former players, baseball executives, politicians, entertainers, and common fans were piled high on a table in the parlor, but one special greeting stood out. The message from President Dwight D. Eisenhower read in part:

> Realization that you now count your years at the four score mark reminds me, with something of a shock, that it is fifty years ago that I used to follow your batting average with the keenest of interest. I venture to say that your name and records you established are as well known to the boy of today as they were to me, and that, I think, must prove that you are truly one of baseball's immortal heroes.

That spring, the Pirates honored Wagner on April 13 at their opening game—the first time the Pittsburgh Pirates had opened a season at home in sixty-one years. Three-year-old Leslie froze when she was supposed to throw out the first pitch, but her mother cheerfully accepted a plaque that read:

> To Honus Wagner, greatest of the great, as an enduring tribute, from the Pittsburgh Baseball Club, in sincere appreciation of an unmatched career, in which loyalty, honesty, high character and sportsmanship were combined with playing skill, to make him a champion and a source of endless good to baseball, the Pirates, and the city of Pittsburgh.

An even greater, more visible tribute was already in the works—efforts were underway to erect a statue in Wagner's likeness to stand outside Forbes Field. As early as 1947, Fred Clarke began urging the National Baseball Hall of Fame to undertake such a project. Six years later, a number of Pittsburgh-area sports figures organized into the

Pittsburgh Professional Baseball Association Inc. for the sole purpose of raising money to commission the work. Pie Traynor and Frankie Gustine were both officers on the board of directors. Frank Vittor, a local artist and Italian immigrant, was selected as sculptor, and he began work late in 1953 with nothing but a verbal agreement, believing that he had just a few months to complete the assignment. As it turned out, he had more than a year.

Needing an estimated fifty thousand dollars for the endeavor, Gustine, by this time retired from baseball and owner of a restaurant in Oakland, personally sought contributions from area businesses. A local steel executive explained that while he was prepared to write out a check for the entire amount, he felt that it would be better to involve the people of the community through their small donations. The association went to the public, mailing out more than forty thousand solicitation letters that explained the goal of erecting a monument adjacent to the left field corner of Forbes Field and expressed the fund committee's "sincere hope that it can be accomplished while Honus is still with us."

Collections took a full year longer than expected. Local models took in $750 at the 1954 opener. Numerous fund-drive dinners were held. The Honus Wagner Sporting Goods Store ran ads in Pittsburgh papers offering free autographed photos in return for donations. In May 1954, the proceeds from an auto race at South Park Speedway were added to the statue fund. And later that summer, the Pirates played an exhibition game raising $6,100. Wagner followed the progress with keen interest and looked forward to seeing his statue completed. By his eighty-first birthday, the dedication date was set for the spring of 1955.

Now thin and frail, Wagner observed the events of Saturday, April 30 from a convertible. He managed to wave feebly toward the crowd of 1,500, but his head was lowered during the brief speeches, including those delivered by Pittsburgh mayor David Lawrence, baseball commissioner Ford Frick, and Pirate president John Galbreath. Even a message from President Eisenhower elicited little response, but Wagner seemed to brighten a bit when greeted by old friends Fred Clarke, George Gibson, and Cy Young, who were among the dozens of former players there. A weak smile briefly crossed Wagner's face as granddaughter Leslie pulled the string to unveil the monument.

The statue, which now stands outside Gate C at Three Rivers Stadium, features a ten-foot-high bronze Wagner, still in his prime, clutching a bat in a high follow-through as his eyes trace the path of the ball. A massive Barre, Vermont, granite base houses a hermetically sealed stainless steel tube containing the names of all the donors listed on a single continuous roll. Carved reliefs depict "the youth of today and the youth of tomorrow" on the pedestal, which bears the inscription:

ERECTED IN 1955
BY THE FANS OF AMERICA
IN HONOR OF A BASEBALL IMMORTAL,
A CHAMPION AMONG CHAMPIONS,
WHOSE RECORD ON AND OFF THE
PLAYING FIELD OF THE NATIONAL GAME
WILL EVER STAND AS A MONUMENT
TO HIS OWN GREATNESS AND AS AN
EXAMPLE AND INSPIRATION TO THE YOUTH
OF OUR COUNTRY.

The ceremony concluded with the playing of "Take Me Out to the Ball Game," but Wagner was not up to it and he was driven home. In a game that Chester L. Smith of *The Pittsburgh Press* said the Pirates "just had to win," the home team staged a ninth-inning rally to beat the Reds 5–4. Honus would have been proud.

◆ ◆ ◆

Wagner's health continued to decline after he was immortalized that spring day in Schenley Park. He was confined to bed after suffering a painful shoulder injury from a fall at home in early October. Many old friends visited him for the last time as he lay in a hospital bed in his living room. When Connie Mack walked in, Wagner's eyes filled with tears, but he managed to talk for a few moments to his onetime idol. As he left, Mack admitted, "I'll feel a lot better now, riding back home."

During the last few weeks of November, Wagner drifted in and out of consciousness, recognizing no one but Leslie. His family remained close by his side, knowing the end was near. Betty had a premonition that her father would die on her birthday, December 5. His heart stopped shortly after midnight—the official time of death being 12:56 A.M., Tuesday, December 6, 1955. He was laid to rest at Jefferson Memorial Cemetery in Pleasant Hills, a southern suburb of Pittsburgh, on Friday, December 9.

For days, baseball notables eulogized Wagner in newspapers around the country. Arthur Daley, veteran sports columnist of *The New York Times*, referred to Wagner as "the perfect shortstop," saying, "There is a simple grandeur to Honus Wagner as a man. As a shortstop he was off in a class by himself." Hank Gowdy, whose firsthand view of Wagner was that of an opposing catcher, stated, "He was without a doubt the finest baseball player I ever saw and one of the best-loved players in the game. There wasn't a thing he couldn't do on the ball field." George Sisler, one of the "eleven immortals" from the inaugural Hall of Fame class, described Wagner as "an institution [in Pittsburgh] and to baseball throughout the country." Former Pirate Ralph Kiner, having just completed the final season of his own Hall of Fame career, called Wagner "the greatest personality I ever met in baseball, and the most humble."

Few would argue that Honus Wagner remains the finest shortstop in history, dwarfing most others in comparison. Was he the greatest ballplayer ever? Certainly he is on a short list of candidates whenever the topic is discussed. In Wagner's heyday, writer Hugh Fullerton called him "the nearest approach to a baseball machine ever constructed." Possibly no other man in baseball history excelled at so many aspects of the game.

Widely respected baseball writer and analyst Bill James wrote in his *Historical Baseball Abstract*:

> Among the great players in the game there are all kinds of men—smart alecks, tough guys, driven men, and heavy drinkers. As gentlemen, there are many who seem worthy of admiration, including Musial, Mathewson, Gehrig, Johnson, and Schmidt. None seems more worthy than Wagner. He was a gentle, kind man, a storyteller, supportive of rookies, patient with fans, cheerful in hard times, careful of the example that he set for youth, a hard worker, a man who had no enemies and who never forgot his friends. He was the most beloved man in baseball before Ruth. . . . Those qualities are part of the reason why, acknowledging that there may have been one or two whose talents were greater, there is no one who has ever played this game that I would be more anxious to have on a baseball team.

◆ ◆ ◆

Wagner had tried his hand at many things, witnessed several of his own ventures prosper then fold, dabbled in politics, and was canonized by U.S. presidents. Ultimately, he was not a farmer or a businessman and never strayed far from the game he loved. During the height of Wagner's career, *The Sporting News* wrote that baseball was his "whole existence, with an occasional automobile trip and hunting excursion thrown in to vary the monotony." Honus himself confessed that he would "annually become possessed of the happy thrill of getting my fingers around a new, white ball."

Throughout his eighty-one years, there were many interpretations of his personality, a number of which survive today. His shy and humble nature was lauded by some and thought by others to be a sign of weakness or even arrogance. He was thought to be noble in certain corners for not being greedy or self-serving, while others simply called him ignorant for not picking up easy money or inconsiderate for hindering their own efforts. There were those who respected his ordinary tastes and calm temperament, while others felt he lacked assertiveness.

No doubt, he would be embarrassed by the publicity surrounding his prized baseball card and other memorabilia, even by the publication of this book. In a time that sports and public figures adore and seek the limelight for self-promotion and gratification, Honus Wagner's modesty should only enhance his achievements—indeed his contribution to the game of baseball.

BIBLIOGRAPHY

This bibliography is divided into both a general listing of sources that proved valuable throughout the work and chapter-specific listings. When faced with conflicts of information, as was frequently the case, preference was most often granted to the accounts of the day or period in question.

GENERAL BIBLIOGRAPHY

In addition to the memories provided to us by the generous people listed in the acknowledgments, we drew upon the following resources.

Archival Resources:

The Honus Wagner clippings and files of: Historical Society of Carnegie, Pennsylvania; The National League, New York; The Pennsylvania Room of The Carnegie Library of Pittsburgh; The Pittsburgh Pirates Baseball Club; *The Pittsburgh Post-Gazette;* The Society for American Baseball Research (SABR); and the Western Pennsylvania Historical Society.

The records of: The Allegheny County Courthouse, Pittsburgh; Cemetery Records of Knox County, Ohio; Chartiers Cemetery Company, Carnegie; Jefferson Memorial Park, Pittsburgh; and the U.S. Census Bureau.

A great deal of important information was obtained in Cooperstown, New York, at the National Baseball Hall of Fame and Museum as well as the National Baseball Library. Files and collections examined at the National Baseball Library include those of Honus Wagner, Ed Abbaticchio, Babe Adams, Ed Barrow, Ginger Beaumont, Bill Benswanger, Kitty Bransfield, Howie Camnitz, Max Carey, Jack Chesbro, Fred Clarke, Wilbur Cooper, John Daley, Ed Doheny, Barney Dreyfuss, Fred Ely, Patsy Flaherty, George Gibson, Frank Gustine, Claude Hendrix, Bill Hinchman, Bill Klem, Tommy Leach, Sam Leever, Lefty Leifield, Hans Lobert, Nick Maddox, Al Mamaux, John Miller, Hank O'Day, Deacon Phillippe, Harry Pulliam, Claude Ritchey, Jimmy Sebring, Harry Smith, Jesse Tannehill, Pie Traynor, Al Wagner, Vic Willis, Owen Wilson, and Chief Zimmer.

Newspapers:

Carnegie Item, 1894–1907.
The Carnegie Signal-Item, 1908–55.
Carnegie Union, 1891–1922.
The Cleveland Leader, 1902, 1904, 1913.
The Cleveland Plain Dealer, 1902, 1904, 1912, 1913, 1925.
Daily Pittsburgh Gazette, 1902.
The New York Times, 1896–1955.
Pittsburgh Chronicle Telegraph, 1900–17, 1922–23.
Pittsburgh Commercial Gazette, 1899–1901.
The Pittsburgh Daily News, 1900.
The Pittsburgh Dispatch, 1900–23.
The Gazette Times, Pittsburgh, 1908, 1912, 1916, 1923.
The Pittsburgh Leader, 1900, 1916.
The Pittsburgh Post, 1893–94, 1899–1917, 1922–25.
The Pittsburgh Post-Gazette, various clippings from 1928–94.
The Pittsburgh Press, 1900, 1907–09, and various clippings from 1916–92.
Pittsburgh Sun, 1922–23.
Pittsburgh Sun-Telegraph, 1933 and various clippings from 1928–55.
The Pittsburgh Times, 1900.

Periodicals:

Baseball Magazine, 1908–48.
Sporting Life, 1893–1917.
The Sporting News, 1893–1950.

Articles:

Biederman, Les. "Circling the Bases with The Flying Dutchman: Life Story of Honus Wagner." *The Sporting News* (November 22–December 6, 1950).
Davis, Sam. "Pittsburgh's Greatest Ballplayer." *The Pittsburgh Press* (February 14–February 19, 1944).

"The Flying Dutchman of the Diamond." *New York Herald Magazine* (January 15, 1911).

Fullerton, Hugh S. "Wagner: Greatest Player in the World." *The American Magazine* (January 1910).

Rowswell, A.K. "The One and Only . . . 'Honus' Wagner." *Tales of the Diamond* (1950: Fort Pitt Brewing Co.).

Wagner, Hans. "Hans Wagner: His Own Story of His Life." *The Gazette Times* (January 16–February 25, 1924).

Wagner, Honus. "I Never Got Tired of Playing." *Collier's* (May 22, 1937).

Wagner, Honus (John H.). "Honus Wagner's Own Baseball Story." *The Gazette Times/Wheeler Syndicate* (January 16–March 26, 1916).

Video:

The Glory of Their Times. Produced by Cappy Productions, 1987.

Books:

Alexander, Charles C. *Ty Cobb.* New York: Oxford University Press, 1985.

———. *John McGraw.* New York: Viking Penguin Inc., 1988.

———. *Our Game.* New York: Henry Holt and Co., 1991.

Allen, Lee, and Tom Meany. *Kings of the Diamond.* New York: G. P. Putnam's Sons, 1965.

Appel, Martin, and Burt Goldblatt. *Baseball's Best: The Hall of Fame Gallery.* New York: McGraw-Hill Book Co., 1977.

Astor, Gerald. *The Baseball Hall of Fame Fiftieth Anniversary Book.* New York: Prentice Hall Press, 1988.

Barrow, Edward Grant, and James M. Kahn. *My Fifty Years in Baseball.* New York: Coward-McCann, 1951.

Bartell, Dick, with Norman Macht. *Rowdy Richard.* Berkeley, Cal.: North Atlantic Books, 1987.

Benson, Michael. *Ballparks of North America: A Comprehensive Historical Reference to Baseball Grounds, Yards, and Stadiums, 1845–Present.* Jefferson, N.C.: McFarland and Co., 1989.

Bowman, John S., and Joel Zoss. *The Pictorial History of Baseball.* New York: Gallery Books, 1986.

Burtt, Richard L., *The Pittsburgh Pirates: A Pictorial History.* Virginia Beach, Va.: Jordan & Company, 1977.

Charlton, James, ed. *The Baseball Chronology: The Complete History of the Most Important Events in the Game of Baseball.* New York: Macmillan Publishing Co., 1991.

Cobb, Ty, with Al Stump. *My Life in Baseball: The True Record.* Garden City, N.Y.: Doubleday and Co., 1961.

Daley, Arthur. *Inside Baseball.* New York: Grosset and Dunlap, 1950.

Danzig, Allison, and Joe Reichler. *The History of Baseball: Its Great Players, Teams, and Managers.* Englewood Cliffs, N.J.: Prentice-Hall Inc., 1959.

Demorest, Rose. *Pittsburgh 1874–1949.* Pittsburgh: The Chamber of Commerce of Pittsburgh, no date.

Dickey, Glenn. *The History of National League Baseball.* New York: Stein and Day, 1979.

Dickson, Paul. *Baseball's Greatest Quotations.* New York: Edward Burlingame Books, 1991.

———. *The Dickson Baseball Dictionary.* New York: Facts On File, 1989.

Durso, Joseph. *The Days of Mr. McGraw.* Englewood Cliffs, N.J.: Prentice-Hall Inc., 1969.

Eckhouse, Morris, and Carl Mastrocola. *This Date in Pittsburgh Pirates History.* New York: Stein and Day Publishers, 1980.

Einstein, Charles, ed. *The Fireside Book of Baseball: First Edition.* New York: Simon and Schuster Inc., 1956.

———. *The Fireside Book of Baseball: Third Edition.* New York: Simon and Schuster Inc., 1968.

———. *The Fireside Book of Baseball: Fourth Edition.* New York: Simon and Schuster Inc., 1987.

Harper, Frank C. *Pittsburgh, Forge of the Universe.* New York: Comet Press Books, 1957.

Hays, Samuel P., ed. *City at the Point.* Pittsburgh: University of Pittsburgh Press, 1989.

Historical Statistics of the United States: Colonial Times to 1970. Washington, D.C.: U.S. Department of Commerce, 1975.

Honig, Donald. *Baseball America.* New York: Macmillan Publishing Co., 1985.

———. *Baseball When the Grass Was Real.* New York: Coward, McCann and Geoghegan Inc., 1975.

James, Bill. *The Baseball Book 1990.* New York: Villard Books, 1990.

———. *The Bill James Historical Baseball Abstract.* New York: Villard Books, 1988.

Kahn, James M. *The Umpire Story.* New York: G. P. Putnam's Sons, 1953.

Kavanagh, Jack. *Honus Wagner.* New York: Chelsea House Publishers, 1994.

King, Sidney A., ed. *The Story of the Sesqui-Centennial Celebration of Pittsburgh.* Pittsburgh: The R. W. Johnston Studios Inc., 1910.

Lieb, Fred. *Baseball as I Have Known It.* New York: Coward, McCann and Geoghegan Inc., 1977.

———. *The Pittsburgh Pirates.* New York: Van Rees Press, 1948.

Lorant, Stefan. *Pittsburgh: The Story of an American City.* Lenox, Mass.: Authors Edition Inc., fourth edition, 1988.

Lowry, Philip J. *Green Cathedrals: The Ultimate Celebration of All 273 Major League and Negro League Ballparks Past and Present.* Reading, Mass.: Addison-Wesley Publishing Co., 1992.

McCallum, John D. *Ty Cobb*. New York: Praeger Publishers Inc., 1975.

McClow, Jeanne, ed. *A Baseball Century: The First 100 Years of the National League*. New York: Macmillan Publishing Co., 1976.

McGraw, John. *My Thirty Years in Baseball*. New York: Boni and Livewright Inc., 1923.

Mathewson, Christopher, with John N. Wheeler. *Pitching in a Pinch*. New York: Grosset and Dunlap, 1912.

Meany, Tom. *Baseball's Greatest Hitters*. New York: A. S. Barnes and Co., 1950.

Mercurio, John A. *A Chronology of Major League Baseball Records*. New York: Harper & Row Publishers, 1989.

Moreland, George L. *Balldom: The Britannica of Baseball*. New York: Balldom Publishing Co., 1914.

Mote, James. *Everything Baseball*. New York: Prentice Hall Press, 1989.

Murdock, Eugene C. *Ban Johnson: Czar of Baseball*. Westport, Conn.: Greenwood Press, 1982.

Nagle, Walter H., as told to Bryson Reinhardt. *Five Straight Errors on Ladies' Day*. Caldwell, Idaho: The Caxton Printers Ltd., 1965.

Neft, David S., and Richard M. Cohen. *The Sports Encyclopedia: Baseball*. New York: St. Martin's/Marek, sixth edition, 1985.

Nemec, David. *Great Baseball Feats, Facts and Firsts*. New York: Signet, 1989.

Okkonen, Marc. *Baseball Memories: 1900–1909*. New York: Sterling Publishing Co., 1992.

———. *Baseball Uniforms of the Twentieth Century: The Official Major League Baseball Guide*. New York: Sterling Publishing Co., 1991.

Okrent, Daniel, and Harris Lewine, eds., with historical text by David Nemec. *The Ultimate Baseball Book*. Boston: Houghton Mifflin Co., reprint edition, 1991.

Pope, Edwin. *Baseball's Greatest Managers*. Garden City, N.Y.: Doubleday and Co., 1960.

Powers, Jimmy. *Baseball Personalities*. New York: Rudolph Field, 1949.

R. L. Polk City Directory. Pittsburgh: R. L. Polk & Co., annual editions, 1897–1935.

Rader, Benjamin G. *Baseball: A History of America's Game*. Urbana, Ill.: University of Illinois Press, 1992.

The Reach Official Base Ball Guide. Philadelphia: A. J. Reach Co., annual editions, 1883–1939.

Reichler, Joseph L., ed. *The Baseball Encyclopedia*. New York: Macmillan Publishing Co., first edition, 1969.

———. *The Great All-Time Baseball Record Book*. New York: Macmillan Publishing Co., 1981.

Reidenbaugh, Lowell. *Cooperstown: Where Baseball's Legends Live Forever*. The Sporting News Publishing Co., 1983.

Rickey, Branch, and Robert Riger. *The American Diamond: A Documentary of the Game of Baseball.* New York: Simon and Schuster Inc., 1965.

Ritter, Lawrence S. *The Glory of Their Times.* New York: William Morrow and Co., 1984.

————. *Lost Ballparks.* New York: Viking Studio Books, 1992.

————, and Donald Honig. *The 100 Greatest Baseball Players of All Time.* New York: Crown Publishers Inc., 1981.

Segar, Charles, ed. *Seventy-fifth Anniversary of the National League.* New York: National League of Professional Baseball Clubs, 1951.

Seidenberg, Mel, ed. *A Pittsburgh Album: 1758–1958.* Pittsburgh: Pittsburgh Post-Gazette, 1959.

Seymour, Harold. *Baseball—The Early Years.* New York: Oxford University Press, 1960.

————. *Baseball—The Golden Age.* New York: Oxford University Press, 1971.

Shannon, Bill, and George Kalinsky. *The Ballparks.* New York: Hawthorn Books Inc., 1975.

Shatzkin, Mike, ed. *The Ballplayers: Baseball's Ultimate Biographical Reference.* New York: William Morrow and Co., 1990.

Smith, Myron J. *Baseball: A Comprehensive Bibliography.* Jefferson, N.C.: McFarland and Co., 1986.

Smizik, Bob. *The Pittsburgh Pirates: An Illustrated History.* New York: Walker and Company, 1990.

Sowell, Mike. *July 2, 1903: The Mysterious Death of Hall-of-Famer Big Ed Delahanty.* New York: Macmillan Publishing Co., 1992.

————. *The Pitch That Killed.* New York: Macmillan Publishing Co., 1989.

Spalding's Official Base Ball Guide. New York: A. G. Spalding and Bros., annual editions, 1876–1906; New York: American Sports Publishing, annual editions, 1907–41.

Spink, J. G. Taylor. *Daguerrotypes.* St. Louis: C. C. Spink & Son, 1934.

————. *Judge Landis and Twenty-five Years of Baseball.* New York: Thomas Y. Crowell Co., 1947.

The Thistle. Carnegie Technical Institute Yearbook, annual editions, 1906–23.

Thorn, John, and Bob Carroll, eds. *The Whole Baseball Catalogue.* New York: Simon and Schuster Inc., 1990.

————, and Pete Palmer, eds. *Total Baseball.* New York: Warner Books, first edition, 1989. New York: HarperCollins Publishers, Inc., third edition, 1993.

Tiemann, Robert L., and Mark Rucker, eds. *Nineteenth Century Stars.* Kansas City, Mo.: The Society for American Baseball Research, 1989.

Toker, Franklin. *Pittsburgh: An Urban Portrait.* University Park, Penn.: Pennsylvania State University Press, 1986.

Turkin, Hy, and S. C. Thompson. *The Official Encyclopedia of Baseball.* New York: A. S. Barnes and Co., second edition, 1959.

Voigt, David Quentin. *American Baseball, Volume I: From Gentleman's Sport to the Commissioner System.* Norman, Okla.: University of Oklahoma Press, 1966.

———. *American Baseball, Volume II: From the Commissioners to Continental Expansion.* Norman, Okla.: University of Oklahoma Press, 1970.

———. *American Baseball, Volume III: From Postwar Expansion to the Electronic Age.* University Park, Penn.: Pennsylvania State University Press, 1983.

Wallop, Douglass. *Baseball: An Informal History.* New York: W. W. Norton and Co., 1969.

Walsh, Christy. *Baseball's Greatest Lineup.* New York: A. S. Barnes and Co., 1952.

Wolff, Rick, editorial director. *The Baseball Encyclopedia.* New York: Macmillan Publishing Co., ninth edition, 1993.

Wright, Craig R., and Tom House. *The Diamond Appraised.* New York: Simon and Schuster Inc., 1989.

CHAPTER-SPECIFIC RESOURCES

Beyond the articles, newspapers, periodicals, and books listed above, which were used throughout the process, the following resources were essential to specific chapters.

PRELUDE

Books:
Smith, Ken. *Baseball's Hall of Fame.* New York: A. S. Barnes and Co., 1947.

Articles:
Vlasich, James A. "A Legend for the Legendary: The Origin of the Baseball Hall of Fame." Bowling Green State University Popular Press (1990).

CHAPTER ONE

Archival Resources:
Burry, L. O. *St. John's Evangelical Lutheran Church Annals.* Carnegie, Penn.: 1955.

Newspapers:
Iron Valley Reporter, Dover, Ohio, 1894.
Mansfield Item, Mansfield, Pennsylvania, 1892–94.
New Philadelphia Times, New Philadelphia, Ohio, 1894.

Ohio Democrat, New Philadelphia, Ohio, 1894.

Ohio State Journal, Columbus, Ohio, 1894.

Books:

Curran, Alfred A. *German Immigration to Pennsylvania 1683–1933*. Columbus, Ga.: Brentwood University Press, 1986.

Fox, Maier B. *United We Stand: The United Mine Workers of America, 1890–1990*. Washington, D.C.: The United Mine Workers of America, no date.

Gilbert, Russell Wieder. *A Picture of the Pennsylvania Germans*. Gettysburg, Penn.: Pennsylvania Historical Association, third edition, 1962.

Porter, David L., ed. *Biographical Dictionary of American Sports: Baseball*. Westport, Conn.: Greenwood Press, 1987.

Articles:

Astorino, Sam. "Would You Believe Manteer? Manstorr?" *The Carnegie Signal-Item* (December 30, 1992).

Drensen, Dorothy. "Superior Steel Corp. Remembered." *The Carnegie Signal-Item.* (October 13, October 20, 1993).

Faires, Nora. "Ethnicity in Evolution: The German Community in Pittsburgh and Allegheny City, Pennsylvania 1845–1885." Ph. D. thesis, (1981).

Video:

Out of Darkness: The Mine Workers' Story. Produced by the Labor History and Cultural Foundation. No date.

CHAPTER TWO

Newspapers:

The Adrian Daily Times and Expositor, Adrian, Michigan, 1895.

Adrian *Evening Telegram*, Adrian, Michigan, 1895.

Akron Beacon Journal and Republican, Akron, Ohio, 1895.

The Evening Democrat, Warren, Pennsylvania, 1895.

The Evening Journal, Jamestown, New York, 1895.

The Hartford Daily Courant, Hartford, Connecticut, 1896.

Mansfield Daily Shield, Mansfield, Ohio, 1895.

Michigan Messenger, Adrian, Michigan, 1895.

New Castle News, New Castle, Pennsylvania, 1895.

Ohio Democrat, New Philadelphia, Ohio, 1895.

Ohio State Journal, Columbus, Ohio, 1895.

Paterson Daily Guardian, Paterson, New Jersey, 1896–97.

Paterson Daily Press, Paterson, New Jersey, 1896–97.

Paterson Evening News, Paterson, New Jersey, 1896–97.

The Steubenville Star, Steubenville, Ohio, 1895.

Sunday Morning Star, Wilmington, Delaware, 1896.

Times-Mirror, Warren, Pennsylvania, 1938, 1946, 1958.

The Warren Mail, Warren, Pennsylvania, 1895.

Washington Observer, Washington, Pennsylvania, 1897.

Wheeling Daily Intelligencer, Wheeling, West Virginia, 1895.

Wheeling Register, Wheeling, West Virginia, 1895.

Wilmington Morning News, Wilmington, Delaware, 1896.

Books:

Baker, Wilma Sinclair LeVan. *Father and His Town: A Story of Life at the Turn of the Century in a Small Ohio River Town*. Pittsburgh: Three Rivers Press, 1961.

Bankes, James. *The Pittsburgh Crawfords: The Lives and Times of Black Baseball's Most Exciting Team!* Dubuque, Iowa: Wm. C. Brown Publishers, 1991.

Baughman, A. J. *History of Richland County, Ohio from 1808 to 1908*. Chicago: The S. J. Publishing Co., 1908.

Doyle, Joseph B. *Twentieth-Century History of Steubenville and Jefferson County, Ohio and Representative Citizens*. Chicago: Richmond-Arnold Publishing Co., 1910.

Herbst, John A. and Catherine Keene. *Life and Times in Silk City: A Photographic Essay of Paterson, New Jersey*. Haledon, N.J.: The American Labor Museum, 1984.

Heusser, Albert H., ed. *The History of Silk Dyeing Industry in the United States*. Paterson, N.J.: Silk Dyers' Association of America, 1927.

J. R. McEldowney's Adrian City Directory. Multiple annual editions and dates.

Articles:

Cashman, William Maurice, and Timothy Michael Gay. "The Flying Dutchman and the Iron and Oil League." *Warren Times Observer* (October 30, 1980).

Geyer, Orel R. " 'Hans,' 'Honus,' 'Dutch' or Plain John Henry Wagner." *Baseball Magazine* (August 1908).

"Hans Wagner's Debut." *The Literary Digest* (June 21, 1913).

MacFarlane, Paul. "Hans Wagner at Adrian, Michigan." Publisher unknown (no date).

McFarlan, Claude. "Discovered Hans Wagner." Louisville *Evening Post* (no date).

Mercer, Sid. "Old Honus." New York *Evening Journal* (no date).

Parker, Dan. "Ed Barrow Reminisces About Honus Wagner." *Baseball Digest* (December 1942).

Suehsdorf, A. D. "Honus Wagner's Rookie Year." *The National Pastime* (1987).

Tarvin, A. H. "Another Wagner Tale." *Baseball Magazine* (February 1948).

CHAPTER THREE

Newspapers:

The Courier-Journal, Louisville, Kentucky, 1897–1900.
Kentucky Irish American, Louisville, Kentucky, 1898.
The Louisville Commercial, 1897–99.
The Louisville Times, 1897–99.

Books:

Bernheim, Isaac Wolfe. *The Story of the Bernheim Family*. Louisville: John P. Morton & Co., 1910.

Hall, Wade, and Nancy Jones. *Louisville: 200 Reflections of a City*. Louisville: Hamilton Printing Co., 1978.

Hetrick, J. Thomas. *Misfits! The Cleveland Spiders in 1899*. Jefferson, N.C.: McFarland and Co., 1991.

McMeekin, Isabel McLennan. *Louisville: The Gateway City*. New York: Julian Messner Inc., 1946.

Phillips, John. *The '99 Spiders: The Story of the Worst Baseball Team Ever to Play in the Major Leagues*. Cabin John, Md.: Capital Publishing Co., 1988.

Articles:

Bailey, Bob. "Four Teams Out: The NL Reduction of 1900." *Baseball Research Journal* (1990).

Wagner, Hans. "Hans Wagner Tells of His First Training Trip." *The Pittsburgh Post-Gazette* (April 17, 1942).

CHAPTER FOUR

Books:

Brunell, F. H., ed. *The American Sporting Manual for 1905*. Chicago: Daily Racing Form Publishing Co., 1905.

Goodwin's Annual Official Turf Guide. New York: Goodwin Bros., Publishers, 1901–04.

Notable Men of Pittsburgh. Pittsburgh: Pittsburgh Printing Co., 1901.

Peterson, Robert W. *Cages to Jump Shots: Pro Basketball's Early Years*. New York: Oxford University Press, 1990.

Spalding, Albert G. *America's National Game*. New York: American Sports Publishing Co., 1911.

Articles:

"Annual Report for 1900." *Street Railway Journal* (March 1901).

Bonk, Daniel L. "Exposition Park Site Survey," self-published (April 29, 1993).

CHAPTER FIVE

Books:

Adomites, Paul D. *October's Game: The World Series.* Alexandria, Virginia: Redefinition Inc., 1990.

Cohen, Richard M., and David S. Neft. *The World Series.* New York: Macmillan Publishing Co., 1976.

Devaney, John, and Burt Goldblatt. *The World Series—A Complete Pictorial History.* Chicago: Rand McNally and Co., 1972.

Lieb, Fred. *The Story of the World Series.* New York: G. P. Putnam's Sons, revised edition, 1965.

Smith, Robert. *World Series: The Games and the Players.* Garden City, N.Y.: Doubleday and Co., 1967.

Articles:

Cava, Pete, and Paul Sandin. "Criger—As in Trigger." Self-published (no date).

Ferraro, William M. "The Institutionalization of the Modern World Series, 1903–1905: An Example of American Progressivism." Brown University (1987).

Graybar, Lloyd. "World Series Rarities—The Three Game Winners," *Baseball Research Journal* (1982).

Kermisch, Al. "Researchers Notebook." *Baseball Research Journal* (1986).

CHAPTER SIX

Books:

Flink, James J. *The Automobile Age.* Cambridge, Mass.: The MIT Press, 1988.

Throm, Edward L., and James S. Crenshaw. *Popular Mechanics Auto Album.* Popular Mechanics Press, 1952.

Watts, Lew. *The Fine Art of Baseball: A Complete Guide to Strategy, Skills, and System.* Englewood Cliffs, N.J.: Prentice-Hall Inc., 1964.

Articles:

Dudley, Bruce. "Louisville Slugger." *Louisville Herald Magazine* (Sept. 27, 1914).

Klem, William J. "My Last Big-League Game." *Collier's* (April 21, 1951).

CHAPTER SEVEN

Newspapers:

Chicago Tribune, Chicago, Illinois, 1908.

Books:

Chew, Peter. *The Kentucky Derby: The First 100 Years.* Boston: Houghton Mifflin Co., 1974.

Fleming, G. H. *The Unforgettable Season.* New York: Holt, Rinehart & Winston, 1981.

Reidenbaugh, Lowell. *Baseball's 25 Greatest Pennant Races.* St. Louis: The Sporting News Publishing Co., 1987.

Articles:

Lonich, David W. "Metropolitanism and the Genesis of Municipal Anxiety in Allegheny County." *Pittsburgh History* (Summer 1993).

CHAPTER EIGHT

Archival Resources:

Prospectus for Hans Wagner Brothers' Circus and Congress of Athletes.

Newspapers:

The Detroit Free Press, 1909.
The Detroit News, 1909.

Books:

The World Series books listed under Chapter Five.

Allen, Irving Lewis. *Unkind Words: Ethnic Labeling from Redskin to WASP.* New York: Bergin & Garvey, 1990.

Benswanger, William E. *Forbes Field Sixtieth Birthday 1909–1969: Pittsburgh Pirates Picture Album.* Pittsburgh Pirates, 1969.

Carmichael, John P., ed. *My Greatest Day in Baseball.* New York: A. S. Barnes and Co., 1945.

Meany, Tom. *Baseball's Greatest Teams.* New York: A. S. Barnes and Co., 1949.

Articles:

Bonk, Daniel L. "Ballpark Figures: The Story of Forbes Field." *Pittsburgh History* (Summer 1993).

Lancaster, Donald G. "Forbes Field Praised as a Gem When It Opened." *Baseball Research Journal* (1986).

Smith, Chet. "Goodbye Forbes Field." *Renaissance* (June 1970).

Watkins, James. "Nothing to Nothing in Overtime." *Baseball Research Journal* (1976).

CHAPTER NINE

Newspapers:

Public Ledger, Philadelphia, Pennsylvania, 1915.

Books:

Creamer, Robert W. *Stengel: His Life and Times.* New York: Simon & Schuster, 1984.

Murdock, Eugene C. *Baseball Between the Wars: Memories of the Game by the Men Who Played It.* Westport, Conn.: Greenwood Press, 1992.

Articles:
Buckley, Steve. "The Real Honus Wagner." *Tuff Stuff* (May 1993).
"Carnegie Peeved Over the Way Pittsburgers Worship Wagner." Dayton *Herald* (May 18, 1910).
"Fred Clarke Invents Cap with Sun Glasses; Help to Outfielders." Dayton *Herald* (June 17, 1910).
Kindl, Christine. "In Wisps of Advertising Art, Cigar Smokers' Legacy Lingers." Pittsburgh *Tribune-Review Focus* (May 2, 1993).
"Wagner a Star at Basketball." Dayton *Herald* (January 5, 1910).

CHAPTER TEN

Books:
Okkonen, Marc. *The Federal League of 1914–1915: Baseball's Third Major League.* Garrett Park, Md.: The Society for American Baseball Research, 1989.
Phelps, Edith M., ed. *Selected Articles on the Income Tax.* New York: The H. W. Wilson Co., third edition, 1917.
Riley, Ridge. *Road to Number One: A Personal Chronicle of Penn State Football.* Garden City, New York: Doubleday & Co. Inc., 1977.
Seligman, Edwin R. A. *The Income Tax.* New York: The Macmillan Co., 1921.

Articles:
Bulger, Bozeman. "A Dutchman's Crown." *The Literary Digest* (March 24, 1917).
McLinn, George E. "One Reason for Honus Wagner's Greatness—A Real Record." Philadelphia *Public Ledger* (May 9, 1915).
Rothe, Emil H. "Was the Federal League a Major League?" *Baseball Research Journal* (1981).

CHAPTER ELEVEN

Archival Resources:
Court records relating to Wagner v. Braunstein, 1933–34, The Court of Common Pleas, Allegheny County, Pennsylvania.
Death Certificate of Elva G. Wagner, January 9, 1918. Pennsylvania Department of Health, Division of Vital Statistics, New Castle, Pennsylvania.

Newspapers:
The Pittsburgh Courier, 1923–25.

Books:

Lenburg, Jeff, Joan Howard Maurer, and Greg Lenburg. *Three Stooges Scrapbook.* Secaucus, New Jersey: Citadel Press, 1994.

Miller, Marvin. *A Whole Different Ball Game: The Sport and Business of Baseball.* New York: Birch Lane Press, 1991.

Articles:

McCue, Andy. "A History of Dodger Ownership." *The National Pastime* (1993).

Welsh, Regis M. "The Cuyler Incident." Publisher unknown (no date).

Wiley, Mary. "Movies: They made 'em here in 1919." *The North Hills News Record* (August 2–3, 1975).

INDEX